Women in Philosophical Counseling

Women in Philosophical Counseling

The Anima of Thought in Action

Edited by Luisa de Paula and Peter Raabe

LEXINGTON BOOKS
Lanham • Boulder • New York • London

Published by Lexington Books
An imprint of The Rowman & Littlefield Publishing Group, Inc.
4501 Forbes Boulevard, Suite 200, Lanham, Maryland 20706
www.rowman.com

Unit A, Whitacre Mews, 26-34 Stannary Street, London SE11 4AB

British Library Cataloguing in Publication Information Available

Library of Congress Cataloging-in-Publication Data

Women in philosophical counseling : the anima of thought in action / edited by Luisa de Paula and Peter Raabe.
pages cm.
Includes bibliographical references and index.
ISBN 978-0-7391-9165-1 (cloth : alk. paper) -- ISBN 978-0-7391-9166-8 (electronic)
1. Philosophical counseling. 2. Women--Conduct of life. I. De Paula, Luisa, editor.
BJ1595.5.W66 2015
108.2--dc23
2015000473

∞ ™ The paper used in this publication meets the minimum requirements of American National Standard for Information Sciences Permanence of Paper for Printed Library Materials, ANSI/NISO Z39.48-1992.

Printed in the United States of America

Contents

Editors' Acknowledgments

PETER: I very much appreciate the enormous effort Luisa de Paula has put into this book project, in soliciting manuscripts from all over the world, in working patiently with the authors who provided the fine chapters in this volume, and in polishing the final version of the manuscript for publication. I would also like to thank the many philosophers, who just happen to be women, who have contributed their time and their thoughts to this project. As well I would like to thank the editors at Lexington Jana Hodges-Kluck, Kari Waters, Natalie Mandziuk, and Jay Song for their patient guidance and advice during the writing and compilation process, and also to Lexington Books for publishing this important work.

LUISA: I thank Peter for his invaluable guidance, for his trust and support, for the work we have shared and the ongoing philosophical dialogue which day after day has been nourishing this book. I have learned a lot from him and his impressive philosophical style. Working with him has been not only a privilege, but also a wonderful formative experience that I will keep and cultivate as a seedling for the rest of my life.

I would like to thank women colleagues in philosophical counseling and practices who have contributed to this book, carried out an intense and mutually enriching exchange, and were patient with all my critiques and my obsession with improvements throughout the whole process.

A special thanks goes to Helen Douglas, who from the other side of the world immediately picked up on the help that I needed at just the right moment, and generously gave her creativity and professional experience in helping me for my introduction and end notes. I also would like to thank all those colleagues who have submitted contributions but, for one reason or another, did not make it to the end of the publication process. Our dialogue was prolific and an inspiration for this book.

I want to express my deepest gratitude to my friend Victor Townsley for his patience and commitment. He came to my rescue whenever I could not find my way while thinking and writing in English, a language that is not my mother tongue. There is not a single page in this book that has not passed through his attentive and sensitive supervision, and I suspect he has been infected by philosophy in these last months.

I would like to thank Barbara Boyd. Luckily for me, she is not only a patient always-supportive stepmother, but also an experienced author and editor who helped me to move my first steps on this book project when I was still very awkward and uncertain about being up to the task. I would also like to thank my cousin and genetics researcher Massimo Zollo for the scientific consultations and inspiring dialogues that have guided me in discovering the fascinating insights in gender differences from the perspective of molecular biology and human genetics.

Together with Barbara and Massimo, I want to express my gratitude to my family and friends, for their unwavering presence at my side. Their tireless commitment for a better life is to me an inexhaustible source of philosophical inspiration.

PETER AND LUISA: We want to thank all the women colleagues who have done important and pioneering work in the field of philosophical practice, in particular to Dr. Vaughana Feary, who paved the way for the feminist perspective on philosophical practice in her groundbreaking article "Virtue-Based Feminist Philosophical Counseling" (http://www.society-for-philosophy-in-practice.org/journal/pdf/6-1%20007%20Feary%20-%20Feminist.pdf).

Introduction

Peter Raabe

There is no doubt that women and men are equal. Unfortunately the political and economic systems of many countries today still refuse to recognize this. But being equal doesn't mean being the same. Women and men are different; they're not the same. In fact, no two people on earth are the same, not even identical twins. And yet people often say we're all the same because we all have a heart, a liver, two lungs, and so on. It's also not uncommon to hear someone say that women are all alike, or that this man is no different from all the rest. But this is where problems often start.

There are, of course, biological differences between women and men, even though these are not always as clear and distinct as social convention would have us believe. At one point in his *Meditations*, the French philosopher René Descartes suggested that reality is that which is clear and distinct within our perception. But the material reality he was contemplating is very different from everyday social reality. The reality that individuals live within a society is often established and controlled by those with power. When it comes to the reality of life for women and men, the powerful have generally dictated that women are inferior to men. This hierarchy, based on what were believed to be clear biological weaknesses in women, has not only had a significant impact on the course of history, it continues to have a significant effect on what is assumed about women today. Women are still considered to be inferior in most societies; girls are valued less than boys; a woman's work in the home is not counted as part of a country's productivity and so on. Negative generalizations about women are common in most cultures, even where sexual prejudice is against the law.

Of course it's sometimes acceptable to generalize. For example, when women share a problem they're often content with having the other person simply listen and empathize. On the other hand, when men share a problem they more often expect the other person to offer some sort of suggestion for fixing that problem. This is, of course, a very simplistic picture, based on broad generalizations. But research in psychology has in fact shown these generalizations to be true for many people in most cultures.

Now imagine that a woman goes to a male counselor to share a problem. She expects him to mostly listen. But, being a man, he offers a number of suggestions on how to fix the problem. Or, *vice versa*, imagine a man sitting opposite a woman counselor or therapist sharing his problem. He pauses, expecting her to offer suggestions on how he might fix his problem, but she sits, listening patiently and empathetically without saying a word. Both the woman and the man in these two scenarios would find the professional's response, or lack thereof, to be frustratingly unhelpful. This is because both the woman and the man had an expectation—they each had a need that was not met in the usual way that women and men interact with others of their own kind. This difference is just one of the many issues facing women and men discussed within the book you're holding.

There's no doubt that women and men are equal. In most nations and cultures this is understood, although this isn't always respected in practice. But women and men are not the same. And this difference must also be respected in practice, especially by mental healthcare services providers who wish to be equally helpful to women and men.

Peter Raabe PhD
North Vancouver, Canada
August, 2014

Introduction

Luisa de Paula

Dear Reader, the book you hold in your hands represents the last step in an eighteen-month project involving ongoing dialogue and cooperation between eighteen women philosophical counselors from thirteen different countries, Peter Raabe, and myself. In this respect, it is a point of arrival. However, we hope it will also be a point of departure for engaging philosophical counselors with the question of *différance*.[1]

I started to work on this book almost by chance and I am now at the last steps before publication. Sitting at the desk where I've been studying and writing philosophy for almost twenty years, I suddenly realize that I have now started to feel entitled to work as a woman and to be a philosopher in every single cell of my body, for the first time in my life. As I run my eyes over my high school philosophy textbooks, always faithfully at hand, the phantom of a thought has begun to take form. It must have wandered restlessly through my mind for a lifetime, but has only become fully perceptible to me today. Right now, it is asking me to perform certain gestures to verify its existence.

I stretch out my hand and frantically browse through the first volume of my philosophy texts, the one dealing with ancient and medieval thought. Despite its 1,216 pages, it does not take me long to verify what I had expected: not a single woman is to be found here. But wait: not altogether true! I find some words put in the mouth of a woman, Sophocles' *Antigone*, who makes a claim for a Law of Nature as opposed to Human Law.[2] She is rolled out as the cliché of Woman-Nature, pre-*logos* (λόγος), representing primordial instinct and bound to yield to the masculine force of intellect and civilization. Woman is called upon to embody the instinctual feeling and empathic connection that, not without paradox, philosophical reason pretends to both submit to and divorce itself from: a sleight-of-hand affirmation of its sovereign independence.[3]

Is this the real origin of philosophical thought or an invention of the history of philosophy? More than one clue invites us to lean toward the second hypothesis. Even though no written work by women philosophers has come down to us from antiquity, a number of sources reveal that women practiced philosophy in both Greece and Rome, and that some of them even ran schools and gained celebrity for their subtle reasoning. In his *De Vita Pythagorica*, Iamblichus tells us of seventeen women who followed Pythagoras's teachings.[4] Diogenes Laërtius exalts the thought of Hipparchia of Maroneia[5], one of the many women who cultivated the Cynic philosophy to strip life of all futile frills and focus it down to its pure essentials. We also know of women who practiced philosophy in less ascetic ways, such as Aspasia's famous salon, which is referred to by Xenophon,[6] Plato,[7] and Cicero[8] among others.

Although history cannot speak of the past other than through the present and from the perspective of those entitled to speak, something has come down to us which does not dovetail with our current perspective of the past.

I bear this in mind as I turn back to my old volume and notice that among Plato's excerpts there are any number of pages devoted to Socrates' heroic death, and to *Meno* and *Theaetetus's* discovery of "true knowledge" as opposed to the world of sensation, while there is no place for Diotima's discourse on Ἤρος (*Eros*).[9] Nor do I find any of the passages from *Republic* and *Laws* where Plato argues that women, having shown themselves to be up to the task, should be granted political and military command.[10] What criteria were behind these choices? This question swirls through my mind as I arrive at the chapter dedicated to Aristotle. A hundred pages are neatly divided into Aristotelian logic, epistemology, physics, ethics, and politics, yet politely leave out any reference to the philosopher's misogynist pronouncements, or his non-systematic, open research on topics that do not lend themselves to simple, linear reasoning, such as dreams.

I will spare the reader further details of this first volume of a highly rated Italian philosophy course for classical high schools. Nor will I dwell on the second volume, which starts with Pico della Mirandola's *Dignity of Man* and ends with Kant's claim for the right of man to subject animal life to his own purposes, in the name of a natural superiority.[11] Picking up the fourth volume, which covers the nineteenth century and the first decades of the twentieth, I eagerly expect my first encounter with a woman philosopher, but am again disappointed. Disconsolate, I fetch down the last volume, only to find not a single word on the thought of Simone Weil, Agnes Heller, Simone de Beauvoir, or Edith Stein. Hannah Arendt rates an appearance in a two-page paragraph on "The rehabilitation of practical philosophy."[12] In addition to that, in another part of the book I find a three-page extract from *Vita Activa*

(*The Human Condition*), which I cannot help but compare to the fifteen pages given to the Italian philosopher Benedetto Croce's ideas on spirit and art.[13]

What is philosophy losing by persistently neglecting and brushing aside women's thought?

From the collection of massive volumes that have been my constant and primary reference for so many years, I shift my eyes to the unbound essays scattered on the right side of my desk. As I flip through them, an underlying thread starts to unwind in my mind. It moves from ἔρος (eros) to φρόνησις (*phronesis*), from the process of giving birth to the cultivation of the art of doubting, passing through emotions that spur rationality through whispers, silences, and narratives.

I find myself at ease with a dimension of thought that a whole genealogy of male Western *philosophes* has completely neglected and dismissed, a dimension now making a powerful return with the experiences of women philosophical counselors that animate the pages of this book. I follow my underlying thread among their topics and arguments, tasting categories that appeal to sense, feeling and emotion no less than to reason, to existence as much as to wisdom and knowledge, returning thought to its restless movement in step with life.

This book lends itself to being read and savored in many ways. I invite the reader to explore its five sections as the steps of a virtual journey in philosophical counseling, sensing the wonderful and unique path that is the life of each of us, opened out wide by philosophy.

By giving philosophical counseling the voices of women from across the globe, this book is also a political gesture in favor of difference and differences. Its purpose is to encourage every reader to invest in and capitalize on philosophical resources as they seek out and develop their uniquely different way of life. Enhancing difference, from within and in relation to others and the world, is essential for both women and men today. We need to leave behind the stifling enclosure of a purportedly self-identical *ego* whose *alter* cannot be but an *alter-ego*, a mirror of the ego's reflections and projections, rather than a source of wonder and discovery.

The closed-off self-identity is perfectly depicted in the Cartesian *ego cogitans*, the Kantian *reine Ich* ("pure I") and *Ich denke* ("I think"), and the Freudian *Ego*. It cannot be by accident that this roll call of big-name historical figures with their project for the self-identical Ego is all male. The one-size-fits-all model has not convinced women, who are biologically designed to give birth and enhance connection and interdependence, and who make sense of their lives by assisting others in need. Nor it is fitted to modern men. This because the identity model—the brand leader for individualistic society—can be effective only in setting out rigid boundaries of the modern individual, a demarcation of *his* culture and *his* society that, by its nature, marginalizes women. Hence the crystallization of *the* Woman and *the* Feminine in static definitions that allow for the exorcism or exile of all those troubling attributes of *being-human.*

As J. S. Mill understood all too well,[14] the subjection of woman to man is also the subjection of man to himself, of body to mind, and emotion to reason. In the same way that the hierarchical divide thwarts women's intellectual potential, it stunts men's emotional and relational powers, depriving them of the *alter* they could meet on an equal footing.

Today, the equivocation between true difference and a simple plus-or-minus scale of sameness has been revealed by what simplistically passes for "women's emancipation." Within a rigidly hierarchical identitarian regime, both men and women need women in order to find their own, and others', *different* voices, voices that are alive and more in tune to their humanity.

Regaining our voices as both women and philosophers is the fundamental first step to regaining our ability for dialogue, which is the royal road to thinking differently. This is what philosophical counseling aims to be: a *via regia* toward *dia-logos* and *con-versation.*[15]

This is also what this book aims to be: a starting point for thinking about difference and the differences camouflaged by in-difference. It is still only a sign along an unbeaten path, an invitation whose appeal rests on the (re)actions it may elicit, within the unpredictable horizons of the future.

NOTES

1. By recalling Derridean *différance*, I address the current and practical issues we face, mostly without even realizing, as we struggle through life wearing identity guises tailored to a very limited range of gender sizes. "The economy of this writing is a regulated relationship between that which exceeds and the exceeded totality: the *différance* of the absolute excess." Jacques Derrida, "Cogito and the History of Madness," in *Writing and Difference*, trans. Alan Bass (Chicago: University of Chicago Press, 1978), p. 75. For further reference: Jacques Derrida, "Interview with Julia Kristeva," in *Positions*, trans. Alan Bass (Chicago: University of Chicago Press, 1981), 15–36.

2. Fabio Cioffi, Giorgio Luppi, Amedeo Vigorelli, Emilio Zanette, *Il Testo Filosofico* (Milano: Edizioni Scolastiche Bruno Mondadori, 1991), Vol. 1, 214–215.

3. Submission is in itself a relation of the submitting and the submitted, involving dependence on both sides, as in Hegel's *Herrschaft und Knechtschaft* ("lordship and bondage," better known as the maste-slave dialectic). See Georg Wilhelm Friedrich Hegel, "Independence and Dependence of Self-Consciousness. Lordship and Bondage," in *Phenomenology of the Spirit* trans. A. V. Miller (New Delhi: Motilal Banarsidass, 1998), 111–119.

4. "[T]he most illustrious Pythagorean women are Timycha, the wife of Myllias the Crotonian. Phyltis, the daughter of Theophrius the Crotonian. Byndacis, the sister of Ocellus and Ocillus, Lucanians. Chilonis, the daughter of Chilon the Lacedenonian. Cratesiclea, the Lacedemonian, the wife of the Lacedemonian Cleanor. Theano, the wife of Brontinus of Metapontum. Mya, the wife of Milon the Crotonian. Lasthenia the Arcadian. Abrotelia, the daughter of Abroteles the Tarentine. Echecratia the Phliasian. Tyrsenis, the Sybarite. Pisirrhonde, the Tarentine. Nisleadusa, the Lacedemonian. Byro, the Argive. Babelyma the Argive. And Cleaechma, the sister of Autocharidas the Lacedemonia." Iamblichus, *On the Pythagorean Way of Life*

(De Vita Pythagorica) ed. Patrick Rousell, Vol. 1 of *The Complete Pythagoras*, retrieved from http://arcaneknowledgeofthedeep.files.wordpress.com/2014/02/completepythagoras.pdf .

It must be emphasized that these seventeen women represent a tiny portion of the 218 remarkable Pythagoreans remembered by Iamblichus. Moreover, in his "Advice to Women," Iamblichus recommend mildness and complete deference to the husband as essential qualities of the perfect Pythagorean woman.

5. Diogenes Laërtius, *Lives of the Eminent Philosophers*, trans. Robert Drew Hicks (1925), Book VI, 96–97, retrieved from http://en.wikisource.org/wiki/Lives_of_the_Eminent_Philosophers/Book_VI.

6. In Xenophon's *Economist*, Socrates says to Critobulus: "I will introduce you to Aspasia, who can explain these matters to you in a far more scientific way than I can." Xenophon, *The Economist*, trans. H. G. Dakyns, retrieved from http://www.gutenberg.org/files/1173/1173-h/1173-h.htm.

7. Plato, *Menexenus* 235e: Socrates refers to Aspasia as his instructor and the instructor of many other eminent men of fifth-century BCE Athens. Retrieved from http://www.perseus.tufts.edu/hopper/text?doc=Perseus%3Atext%3A1999.01.0180%3Atext%3DMenex%3Asection%3D235e .

8. In Cicero, *De Inventione* I: 51–52, Aspasia shows dialectical and rhetorical skills, together with smart intelligence and refined cunning. Retrieved from http://www.thelatinlibrary.com/cicero/inventione1.shtml.

9. Cioffi, Luppi et al., *Il Testo Filosofico*, 400–447.

10. In *Republic*, Socrates argues for the inclusion of women within the upper ranks of military forces and political government. "Women are the same in kind as men, and have the same aptitude or want of aptitude for medicine or gymnastic or war, but in a less degree. One woman will be a good guardian, another not; and the good must be chosen to be the colleagues of our guardians." Plato, *Republic* V, 451c–452a, trans. Benjamin Jowett, retrieved from http://www.pinkmonkey.com/dl/library1/republic.pdf.

Also, from *Laws*: "There was one main point about which we were agreed—that a man's whole energies throughout life should be devoted to the acquisition of the virtue proper to a man, whether this was to be gained by study, or habit, or some mode of acquisition, or desire, or opinion, or knowledge —and this applies equally to men and women." Plato, *Laws* VI, trans. Benjamin Jowett, retrieved from http://classics.mit.edu/Plato/laws.6.vi.html. See also Françoise Collin, Evelyine Pisier, and Eleni Varikas, *Les Femmes de Platon à Derrida: Anthologie Critique* (Paris: Plon 2000); Mary Briody Mahowald, ed. *Philosophy of Women: An Anthology of Classic and Current Concepts* (Indianapolis, IN: Hackett 1994).

11. Cioffi, Luppi et al., *Il Testo Filosofico*, Vol. 2.

12. Ibidem, Vol. 3:2, 738–739.

13. Ibidem, Vol 3:2. Pages 746–749 contain the extract from Arendt, *Vita Activa*; 76–100 are dedicated to Croce's *Aesthetics*.

14. John Stuart Mill, *The Subjection of Women* (London: Longmans, Green, Reader, and Deyer, 1869).

15. The word "dialogue" originates from the ancient Greek words διά (dia), meaning "in-between, through," and λόγος (logos), meaning "reason, word, language, norm, principle." The word "conversation" is derivative of the combination of the two Latin words cum, meaning "with" and vertere, meaning "to turn towards." It is interesting to note that the word "conversion" has the same etymon: an authentic conversation can be thought of as a kind of conversion.

I

Listening to Whispers

Chapter One

Women Think in Whispers in a Developing Country: A Glance through the Lens of Philosophical Counseling

Riella Morhayim

SOME CASE STUDIES

Have you ever wondered whether women in developing countries[1] experience philosophical counseling?[2] Surprisingly, Philosophical Counseling is not only practiced in developed regions like the United States, Canada, Great Britain, and Europe (Netherlands, Norway, Austria, France, Switzerland), but also in countries like Israel, Turkey, Argentina, South Africa, Serbia, and Russia to name but a few. Before going into more details, I would like to share some of my philosophical counseling experiences in Turkey.

No Right to Study and Work

One of my first woman clients,[3] Sinem, was suffering from injustice and discrimination against her identity as a woman. When she came to me, she was twenty-six years old and had no right to work and study outside her home. Although her father and brother were working in their own private company, her mother, her sister, and she were not permitted to work. She could leave the house just to shop for groceries or to meet certain friends. She visited me through her best friend without the knowledge of her parents.

I should admit that for the first meeting it was very hard for her to talk about herself and her family with someone she did not know. Only after some general talk (more than forty minutes) and as a result of my receptive attitude, she felt a bit more comfortable in telling me she was very upset and depressed about her unfair life circumstances, where her family did not allow her to work or go to university.

As soon as she made these first intimate revelations, I thanked her for overcoming barriers and expressing herself. I find it crucial to show your appreciation when the counselees share their inner thoughts and feelings.

Initially, we talked about her family and their conservative background. The more she objectively focused on her parents' lives, the more understanding she became. There we utilized a saying from Søren Kierkegaard, "Life can only be understood backwards; but it must be lived forwards." She started to develop more sympathy for her family, their old-fashioned religious principles, and their ethical obligations. We arrived at the point where she recognized that an inner conflict between religion and an educated lifestyle is commonplace in her circumstances. Instead of feeling miserable and depressed, she became hopeful about her situation and life.

We then questioned her inner thoughts and sensations regarding her conditions. We also analyzed how many external elements such as social expectations, parental pressure, and religion made her feel depressed. I introduced William James's assertion that "the greatest discovery of my generation is that human beings can alter their lives by altering their attitudes." Hence, she first realized that her attitude to her conditions, her deep feelings and thoughts were making her sad; then, she realized that actually she could overcome them. She agreed with Gautama Buddha, "no one saves us but ourselves. No one can and no one may. We ourselves must walk the path." This philosophical thinking enabled her to examine her life from a different perspective from which she could then address her problems and life issues. When she stopped putting pressure on herself with all her expectations, comparisons, and disappointments, she began to contemplate the positive components in herself and her life. With this motivation, she realized that she had never expressed her desires and views to her parents. As Séamus Heaney said "If you have the words, there's always a chance that you'll find the way." She decided to talk the issue through with her family. Luckily, she expressed herself so well that her parents were convinced to let Sinem study and work a few days a week outside their home.

The philosophical counseling sessions with her had lasted three months; however, it was vastly beneficial for her in examining her circumstances, realizing the most appropriate perspective from which to address her problems, and developing a constructive attitude toward them. Philosophical inquiry about her family, her conditions, and herself motivated her to gain a different and broader perspective of her life. Therefore, she succeeded in solving her concrete and personal problems.

Woman Image

I would like to share a case of a young woman who came from a very religious Muslim family and was living in Şanliurfa, in southeastern Turkey with her family. She had found me through a blog I was writing about philosophical counseling. She wrote me an email complaining that her life was a prison and that she was feeling very depressed, dissatisfied, and uncomfortable with herself.

She complained about control, restrictions, and pressure over her appearance. She had to wear a veil that covered her body from head to foot or a scarf covering her neck and hair. In addition, she could only wear skirts reaching to her knees and loose, long-sleeved blouses. On top of it all, she was very distressed since she could not even choose the color and texture of her clothes and was supposed to wear only dark colors in a non-decorative way. She also grumbled about the strict requirements and interpretations of *hijab* (Islamic dress), which forces women to conceal their hair and skin in public. She expressed her inner reaction very openly, "I feel unhappy living in this atmosphere as a woman. I do not understand why I need to hide my beauty and repress my original identity. I feel really alone and depressed as none of my friends and family members think like I do, or approve of my thoughts. I do not know how I can overcome these obsessive thoughts I have. Can you please help me deal with myself and my situation?"

I should highlight that in this at first email there was no name or contact information. At that time online counseling was not common in Turkey and I was not really sure whether it was a fake request. I wrote back to her that I could help her deal with this situation and asked her to give me some more details about herself and/or call me on my mobile phone. She called me the next morning and spoke in a whisper because she was calling me secretly, then introduced herself and asked me how I could help her. I simply explained to her the basics of philosophical counseling and we agreed to start her counseling via email and via phone if necessary.

In her counseling, we conceptually analyzed her emotions and thoughts concerning herself, her identity as a woman, and her environment. In the beginning, we focused on her own judgments and sensations about herself. During this work of reflection I helped her realize that she was able to express her emotions and reactions explicitly, but in doing so she also showed herself as disoriented, and not aware of the reasons behind her negative feelings and emotions. I showed my appreciation of her self-expression and self-awareness and encouraged her to reflect on why she experienced such negative feelings. Furthermore, we discussed the links between her gender identity and her current state as she wrote that she was feeling unhappy living in this atmosphere as a woman. We differentiated the internal reasons (her insecurities, sense of solitude and isolation, feeling of being different, low-self-esteem) and the external reasons (family, environment, cultural and religious obligations). She decided to work on her own priorities with respect to different and not necessarily compatible values and life attitudes: the value of happiness with respect to the praise for appearance, flexibility as compared to a confrontational attitude. With this philosophical analysis she noticed that many intrinsic causes and a few external factors had contributed to her feelings. Instead of complaining and accusing other people and outer causes, she decided to point her finger at herself and her personal life perspective. She understood that it all depended on her attitude and point of view. She shared the insight that she had gained in these words: "If I could be secure with myself and my identity as a woman, and if I could accept the norms of my conservative environment, nothing and no one could make me feel depressed." After in-depth analysis on the reasons that she was not happy with herself, her identity, and her environment, she wrote to me, "I have decided that my happiness should not be influenced by any external factor and actually my gender and beauty cannot be hidden." Then we considered a few views about happiness and the meaning of life. She fully agreed with the Dalai Lama's perspective on happiness as an art of living which is a mental attitude, a state of mind and not primarily dependent on external conditions.

By the time that she had found her inner happiness and accepted her surroundings, she started to feel less pressure over her appearance. Her friends and family members noticed her calmer attitude and her increased acceptance of external obligations; they even started to approve her thoughts. In her last email, she wrote that she had been shopping with her family and they had approved of her buying colorful clothes and veils that made her very happy and hopeful about the future.

I have always found this example philosophical counseling so inspiring that I have told it to many women counselees to help them realize they can solve all of their problems if they want to. I would like to emphasize that an appropriate framework for a comprehensive view of the situation we find ourselves in is the first big step in shifting perspectives and moving ourselves into a better position to change what we can. After that, it becomes easier to comprehend the personal belief system, way of thinking and components of problems by the means of philosophical understanding and creative thinking. Finally, the discovery of the best philosophical perspective to be matched to personal values provides the appropriate approach toward life.

Compelled to Marry and Live with Someone She had Never Seen

The other case that I wanted to mention was Zeynep, who came to talk with me just before her arranged marriage. She was nineteen years old and had to marry a thirty-four-year-old man who had chosen her to be his wife. Although arranged marriages in Turkey are very common, it was hard for her to understand the situation and accept this coercion. She was really concerned about the fact that she had to marry and live with someone who she did not even know. She told me that from the day she heard that she was being forced to marry someone she did not know, she was so sad that she was always crying and even contemplated suicide. One day, while she was crying, her neighbor came and advised her to meet with me. When Zeynep felt strong enough to take this step, her neighbor brought her to me.

When she came to the first philosophical counseling session, she was very quiet, tense, and anxious. Obviously, she had many things to tell me but in one hour she could not express anything about herself. However, as I was familiar with this situation I did not push her to speak, I just proposed a few questions to think about. It was only in the second and third meetings that we started to have proper conversations. After talking about concepts like happiness, freedom, faith, and success, we explored her inner feelings as well as her thoughts about herself, her family, and her life in general. Then we read and developed a reflection on the "The Serenity Prayer"[4] by the religious thinker Reinhold Niebuhr: "God, grant me the serenity to accept the things that I cannot change, the courage to change the things that I can, and the wisdom to know the difference between them." She was so impressed by this quote that she totally opened herself up to me and to philosophical counseling. We focused on the categorization of things that she could change and she could not, so that she became more patient and persevering toward her life and her conditions.

Additionally, she realized that she felt anger toward her family in that they had approved and arranged this marriage without her consent or knowledge. At this stage, she followed Emma Goldman's advice, "Before we can forgive one another, we have to understand one another," which helped her liberate herself from negative emotions toward her parents. By considering her parents' background and education, she started to empathize with the value system behind their decision. She realized that, from their limited perspective, they just wanted her to be happy. At the same time, she became aware of her lack of communication and self-expression toward her family, who were so happy about arranging this marriage that they could not really understand why Zeynep had been reacting in such a way.

Subsequently, we focused on Susan Sarandon's theory about the effort to understand people, "When you start to develop your powers of empathy and imagination, the whole world opens up to you." Rather than ruminating on suicide, she decided to seek her own way as to make her world open up to her. She decided to talk with her parents and express her inner feelings. Once she had spoken with her parents and explained her concerns and discussed the situation with them, they told her that they understood her worries and would try to find some solutions. They then decided to invite the potential husband to dinner and have them get to know each other, and only after she approved of being with him did they think about the next steps to take. When she visited me the next time, she regarded all these updates as "miracles" of philosophical counseling. At that point, I wanted her to understand that whatever had happened was the success she herself had achieved by exercising and learning to take advantage of philosophical reflection, so that she should feel more self-confident. Eventually, she was satisfied and happy and decided to marry the man of her own free will.

PHILOSOPHICAL COUNSELING FOR WOMEN IN DEVELOPED COUNTRIES

As you will have realized from the report of my philosophical counseling experiences above, women who live in my country have to confront a range of problems that far exceed the more limited sphere of emotional and psychological concerns faced and discussed in philosophical sessions by women in Western Europe, the United States, Australia, and Canada. As a woman and a philosopher, I would like to emphasize one of the major problems of living in a lesser-developed country where women are often unable to express themselves freely. Commonly, in these kinds of environments, women have no primary control over their daily lives. They cannot choose how to live and spend their time, nor can they articulate their desires free of constraint. They feel, and/or *are*, controlled, abused, or manipulated most of the time. They feel that they are not heard, accepted, loved, and respected. Living in an environment that exposes them to emotional, sexual, and physical abuse, women cannot but experience communication and relationship problems. They also experience loneliness, isolation, and low self-esteem. All in all, it is no surprise that most women from less-developed countries suffer from depression and anxiety. Philosophical counseling can be a decisive step in helping these women seek, find, and express their voices.

It should be emphasized that, although more and more people have started to hear about philosophical counseling, in countries that are often considered backward in terms of social and economic development, the layman is still not at all familiar with its framework and may not even not know what philosophical counseling is. If we look at the actual status of philosophical counseling in Turkey, for example, we can see that it has not yet developed as a professional field. There are very few counselors who are interested in developing a philosophical approach, and when they do show an interest, it is more often to give a veneer of philosophy to their practice than to make proper use of its specific tools and contents.

Women in Turkey have recently started to educate themselves and have taken up employment, which means: they have begun to notice the need for counseling and for seeking and expressing their own voices. However, cultural barriers preventing women from undertaking a philosophical path and gaining awareness of themselves are still very hard and difficult to break in Turkey. In the same way, both in my own country and in others such as Israel, Taiwan, Argentina, South Africa, Serbia, and Russia, most women feel inner barriers that prevent them from talking about their feelings, thoughts, and problems.

Having said all this, it might be that philosophical counseling in Turkey and other countries at the tail-end of the global chessboard face very different tasks from the ones it is committed to in regions such as North America, where, at least in theory, everyone has equal freedom to any kind of counseling services.

TO BE A WOMAN IN DEVELOPING COUNTRIES

Although we are in the twentieth century, in many countries women are exposed to very conservative and immature attitudes. In many areas, from West Africa to Central Asia, women are still second-class citizens and are expected to be content with their traditional roles of mother, wife, and housewife. In Egypt, Iran, and Saudi Arabia women find themselves in the worst possible conditions, since their word counts for nothing and is entirely disregarded. To be more specific, I would like to spell out the most problematic issues women encounter in a number of countries:

Employment

In many countries women experience significant discrimination in employment. First of all, a husband can prevent and prohibit his wife from working outside the home, or a father can decide on behalf of his daughter whether she is allowed to work or not. Most of the workplaces prefer to hire men instead of women. Across a larger perspective, the highest levels of participation for the native female labor force in so-called developing countries are found in Lebanon, Morocco, Turkey, and Yemen, where women constitute 25 percent of the labor force.[5] According to the U.S. Bureau of Labor Statistics 2011,[6] in the Middle East women make up only about 10–15 percent of the working population, far below percentages found in Western Europe, Australia, Canada, and United States.

Education

Despite the great expansion of educational opportunities worldwide during the last thirty years, women in most so-called developing countries still receive less schooling than men.[7] That may be unbelievable for some people who come from countries where equal rights to education were acquired a long time ago, but it is true: in a number of countries, girls are still excluded from education. Statistics show that nowadays more than seventy-five million illiterate adults are to be found worldwide, and more than half of them live in Egypt, Iraq, and Morocco. Research has also shown that education has a direct impact on the overall life situation of a human being. For example, Turkey's 2010 Demographic and Health Survey (DHS) showed that 72 percent of girls fifteen to nineteen years old who had no education or had not completed primary school were already mothers or pregnant, compared with only 2 percent of girls who had completed secondary or higher education had had children at so early an age.[8]

Gender gaps in literacy and school enrollment can be observed in both rural and urban areas without significant distinction. Gender gaps in school enrollment are especially wide in Egypt, Iraq, Turkey, and Yemen. Moreover, women in MENA countries are twice as likely to be illiterate as men are and make up two-thirds of the region's illiterate adults.[9] The gender gaps in education vary widely across countries in the region, but generally are proportionate to the overall level of schooling and literacy, wider in countries where general literacy and school enrollment are lower. In Yemen, for example, the illiteracy rate among young women (54 percent) is triple that of young men (17 percent).[10]

Inequality of Rights

In contrast to countries at the forefront of the global economy, in many areas of the world women experience human rights violations and different forms of violence. They suffer from the gender inequalities due to the traditional structure of their societies and their conservative mindset. In some countries gender discrimination is not only a part of everyday life, but is also legitimized and codified by laws and civil codes. In most cases women have hardly any rights in the fields of divorce, custody, and inheritance. Not only can women be forced into marriage at really early ages like twelve or thirteen, but they also need permission from a male relative, usually a husband or father, if they want to seek employment, request a loan, start a business, or travel. Women cannot get a passport without the permission of a husband or male relative, and a woman's testimony in court is technically worth half of a man's, while a woman can still be stoned for adultery. In addition, domestic violence generally goes unpunished. Unfortunately, such laws and their mentality limit women's engagement in society and in their own families, as well as fostering the subjugation of women. Women are often unaware of or even confused about their rights because of the gap between formal law and customs.

There are some more issues that cannot be underestimated which relate to women in developing countries. The violence that women face may include: honor killings, dowry-related violence, forced and early marriages, female genital mutilation, female infanticide, and enforced sterilization. For instance 'honor killings' are customary in more than a few countries, endorsed by extremist Muslims and occasionally practiced by Muslim immigrants in non-Muslim countries. There are areas and countries in the world where it is the custom for members of a family or a social group to kill a woman member for the reasons such as being the victim of rape, refusing to enter an arranged marriage, being in a relationship that is disapproved by relatives, or dressing in ways deemed inappropriate. The murder of women who 'dishonor' the family is commonly encountered in formal law courts, where men who kill female relatives are often acquitted.

Another kind of violence imposed on women that is still in use is dowry-related subjugation. Dowry-related murders or suicides occur predominantly in India and South Asia, where women are treated as property. Brides unable to pay the high 'price' to marry are punished by violence and often death at the hands of their in-laws or their own husbands. Lastly, in many countries it is still a common practice to force underage girls into marriage, which means they lose their opportunity for education. This is an acute problem as girls who are not physiologically and psychologically ready to bear a child are put at risk through marriage or pregnancy-related complications.

TO BE A WOMAN IN A SESSION

From the Client's Perspective

The cases reported from my practice and the general picture given of the situation in which women in some countries find themselves will have led the reader to understand that violence and violation against women are rampant in every corner of that region. First of all, it has to be said that in systems where political, economic, social, cultural, and civil oppression of women is the rule, it is not an easy step for a woman to go to a philosophical counseling session. In addition, women who find themselves in various degrees of social or domestic incarceration are typically invisible and inaudible to wider society. Most of them do not even think it is worth their while to work on themselves in philosophical session, and they hardly find the spirit to whisper their stories, as if they are talking into their counselor's ear. The first couple of sessions are therefore very critical and crucial in making sure a woman counselee feels comfortable.

Imagine you are a women client who is about to walk through the door of a philosophical counselor's office for your first visit. You are living in a poor country where you are treated unfairly and it is really hard for you to find the time, motivation, courage, or opportunity to go to a counselor. You have arrived in secret to talk with someone about your intimate problems and inner dilemmas. You have thought many times about going to talk to someone, but fear and anxiety have kept you from seeking help. You are worried that somehow your family will find out what you have dared to do, that the counselor might judge you or let slip something about your problems to someone in the community. You are doubtful as to whether the counselor is really able to help you and can do anything to improve your situation. Perhaps you can now begin to feel how hard it is to make the decision and attempt to go to a counseling session. The fact that philosophical counseling is so unusual and little known in the general culture does not encourage you to take the step. However, despite this you have made the decision to see a philosophical counselor, to share your inner secrets, to obtain professional and philosophical help, and to walk through that door with courage.

At this point, what becomes very important on the part of the counselor receiving you as a courageous, audacious woman is that they build on your trust and that you have trust in their confidentiality. For a woman coming from a conservative and uneducated environment, the building up of trust plays a key role in helping them to open up and go from whispering to being able to talk freely. That is to say, once women in counseling have inner security and feel that what they are saying is in confidence, they can be comfortable in opening up and expressing themselves.

Your philosophical counseling session has already started. You are still feeling nervous sitting with a trained philosophy graduate person who seems trustful, sincere, and willing to help you deal with your problems and concerns. Can you visualize yourself as that woman who is so accustomed to be repressed that she is hardly able to express herself? This could be your one big opportunity to share all your thoughts, dilemmas, emotions, and complaints. Would you really feel comfortable enough to reveal things that you have kept trapped inside yourself so many times? It will not be so simple at the beginning. You will need to make a real personal effort just to raise your voice above a whisper. After passing that barrier of talking more comfortably about your life and yourself, the philosophical counselor can facilitate you to analyze your thoughts, feelings, beliefs, roles, and behaviors. Would you be able, step by step, to realize how expressing yourself, being heard, self-reflective philosophical assistance are beneficial and can make you feel liberated and healed? As can be clearly sensed from such a confrontation with philosophy, it leads to greater self-acceptance and empowerment in many aspects in your general life, everyday decisions, and relationships.

The other aspect is to build a 'helping relationship,'[11] which involves advanced empathy skills and closeness. As a woman who gets used to impartial attitudes in society and imbalanced power relationships, it is greatly significant to feel empathy in the relationship for exposing her inner strength and self-reliance.

Moreover, an effective philosophical counseling entails the challenging skills that facilitate self-awareness and confidence of counselees. In a session with women, this tool should be used sensibly so that the consultation can create a mature woman who possesses the ability to find ways to accept her situation as well as succeeding in a smooth and positive change.

All in all, philosophical counseling, which builds strong and professional bonds with women counselees along with the proper use of the skills mentioned above, creates therapeutic changes in a woman's life. Additionally, philosophical counseling helps people (especially women) to develop self-esteem and the ability to set clear boundaries. By having more control over their lives and relationships, women can learn how to make changes that they need to make. Last but not least, philosophical counseling facilitates people to find the appropriate decisions for themselves, their lives, careers, family, and future as well as feel confident about these decisions.

From the Consultant's Perspective

At this point, we can go further and envision the situation from a different perspective. Imagine that you have now changed seats and switched roles. Having empathized with the problems you faced as the counselee, now you are positioned as the philosophical counselor, seated as you greet your counselee.

As a philosophical counselor, you know that the majority of people are relatively capable of solving most of their problems either by themselves or with the guidance of philosophy. You are able to imagine, especially for women in so-called developing countries, that the role of the counselor is highly important and critical. First of all, as a counselor you are expected to understand women's problems, dilemmas, and desires within their social environment. With the aid of philosophy, you help each woman discover a proper constructive attitude, their inner strengths and capabilities to overcome their struggles. In addition, you facilitate the client in developing unconditional happiness, life satisfaction, and motivation. As a counselor you guide the counselee in a consequential manner along the path of philosophical counseling in order that they find the appropriate approach to deal with everyday problems according to their own personality, values, background, and culture.

The Approach

In this paragraph I will present some important aspects of philosophical counseling which I deem particularly relevant in working with women in so-called developing countries.

To start with, generally clients in philosophical counseling are in need of being listened to. One of the most crucial roles of the philosophical counselor is to be a good active listener where the counselor speaks little but conveys a great deal while listening. Even though philosophical counselors may not speak a lot verbally, they communicate consciously with their body language. A women counselor, in particular, knows how to use her facial expressions, position her body, and adjust the tone of her voice in a balanced and sensitive way.

In addition to being an active listener, a philosophical counselor must be well trained in sensing when, how, and what to ask in terms of addressing questions to the counselee. Questioning has to be performed while maintaining an open and non-judgmental attitude. The counselor should not pretend to have all the answers; giving the answers is not their job, but asking the right questions is. If the questions are effective, they will help the counselee think their experience through, and define their problems more clearly, as well as realize where they stand. The right questions are the gateway to self-discovery and they can help the counselee uncover what they might be unaware of. At this point, the philosophical counselor can draw on the Socratic method of questioning to stimulate critical thinking and bring to light new insights and perspectives. In the course of the dialogue, the philosophical counselor can ask open questions in order to elicit from the counselee a long answer providing implicit and explicit hints of their mindset. The counselor can also make use of closed questions in order to gather necessary specific information. In any cases, it should always be kept in mind that one of the main roles of the counselor in a philosophical counseling session with a woman (especially in so-called lesser-developed regions) is to make her feel comfortable so that she can think and freely express herself.

Furthermore, establishing a well-built and linking (philosophical) relationship between counselor and counselee is crucial. When following the Socratic method, the therapeutic process is based on a dialogue that enables self-examination through mutual trust and transparency. With this curing dialogue and relationship, the consultant broadens the clients' awareness of themselves, their motives, feelings, thoughts, actions, environment, and life. Through this relationship counselees are stimulated and guided to work out new insights and perspectives with respect to themselves, their surroundings, and their life's events. In dealing with women and their tendency to self-blame, this relational structure is particularly important in reducing their sufferings and rethinking their lives in general.

In many of the countries we are analyzing here, another important aspect of philosophical consultancy (therapy) with respect to women is the need to take attentive and sensitive note of the social, political, and moral values of the counselee's environment. It is undeniable that the problems that women are facing in so-called developing countries are not just caused by specific personal factors but are also significantly fashioned by external factors like ethical systems, culture, customs, social surroundings, and family structures. In this sense, the consultant should be sensible in guiding the counselee to reflect on the causes of their problems and neatly distinguishing and dealing with their intrinsic and extrinsic components.

To return to our session where you find yourself in the role of counselor, you realize as your client (a woman) talks about her everyday problems that she is neglecting all external constrictions relevant to her situation and is putting all the blame on herself. Or it may be the other way round and you realize she is accusing the external factors so much that she is failing to notice her actual position and her potential for working with personal issues and changing them for the better. In either case, you let her express her thoughts and emotions frankly, and then help her comprehend ways in which she can overcome her one-sided perspective and distinguish between external and internal dynamics and how the two are interrelated. Your guided questioning as the session unfolds should enable your counselee to understand how her self-perception, emotions, thoughts, decisions, conflicts, family, and society shape her life and cause her to feel a certain way.

Did you just notice a particular moment when her breathing eased and there was a release of tension? This is a key stage in philosophical counseling where your counselee essentially and objectively changes her life insight. It is an awareness of the apparent connection between her basic personal problems and the environment she lives in which helps her accept herself as she is and empower her with the skills she requires to actualize her potentials in all areas of her life.

The Technique

Unlike other forms of counseling, there is no absolute method in philosophical counseling that can be successfully applied to all cases. Although I have mentioned some of the general dynamics that can develop, it is worth specifying that all philosophical consultants have their own preferred approaches in dealing with their different cases. On the one hand, philosophical counseling strategies vary from counselor to counselor due to their backgrounds and life philosophy, while on the other each client differs depending on their specific situation, personality, and value system. Even though similar problems could be discussed in different philosophical counseling settings with different people, the contents of the sessions would be thoroughly different since everybody has a different way of dealing with life.

In my philosophical counseling meetings, I always find it beneficial to focus on the client's way of thinking before mentioning views from particular philosophers. During the session, I aim to analyze the components of my counselees' thoughts, beliefs, attitudes, and even actions. Through this exploration, I figure out the best philosophical approach that matches the client's values and principles. Very often, the discovery and developing of the personal philosophical potential of the counselee enables them to examine their life attitude, better understand their problems, and appropriately deal with them. At that point, the guidance of a philosophical counselor plays a critical role in providing a wide range of philosophical perspectives and tools for the counselee and suggests unseen aspects of the situation. In other words, I believe that philosophical consultancy enables counselees to examine their life as to live in more conscious, constructive, and creative ways.

As already mentioned, in my guidance to counselees I often refer to a saying of William James: "The greatest discovery of my generation is that human beings can alter their lives by altering their attitudes." I use this to emphasize the significance of their approach toward their lives and problems. It is always useful to keep in mind that people cannot easily change their circumstances, but always change the way they interpret them. Besides, not every problem has an immediate solution, but a counselee can reconsider the problem from a certain or different perspective. For women counselees who live in a so-called lesser-developed environment where they cannot really change their conditions, this insight can help them cope with issues so that they are no longer the source of their problems.

CONCLUSION

Taking everything into consideration, it is undeniable that philosophy can change lives positively and guide people to think and deal with their problems by themselves, and that this philosophical potential can play a key critical role with respect to women who find themselves in the particular circumstances we have described. In philosophical counseling, counselees learn to deal with their concrete and difficult problems in increasingly sophisticated ways. Philosophical inquiry about the life and the self enables people to reconsider and understand their environment and conditions from different viewpoints. As Albert Einstein stated, "Problems cannot be solved by the same level of thinking that created them." In order to overcome a problem, it has to be looked at in a different way. Thus, philosophical counseling could be regarded as a kind of wand for transforming problems into wisdom through the magic of changing personal attitudes and perspectives.

NOTES

1. It would be useful to define briefly what I mean by the developed and developing countries. Although there is no common, agreed-upon standard for what makes a country developing versus developed, some statistical indexes, such as GDP per capita (Gross Domestic Product), HDI (Human Development Index), life expectancy, the rate of literacy and so forth are used to measure the development of a country. Most commonly, a developed country or an industrialized country has highly strong economy with high level of industrialization and advanced general standard of living. In common practice, Japan, Canada, the United States, Australia, New Zealand, western and central Europe are considered developed countries. On the other hand, a developing country or a less-developed country is a nation with a lower living standard, underdeveloped industrial base, and low Human Development Index (HDI) relative to other countries. In the article, while using the term "developing countries," I referred to these counties with more conservative backgrounds like South Africa, Singapore, South Korea, Israel, China, Russia, Slovenia, Slovakia, Indonesia, Malaysia, Brazil, India, the Philippines, Thailand, Turkey, Egypt, Iran, and so on.

2. Philosophical counseling is a relatively new movement which was developed in the 1980s and which is generally practiced by professionals who hold a doctorate or at least a master's degree in philosophy. It involves sincere dialogue between counselor and client, which brings philosophical understanding in everyday problems. It could be assumed that although philosophical counseling is a modern approach, it is originated from older history and today's philosophical counselors could resemble the Pythagoreans, Cynics, Stoics, Epicureans, or the first philosopher in ancient Greek. To illustrate, just like in philosophical counseling, Socrates and his followers perceived philosophy as a method to examine the life through thinking and questioning. He also practiced philosophy in everyday and common places with ordinary people in order to encourage his discussion partners to think and question their assumptions and beliefs. In addition, the Stoics always portrayed philosophy as the wisdom or the art of living, not as the memorization of words of the philosophers or abstract texts. In line with the sophist movement, philosophical counselors use philosophy in pragmatic way to manage everyday problems for the sake of happy and fulfilled lives. See Pierre Hadot, *What is Ancient Philosophy?*, trans. Michael Chase (Cambridge Mass.: Harvard University Press, 2004); Pierre Hadot, *Philosophy as a Way of Life. Spiritual Exercises from Socrctes to Foucault* trans. Michael Chase ed. Arnold Davidson (Oxford: Blackwell, 1995).

3. It is highly controversial question how to name the person who receives a counseling service. In the mental health literature, the terms 'client' and 'patient' are commonly used. Most of the philosophical counselors would agree with me that neither patient nor client is agreeable in counseling. As it is known, the word 'patience' is highly affiliated with the medical context and the doctor-patient relationship, which conflicts with the nature of philosophical counseling. The word 'client' is also problematic in that it has capitalist connotations of business and money; however, many professionals agreed upon the use of this term as the 'client' in counseling pays to receive a service and has the freedom to leave the service that he has paid for. Additionally, lately, the terms 'counselee' and 'host' are used. The first one is not prevalent yet and the second one has just known by philosophical counselors who follow and read Achenbach, the founder of philosophical counseling. In this article, I use the terms 'client' as it is well known in the literature and 'host' as it involves the reciprocal relationship where the person in counseling opens himself to the philosophical thoughts and to the guidance of the counselor.

4. Reinhold Niebuhr, *The Essential Reinhold Niebuhr: Selected Essays and Addresses,* ed. Robert McAfee Brown (New Haven: Yale University Press, 1986), 251.

5. Farzaneh Roudi-Fahimi, and Valentine M. Moghadam, *Empowering Women, Developing Society: Female Education in the Middle East and North Africa* (Washington, DC: Population Reference Bureau, 2004).

6. BLS (Boreau of Labor Statistics), *Women in the Labor Force: A Databook for World Demographic Index* (Washington DC: Boureau of Labor Statistics, 2011).

7. Elizabeth M. King and Anne M. Hill, *Women's Education in Developing Countries: Barriers, Benefits, and Policies* (Baltimore: John Hopkins University Press, for the World Bank, 1993).

8. Turkey Demographic and Health Survey 2010 Final Report. Ankara, Turkey, and Calverton, MD, USA: Hacettepe University, Institute of Population Studies, and ORC Macro, 2011.

9. King and Hill, *Women's Education in Developing Countries*.

10. May Rihani and Cynthia Prather, *Strategies for Female Education in the Middle East and North Africa* (Amman, Jordan: United Nations Children's Fund, 2003).

11. Carl S. Rogers, "The Characteristics of a Helping Relationship," *The Personnel and Guidance Journal* 37 (1958): 6–16. doi: 10.1002/j.2164-4918.1958.tb01147.

BIBLIOGRAPHY

BLS (Boreau of Labor Statistics), *Women in the Labor Force: A Databook for World Demographic Index* (Washington DC: Boureau of Labor Statistics, 2011).

Hadot, Pierre. *What is Ancient Philosophy?* Translated by Michael Chase. Cambridge, Massachusetts: Harvard University Press, 2004.

Hadot, Pierre. *Philosophy as a Way of Life: Spiritual Exercises from Socrates to Foucault*. Translated by Michael Chase. Edited by Arnold Davidson. Oxford: Blackwell, 1995.

King, Elizabeth M., and Hill, Anne M. *Women's Education in Developing Countries: Barriers, Benefits, and Policies*. Baltimore: John Hopkins University Press, for the World Bank, 1993

Niebuhr, Reinhold, ed. McAfee Brown, Robert. *The essential Reinhold Niebuhr: Selected essays and addresses*. New Haven: Yale University Press, 1986.

Rihani, May, and Prather, Cynthia. *Strategies for Female Education in the Middle East and North Africa*. Amman, Jordan: United Nations Children's Fund, 2003.

Rogers, Carl S., "The Characteristics Of A Helping Relationship." *The Personnel and Guidance Journal* 37 (1958): 6–16. doi: 10.1002/j.2164-4918.1958.tb01147.

Roudi-Fahimi, Farzaneh, and Moghadam, Valentine M. *Empowering women, developing society: Female education in the Middle East and North Africa*. Washington DC: Population Reference Bureau, 2004.

Chapter Two

Therapy in Serbia from a Gender Perspective

Natasa Radovanovic

This chapter looks at gender differences in therapy starting from my experiences as a professional in Serbia. To begin, I would like to give the reader some information about how counseling is generally conceived in my country.

In Serbia, philosophical counseling has not yet gained a distinct autonomous physiognomy with respect to other forms of counseling. Moreover, counseling and philosophical approaches have not even really acquired their specific recognition with respect to psychoanalysis and psychological oriented therapies. As opposed to other countries in Europe and in North America, in Serbia the field of the professions designed to deal with personal and existential discomforts has not branched out into a multiplicity of different approaches and options from which potential beneficiaries can choose. Counseling, philosophical or otherwise, has started to develop just in the last years, at the same time as traditional psychotherapy. That's why in Serbia the rise of philosophical counseling can be regarded as part of the revival of psychotherapy, as it was conceived of in the antiquity: a therapy of the soul.

As Carl Gustav Meier and James Hillman remind us, the word "psychotherapy" is the compound of two Greek words: ψυχή (*psyche*), meaning vital force or soul in the original Greek sense of a fully embodied entity, and θεραπεύω (*therapuuo*), whose original meaning is 'to serve' referring to the priest's service to the divinity.[1] Thus, the word 'therapy' would suggest a process in which two parties, a client and a therapist, are equally involved. It is structurally guided by the therapist, with an aim to helping the client gain deeper insight into his or her problems and deal with them in an appropriate manner, one which induces self-awareness and personal growth. It requires confidence in the therapist and the therapeutic process, a trust-based relationship, and the therapist's caring guidance of the client through the therapeutic process.

The history of therapy, which can be dated back to the ancient Greeks, has seen the development of many psychological schools in the field of counseling. In fact in the 1960s there were around sixty different types of psychotherapies in Western countries, including psychodrama and guided imagery.[2] But Serbia has been late in its development.

In Serbia, psychotherapy is still a young discipline and a relatively new profession compared to other European countries. Its effects aren't yet visible and probably won't be for many years. Considering the historical development of psychotherapy in Western Europe and especially in North America, it can be concluded that Serbia is about fifty years behind. That is to say that in the past decade psychotherapy in Serbia went through the equivalent of the 1960s in Europe.

Philosophical counseling is a new and almost unknown field in Serbia even among counselors. The Serbian layperson would not be able to distinguish philosophical counseling from psychotherapy. That's why this chapter will focus on gender differences with respect to the general framework of therapy rather than in the specific discipline of philosophical counseling. The development of nonpharmaceutical approaches to mental and existential discomfort is just at its beginning in Serbia. Both the social context and the cultural debate on different alternatives to mental healthcare are not mature enough to allow me to reflect on the peculiarities of philosophical counseling in comparison to psychological approaches. On the other hand, however, because philosophical counseling is just taking its first steps here, Serbia may provide a good vantage point for observing the impact of gender differences on therapy.

To develop my reflection on the matter of psychotherapy among Serbian people, I will rely mainly on my professional experience as a school counselor, and on the data collected in the informal research I conducted for the purpose of this chapter.

In taking a broader look at Serbia as a country, the following facts are noteworthy: the country has been afflicted by wars in the past, it has been in transition for more than two decades, its economic situation is poor, the young are raised within a patriarchy and by a predominantly older population that is closed to the perspectives of other contemporary societies. Considering all these facts there will likely be long delays in the development of all forms of counseling and therapy. In this respect, philosophical approaches are no exception.

The labored development of the therapy in Serbia and its hardships in gaining acceptance by its people is also a consequence of a lack of the system's attention to this field. Mental health services are not supported by state medical insurance and must therefore be privately paid for by services' users.

It is possible to visit a psychologist in a state medical center, but this will be more the result of a protocol, than from a request for personal therapy. In such a case a psychologist gives a diagnosis or offers advice to an individual in compliance to a formal application by an institution such as a school. While state insurance will cover a visit to a psychiatrist, the function of these therapists is merely to prescribe drugs without offering any sort of discursive approach to counseling.

Like in many other parts of the world, in Serbia people still harbor prejudices about visiting a therapist or a counselor, and asking for this sort of help in dealing with their problems. In Serbian society there is still a tendency to associate the attendance of a psychotherapeutic session with pathological mental conditions or even insanity. Just the simple idea of visiting a psychologist or a psychiatrist is bound to trigger fears and discomfort, suggesting that there is something wrong in the person who wishes to work with a therapist. The pressure of those thoughts is enough for people to give up the therapy and rely only on themselves. People aim to stay 'untouchable' in other people's eyes at any price even when the price is their very health and peace of mind. This phenomenon shows how intense the pressure of the social environment can be. The pressure is greater on men, because they are expected to be tough, strong, self-reliant, and supportive providers for others; their weakness is more prone to be disapproved of, and their failure is more visible in the eyes of other people.

One more difficulty hindering the development of therapy is that while bigger cities have become as accepting of the professions of psychologist, psychiatrist, counselor, and psychotherapist as any other occupation, and while they try to stay open to innovations in this field, this has not occurred in smaller cities. In rural areas these professions are still totally unaccepted. Most people resist help from these professions and use these services only if absolutely necessary—that is, when ordered by the courts, or when it is a requirement to getting a license or a job. When such a service is externally imposed by some protocol or by law it cannot be refused. A mandatory requirement to visit a therapist often carries a stigma for the service's users and shame for their families, even more so when a person chooses to visit a therapist on their own. When you ask people if they have ever visited a psychologist they will usually answer that they haven't, even if they have.

I draw this picture from my own experience as a school counselor who works with pupils from seven to fifteen years of age, and with teachers and parents. Pupils have minimal resistance toward counseling regardless of their sex, but with growing up the differences appear influenced by their gender identities. I would trace prejudice toward therapy to gender identity as a result of education and social influence rather than to sex as a biological *datum*. As children mature the resistance becomes stronger under the pressure of public opinion. Teachers and parents prefer to use the services of an 'in-house' counselor, and only under a condition of strictest confidentiality. For example, teachers who work in school will use the help of a school counselor. The gender gap increases as children become adults because of the roles that mature men and women are expected to take on as adults and their accompanying social expectations. Parents usually come to a therapist for the sake of their child when they have tried almost everything else without success; children talk to the counselor because their teachers insist they should.

Most Serbs are not self-motivated to visit a psychologist or psychotherapist with the desire to better understand their problems, or for personal growth. They are under the powerful influence of tradition, which requires that men be brave and strong—both physically and emotionally—and never complain or show emotions in front of others, even in front of their spouse. Women are also expected to be strong, but only in some limited psychological respects, and therefore in a more circumscribed and less demanding sense. More specifically, they are expected to be an example to their children, to do their housework, to fulfill their maternal obligations, and to deal with problems inside the family.

I suppose that a similar situation is to be found in other countries that are experiencing a time of transition due to wars in their recent past and economic problems. Countries vexed by post-war reconstruction and socioeconomic difficulties are unlikely to have either the strength or the wish to break free from a conservative and patriarchal power structure. They are also likely to stubbornly resist any innovation, even to the point that progress is unwelcome. There is a certain fear of any change which could disturb the existing 'solid' societal structures: a collective fear usually most easily visible within family units. It is the fear of the unknown. When faced with unknown situations it takes effort to adapt to them and to accommodate changes.

In order to reveal why women and men have different points of view and why they tend to reject therapy, it is necessary to find out how they were brought up. As it is well known, society and family are the two most important and most influential factors in a child's development. What children learn at an early age shapes their attitudes and behavior in adult life. The basic need of every human being is to be accepted. So it is common for children to want to be accepted by their parents and friends, and adults to want to be recognized by society. Children learn at an early age what they must do in order to be accepted. For most people this becomes their most important guide in life. They think, "What will other people say; what will society say and think about what I do?" Therefore, if a family, under the pressure of tradition, educates its young that boys should behave differently from girls, the children will internalize this as their mental 'program.' This will then shape their behavioral patterns during most adult life situations.

In Serbia, young children get different behavioral instructions depending on their sex. Boys learn that they mustn't cry or otherwise show emotions or any sign of weakness; they must not to talk too much, and must not complain because that is what girls do. Later in life they should be the support for their family, so they must learn how to rely only upon themselves. It sends the latent message to boys that it's not appropriate for them to ask for help. A man should prove himself to society, especially in his career and the support of his family. And he should invest his energy and time in hard work.

Girls learn that they are expected to be emotionally warm, sensitive to the needs of family members, but yet strong at their core being. So it is common for girls to talk, to show signs of weakness, to cry, and to complain. This is not just common behavior for girls but in fact the expected behavioral pattern. Girls learn to rely upon other people, either on a partner, a friend, or a counselor and they are free to ask for help and support.

These sex differences in the behavioral expectations from an early age form the basis for the view on gender differences in emotions and logic later in life. When we understand these two patterns we can see that the gender differences are inevitable, and we can also better understand why men and women see psychotherapy differently. It was the aim of psychoanalytic feminists to alter the experiences of early childhood and family relations with therapy, as well as the social linguistic patterns that continue to produce and reinforce masculinity and femininity. Likewise, radical feminists saw early childhood experiences as key influences on sexual 'difference' and the perception of women's 'otherness' in relation to men.[3]

Since philosophical counseling is still unknown in Serbia, I conducted an informal research project on the topic, "What men and women think about undertaking a therapeutic process for dealing with life problems and existential discomfort." The participants consisted of fifty-two individuals: eight men and forty-four women (15 percent men and 85 percent women). They were mostly teachers and counselors. The women were generally more willing to answer the questions.

Participants were asked to respond to seven questions and tasks:

1. What do you think about the profession of psychotherapy?
2. Have you ever wanted or needed to visit a psychotherapist?
3. Why? Explain your answer to the second question.
4. Name some common reasons for visiting a psychotherapist.
5. Name what might be your reasons for visiting a psychotherapist.
6. Name benefits and drawbacks of visiting a psychotherapist.
7. Who visits the psychotherapist more often, women or men, and why?

The results aren't statistically significant because of the small sample size, but can be descriptively interesting. The various answers to the questions and tasks are discussed below by decreasing percentages.

In the first question they were asked to share their opinion about the profession of psychotherapy. Men (50 percent) said that this profession is unjustifiably neglected, but very sensible and important, that it takes too much emotional strength, that it is useful for people with psychological problems, and for lonely people without anyone to support them. 11 percent of the sample, two thirds of them women, said there are too many psychiatrists. Women also said that being a psychiatrist is very useful and interesting, humane, responsible, even creative, and that it represents the profession of the future. They considered the profession very mentally and emotionally exhausting, and feel that it requires continual self-improvement and dedication. Only a small number of the women in the sample stated that there is prejudice toward that profession (6 percent).

As we can see from the answers above, men tend to focus on the practical side of the profession, while women are more inclined to connect the profession to emotions, creativeness, personality traits, and personal development. That is to say women are more projected to the future of the profession and its potential for further self-development.

In the second question participants were asked if they have ever wanted or needed to visit a psychotherapist, or actually visited one. (I felt the question of 'need' might produce more honest answers). 52 percent said that they have wanted to, or actually did visit a therapist, thereof only 4 percent were men. Additionally, they explained why they visited or wanted to visit a therapist. Most of the participants identified the main reasons for going to therapy as stress at work and need for support in painful circumstances and critical life moments, marriage crises *in primis*. 6 percent, all of them women, said that they wanted to visit the therapist but actually didn't, a few named medical reasons, personal development, and formality as reasons why they visited or wanted to visit a therapist.

The rest of the participants (48 percent) said that they have never needed to visit a therapist—more than two-thirds of men from the sample and one-third of women. They named the following reasons for that: some of them like to rely upon themselves (mostly men's reason); some couldn't say why; some consulted friends instead of a therapist; some didn't know any therapist or how to get to one (men); some thought that visiting a therapist is just for seriously difficult life situations which they have not experienced; some said they didn't believe in therapy (women).

In the third task many of the participants connected seeking the help of a therapist either with a life crisis or a formal requirement to do so. Only a few were aware of therapy's potential for personal growth (women). The answers and comments have confirmed the hypotheses mentioned at the beginning of this essay about people's lack of understanding about the profession a prejudice against it, and a fear of disapproval from other people.

In the fourth task only one person, a man, said that there is no need for visiting a therapist at all, because that is what friends are for. The others named the following situations:

- When someone cannot confront the problems or difficult situations by him or herself. 46 percent of the participants chose this as a reason. Of this 46 percent, 42 percent were women, 4 percent were men.
- Harsh life situations: crises, marriage problems, losses (33 percent; this was a legitimate reason for counseling for most men and just one-third of women).
- Psychological problems—dissatisfaction, tension, fears, helplessness, depression, traumas. 17 percent of the participants chose this as a reason. Of this 17 percent, 13 percent were women, 4 percent were men.
- For advice, support (4 percent, women).

The participants named situations which tend to be the most common reasons for visiting a therapist, but the women mostly named situations in which people cannot fight the problems by themselves, while men generally didn't see that as a legitimate reason for visiting the therapist. Only a few of the participants—mostly women—considered seeking the advice or support of a therapist even before problems have piled up. Given these responses, it seems obvious that men depend on themselves much more than women, and expect the same from other men.

The fifth question which asked about personal reasons participants had for visiting a therapist elicited answers which appeared more specific and concrete, such as for getting help in solving big life problems related to:

- Trauma because of death of a close person: 17 percent (equal frequency in the responses from men and women)
- Mental health: 13 percent of the participants chose this as a reason. They were all women.
- Marital problems and divorce: 12 percent of the participants chose this as a reason. Of this 12 percent, 10 percent were women, 2 percent were men.
- Everyday stress: 10 percent (an equal number of men and women)
- Job: 4 percent of the participants chose this as a reason. Of this 4 percent, 3 percent were women, 1 percent were men.

Women also named the following reasons: getting professional advice, personal growth, loss of interest in everyday situations, and communication problems. Only men named 'curiosity' as a reason.

From these answers it can be seen that despite the obvious need to visit a therapist, over 40 percent of participants said they wouldn't visit one. In spite of that women would visit the therapist only if they couldn't do anything more by themselves (three times more women said this than men and 25 percent of men wouldn't visit one even then). Both sexes are more willing to visit the therapist for personal reasons than for anything else. Men said that they would visit the therapist more often because of practical and intellectual reasons; women said they would do that because of healthcare, personal growth, and problems with children. It is obvious that both sexes need emotional support in difficult life situations, although women are more willing to admit this.

For the sixth task—the benefits of visiting a therapist—participants named the following:

- Getting professional help in solving problems: 75 percent (an equal number of men and women)
- Increasing level of awareness: 14 percent (an equal number of men and women)
- Life coaching: 8 percent (more women than men)
- Emotional relief: 6 percent (women)
- Confidentiality: 2 percent (men)

For drawbacks they named the following:

- Time wasted because of unethical behavior—an unprofessional approach which aggravated the problem; a misuse of confidential data and a consequent loss of self-confidence 31 percent of the participants chose this as a reason. (They were all women.)
- Social stigma and abusive labeling: 23 percent of the participants chose this as a reason. Of this 23 percent, 10 percent were women, 13 percent were men.
- Danger of becoming dependent on the therapist, and abdicating responsibility for the problem-solving process: 21 percent of the participants chose this as a reason. Of this 21 percent, 18 percent were women, 3 percent were men.
- Financial losses: 2 percent (men).

Most participants were aware of the potential benefit in therapy but some of them had fears related to visiting a therapist. Some of the fears are linked to the therapist's approach, some to the process, and some to the society's reactions. The first two fear categories can be easier to overcome than the third, because the choice of a therapist, and thereby the process encountered, can be controlled by the individual to some extent while the third—society—

cannot. Fear of disapproval from other people can be explained in terms of their fear that a visit to a therapist will be viewed by others as a case of insanity. However, it takes great personal strength to face social stigma or taboo, to overcome that obstacle, and to get the help that is needed. The paradox is that in situations in which people need help, just when they feel most vulnerable, extra energy is required of them in order to get past the social taboo.

The seventh task asked participants who they thought visits the therapist more often, women or men, and why. Almost all the men said women. Some of men said that they are stronger than women, that a stereotype is that women have always asked for help throughout history which leads them to the belief that women's psyche is more complex requiring them to need help more often than men. The various explanations offered by the men simply illustrate different ways of pointing out the same attitude: women are those who need help, which makes them the weaker sex. Some of the men said the reason why women tend to visit therapists more often may be because women follow trends or fads; they go with what is 'in' more often than men do. Others said it is because men treat women badly more often than *vice versa.* Those answers also confirm the traditional beliefs within Serbian society.

The most frequent reasons for visiting a therapist given in the answers from women was women's readiness to see problems, to talk about them, and to face them. Women also considered themselves as more complex, more rational and emotional, and more profound than men. They actually considered men the weaker sex, despite the opposite point of view common within society. Women said they have more responsibilities, so they are more burdened. A less frequent answer seemed to be influenced by social stereotyping: because women are considered the weaker sex it is easier for them to ask for help. Only a few answers were about women being more serious and more responsible than men, having less prejudice, or finding it easier to trust other people.

The participants tended to agree that women see problems more profoundly and share them with others more easily. The fact that women are considered the weaker sex could make it easier for them to ask for help and talk about their problems. This may be just a social myth, but it affects women's and men's behavior, nevertheless. This generalization about women raises the question: "*Can someone be weaker in every aspect just because of their sex*?" The fact that women haven't agreed that they are the weaker sex seems to indicate that they are more aware of social stereotypes, and have learned how to use this stereotype to their benefit.

While there are many agreements in these responses from the men and women participants, such as in the reasons for visiting a therapist, there are also a few contradictions. Men see women as more complex beings than themselves, and in spite of the fact that they acknowledge that women must deal with so many different roles in modern times, men still think women are the weaker sex. Granted, it seems reasonable to consider women as 'weaker' than men in reference to their social position—according to their gender—which is a socially generated category, but not so according to their sex, which is a biological category.

Men often based their arguments for readiness to visit, or not to visit, a therapist on what women are like, while women in their argumentation didn't state what men are like, naming only their own personal reasons. It may be a sign that women are more self-aware and more ready to reflect on themselves, while men identify asking for help with what women do.

So the key factors to understanding and improving men and women's relationship to therapy include ongoing traditional gender roles, social expectations, and fear of social disapproval. Even today men are better positioned politically and in careers; they are better paid for the same job positions than women. That is especially the case in traditional societies. There visits to the therapist by women could be seen as their attempt to compensate for their unequal social position. In more open societies, where the position of women is better, where their political rights are almost equal to men's, and where they are allowed to have a career and are well paid for the work they do, men are likely to be clients in therapy in greater numbers.

Today women are burdened with many different roles: they are mothers, housewives, and managers of a career. But they still have the 'social permission' to ask for help. On the other hand, men are more oriented toward a career, earning lots of money, and involved in other roles which imply strength. A man asking for any kind of help is still seen as being a weakling in most societies today, and especially in a traditional one such as Serbia.

Gender roles, social expectations, and the fear of contradicting them, along with social stereotypes, shape human behavior, and thus sex and then gender are significant influences on the approach to therapy. It starts from an early age, when adults transfer all this onto the younger generation. In my experience as a school counselor I have found that parents often don't allow their children to visit a counselor because society considers it socially inappropriate. This illustrates the social fear surrounding therapists and similar professions which leads to prejudice against making use of this sort of help.

For a complete perspective on this problem social stereotypes must be taken into consideration, but not as the sole factor. Different gender-specific preferences and reasons for visiting the therapist must be added to the picture. When examining the relationship of men and women toward therapy one needs to bear in mind what has previously been explained about early family upbringing and social stereotypes. This leads to a consideration of basic human needs—for understanding, respect, and acceptance—which aren't determined by sex. Although these are the same for both sexes, they are displayed differently because they are under strong social and educational influences. It is therefore more justifiable to observe the differences as conditioned by gender. Thus, it's not just a question of who visits the therapist more often, men or woman, but why this is so. This will lead to the answer as to which kind of approach better suits women and which better suits men.

Encouraging is the fact that the fear of social stigma has decreased for some people in the past few years, but it remains strong among the majority of the Serbian population. The younger generation is less afraid and their acceptance of the professions improves as they mature. This suggests that children should be taught not to fear the social stigma surrounding therapy during early school years, and that both the schools and the state system can play a significant role in this process.

The call for change in attitudes toward therapy raises the question of what should be changed first, society or the individual members of that society. This is like the perennial dilemma: "Which came first, the chicken or the egg?" Society is an invisible entity that doesn't exist without individuals. However, individuals are shaped by the contexts to which they belong, and are bound to share and conform to their assumed worldviews and perspectives: in a certain sense, it is society that forms the individual by providing him with his own frames of reference, formal and informal rules codes of values, and so forth. Individuals within any society each contribute a small piece of collective awareness which consequentially and positively affects the collective or social consciousness.

Individuals can be the initiators of change, but when a person starts an idea it takes time to develop and grow into a change in society. For a change to set in, a lasting process of growth and transformation in mindset is necessary. This would involve individuals and their social context in a virtuous circle of mutual endorsement and gradual recognition.

The question is: "*What sorts of changes are required in order to stimulate changes in women's and men's attitude toward therapy*?"

If we take a wide perspective in the approach to therapy it surely can be said that state system support is very important for social acceptance of the professions related to psychological counseling of any kind. A social attitude is very powerful; it can either help or obstruct a positive personal attitude toward therapy and therapists. Furthermore it means that one of the system's methods for stimulating visits to the therapist should be the inclusion of those visits within the state medical insurance plan. This would be a fundamental systemic solution that would lessen the resistance to therapy and encourage individuals to accept psychotherapy just like any other kind of medical help. It would affirm the state's positive attitude toward therapy.

My professional experience shows that the key personal motivation for accepting the help of a therapist, besides being able to afford it of course, is overcoming the prejudice and social fear of asking for the help of a therapist. In my opinion an individual's readiness to visit a therapist is directly related to their level of awareness of therapeutic benefits. As this awareness is developed the individual becomes more willing to consider the possibility of therapy, and eventually to take that step. Rather than say that one's readiness for visiting the therapist depends on his educational level, it seems more appropriate to say that persons who would not even consider visiting the therapist are so inclined due to their educational level. The less educated usually can't visit a therapist because of economic reasons, but those with a higher education don't do so because they are afraid that the visit could endanger their social status. In my experience, educational levels have less of an influence on women; they are simply more willing to accept therapeutic help.

Individuals, who are self-aware and show a willingness to work on themselves, including visiting the therapist, could be the main contributing factor to progress in this field.

The second important step toward better acceptance of therapy is the counselor's positive attitude toward both the client and therapy itself. That attitude must be cultivated in every kind of counseling, even while possible future clients are still attending school. School counselors should present their helping profession in the best possible light. Psychotherapists should do this in two ways: *in a direct way* by doing their jobs in a professional manner, with dedication to their clients, and *in an indirect way* by constant professional development.

The third important step is for therapists to take different approaches to their various clients according to specific and socially conditioned gender needs. Although individual requirements vary, a predominantly discursive approach might be most helpful to women, while therapy for men could include more practical tasks. In countries in which the field of psychotherapy is more developed, such as in Western Europe and especially in the United States, gender differences and the need for adaptation are already always taken into consideration. But even in those countries women clients are still more numerous than men.

In conclusion, there are many factors and numerous perspectives that must be taken into consideration when developing any field of practice. To achieve improvements in psychotherapy societies should start from a broad perspective and narrow this down to a very specific and individual level. That is to say, in order to stay open to progress in therapeutic approaches, with an ability to face new problems and questions, and still remain sensitive to the variety of individual needs, it is necessary to incorporate philosophy into psychotherapy. A philosophical approach is a stimulus to progress because with it questions become more important than answers. A closer cooperation between psychological and philosophical approaches may be the key to further development of psychotherapy, and for decreasing resistance toward therapeutic help which still exists today within both genders.

These are some questions to be considered from a philosophical perspective:

- Are women and men really substantially different, or is gender just a surface upon which social fears are projected?
- Who do we fear the most? Who is our strongest judge?
- Is it time to look in the mirror, to meet society by ourselves, to face it with our true being, and to question it?
- Is the resistance to therapy just a way to hide from oneself?
- Is it time for a multidisciplinary approach?
- Why did the oracle at Delphi advise, *"Know thyself?"*
- Perhaps today it may be more helpful to ask: Which therapy is the best way to know yourself?

NOTES

1. Carl A. Meier, *Healing Dream and Ritual: Ancient Incubation and Modern Psychotherapy*, (Zurich: Verlag 1985).
2. http://psychcentral.com/lib/history-of-psychotherapy/000115.
3. http://www.oakton.edu/user/2/hgraff/WGSSummaryPsychoanalyticFemminismS12.html.

BIBLIOGRAPHY

Hillman, James. Anima. *An Anatomy of a Personified Notion.* Dallas: Spring Publications 1985.

Hillman, James. *Suicide and the Soul.* London: Hodder & Stoughton 1964.

Meier, Carl Alfred. *Healing Dream and Ritual: Ancient Incubation and Modern Psychotherapy.* Zurich: Verlag 1985.

http://www.oakton.edu/user/2/hgraff/WGSSummaryPsychoanalyticFemminismS12.html

http://psychcentral.com/lib/history-of-psychotherapy/000115

Trebjesanin, Zarko. Recnik psihologije. Belgrade: Stubovi kulture 2008.

Chapter Three

The Awakening of *Anima* in Philosophical Counseling

Silvia Bakirdjian

> You define yourself as a woman who is "very moderately gifted from the intellectual point of view" who "has never sunken into any metaphysical reflection whatsoever." As shown throughout your life story, your Animus projection was made on "an internationally renowned psychiatrist" because you should have more psychological knowledge. A deeper knowledge of the soul and its mysteries could deliver you from the fascination that captured you. In the second half of our lives, we should learn to know the inner world. This is quite a general problem. —Carl Gustav Jung[1]

I would agree with Professor Lou Marinoff when he states that the more elevated spiritual practices are not gender exclusive. In his book, *Therapy for the Sane* (formerly, *The Big Questions: How Philosophy Can Change Your Life*), he points out, for example, that to selflessly help another to meditate, to apply a philosophical principle, to achieve a more encompassing and higher worldview of reality, and so on, have no gender. He literally says: "*The soul has no gender*."[2]

However, in the dialectics being played in the inner life of the human spirit—in its broadest sense—the distinction between spirit as a masculine pole, and soul as a feminine pole, constitutes a topic that has spanned the entire history of our Western culture: the classic '*anima*' and '*animus*.'

What is my own experience with respect to this exquisite counterpoint?

I cannot speak only as a female philosophical counselor. In this I am bound to refer to experiences with male colleagues as well, not only as fellow students, but also as it applies to academic life.

When a young woman begins to study philosophy at university, she often finds herself amidst fellow male students whose peripatetic debates impress her, and, in order to be at their level, she proceeds to collect grandiose concepts, which she safely keeps and polishes, ready to bring out at the most opportune moment. Thus, she quite often succeeds in shining as much as the young men. This same attitude, the very same pattern, still prevails in the teaching profession, in the field of research, as well as in the whole paper writing process, and beyond.

This stage is only the beginning of a feminine life that is being conditioned by a central dominant cultural pattern.

Long before he or she become a counselor and chooses a philosophical practice, they have begun to take different paths, perhaps not with respect to the topics they work with, but certainly as far as concerns and details that have to be considered.

Of course, I cannot generalize and I speak only from my own experience. But bearing in mind these considerations is crucial if what follows—in itself relative—is not to be misinterpreted.

Often, men seek to demonstrate a certain doctrine and then persuade us. Women, on the other hand, take a long time reaching full awareness of a subject's inherent complexity, and upon reaching it, many times prefer to leave various doors open to allow the other to advance at his own pace. The women commonly tend to aim at fostering others to think for themselves.

Men frequently prefer to make others think what they think, and once they achieve this, they often feel satisfied that they have completed the task!

Life goes on, and as women get older and mature they re-find themselves and many times, and even though common codes persist, they feel they have had enough of the same old ambitions for fulfillment and the need to verbalize and make evident every argument in the discussion.

What has happened?

No activity can be separated from life, from a life story, and women have experienced life from such depths that it is difficult to verbalize, compare, classify, and so on.

Then, in a manner entirely different from the days of their youth, women no longer feel the pressing need to overwhelm with words, and they learn to speak less, perhaps saying more or pointing in the direction of more significant places, where no words reach.

Just like in a *Zen* state of consciousness, a mere gesture, a listening ear, a well-timed silence, the right *tempo* in the inner play between words and silences, a generous emptiness, all become for women the most valuable philosophical treasure they could offer.

However, it is important to add—in order to avoid any misunderstandings—that many men themselves achieve this very same even temperament, with which it becomes evident that when it comes to philosophical counseling, I find it altogether impossible to draw a clear dividing line between male and female counselors.

From reading transcripts of sessions attended to by male counselors, and through shared experiences with colleagues, I have nevertheless observed certain marked differences which in no way affects their professional competence or its effectiveness, given that the success of the consultations—its potential for lessening the suffering of the other—has been very high in every case. I often tell my clients (as well as other people) that things can never go wrong. It's not sheer optimism but rather the intention of selflessly helping another (compassion) that fulfills its purpose beyond how insightful or skillful we are at the time.

It is also necessary to refer to the *anima* or *animus* of the client, given that he or she is not merely the passive guest invited to this banquet, but the main protagonists in his/her own recovery.

Some male philosophical counselors, while listening, are already thinking of the different philosophical doctrines that they can offer their clients to help them take adequate decisions —or at least the one best possible. Decision-Prescription appears to be their outstanding feature and many times they manage to fully satisfy their clients.

When female philosophical counselors listen, they *listen*. They empathically auscultate the client's emotions while at the same time coming up with highly customized strategies to overcome the very particular inertia and resistance of the other to undertake some changes. Only when empathy climaxes, they resume speech and use philosophical explanations to endorse and obtain acquiescence in relation to the proposed changes.

Also, I wish to point out an interesting difference stemming from a well-known idea referring to epistemology of gender. Men are fascinated by things and how they work. They perceive themselves as objects separated from other objects with which they establish relationships of threat, friendship, enmity, and so on. Women focus more on the relationships between people and with themselves. They are more interested in emotional links, and when dealing with objects, include them also in their own emotional world.

We are born either male or female. Through culture we become men or women. But biology is not destiny and I would add that psychosocial conditions are not either. Even when differences persist, as was pointed out earlier, these tend to vanish within the field of a higher activity such as philosophical counseling.

I must admit that I do not feel entirely comfortable writing some of these somewhat reductionist descriptions. Many times, a new practitioner doesn't bear in mind the considerable amount of time that needs to be given to a consultation's emotional unfolding, both for men and for women. In face-to-face encounters with clients, time allows for a fine sensitivity to mature: this is a clear example of *learning by doing.*

All types of clients approach philosophical counseling. There are those who come because of some unresolved existential concern; others because they are about to take a decision or have an important choice to make, and some are people who, having suffered much, seek help to heal what remains of their lives. But in neither of this do I find any predominance of gender.[3]

I want to make a punctual but interesting observation. Males, of all ages, 'pour their hearts out' without hesitation and expose their most jealously guarded intimacies both to female and male counselors alike. And the most interesting thing is that they do this with a naturalness, intimacy, and clarity about themselves such as they would never do sitting with their friends in a café, where a set of codes and common places are in force and which a group of 'macho' men would never dare violate.

In any case, I have observed that in many cases the male client is more inclined to hold on to the solutions that he has already brought with him and which he has only come to confirm, so to speak; women, on the other hand, bring to the consultation some lucid thoughts about themselves that they have managed to string together, but which have not convinced them and which they don't fully believe and so they ask more than men what they should do and how to act. They come, for the most part, to construct a plan of life that would procure them a greater sense of well-being. Men, on the other hand, usually approach counseling already toting their own agendas, and in informal gatherings with fellow counselors, we agree that it then proves to be more difficult than with women to propose changes and discourage their preconceptions as to how they are dealing with a certain crossroads in their lives.

However, I have written some books for my clients in order to make them reflect on the paragraphs that they have found more touching, and I must admit that according to my experience men are more enthusiastic and compliant than women in this type of task.[4]

After these rather random observations—which are, nonetheless, not altogether without interest—I wish to return to the subject of *anima* and *animus* within a different setting. And here I suggest the reader become used to thinking of these two faces of the spirit living within the human being, without the division between men and women, but as faces of the soul that can be further developed, one at the expense of the other, or harmonically balanced, whether it be male or female.

Even more, I would wish to explore the subject from the standpoint of two great Western philosophers who have taught and motivated us to profoundly reflect on what it is to think well, deeply and by ourselves. I am referring to Martin Heidegger and Emmanuel Levinas, despite the fact that they have never before been presented as complementary philosophers. This perspective is particularly interesting to me when we consider that the environment within which the consultation is played and unfolds, is precisely this: our thinking.

If we were suddenly confronted with the question 'What is thinking?' we would hesitate a little and then respond in various ways, referring to the different, more commonly used instances of the term. In any case, at first, we would most probably be taken aback because we are used to believe that we think all the time, and that this being something so natural, the question is too obvious.

However, following the thread of thinking of the meditations of the mentioned contemporary philosophers, we see that we do not think as we think we do—for instance, we do not think in an authentic and essential manner. That it is altogether probable that we might go through our entire lives without even having truly *thought*; that we have lived trapped in a tapestry of mental patterns that have quashed our deepest and most real consciousness; that we have unconsciously thought in spite of ourselves and even against ourselves (that being the source of all the maladies that the counselor endeavors to address) that a parasitic mind took over our essence and our destiny. That we never thought what is worth thinking.

Heidegger and Levinas point the way of a more genuine path, to a more genuine way of thinking. But it would be of no use to take those indications as 'prescriptions' to practice, if an inversion of the ordinary consciousness hasn't taken place before (such as can be encouraged in counseling). First it is necessary to become aware of this, and then to surrender to the vertigo that any true inversion of consciousness demands. What I aim to show as shared by these two authors (which have, apparently, no evident common ground that would merit a comparison) is that the jump into the abyss which deep inner change presupposes has much to do with silence.[5] And it is at this point, that the reader might notice that I am speaking from the pre-eminence of my *anima* side.

I'm redeeming the silence where the alert and vigilant waiting, as well as the recognition experienced when faced with the other's gaze, converge. The essence of speech, of language, appears more as silence than as words or excess of speech characteristic of a representative, instrumental, categorical thinking.[6]

In the consultation, it is not about nonverbal silence, of having to opt between speaking or keeping quiet. It's rather about a silence beyond language, beyond words, because when words are uttered they don't feel sufficiently expressive. They are not quite enough. And the same happens with the mental images that are evoked with merely words. When we liken it to a vacuum, we should understand it as a vacuum we are conscious of. A vacuum within the gaps of our conversation, which even as a vacuum, whispers messages to us. We have entered the realm of the unutterable, even if we continue to speak. But as we have said above, first we must *become aware* of the difference and accept it consciously in order to allow for a Presence that transcends the subjectivity of pure rational speculation.

Although in Levinas the metaphysical absolute distance is given, "a relationship absolved of all relationship," between 'I' and the other—in contrast with Heidegger's comprehensive ontology, where the being re-appropriates itself as *Da-sein*—a common form of transcendence persists: the *decentering* of the self.[7]

This decentering is an absolute transcendence of the ego consciousness with respect to itself. It is the forgetting of oneself. And the abandonment of consciousness characteristic of modernity by which we have all been formed, demands that the male or female philosophical counselor humbly allow a transcendent presence to emerge in the middle of the dialogue. This transcendent Presence does not dwell in a separate world—such as is referred to in the Platonic archetypes—but in the deepest confines of this world, in the depth of our immanence. Here and now (within a session), and in the depths of our hearts.

We are used to living on the surface of our being, where we like to interpret starring roles in which we can stand out. And we live it as a rational individual separated from its object, this establishing and reinforcing a consciousness pattern based on duality and separation. From this duality mutual understanding becomes impossible, unless counselor and client come to some kind of forced solution, but which is neither lived nor felt. Our basic illusion is that of being individuals who gather objects, ideas, and forms, be they sensitive or intelligible. In the outer layers of our being, we experience ourselves as the center of the universe. When we mention the necessary 'inversion' of consciousness, to allow for real thinking and for real language, we refer to a radical inversion. It is also likely that modern man may think of himself as *not* being the center of the universe. But this thought means nothing without a genuine '*become aware.*'

First it is necessary to 'become aware,' and then to surrender to the vertigo that any true inversion entails, as said above. This is why Heidegger called it 'extremely serious' to forget that we forget, not even noticing the basic dysfunction that keeps getting in the way of real thinking and of true uttering, whose grooves are even less pretentious than the grooves left by the farmer in the field.[8]

We live as if all things are at our disposal to be controlled and classified as knowable elements or issues in the Kantian sense; as if we were not aware of the tyranny of our—very often imaginary—passions, and the distress that this provokes in us—making us seek help because we can no longer cope alone.

Living in this *consciousness dysfunction* keeps us from gaining access to a more essential dimension, even when we seek help. In that more essential dimension, the wrong perceptions would inevitably break down and our look—until then focused on a distressing object or obsession—would benefit from the gift of a radical 'conversion:' a μετάνοια (*metanoia*)—from μετά (*meta*), meaning 'through,' and νοῦς (*nous*), meaning 'mind,' 'intellect'—so amiable toward *animus* and so treacherous to our *anima*).

What does 'a new look' mean? It does not occur simply as the result of subjective will. It is an occurrence that happens suddenly, an experience. It is an event, it happens. It is no longer us who think and speak while remaining in control and indicating something. It is the being-other who thinks *himself* and manifests *himself* in us. This is why Levinas also speaks of this experience as an asking, a questioning or an approach toward us from the other, the being (depending on which of the two philosophers we take as reference).[9]

If we had to describe the attitude that best corresponds to a man, in this asking/questioning by the other (Levinas) or by the being (Heidegger), perhaps silence—necessary for listening and for being able to recognize it—would be the most appropriate. From silence and inner stillness one can really, truly inquire, pay attention, be present in the experience of the encounter. Accustomed as we are, to doing and producing, we think of silence as nothing. And it *is* just nothing in relation to our habitual behaviors.

As Kafka beautifully said, and then Deepak Chopra reported, becoming a spiritual metaphor of mankind:

> There is no need to leave the room. It is enough to just sit at the table and listen. One doesn't even have to listen, just wait. One doesn't even have to wait; only learn to remain silent, still, and alone. The world will freely offer itself to be discovered. It has no alternative; it will drop in ecstasy at your feet.[10]

It is a brilliant and bold statement that values the wisdom of asking, paying attention and being present as a nondoing, paradoxically emphatic between counselor and client.

Heidegger speaks us of the '*Khere*' ('the turn') and I would add: toward depth Levinas alludes to discovering oneself as a responsible being before the eyes of the other, while facing the other; discovering himself no longer purely as an action subject, but as someone touched by a superior initiative that transforms him and turns him inside out.[11] He is born again in a different way; in a dimension of himself he has never previously known.

Both thinkers are exponents of what we could describe as a philosophy of the '*ear*' as opposed to classical philosophy, which since the days of Plato—and his theory of ideas has been likened to a philosophy of '*sight*.'[12] We can hear silence more easily with our eyes shut.

In philosophical counseling we need consciousness, we need to be here or there but present, so that we may be able to listen and give of our attention freely. It wouldn't do to be looking at things from the past, future, or even heavenly or transcendental, with our real being somewhere else. The philosophy of the '*ear*' most appropriate for counseling, is the one of 'the being's calling,' the one with the commanding 'Speech' of the other. Both converge in the experience of listening to silence as a means of quieting the voices of the mind with which man is familiar, in order to allow for other different, more genuine and essential voices to resound in one.

It is a question of listening to that which is worth listening to: silence, which nevertheless, utters the purest truth; so much so that we deem it to be the way the Absolute manifests itself—that which is free of all limitation and dependency, the infinite and Numinous which resides in the deepest part of each one of us, counselors and clients alike.

If after all that has been said, gender difference in philosophical counseling is still considered radical—which may have become evident that I do not subscribe to, preferring to speak to the feminine aspect of men and the masculine aspect of women—I invite the reader to read a quote from Paul Claudel's *Parabole d'Animus et d'Anima: pour faire comprendre certaines poésies de Rimbaud*:

> One day when Animus came home unexpectedly, or perhaps he was taking a nap after dinner, or perhaps he was absorbed in his work, he heard Anima singing all alone, behind the closed door. An unusual song, something he did not know, and there was no way to find the music or the words or the key; a strange marvelous song. Since then he has tried slyly to make her repeat it, but Anima pretends not to understand. She shuts up as soon as he looks at her. (. . .) Gradually Anima relaxes, looks about, listens, breathes, believes she is alone, and noiselessly goes to open the door to her divine lover. But the eyes of Animus, as they say, are in the back of his head. [13]

NOTES

1. Carl Gustav Jung, *Correspondence, tome 4, 1955–1957*, (Paris: Albin Michel, 1995), 240 .
2. Lou Marinoff, *Pregúntale a Platón,* (Barcelona: Edicitiones B, 2004), 278.
3. Regarding the epistemology of gender, my experience as a consultant on environmental issues, in which I work both in the office and in the field has enabled me to note that men, even if they live within an ecosystem, fail to connect deeply with the meaning of the 'ecosystem' concept. However, women have a more organic, more holistic, almost spontaneous knowledge—which is transmitted ancestrally—about the cycles that are the hallmark of an ecosystem. For example, ahead of an alteration of nature they recognize the signs earlier than men, and act accordingly. This female perception implies a respect for life and nature, a connection to all living beings, without forcing solutions to problems but looking for non-invasive or abusive operating alternatives, to conserve natural resources and ensure food for their peers. In that sense women play a prestigious and valued role in front of the people of their community.
4. See Silvia Bakirdjian *El Secreto de los Filósofos* (Ushuaia: Editorial Utopías, 2010) and Silvia Bakirdjian, *El Pensar, el Habla y el Silencio* (Ushuaia: Editorial Utopías, 2011)
5. See Bakiardjian, S., 2011, 99–104.
6. Heidegger, Martin, *¿Qué significa Pensar?* (Buenos Aires : Nova, 1972), 47.
7. Emmanuel Levinas, *Totalité et Infini* (The Hague: Martinus Nijhoff, 1971), 35.
8. Heidegger, *¿Qué significa Pensar?,* 32.
9. Levinas, *Totalité et Infini,* 9.

10. Deepak Chopra, *Las siete leyes espirituales del éxito* (Madrid : Edaf, 1994), 9.
11. Bakirdian, *El Secreto de los Filósofos,* 107–113.
12. In ancient Greek *òida* (οἶδα) means 'I know' and it is the past aorist of *oráo* (ὁράω), meaning 'I see.' For the ancient Greeks 'to know' is 'to have seen.'
13. Paul Claudel, *Positions et Propositions, I,* in XXe Siècle (Paris: Collection A. Lagarde & L. Michard, Bordas, 1966), 218.

BIBLIOGRAPHY

Bakirdjian, Silvia. *Decatlón para ejercitar el alma. Endorfinas filosóficas.* Ushuaia: Editorial Utopías, 2009.
———. *El Secreto de los Filósofos.* Ushuaia: Editorial Utopías, 2010.
———. *El Pensar, el Habla y el Silencio.* Ushuaia: Editorial Utopias, 2011.
Chopra, Deepak. *Las siete leyes espirituales del éxito.* Madrid: Edaf, 1994.
Claudel, Paul. *Positions et Propositions, I,* in XXe Siècle, Collection A. Lagarde & L. Michard, Bordas, Paris 1966.
Jung, Carl Gustav. *Correspondance, tome 4, 1955–1957.* Paris: Albin Michel, 1995.
Heidegger, Martin. *¿ Qué significa Pensar ?* Buenos Aires: Nova, 1972.
Levinas, Emmanuel. *Totalité et Infin.* The Hague: Martinus Nijhoff, 1971.
Marinoff, Lou. *Pregúntale a Platón.* Ediciones B, Barcelona 2004.

Chapter Four

Philosophical Counseling at the End of Life: A Gender Perspective

Luisa Sesino

AN ALL-FEMALE JOB

For almost twenty years, I have supported people at the end of their lives, as well as their families and health workers, assisting them with my philosophical counseling. I try to listen to their suffering and to their questions. I live the experience of supporting both men and women as a woman, obviously. This means that I spontaneously focus on certain work methods which, by their very nature, suit me: acceptance, listening, the comprehensive understanding of a person and, in terms of thought, the consideration of the emotional and affective dimensions of the other person.

I am fully aware that an analysis of the feminine role in philosophical counseling, in particular in the context of the end of a life, deserves a more comprehensive and in-depth study than the present chapter has been able to include. The very definition of *feminine* would need more extensive research and a more detailed discussion. However, I will try to highlight some of the characteristics which, in my opinion, are specifically feminine in the practice of philosophy with people.

There are several characteristic aspects of philosophical counseling that I believe have an important and productive role in the field of terminal medicine: giving voice to the experience of the limit and of impotence; having the courage to accept problems rather than attack them, waiting for the light that is needed to truly change, having an attitude of listening to what opens to life, and a disposition to explore the space of *mystērĭum*.

I will therefore attempt to illustrate my work starting from these feminine perspectives, in which dimensions like nakedness and treatment, the primacy of being over doing, the importance of interior gestures and of giving the soul more space can all fully express their potential. Actions like meeting and watching over, accepting and offering, giving voice, broadening horizons and exploring what is vital, can then become paths in a journey to understanding and transformation.

NAKEDNESS

Illness, suffering, and the prospect of death are among the most challenging and significant chances to embark on a journey in search of meaning. Everyday routine and challenges usually make us lose sight of this meaning. Pain closes our eyes, diverts our attention from outside, and forces us to look inside ourselves so that we can listen and concentrate on the essential. Questions about the multiple dimensions of life which everybody, more or less consciously, asks themselves throughout their lives are often postponed or buried by things that take precedence or are more urgent. When illness begins, however, these questions often become more pressing and distressful. This is a time of difficult questions, which pour out like a scream demanding to be heard.

Terminally ill is used to define, and often label, a person who has entered the last stage of their life. It is almost as if they have a new role to play. Their hunger for meaning is great, urgent, and intense. In practice, however, terminally ill patients see and understand themselves mostly through the eyes of the people who are close to them. Yet family, friends, and health workers often feel increasingly uncomfortable in the relationship and prefer to relate to their sick bodies rather than to their interior suffering. [1]

Excluded from the everyday routine of doing, producing, and searching for well-being, the terminally-ill person is deprived of their social identity. "I was a manager. I ran an important insurance company and now I need to be fed by others." Face-to-face with the naked person, with the core of human being, we often find ourselves without words, images, ideas, or points of reference.

To think of ourselves as acting beyond our roles is a very delicate and difficult passage, but it can greatly broaden our understanding of life and of our ultimate choices. While all the others relegate the terminally-ill patient to a new role, it is important that the philosopher make sure that they are not denied the chance to experience their own identity at a deeper level.

"Not everything is without meaning. Now I have the chance to ask myself who I am beyond the roles I have to play. Who I really am." "You can't live depending on what you previously judged important but then realized wasn't.

For example, what others think of you. Those few *others* aren't even the ones you care about the most . . ."

LISTENING TO THE "WHYS"

"Why me?" This tragic question needs to be asked and listened to. We often don't know how to question pain, suffering, illness, and death. We can hardly expect, then, to be able to share these questions, so we are constrained and confined to a few trivial and inadequate stereotypes.

It is the so-called *conspiracy of silence* of relatives and friends who neutralize the ill person's questions by eluding, postponing, and opposing them. "What are you talking about?" "Come on; don't think about it, the doctor's coming!" "Stop saying these things, I'm sure you'll get over it." The ill person feels alone and ignored, or confined to the suffocating space of limited and ready-to-use Band-Aid answers, which are supposed to relieve or at least ward off his existential suffering.

Philosophical work often starts by listening to a person's deep questions, to their *whys* without answers, in an open and friendly space. This space is not pre-defined, pre-categorized, or jeopardized by perspectives suggesting or imposing meanings given initially by others.

At first, ultimate values are seldom tackled. The starting point is what the person tells, what they feel as urgent. Their vision emerges from the way they talk about life and its difficulties. We are not working with a problem, but listening to a person. We are dealing with individuals who have their own unique way of seeing and constructing the world, and who are asking us to live temporarily in their universe, allowing them to somehow be the center of ours for a while. It is a matter of firstly identifying the ill person as a face.[2]

GIVING VOICE TO THE LIMIT

We first need to give voice to the limit, to impotence, and to the hunger for meaning. Only by announcing them can we actually look at them. Only by giving them space we can explore a different dimension in which the time of death—as one of the most important and significant human experiences—can be seen as a precious and meaningful opportunity to find a deeper sense in life.

"I have an urge for truth which the people close to me can't satisfy." The terminally ill need truth; they want to live at all costs, even if this implies suffering. No matter how difficult, exhausting, or full of anguish it can be, it still remains the fundamental experience of their life.

According to the mentality of the people surrounding the dying person, this often appears difficult to accept, almost scandalous. "I understand them.

After all, I'd also rather have a drink than think about certain things. But now my horizons have broadened enough to make me see what's happening to me as worth living. I think that this is much more interesting for me now."

Widening our perspective on things to actually live what happens to us. I believe this is a good definition of philosophical work. The time of illness, then, is no longer a meaningless time subtracted from life, but it becomes—for some people at least—a time of deeper understanding and experience of life itself. Although we are used to interpreting them as a denial of life, both illness and pain can in reality be lived as an essential part of our story.

"In this work, it is life that I'm discovering. And I am also discovering that I can actually live my illness and, maybe, death."

MAIEUTICS

A person's narration is the fundamental basis for the counseling which will begin. The quality of listening to this narration is the necessary precondition for the development of all the following stages. The starting point of the work is to make sure to listen to the ill person with an open mind. Thanks to this, the concepts used by the individual to describe their existence and interpret their life become doors to reach their deeper condition.[3] It is exactly this depth that generates their words and tinges them with personal hues. Through these words, in a sort of maieutic process, it is possible to reach the core of their experience and, little by little, allow it to reveal itself.

Through the ways it is expressed, we can somehow save the reality that the person is living. Deciphering it in the deep texture of their life and of their suffering, we can see and try to understand their reality in the same way that the person sees and understands it.

I think it is important to consider that the main observers of the situation are the patients themselves. They are the ones who look, contemplate, interpret, and are reached by what they are living. My job as a philosopher is first of all to focus on the process that their own observation triggers inside them and to allow it to develop. Only then we can explore together the fruitful opportunities it offers. I think it can be said that philosophical counseling starts with this self-contemplation; sharing the same—so to say—solemn and inviolable space that is the other person's life.

THE COURAGE TO INHABIT QUESTIONS

The person needs to be accompanied in their exploration of the wonder of their existential world and helped to move within it, to go a little farther every time and expand its boundaries. In order for this exploration to reveal new and genuinely creative possibilities for real change, our duty as counselors is to accept and respect that world without invading it with our own self, our presumed knowledge or ability to help people know.

It is a matter of learning how to inhabit questions, whether they are explicit or implicit, of finding out that we can start to move within them and that, by searching—perhaps through short and uncertain answers—we can grow as human beings and reach a deeper meaning. There are not ready-made, unequivocal, and definitive answers. And rightly so, for this guarantees the depth and richness of existence considered in a broader perspective—to actually release its vital energy. This doesn't happen immediately. We need, then, to be ready to accept silence and to inhabit the uncertainty.

This invitation to welcome waiting and remain inside it is difficult; perhaps more for the counselor than for the patient. It means living in a deserted space, accepting a nakedness of concepts, a scarcity of operational tools, and sometimes limits to our resources.

It takes courage. A feminine version of courage, I would say. Not the courage to face problems in order to solve them, but the courage to stay and support in order to foster a creative environment which leaves space to the other and the new.

MEANINGFUL WORDS

If we resist the temptation to draw immediately, without mediation, from our own conceptual knowledge, it is the unique and original self-interpretation of the person that will eventually emerge. The interior resources used by people to interpret their life experiences are always a source of wonder and fresh knowledge for me.

By way of an idea, a recurring image or a deeply meaningful word, their accounts eventually offer a key which can help us broaden our horizons in order to explore new dimensions. Sometimes, it is an expression that surprises us. This is, perhaps, because the expression is not one that we would give much importance to, or would even take into consideration as it is seemingly far from the path we would have followed as counselors.

I met a woman, for instance, a little after the death of her forty-two-year-old daughter. She herself had been widowed when she was very young and her daughter had been a source of strength and reason for most of her life. I was in a difficult position, because given the delicate situation, I was afraid I could not find an adequate starting point to tackle her suffering.

Absorbed in my own discomfort, I did not realize that she was repeatedly expressing the crucial concept around which she had gathered all her strength to live with the expression "life goes on." It was probably the one thing I would have never dreamt of saying to a person hit by such a bereavement! To me, it sounded stereotypical, stupid, and potentially devastating. The fact that it was exactly what I would never want someone say to me in a similar situation was preventing me from detecting the actual clue the woman was offering. It was exactly this that the woman was formulating and living as a source of life.

In the tangle of emotions, images, and ideas that a person conveys, we can choose to start from that little bright spot perceived as vital and dynamic, which somehow introduces an element of novelty into the system.

Starting, therefore, not from what appears to be relevant and right to us, but from what stimulates evolution and change in the individual: It is this attitude that allows us to meet the person within, that almost sacred space which is their interiority, and move consistently with the form and colors of their unique and personal way of living, feeling, and understanding things.

LISTENING TO WHAT OPENS TO LIFE

Listening to what opens to life: this is also a specifically feminine attitude which can protect us from those aggressive temptations of thoughts that want to break in from the outside in order to explain rather than understand. This is the only way actual philosophical work can really start. The moment of conceptual clarification has finally arrived and we can tailor it in a truly personalized way.

Now the person's language and meanings can be examined, ordered, and expressed. They can be interpreted on different levels, opened up, and enriched with new alternatives. They can be taken further to explore their perspectives and stimulate their productivity, and possibly put aside in favor of more creative paths. Because they can no longer be used in a trite and uncritical way, they unveil a hidden vitality.

Confused ideas often result in contradictory attitudes, forcing a person to be in situations in which they would usually never find themselves. Through the analysis of meanings and their expression, the individual becomes more transparent to themselves and more aware of their situation. By searching for alternatives they are freer and more capable of making choices. The quality of their access to reality changes, and new dimensions of acceptance and responsibility toward life open up. It is the mysterious result of the deep contact between thought and existence, and between thought and action.[4]

MEETING THE MEANING

More than about death, people wish to talk about life; the life which was, and the life which is left. Many terminally-ill patients—more or less explicitly—express the fear that their life may somehow have been wasted, missed, scattered, or not lived to the fullest.[5] Much more frequently than expected, the origin of their desperation is simply the feeling of meaninglessness. "If nothing makes sense, then illness becomes really unbearable." If we talk about *sense*, this doesn't mean that we have to understand the illness completely, explain it, or find a reason or purpose for it. It is sufficient to find a direction to follow. We therefore feel the need to put in order, or to read our personal story in order to decipher its meaning. This meaning is often discovered not as something created by us, but as something we've found. "I've always believed that I was the one who gave meaning to the things I lived, but now I see that life has its own meaning. It's something I've never been aware of." Meaning is not given; it is happened upon.

Some people need support in their search of what really matters. "What is really important?" In selecting what things are essential, relationships have always had a crucial role. Other values, perhaps long and tenaciously pursued like success or respectability, having or succeeding, usually fade away. We discover the importance of putting people before things.

One day, a young woman staying in a hospice was writing some notes and piling them up with difficulty on her bed; some to her right and some to her left. "What are you doing?" I asked her. "I'm separating what I'll keep from what I'll throw away," she responded. "May I ask you what you are throwing away?" "My gold Rolex, for one!" "And what are you keeping?" I inquired. "These are my grandmother's lullabies."

TRANSFORMATION

Within this process, which is at times liberating, at others exhausting and painful, problems can turn from insurmountable and overwhelming difficulties into precious opportunities. We don't face them together only as obstacles to overcome, or with the sole objective of solving them. Rather, we see them in terms of the prospects they open up; of their fertility and of their intrinsic capacity to enrich life. If pursuing a mere practical purpose leads to suffocation, searching by definition implies by its nature a concept of space, and thus the possibility of movement.

Pain, which is often rejected as something 'other' that cannot be understood or explained, can now find its own expression. The ill are frequently left alone with their suffering as a result of the fear and sense of inadequacy felt by the people who are close to them. Through philosophical reflection, however, suffering can be not only expressed and contained, but can be oriented toward a direction perceived as growth.

By reinterpreting one's own story, the time of illness can be turned into a favorable moment, and into a chance to learn and collect. Perhaps the person is able to discover that there are still some important cards to play. Trying to do what is still possible in order to change direction is an excellent way of preventing regret or remorse from having the last word.

Many people can therefore arrive at fundamental decisions, which are essential for them in order to make peace with life, the people they live with, and themselves. These decisions have often been postponed for years. In fact, when you don't have anything to defend anymore, it's easier to act, and to let yourself go. Some people ask for, offer, and receive forgiveness. They discover that they would rather be happy than right.

Unfortunately, the course of illness and subsequent death may have a different pace from that of philosophical dialogue and life changes. They can make the process of dialogue and change increasingly more difficult, or interrupt it in an abrupt way. We are forced to face the ultimate limit. "When death comes, there are still a lot of things to do. It would be enough for me to not leave something important unfinished."

At this point even the smallest thing can become really important: saying or writing something which has not been said or written before, doing something new or finishing something, giving a precious belonging to someone else. A kiss or a hug that until this moment has been denied or delayed can offer the terminally-ill person a sense of completion. These small actions can be enough to dispel the fear of the unfinished, or to discover a mysterious value within them.

THE SPACE OF *MYSTĒRĬUM*

I have often wondered about the ultimate horizon of such work. "Now that I'm at the end, I'm interested in looking at what is greater than me, and in trying to understand my part in it." This is a wish that, in some way, concerns all of us and probably defines the ultimate scope of philosophical counseling and its essential meaning.

This work allows us to explore with increasing depth that dimension within the existential experience of a person, which ancient philosophy defined with the word *mystērĭum*. It is not just what is not known or cannot be known based on reasoning, but rather the very essence of life which necessitates our participation in order to exist. It is a dimension that goes beyond the now and invites us toward a continuous path of growth, evolution, and discovery. Life and death, love and pain, knowledge, beauty and liberty; these are just some of the many *mystērĭa* which are interwoven within life. They are revelations of the *mystērĭum* animating the world and hidden in history, situations, and events.[6]

It is necessary, however, that we do not become distracted. Many people have taught me that truly living is not done by keeping our distance from pain and illness, but when we cultivate a vivid sense of reality. This means to experience all its dramatic aspects without wanting to extract ourselves from them. We can feel comfortable in the world when we have the courage to move further into life with all our limits and suffering, thus reaching its heart.

The further we delve into the knowledge of human nature and life, the more the characteristic traits of the *mystērĭum* which envelops everything emerge. It is a revelation of the depth concealed in things themselves. Rather than investigating the world after death, philosophical inquiry focuses on the mystery permeating the world we live in.

Wisdom, an intimate and intrinsically feminine quality, proves itself to be eminently practical in the ability to communicate with this mystery.

A certain contemporary tendency to trivialize existence leads people to live concentrating on their daily routine, to stop at partial meanings which do not go beyond the immediate and exclude a wider scope of meaning.

The material dimension and well-being are commonly emphasized, which is quite different from being happy! Giving space to the category of *mystērĭum*, the dimension in which reality precedes, transcends, and always surprises us, can be a way of listening to perhaps one of mankind's most urgent interior needs.[7]

Otherwise, our lives and the lives of the others are lived and treated like objects. Illness is no longer an existential—though painful—experience but a condition which prevents us from living. Death is no longer the scandalous reality that somehow determines the meaning of life, but just an absurd event marking its end.

Our vision of life is very likely to affect our vision of death, and the other way round. Constantly referring to each other, life and death are two sides of the same reality in which we are inevitably immersed. A society where people run away when faced with looking at or talking about suffering and death displays its cultural poverty. This explains why, on the threshold of death we are usually caught unprepared.

Yet multiple people have taught me that being ready for this moment is indeed possible. It is, however, an experience which is somehow granted. Only in this way we can discover that there is meaning and especially an enthusiasm for life that does not depend on the passing things.

A MEDICINE THAT UNDERSTANDS

Palliative care is perhaps the only branch of medicine which explicitly refers to a model of medicine that is largely feminine. The strength of its therapeutic approach is that it offers an all-encompassing treatment focused on the sense and quality of the patients' lives when their illness does not respond anymore to specific treatments and progresses toward its fatal conclusion. Palliative care does not simply consist of controlling the physical symptoms, but includes providing psychological, social, spiritual, and, in our case, philosophical and existential support. The word "palliative" has its origin in *pāllĭum*, meaning cloak. Wrapped around the body, it creates a comfortable and protective space for a person.

Several professional and non-professional figures are involved in the treatment process and act together to pursue an organic strategy that is consistent with the patient's view of life and well as his habits, history, and aspirations. Until the last moment, terminally-ill people are themselves, and are capable of accepting and giving sense to their lives and to the lives of the people they will leave behind. They are alive and have to be able to live the experience of death, giving space to life even at the end of life itself. When recovery is impossible, treatment becomes the dimension in which the terminally ill person is accepted and supported in all aspects of the variety and depth of their needs. When a clinical practice centered on acting at all costs recognizes that "there's nothing left to do," a new, extraordinary and potentially rich time begins.

Why postpone it to the end of life? Why not export this vision beyond the limits of the end-of-life stage and spread it within other fields of medicine, in order to re-examine them in a more global perspective?

A more in-depth consideration of the central role patients play and the importance of their life experience is a crucial issue in therapeutic relationships and care practice. Over the past decades, the consequences of the gap created between the scientific and human dimensions have been increasingly denounced as a reaction to the predominant role the technical dimension has acquired through the great progress of biomedical science. As a result, a need to recover the *human* dimension in the treatment process has now emerged.

Emphasized by a scientific-technological mentality, the technical aspect cannot be separated from the wider and comprehensive existential one. The modern vision of medicine that is exclusively centered on scientific method needs a broader perspective.

THE ART OF TREATMENT

The scope of treatment has traditionally gone beyond the mere dimension of technical intervention. There has always been a keen awareness that the art of medicine is only partly derived from fields of knowledge related to exact sciences, and cannot be limited to sectors and specialized procedures. Medicine has to consider each person as a whole, as a unity which is not only biological, but also psychological and spiritual. Taking into account each of these different dimensions means broadening the horizons of knowledge and establishing a dialogue between different disciplines. Their interaction in the therapeutic relationship can enrich our view of human beings.[8] The ill are not just biological entities, but creatures endowed with reason and who express their own significant visions of the world as well as their values and their aspirations toward life goals and purposes. They are individuals who are responsible for their own thoughts and actions. The professionals who take care of others should focus their attention on considering patients' different needs and listening to the questions prompted by their suffering, as well as their personal search for recovery.

However, even caregivers are human beings. Consequently, they can also receive training and support through a philosophical journey. The therapeutic approach is consistent with a more or less explicit anthropological vision. In medicine the focus is on people. We treat them according to how we look at and consider them. Exploring the space in which we move and understand the idea of support in order to try to broaden its scope and horizons is certainly a fruitful opportunity for the individual caregivers as well as for health professionals.

Recovering more eminently feminine dimensions is thus perceived as an urgent need in the debate regarding patient care. There is certainly a need for a *supplement of soul* and for the development of new modes of thinking, loving, and contemplating. There is an explicit need for a model of care focused on the being, rather than on the doing. For a life that is simply more human.

NOTES

1. For an in-depth analysis of end-of-life issues see Elizabeth Kübler-Ross, *Questions & Answers on Death and Dying* (New York: Simon & Schuster, 1972).
2. The role of the face in the relation to the other has been emphasiezed by the philosophy of Emmanuel Levinas. E.g. Emmanuel Levinás, *Éthique et Infini* (Paris: Fayard, 1977).
3. Elizabeth Kübler-Ross, *Death: The Final Stage of Growth* (New York: Simon & Schuster, 1974).
4. For further reference see Luisa Sesino, *Ho bisogno di pensare: esperienze di Consulenza Filosofica nelle Cure Palliative* (Milano: Società Italiana di Medicina Pallaitiva, 2006).
5. De Hennezel, Marie, *La mort intime* (Paris: Éditions Robert Laffont, 1995).
6. Luisa Sesino, "Cercando senso. Esperienze di accompagnamento filosofico nella malattia e alla fine della vita," in AA. VV., *Sofia e Agape* (Napoli: Liguori Editore, 2013)
7. About the need to give space to *mystērĭum* in the last stages of life see Geoffrey Hanks et al., *Oxford Textbook of Palliative Medicine* (Oxford: Oxford University Press, 2011).
8. For further reference see Sandro Spinsanti, *Curare e prendersi cura: l'orizzonte antropologico della nuova medicina* (Roma: Cidas, 2006).

BIBLIOGRAPHY

De Hennezel, Marie. *La mort intime*. Paris: Éditions Robert Laffont, 1995.

———. *La Quête du sens*. Paris: Éditions Albin Michel, 2004.

Hanks, Geoffrey et al. *Oxford Textbook of Palliative Medicine*. Oxford: Oxford University Press, 2011.

Illich, Ivan. *Medical Nemesis*. London: Calder & Boyars, 1974.

Kübler-Ross, Elizabeth. *Questions & Answers on Death & Dying*. New York: Simon & Schuster, 1972.
———. *Death: The Final Stage of Growth*. New York: Simon & Schuster, 1974.
Levinas, Emmanuel. *Éthique et Infini*. Paris: Fayard, 1977.
Sesino, Luisa. "Cercando senso. Esperienze di accompagnamento filosofico nella malattia e alla fine della vita." in *Sofia e Agape*, edited by AA. VV. Napoli: Liguori, 2013.
———. "Philosophical Practice at the End of Life," in AA. VV. *Philosophical Practice in Italy*, Di Girolamo Editore, Trapani 2008.
———. *Ho bisogno di pensare: esperienze di Consulenza Filosofica nelle Cure Palliative*. Milano: Società Italiana di Medicina Pallaitiva, 2006.

II

Enhancing Doubt

Chapter Five

The Eros of Doubting

Heidi Salaverría

I am so tired of fear.
—Michelle Obama[1]

"But—who then, Diotima," Socrates asked, "are the lovers of wisdom, if they are neither the wise nor the foolish?" "A child may answer that question," she replied; "they are those who are in a mean between the two; Eros is one of them."
—Plato[2]

. . . a sort of flirtation with meaninglessness—[. . .] trying to plumb abysses which are generally agreed not to exist.
—Marilyn Frye[3]

One of the biggest problems of our civilization is a misguided idea of the self. Conceptually, as well as in everyday practices, the general expectation is to display a self-certain, determined posture, and to act correspondingly. The *phantasm* of the self-certain, autonomous, and impermeable ego has been proven to be dangerous and fictitious long ago. And it has been linked to the—likewise fictitious—idea of masculinity, which—proving its alleged autonomy wrong from the beginning—has always been dependent on its complement in the equally fictitious idea of femininity as self-uncertain, heteronomous, and permeable. Notwithstanding its fictitious character, this binary gender model has been very powerful and continues to be so. It seems very difficult to think, to feel, and to act outside of this frame, as on a deeper level, our Western philosophy is pervaded by this violent dualist paradigm.

The *Quest for Certainty*, which the pragmatist philosopher John Dewey considered one of the most dangerous attitudes of modernity, has suffused our Western everyday thinking and ways of acting. Doubt nowadays is considered mainly an obstacle to avoid (or to be rapidly overcome) for maintaining a strong position in the world, toward oneself and toward others. The position of the doubter is seen as a position of weakness, accompanied by suffering, exclusion of recognition, and the inhibition to act decisively. The mainstream climate in politics and in public debates, as well as in private life, is one of a vague, but nevertheless powerful pressure: the pressure to be sure of one's own position, to know what one wants, to come up—at best instantly—with solutions to given problems, to have an opinion on any topic at stake. In short, it is the fantasy of inhabiting the God's-eye view.

Of course, as we aren't gods, this climate of certainty-pressure does not *resolve* any doubts or make them disappear, it only *suppresses* them. And suppressed doubts suppress judgment-formation as well. As a result, common sense and the public media are marked by an alarming lack of a thoughtful and responsible formation of judgment, one of the most precious capacities of human beings.[4] With the increasing velocity of digital communication and information flow we are even more in dire need of cultivating our opinion-formation; instead the increase of information is accompanied by a decrease of adequate coping. The consequence is the prevalence of a posture which could be called the *pro-con-whatever-posture*: either being instantly in favor of or instantly against something, or, if neither one of those options seems fit, not to care at all—which, in the end, amounts to the contra position, except for the fact that the manifested indifference doesn't even bother saying no and saves the effort of taking responsibility. The *pro-con-whatever-posture* seems to suppose that being impermeable and self-satisfied leads to success and happiness. And, at first sight, it in fact does seem to lead to success, as this posture makes people functional within most of the given globalized economic and political systems. But it represents a functionality in the sense of the functional drug addict or alcoholic who, viewed from the outside, succeeds in behaving as expected, while, viewed from the inside, fights a war against all kinds of desires and doubts which, having been cut off from conscious reflection, become less and less controllable, until one day the system collapses. Repressed doubts and desires turn into aggression and exponentially increase the violence that originally caused them. This mechanism not only applies to the psychological microstructure of the individual, it applies as well to the macrostructure, for example, of nations. The more impermeable a nation claims to be, the stronger the fictitious 'we' is being opposed to the 'others' by building a fortress, the more likely a collapse of civilization is to be expected.

Underneath all, this posture is nurtured by a profound fear. Fear that anything else but certainty amounts to nothing and renders one's existence worthless. If you are not determined in your own position, fear seems to ask, isn't everything just random? If there is no absolute evidence, isn't everything just a joke? This either-or-claustrophobia is partly a remnant of Christianity, partly it reflects our deeply ingrained Cartesianism—namely to feel and to think in a binary logic: body/soul, male/female, nature/culture, good/bad, yes/no, everything/nothing.

The translation of the Christians' fear of God into our own times is this: if one does not partake in infinite certainty, one ends up living in the hell of insignificance. The own being, seen from this perspective, will then effectively amount to nothing. In a strange way, the *pro-con-whatever-posture* holds itself captive in some kind of purgatory, trying to avoid at any price the role of the doubting lost soul by adopting the position of a God's-eye view (instantly knowing what is certain) while simultaneously accomplishing the role of the devoted believer desperately trying to know what God would want without daring to ask. As these two roles are completely irreconcilable, an inner war (of course not admitted) is inevitable and simultaneously unsolvable.

Denying doubts and denying the value of doubts is disastrous, because unchanging and indubitable identity is a fiction, which can only be established and maintained through structural, indirect, or direct violence. Instead, it seems less violent, more realistic, and more fruitful to acknowledge that subjects are living organisms, as much as political systems, science, language, and relations are. These living organisms constantly alter. Trying to fix them into a static position is like cutting off every branch a tree grows. If not shaped in a friendly and very skillful manner—as in the art of bonsai—the result will be a crippled plant with very low life expectancy. Also the question would remain: who should be the bonsai artist cutting our tree?

In this chapter I am going to outline the significance of what I call the *Eros of doubting*, by following some of its traces in philosophy, thereby proposing a concept of the self beyond stiff impermeability/permeability. Its cultivation is crucial for the (always ongoing) process of creative and responsible positioning of the self.

ON A DIVING BOARD

Doubting is like standing on a diving board: a delicate situation, in which it is necessary to sharpen one's own perception and to develop the right amount of momentum in order to dare to jump into the unknown. On a diving board, one easily gets the feeling of losing a grip on the ground, because the board gives way quickly. And in fact, one does not stand on firm ground, but is instead only held by a thin elastic plank in the air, about to move from one element into another, leaving behind one unstable standpoint for an even more unstable one: plunging into the water, hoping—in the moment of *jumping-falling*—that the transition will be smooth and painless. The same holds true for doubts. Suddenly you find yourself on precarious and questionable grounds, vacillating between returning to the old and turning to the new. Something says no to the old but fears the new, something says yes to the new but fears to let go of the old. You are about to change, or, even better, something already has started to change, which led to the doubt altogether (you already stand on the diving board, and something brought you here).

But what is it that leads to the situation of doubt? A colleague of mine, who discussed this chapter with me, raised the question if it weren't more adequate to talk of a 'state of doubt' instead of a 'situation of doubt:' a state of doubt, as she argued, designates an internal or mental process, whereas a 'situation' rather designates some external event. But then again, I wondered, isn't the characteristic feature of doubt precisely that the self becomes permeable? Doesn't it happen that in the process of doubting the supposed borders between the self's identity and something yet unknown become porous, dissolving temporarily the separation of the 'internal' and the 'external,' even suspending temporarily the status of a self-contained identity? From the point of view of pragmatism (comparable in that sense to the one of phenomenology and existentialism) the dichotomy of the internal/external appears to be part of the virtual binary logic. Couldn't one describe the moment of doubting instead in terms of "I've got a situation here," thereby questioning the whole setting one finds oneself in?[5]

It seems to have to do with this transitory blurring between the self and the outer world that one never knows exactly what caused the situation of doubt. Of course, there are harbingers, like a repeatedly felt tension or nervousness in the face of particular occurrences or persons. But these harbingers can go on unnoticed for quite a while. Afterward, it seems puzzling how long one could endure a political or a personal situation, a situation in a company (or any other constellation), not only without changing or saying anything, but also without even being aware of it. In retrospect, the taken action seems so clear. But this clearness only becomes discernible after the undergone 'change of elements,' when a new contour between the self and the world becomes tangible after having lived through a new experience. There is an existential dimension about doubts that always remains partly opaque. What becomes clear transitorily (until the next doubt shows up) is the outcome, not the process itself.

Once you took the first step to do something you have been intending to do for a while, you need to overcome the long guarded doubt, and before that, you need to carefully nurse those uncertain impulses in a process of finding out what you want and don't want. Or, put more precisely: it is a process of finding out, again and again, who you are. Practicing this finding-out is indispensable, since it signals how and in which direction to jump. The point is: *we don't really know us*. And as the idea of a defined and self-contained identity is completely fictitious, doubts do not function as an indicator of something distinct and definable, which had been there all along (say, like a stone in the water) and simply needed to be retrieved, but on the contrary: doubts *generate something new* about us, about our relation to the world and thus, generate something new in the world itself.

Doubting is a deeply ambivalent state, somehow painful and a reminder of our finitude (gods and angels don't doubt), yet simultaneously revealing, and in that sense a reminder of our singularity (stones or robots don't doubt either). In doubts, something new is being experienced which does not fit within our own commonsense conglomeration of belief-habits, something makes us question the beforehand taken for granted ground on which we stand. Because doubts reveal something new, they are not completely controllable or foreseeable (as pretty much everything in life, only that doubts remind us of that fact). However, this perceived lack of control often leads to the conclusion that doubts are not only unpleasant, as they are accompanied by feelings of insecurity and uncertainty, but that they are also dangerous, as they seem to weaken the self's position. And indeed, doubting *is* a manifestation of uncertainty, and it is, in that respect, a relative of fear and pain. Yet, at the same time, doubting is exciting, and this is where Eros comes into play. Doubts are as much related to fear, as they are to desire: an inner conflict takes place between something wanted and something unwanted, both sides not quite graspable, yet nevertheless pressing. But it is fear of uncertainty, which many times inhibits us from enjoying the doubting, thereby restraining the creative potential of the process.

It is not simply that doubts *unsettle* the self, signaling a problem or an error committed by the self or experienced in the environment (e.g., the structures of society). They also *resettle* the self by signaling an emerging new contour of the own positioning. Some part of the self, allegedly known, is being weakened, and simultaneously some part of the self, yet unknown, is being encouraged through the enjoyment of the uncertain. The *Eros of doubting* enables the self to experience the seeming 'lack' of temporarily being uncertain in an abundant way, inviting a diving into unknown terrains, which might bring up something helpful. Doubting invites the self to (re)positioning, its singularity being at stake by connecting to something new. It opens up new possibilities.

Therefore, to face doubts does not mean to be overwhelmed by them as if they were a violent force of nature, too strong to counter, leading to paralysis and despair. It means instead to ally with them. If one tries, however, to maintain absolute control over situations and thereby to push aside every hesitation, one will end up repeating stiff routine patterns of behavior, which simply do not match the given circumstances, and will bring about more stiffening of one's own identity. Being controlled by fear of the unknown will, moreover, result in inflicting aggression upon oneself, upon the situation, and upon everybody involved, by trying to squeeze a new situation into an old inflexible template. It is, as if someone forces her or himself to wear shoes which they grew out of long ago. In political terms doubting of course appears scary to authorities when expressed by groups of people claiming their rights. And from the point of view of persons or institutions, which prefer to let other people wear their worn-out shoes for them, doubts definitely represent a danger that needs to be repressed. However, as history has shown, doubts won't go away through repression. Here again, the solution consists in allying with them, because every other alternative, in the long run, will turn out worse. The longer that doubts are repressed, the more rage accumulates and causes all the more violence, which then is much more difficult to resolve.

The fear of being weakened by doubt is caused essentially by the erroneous premise of a fixed, self-satisfied ego and the objective of strengthening this ego. But the real danger does not lie in the doubting. It lies in this premise of a strong indubitable self (and, for that matter, a strong, indubitable state or corporation) which not only is false, but causes even more fear, not less, and which, in the end, results in nothing but (direct or indirect, passive or active) violence up to and including war.

Not only does this posture produce violence, it also gives away the possibility to cope with problems in a new and potentially better way. It also gives away the opportunity to enjoy experiences in ways previously unknown, which could extend the scope of action. Adhering to control and stiff routine scotches the option of making acquaintance with the new and of experiencing profound joy. Profound joy always has to do with an element of surprise, with an unconstrained modification of our criteria. Warding off doubts means warding off key experiences and paradigm chances of any sort. Put the other way around: the more we cultivate fertile doubts, the more we allow the emergence of new perspectives on oneself, on others, and the world. We seem to have lost sight of the fact that doubts not only broaden the range of problem solving, but also the range of experiences, enabling thereby deeper fulfillment. And the serious seeking of joy and fulfillment is far from being a luxury theme. Taking seriously the uncertain joy of Eros means, on the contrary, finding the courage of seriously listening to the soft inkling of one's own orientation and judgments—and the ones of others, which are the base of any responsible posture, and which represent the core of Kant's political philosophy of enlightenment. "*Dare to know!* Have the courage to use your own understanding."[6]

METAPHYSICAL LOVE AFFAIRS

For too long uncertainty, and for that matter doubting, has had a bad reputation in Western philosophy. The prevailing thread of Christianity over centuries regarded doubt as a sin, since doubting meant questioning God's will.

Therefore, unshaken belief was demanded. The impact of that powerful tradition still resonates in our own times. The dawn of the idea of modern subjectivity is inseparable from this tradition: with Augustine's *Confessions*, synthesizing Christian theology and Platonism, for the first time a subject-position had been articulated by way of a self, which starts to internalize divinity through the desired love of God. Exercising its belief made the finite individual partake in God's infinite realm and, thereby, evolving its own status as a subject, its subjective point of view in the world. By loving God back, the believer established a connection between her or himself and the divine. The inner life of the believer emerged, became graspable and, by this, started taking shape as the *mind*, a secularized version of the immortal soul. In that way, the internalization of God's love led to the first rising of the idea of freedom of thought or autonomy, an introjection of a spark of eternity, which liberated the human being from its supposed sinful absorption by carnal desires and limited self-interests.

In the famous eleventh book of his *Confessions*, Augustine testifies before God his struggle with the question what time is, particularly with the problem of understanding the difference between finite human time and divine eternity. The only solution he can think of is that there "was no time, therefore, when thou hadst not made anything, because thou hadst made time itself."[7] It turns out—as he convincingly analyses in a detailed survey of the impossibility of measuring time—that the concept of time is incomprehensible without *somebody* perceiving it. He concludes, therefore, that there are:

> neither times future nor times past. Thus it is not properly said that there are three times, past, present, and future. Perhaps it might be said rightly that there are three times: a time present of things past; a time present of things present; and a time present of things future. For these three do coexist somehow in the soul, for otherwise I could not see them. The time present of things past is memory; the time present of things present is direct experience; the time present of things future is expectation (C, XX, 26).

But what is perceived when one perceives time? Time does not represent anything distinct, and therefore no object. The point Augustine makes is that time is not to be found in an object, but in the subject! He puts it in the following way: "From this it appears to me that time is nothing other than extendedness [*distentionem*, spread-out-ness]; but extendedness of what I do not know. This is a marvel to me. The extendedness may be of the mind itself" (C, XXVI, 33). What does this have to do with doubting? The extendedness of time Augustine speaks of is not something to be known, for if it were known, it would be some kind of epistemological object (and note that Augustine himself seems to be unsure of his conclusion). *Time is the way in which the mind thinks*, and it is a way of relating the presence of the past (memory) with the presence of the presence (direct experience) and with the presence of the future (expectation). Now, this relating does never know in advance what is going to occur. It's a process of processing and connecting. This process can never be definitively completed, never consummated and therefore, never certain. In other words, the activity of the mind or of the subject is impregnated with doubts. If we knew everything from all times, we would not be subjects, but gods. The core of subjectivity is, formally as well as with regard to any content, uncertainty. Formally, because the effort of connecting memory, experience, and expectation is an effort of holding the ends together, of stretching the 'now' of the 'I,' which can always be disrupted and therefore is never guaranteed. Kant later transformed this idea into the "I think" that "must be able to accompany all my representations."[8] Content-wise, we don't know indubitably what we are going to think next. If we knew, then we weren't thinking.

An example of this is seen with persons who suffer from severe Alzheimer's dementia and lose their short-term memory. Therefore they are unable to connect the recently experienced past with the present, and because they do not remember what they just said or thought they are unable to anticipate what could come next. Philosophically speaking, they lose the company of their 'I think.' The experience of an interruption in the mental spreading-out between past and future is very common, only that these momentary slips usually are being overcome quickly. However, the extent of the mental stretching or spreading varies very much, depending, for example, on how relaxed, tired, or nervous we are. But it is not the interruption of the mental flow doubting consists in. *Doubting consists, in contrast, in experiencing the tentative movement of the mental stretching itself.* It is the conscious art of extending and relating time. In that sense, thinking always means mildly doubting, as we can never be sure of what comes to mind next. The experienced time of the subject always continues and the continuation of that time is beyond our control. An image to describe this process could be the movement of a flying plane. There is the momentary stance of the subject (that would be the plane), there is the presence of the past (that would be the vapor trail) and there is the presence of the future (the course the plane takes).

A musician or someone who has developed a sense for music will be able, by playing or listening to music, to stretch her memory and anticipation of a musical piece very far. While playing or listening she will constantly connect the just heard with the notes just about to arrive. The metaphorical vapor trail of the plane will then be very long. The Alzheimer's patient, at worst, does not have a vapor trail of memory at all. It seems that music is particularly suitable to bind memory and anticipation. Studies have shown that listening to music, particularly to familiar pieces of music, can help dementia patients to recover their diminished and compromised capacity to connect with the world (and to themselves).[9] By remembering the course of a song, they remember its progression and thereby the stretching and binding of subjectivity. Through the song their 'I think' temporarily awakens, they are, so to say, able to take a short trip and fly their plane again.

Yet, this capacity to reconnect through music is not cognitively reducible. The transitory awakening of the patients also has to do with another factor: music awakens their Eros, and so do doubts. By listening to music not only the formal capacity to bind memory and anticipation comes into play, but also the content of their beloved memories is being revived. One might recall a sunny spring afternoon when he fell in love with his wife, another one might remember turning on the new radio-receiver she had bought for the living room, the delight of hearing music at her home with friends for the first time. And doubts awaken things, too: a new wish, a new possibility.

It is no coincidence that Augustine himself talks about music and verses in his reflections on time (he also wrote a whole book on rhythm). The rhythmical and/or melodic structuring of music and poetry (and, for that matter, of any other art) itself already displays an aesthetic type of time binding. The aesthetic form, the aesthetic '*how*' of the distribution and modulation of the elements (e.g., notes, words) in time, coins the '*what*' of the artistic result. It presents a form of time binding experienceable to us, while at the same time going beyond our clear understanding. And there is an important aesthetic element in doubts, too: they appeal to something, which we do not yet completely understand and thereby broaden and modify our understanding.[10] For Augustine, aesthetic and religious experiences are inseparable. Indeed, beauty and the love to God seem to be the same. The Augustinian version of the subject is not a formalized structure (as Kant

Figure 5.1. Vapor trail. © Daniel Bomze.

conceived of it much later, particularly in his *Critique of Pure Reason*), but it is the whole bodily self being tormented and simultaneously enchanted by the realm of possibilities opened up through God, and an experience that reminds him time and again of his uncertainty. Thinking for Augustine is longing, and longing always is doubtful.

> My soul burns ardently to understand this most intricate enigma. O Lord my God, O good Father, [. . .] do not close off these things, both the familiar and the obscure, from my desire. Do not bar it from entering into them [. . .]. Of whom shall I inquire about these things? And to whom shall I confess my ignorance of them with greater profit than to thee, to whom these studies of mine (ardently longing to understand thy Scriptures) are not a bore? Give me what I love, for I do love it; and this thou hast given me. (XXII, 28)

The self immerses into the divine realm like the plane immerses into the infinite sky. To this, one could object in a bureaucratic voice that a pilot needs to be sure of his course: "If he is filled with doubts, perhaps he should better be reading Augustine instead of navigating an aircraft, risking its security through his own insecurity." But that depends on the interpretation of doubt. Doubting doesn't mean insecurity in the sense of stressful anxiety. Stressful anxiety is mainly caused by pressure to complete a task from which one has become alienated, for example if one fears not being good enough. It is a symptom of an authoritarian thinking, which today still predominates, being fueled by very real fears—fear of the superior, fear to lose one's job. As a result, one loses the connection to the given situation, loses the confidence in being entitled to deal with the circumstances.

Doubting in Augustine's sense instead would mean to maintain the connection with the situation, to extend into the uncertain and to take charge of it. The secularized translation of Eros as metaphysical longing would then mean expectation and anticipation (with the resource of memories), a somehow paradoxical doubtful trust. The pilot flying the plane needs to accompany his actions by a mild form of doubt in that he remains partly skeptical yet still confident about the expected course and the measures he is taking, without this turning into anxiety or desperation. He needs to draw his attention to possible changes in the atmosphere and in the plane, as well as in his own mental state. But the best way to do so is by *loving what he does*. Should he become too tired or unsettled by some turbulence, he would be ill advised not to consult with his co-pilot or to change seats, because his main interest would not be to fit into an inflexible image of the infallible pilot, but to make the best out of the situation.

The misleading idea of instrumental or 'identarian' thinking, which Adorno so vehemently criticized, assumes that the subject could control the objects by identifying them. But the "more relentlessly our identarian thinking besets its object, the farther will it take us from the identity of the object."[11]

The view Augustine develops questions instead its own 'identarian position' and *thereby positions itself as a self.* He even claims, anticipating Descartes, that if "I am mistaken, I am."[12] But Augustine was not a skeptic. On the contrary, he criticizes the antique skeptics for trying to immunize themselves against "the appearance of error in themselves [. . .] by not positively affirming that they are alive" (E, 7, 20). The strategy of stoic indifference denies its own permeability at the price of denying being alive, and thereby denying their Eros. It seems, to summarize, that the *Eros of doubting* for Augustine consists in the irresolvable tension between being alive and loving life (as a gift of God), while at the same time admitting the self's own fallibility as the necessary core of the own existence. The certainty of human existence is felt *through uncertainty*, and this uncertainty is not static, but a relentless extending of the self's own finitude into the infinite.

One thousand, one hundred forty years later, still closely intertwined with religion, Descartes crystallized the core of the modern subject in his *Meditations* as the famous *ego cogito, ergo sum*: "I think, therefore I am," a conclusion he developed with his method of doubt: everything, Descartes assumed, can be doubted, but "we cannot doubt of our existence while we doubt."[13] Doubting represents a necessary means to achieve certainty of the irreducible principle of the thinking subject. But it was certainty and not doubts that became the focus of philosophical developments from Descartes on—a notion that in a way translates the faith in God's infallibility into the human world and its quest for epistemological and moral truth. However, whereas Augustine confides in being loved by God of all things for his faithful uncertainty, Descartes changes the perspective. Somehow, he seems to have fallen out of love with God. Their relation transforms rather into some kind of marriage of convenience. Trying to find an unshakable principle of certainty to base knowledge on, Descartes in his *Meditations* carries out the mentioned thought experiment by doubting everything that is possible: the existence of the outer world, of his own body, of other minds, and of his own beliefs. And he feels compelled to do so by supposing the possibility of an *evil demon*, "as clever and deceitful as he is powerful, who has directed his entire effort to misleading me" (Med. 1).

But it is a strange argument Descartes puts forward: he claims to *only theoretically* assume its possible existence, just in case his assumption of an *evil demon* might turn out to be true. His assumption serves, in other words, as some kind of insurance, like a pre-nuptial agreement. And as we know, that is not the best start for a marriage, because it is like saying: "I think I love you, but I don't trust you, because you might use and deceive me. So let's, just in case, make a divorce-contract before we get married." In contrast to Augustine's passionate stretching of doubts, Descartes's argument seems like a slightly paranoid power game, led by mistrust to, then, surprisingly, culminates in an alleged proof of God's existence. The *Eros of doubting* is being abandoned in favor of an instrumental doubt used to gain absolute certainty, guaranteed by God. The argument winds up finally in the somehow possessive twist of capturing the idea of God inside of him.

And although Descartes admits that God remains ungraspable, his train of thought is rather colonizing and much different from Augustine's. While Augustine finds himself in a relation of permanent metaphysical heartache with God, Descartes secretly seems to wish to become God himself. "I recognize that it would be impossible for me to exist with the kind of nature I have—that is, having within me the idea of God—were it not the case that God really existed. By 'God' I mean the very being the idea of whom is within me, that is, the possessor of all the perfections which I cannot grasp, but can somehow reach in my thought, who is subject to no defects whatsoever" (Med. 3). The dream of unassailable autonomy has its roots in this line of thinking Descartes initiates. But it remains a dream, because, paradoxically, autonomy only works as long as the other remains intact *as other from the self*, no matter if it is god or another person. As soon as one seeks to appropriate the other, the relation is dead, and, for that matter, Eros too.

RECOGNIZING DOUBTS

This appropriative posture toward the other not only dominated Western philosophy and the particularly violent politics of colonization, slavery, and suppression over centuries, but it also became part of our common sense and still continues to do so. One aspect of this development was that, with the growing secularization of modernity, the love for God progressively became replaced by the love for another person—which then, weirdly enough, was deified and disenchanted at once: at the latest with the appearance of the bourgeoisie, the romantic fantasy of the two complementing sexes and their respective roles was invented. From that point on, women were considered 'the other' of men. Women began being transformed into some kind of allegory (which was practical, because allegories don't talk) for whatever seemed fit—for example, of purity, beauty, life. At the same time, much like with Descartes, this process was accompanied by the invention of some kind of *female evil demon*, serving as a corrective threat and simultaneous insurance to the male phantasm: femininity now also represented impurity, ugliness, death, and so on. As Simone de Beauvoir once said: the function of representing the 'other' had become "so necessary to man's happiness and to his triumph that it can be said that if she did not exist, men would have invented her. They did invent her. But she exists also apart from their inventiveness. And hence she is not only the incarnation of their dream, but also its frustration."[14]

It is a strategy which tries to escape uncertainty by forcing every person into a binary template with predetermined features, and although male persons generally have been and are being privileged by this construction, the structural violence is imposed on both sides. The structural violence of patriarchy consists in that it objectifies Eros, ascribing it to one sex (female), thereby also ascribing powers to it, which then simultaneously are being desired and hated, because they cause doubts, as a result of which they lead to an irreconcilable split between a *good* and an *evil demon*. Pornography is the parody-like exaggeration of this construction—trying to maximize Eros by minimizing doubts, punishing, and depreciating women for being the incarnation of male sexual desires. For Socrates it was a different story: Eros is the child of plenty and poverty, neither god nor human. He is an *imperfect demon*, neither good nor bad, whose creativity is being kept alive by his unstable position between given identities and by his continuous striving toward 'the other,' namely the idea of the beautiful itself.

Objectifying the other as "other" makes recognition and love as impossible as the idea of the other as a 'self-identical' mirror of one's self. The problem with the mirror metaphor is that basically the same would have to be confirmed by the same, reflecting one's self-identical ego in the other, thereby gaining self-affirmation. In fact, this metaphor is exemplified in the myth of Narcissus, which, as we know, didn't turn out very well. He drowned in the attempt to unite with his mirror image, in which he had tragically fallen in love by looking into the pond. However, it isn't self-identical affirmation we yearn for, but the other of our self *in its otherness*. Otherwise, it would be sufficient to activate the camera screen on the computer and listen to oneself while speaking. This narcissistic dream can turn out quite nightmarish, as was shown for example in the movie *Being John Malkovich*. Malkovich therein climbs into his own head to find himself in a psychotic scenario where everyone is a duplication of him, shouting out nothing but "Malkovich, Malkovich." And he is not very happy about it.

The first philosopher to show why narcissism doesn't work was Hegel. He outlined convincingly that the identity of the self needs the recognition of the other to become self. The self *needs to become other than itself to become self!* The dynamic he describes could be named the *Hegel-Hollywood-Model*.

Let's call our protagonists *Left* and *Right*: when *Left* falls in love with *Right*, it starts longing for *Right*, so much so, that it turns kind of porous. It loses its self-certain position, in Hegel's terminology: "Self-consciousness is faced by another self-consciousness; it has come *out of itself*."[15] *Left* has lost its heart to *Right* (Panel 2). This is the *Eros of doubting par excellence*. The entire history of literature (especially romantic literature) depends on that moment, and no Hollywood industry would exist without it either. It is a painful, yet profoundly joyful experience, as long as there is hope that *Right* will love *Left* back. And we are lucky: *Right* falls in love with *Left*, too. So it

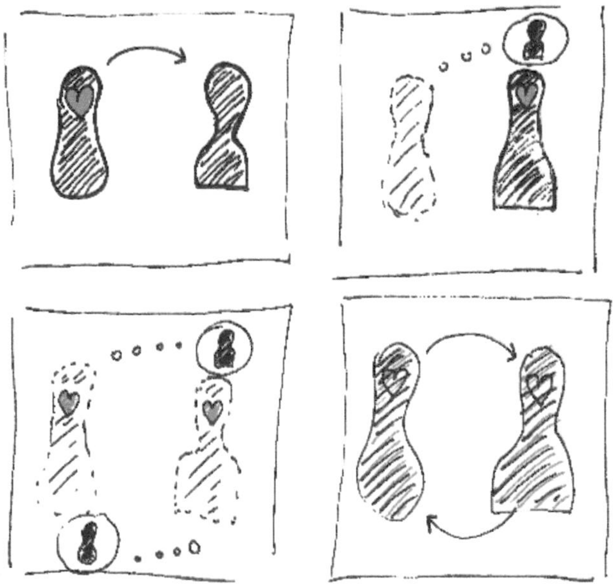

Figure 5.2. Hegel-Hollywood-Model. © Heidi Salaverría.

loses its heart to *Left* as well and also becomes porous, still without knowing if the love is mutual (Panel 3). Each one of them now is *out of itself*, until finally, they confess their love to one another, or, in Hegel's words, they "*recognize* themselves as *mutually recognizing* one another" (Panel 4).[16] The whole point of it is, however, that there is no shortcut to the process. It is necessary for the self to transitorily lose itself in the other *in order to become a recognized self.*

This applies not only to intersubjective dynamics. It applies to every relation between the self and the world. William James once described the situation of doubting as an "inward trouble," which could be compared to the trouble of being *out of oneself*—in Hegel's sense. One "meets a new experience," which doesn't fit within one's own belief-system, be it a contradiction, a new desire, something confusing or else.[17] What then happens is a tension between old belief-habits and the uncertain new. This tension is not being resolved by eliminating violently either the old or the new, but by bringing them together in the best possible way. This bringing-together in the best possible way is what James's famous definition of truth consists of: "New truth is always a go-between, a smoother-over of transitions. It marries old opinion to new fact so as ever to show a minimum of jolt, a maximum of continuity. [. . .] The reason why we call things true is the reason why they *are* true, for 'to be true' *means* only to perform this marriage function."[18]

Now, this idea is applicable to Hegel's description of recognition: doubting consists in an erotic entanglement of 'old' and 'new'. Accordingly, *Old* falls in love with *New*, hoping that *New* will love it back, and hoping that they will fit together well and that their relationship will last. But their relationship will only last if *Old* and *New* always continue to start over, thus establishing a lasting positive tension over time, which implies doubts with respect to the uncertain future and the question over how the matter will play out. For the problem with the *Hegel-Hollywood-Model* consists in that it focuses too much on the Happy-End, or in Hegel's words: on the *reconciliation* of self and other. Once *Left* and *Right* finally found each other, the Hollywood story is over—"after they married, they lived happily ever after." But when Hollywood ends, real life starts. Overcoming fixed images and ideas only is possible when *Old* and *New* fall in love with each other again and again. And this means, never stopping to fall in love with the uncertain, but instead a stretching-out and extending from *Old* and *New* in Augustine's sense.

As I have shown, it is only through doubts we learn who we are. They mobilize our judgment and sharpen our perception, raising the awareness for our habitual patterns of judgment and action, which without doubt would go on unnoticed and automatically. Through doubting habitual patterns and judgments become negotiable and changeable. In other words: Every reflectively undergone (re)positioning and criticism is based on doubts, otherwise it is only thoughtless adoption of the position of others. And this applies not only to individual development. Every social, economic, scientific, and artistic invention or discovery is based on doubt. Doubt is the foundation of creativity; it brings the new into the world. Admitting the dubitability of our own positioning at first sight seems to be a dangerous path. But, in the long run, it proves not only to enhance stability, because elastic systems are more resilient than static ones, but also to prevent and oppose violence—against oneself and against others. And, besides, it simply is less boring.

NOTES

1. Michelle Obama, *To Live Beyond Our Fear* (speech introducing her husband at a campaign rally, Des Moines, Iowa, 16 August, 2007), accessed September 11, 2014. http://www.youtube.com/watch?v=nqCYFpUAJ2Q

2. Plato, *Symposium*, transl. Benjamin Jowett (The Internet Classics Archive), accessed September 11, 2014.http://classics.mit.edu/Plato/symposium.html.

3. Marilyn Frye, *Politics of Reality* (Trumansburg, N.Y.: The Crossing Press, 1983), 154.

4. For a discussion of the relation between Kantian reflective judgments and pragmatist doubts, see Heidi Salaverría, "Critical Common Sense, Exemplary Doubts, and Reflective Judgment," in *Confines of Democracy. The Social Philosophy of Richard Bernstein: Essays on the Philosophy of Richard Bernstein*, ed. Ramón de Castillo, Ángel M. Faerna, Larry A. Hickman (New York: forthcoming).

5. I am grateful to Dr. Laura Odom for fruitful discussions and inspiring suggestions.

6. Immanuel Kant, "An Answer to the Question: What is Enlightenment?" in *Perpetual Peace and Other Essays*, trans. Ted Humphrey (1784; repr.) (Indianapolis: Hackett, 1983), 41.

7. Augustine of Hippo, "Confessions," in *Confessions and Enchiridion*, transl. and ed. by Albert C. Outler, (Philadelphia: Westminster Press, 1955), XIV, 17, hereafter referred to as C and E.

8. Immanuel Kant, *Critique of Pure Reason*, B 131–32.

9. There is an abundance of publications on that topic to be found. See, e.g., Sharon Smith "The Unique Power of Music Therapy Benefits Alzheimer's Patients." *Activities, Adaptation & Aging* 14 (4) 1990: 59–64.

10. For a first draft of an "Aesthetics of Doubts," see: Heidi Salaverría, "Enjoying the Doubtful. On Transformative Suspensions in Pragmatist Aesthetics," *European Journal of Pragmatism and American Philosophy* 4 (2012): 1, http://lnx.journalofpragmatism.eu/?p=571 .

11. Theodor W. Adorno, *Negative Dialectics*, transl. E. B. Ashton, London: Routledge & Kegan Paul, 1990, 149.

12. Augustine of Hippo, *The City of Gods*, transl. Marcus Dods, Hendrickson Publishers: Peabody Massachusetts 2009, XI, 26.

13. Rene Descartes, *Meditations on First Philosophy*, ed. and transl. John Cottingham, (Cambridge: Cambridge University Press, 1986).

14. Simone de Beauvoir, *The Second Sex*, trans. Constance Borde and Sheila Malovany-Chevallier (New York: Vintage Books 2009), 203.

15. Georg W. F. Hegel, *Phenomenology of the Spirit*, trans. A. V. Miller (Oxford: Clarendon Press, 1977 [1807]), 111.

16. Ibid, 112.

17. William James, *Pragmatism: A New Name For Some Old Ways of Thinking*, ed., with an introduction by Bruce Kuklick (Hackett: Indianapolis/Cambridge, 1981), 31–33.

18. Ibid.

BIBLIOGRAPHY

Adorno, Theodor W. *Negative Dialectics*. Translated by E. B. Ashton. London: Routledge & Kegan Paul, 1990.

Augustine of Hippo, *Confessions and Enchiridion*. Translated and edited by Albert C. Outler, Philadelphia: Westminster Press, 1955.

———. *The City of Gods*. Translated by Marcus Dods. Peabody Mass.: Hendrickson Publishers, 2009.

de Beauvoir, Simone. *The Second Sex*. Translated by Constance Borde and Sheila Malovany-Chevallier. New York: Vintage Books, 2009.

Descartes, René. *Meditations on First Philosophy*. Edited and translated by John Cottingham. Cambridge: University Press, 1986.

Frye, Marilyn. *Politics of Reality*. Trumansburg, N.Y.: The Crossing Press, 1983.

Hegel, Georg W. F. *Phenomenology of the Spirit*. Translated by A. V. Miller. Oxford: Clarendon Press, 1977 [1807].

James, William. *Pragmatism: A New Name For Some Old Ways of Thinking*. Edited with an introduction by Bruce Kuklick. Indianapolis/Cambridge: Hackett, 1981.

Kant, Immanuel. "An Answer to the Question: What is Enlightenment?" in *Perpetual Peace and Other Essays*. Translated by Ted Humphrey (1784; repr.). Indianapolis: Hackett, 1983.

———. *Critique of Pure Reason*. The Cambridge Edition of the Works of Immanuel Kant. Edited by Paul Guyer, translated by Paul Guyer and Allan W. Wood. New York: Cambridge University Press, 1998.

Obama, Michelle. *To Live Beyond Our Fear* (speech introducing her husband at a campaign rally, Des Moines, Iowa, 16 August, 2007), accessed September 11, 2014. http://www.youtube.com/watch?v=nqCYFpUAJ2Q

Plato, *Symposium*. Translated by Benjamin Jowett (The Internet Classics Archive), accessed September 11, 2014. http://classics.mit.edu/Plato/symposium.html

Salaverría, Heidi. "Enjoying the Doubtful. On Transformative Suspensions in Pragmatist Aesthetics." *European Journal of Pragmatism and American Philosophy*, Volume 4, Number 1, 2012. http://lnx.journalofpragmatism.eu/?p=571.

———. "Critical Common Sense, Exemplary Doubts, and Reflective Judgment." In *Confines of Democracy. The Social Philosophy of Richard Bernstein: Essays on the Philosophy of Richard Bernstein*, edited by Ramón de Castillo, Ángel M. Faerna, Larry A. Hickman. New York, forthcoming.

Smith, Sharon. "The Unique Power of Music Therapy Benefits Alzheimer's Patients." *Activities, Adaptation & Aging* 14 (4) 1990: 59–64.

Chapter Six

Philosophic Humor for Women—(and Men): Fighting Shame and Disgust

Lydia Amir

Society puts a high premium on humor, yet self-directed humor is rarely addressed by feminists and other theoreticians of humor, and even less so by philosophers and philosophical practitioners. A highly efficient tool for gradual change, self-directed humor can be effectively used in the practice of philosophy to attain various philosophic ideals, such as self-knowledge, authenticity, rationality, virtue, and autonomy. In this chapter, I concentrate on self-acceptance and self-liberation by examining how humor's benefits are helpful for acknowledging and gradually freeing oneself from shame and disgust. Attitudes associating women with human vulnerability, animal nature, and death, may be interiorized as shame and disgust toward women's bodies and inner vulnerability. This chapter, especially relevant for women, is also pertinent for men who perpetuate these attitudes, and eventually for all of us who resist our vulnerability, materiality, and death. It is important to come to terms with these inevitable features of life, as their acceptance enables compassion along with a deeper awareness of our common lot, which is also bound to promote well-being for ourselves as well as others.

While humor can play an important role in philosophy, the interiorization by women of stereotypes about their (in)capacity for humor may hinder its implementation in philosophical practice. I probe the validity of the view that women suffer from frigidity of the funny bone by introducing feminists' response to it, I examine the origins of disgust and shame and explain how it is possible for women to interiorize these emotions. Finally, I propose an effective way to counter these emotions through a gradual process that uses humor as a tool in the practice of philosophy.

WOMEN AND HUMOR

As helpful as humor may be for philosophy,[1] encouraging women to use humor may not be an easy task. This is so because they often interiorize stereotypes about their (in)capacity for appreciating and creating humor. As this issue is often brushed aside, I probe the view that women have no sense of humor as well as feminists' response to this charge.

Our societies put a high premium on humor. "The Best Medicine,"[2] laughter is supposed to be good for us. Current research indicates that we prefer to be considered stupid rather than humorless, which explains why only about 2 percent of the population confess to lacking a sense of humor (Ziv 1984, 3).

Since the word 'humour' began about three hundred years ago to denote a capacity for laughter rather than a bodily fluid,[3] men, and some women, have been reiterating that women have no sense of humor. At the end of the seventeenth century, William Congreve claimed, "I have never made any Observation of what I apprehend to be true Humour in Women."[4] More recently Reginald Blyth has declared that "women have not only no humor in themselves, but are the cause of the extinction of it in others" (Blyth 1959, 14). When in disrepute, however, laughter is attributed to women (and children). Francis Gray explains,

> Like sexuality, laughter has been sometimes highly valued, sometimes denigrated; but like sexuality and indeed, with it, laughter has been closely bound up with power. Cultures which did not exalt humor to its current overblown status could attribute it to women. . . . Only when laughter is the sign of the civilized man . . . do women appear to suffer from a mysterious frigidity of the funny bone.[5]

The civilized man's mark is rationality, and many have associated rationality with humor. Arthur Schopenhauer adds that humor requires a keen sense of ethics, which women notoriously lack.[6] The list of philosophers, authors, and thinkers that deplore women's lack of rationality, ethics, and humor is long; however, this issue needs not be further pursued here.

Contemporary feminists have devised two main strategies to address the claim that women have no humor.

1. The Claim Is False: Several writers have explored questions about gender and humor. Regina Barreca stands out for her persistence: for the last twenty years she has been arguing against the idea that the creation and enjoyment of humor are a masculine privilege.[7] Audrey Bilger notes that humor has historically served as a simultaneous psychological survival skill and an emancipatory strategy for women in sexist societies. Politically, women have used humor as a method for conserving community principles and subverting community expectations. While nineteenth- and early twentieth-

century women were seen as 'lacking' a sense of humor, twenty-first-century women who use it must strike a particularly sensitive balance so as not to be seen as too cerebral, forward, frivolous, or antagonistic.[8]

2. The Claim Is True, But . . . : To fully understand women's use of humor as cultural production, Barreca argues that we need new definitions for assessing their comic output and for evaluating their role as "de-centering, dislocating, and destabilizing" cultural authority.[9] In her introduction to *Last Laughs*, she challenges the "universal" standards for identifying humor. She does so not to outline the allegedly essential elements of "feminine" humor, but rather to argue that we should not overlook humor produced by women when it does not conform to established standards.

What would be, then, the criteria for feminine laughter? In *Sexes et Parentés,* the Belgian philosopher Luce Irigaray argues that as yet no female values exist, and hence that feminist humor is inauthentic in that it merely apes the power structures of phallocracy and the assumptions of phallocentrism.

Another prominent French contemporary philosopher, Hélène Cixous, recognizes laughter as a feminist strategy.[10] Because Cixous is as much a novelist and dramatist as a theoretician, her theory of humor is coextensive with her comic writing. Her work has been characterized as "full of humour;"[11] indeed, she talks of a *nouvel art de rire* as if it was coterminous with a *nouvel art de vivre*, yet does not theorize about it.[12] Cixous's novels end with paradoxical and inexplicable gales of laughter, a laughter from which those who feel themselves excluded might well condemn as hysterical. For her, Freudian psychology directs its entire energy against hysteria and therefore against femininity, while she claims solidarity with hysterics, and one of the most obvious, striking, and perhaps disturbing features of hysteria is uncontrolled and unexplained laugher. She sees it as significant and appropriate that this laughter disturbs, for it is "the moment at which the woman crosses a dangerous line—the cultural demarcation beyond which she will find herself excluded."[13]

The "laugh of the Medusa" advocated by Cixous demolishes hierarchies by rendering nonsensical the aggression between father and son which is at their origin. Laughter thus removes the difference between margin and center. Women cease to be outsiders, because of the resulting meaninglessness of the very concepts of 'outside' or 'inside.' This is why Cixous summons the woman's text to "shatter the framework of institutions . . . blow up the law . . . break up the 'truth' with laughter."[14]

Laughter is seen as a strategy whose goal is to dismantle power structures through writing. But French post-structuralist feminists have been charged with neglecting actual political action. Building on conservative feminists' view that there is no other revolution than the revolution every woman makes by herself, I argue that self-liberation is a pre-condition of political action.

Rather than recommending the dismantling of power structures through writing, however, I suggest that humor can be useful for feminists because humor is a significant philosophical tool of *self*-liberation. Before considering how humor also liberates women from shame and disgust, let us understand how these emotions are produced.

SHAME AND DISGUST

Human beings are plagued by an uneasy tension produced by their perceived dual nature. This duality is expressed in various ways—soul or mind, on the one hand, and body, on the other, angels *versus* animals, infinite and finite, spirit and matter, and so on. But this dualism is not neutral or egalitarian: the body, matter or animal part has traditionally been, and still is, mostly rejected. This explains both our attitudes toward bodily functions and animals. So powerful is the desire to cordon ourselves off from our animality that we do not stop at bodily functions and animals, but need a group of humans against which we can unite.

The *locus classicus* of group-directed projective disgust is the female body, Martha Nussbaum explains.[15] As receivers of semen and closely linked, through birth, with the mortality of the body, women in more or less all societies have been the expression for male loathing of the physical and the potentially decaying. Taboos surrounding sex, birth, menstruation—all these express the desire to ward off something that is too physical, that partakes too much of the secretions of the body. In his recent *Anatomy of Disgust*, legal theorist William Miller describes these male attitudes toward women as inevitable aspects of male sexuality: woman becomes the sticky mortal part of him from which he needs to distance himself. Both misogynistic and homophobic disgust have deep roots in ambivalence about bodily products and their connection with vulnerability and death.

Disgust focuses on reminders of our mortality, while embodiment is seen as sources of contamination for the self. It thus distances us from what we actually are. It is an inherently self-deceptive emotion whose function is to conceal from us, on a daily basis, facts about ourselves which are difficult to face.

The disgust with one's softness and mortality that prevails in Western society dates back at least to Plato's *Symposium*. Aristophanes points there to a kind of primitive shame at the very fact of being human and non-whole which underlies more specific types of shame.[16] Shame is a painful emotion responding to a sense of failure to attain some ideal state; as a painful awareness of inadequacy, shame focuses on the sexual because our sexual organs are symbols of our animality and mortality.[17]

Shame can arise out of feelings of neediness. Boy-culture encourages young people to hide their need for others and avert their own gaze from their inner world, leaving it as uncharted territory. This can become a vicious cycle as unstudied and underdeveloped emotions remain at an infantile level and are therefore felt to be all the more shameful, all the more out of step with the appearance of the controlling adult self. Thus, boy-culture denigrates all aspects of personality that are viewed as female: emotions, need, sadness, and compassion. The multiple experience of shame which marks boys' lives is often channeled into hostility toward women and toward their own vulnerability.

"Primitive shame," the demand for perfection and the constant inability to tolerate any lack of control or imperfection, is a specific type of shame. It is closely connected with narcissism or infantile omnipotence.[18] It is a paralyzing shame of all that is human in oneself which acts as a barrier to compassion. Pathological narcissism can affect both males and females, but Nussbaum insists that "we have reasons to think that the tendency is often connected with common patterns of male development." She emphasizes possible differences in sexual development. This kind of frenzy for control has been variously traced in a number of recent analyses of the origin of misogyny, a narcissistic refusal to tolerate the reality of something different from oneself, especially if it is at the same time a reminder of one's bodily vulnerability.

Along the same lines, Elizabeth Young-Bruehl studies the psychological origins of sexism and shows how it is particularly closely connected to narcissism. It stems from the inability to tolerate the existence of the mother as separate, rather than a part of the child himself and subject to his control.[19]

Although these are extreme cases, normally functioning people have these traits to a degree which encourages self-deceptive thinking about one's own vulnerability. In *Upheavals of Thought*, Martha Nussbaum explains how narcissism is connected with the female body:

> Because the child aiming at omnipotence does not accept the soft, fleshy, fluid aspects of himself, which are so many signs of weakness and mortality, these must be repudiated from the self, as a violent gesture of differentiation and subordination. What Theweleit's *Freikorps* officers loathe is "mire," slime," "swamps," "floods," "stench"—all, he plausibly argues, metaphors for the female body, and ultimately for the vulnerable aspects of their own.[20]

Women interiorize these views of themselves and their bodies, which often translate into low self-esteem and difficulties in exploring their sexual and emotional needs.

The female side of the shame-inducing cultural ideals contains other destructive elements, in particular the continual emphasis on an inflexible ideal of female beauty that emphasizes thinness as a key to desirability. There is a connection between these ideals and the eating disorders that are prevalent in adolescent and preadolescent girls. Andrew Morrison has associated these problems with the hypertrophy of shame: shame at imagined bodily imperfections is a frequent vehicle for earlier and more general feelings of infantile shame, further feeding the tendency to a destructive type of narcissism.[21] The eating disorder, initially aimed at restoring control over the body and achieving the desired perfection, becomes a new source of shame. A lesser yet significant problem may occur after birth and motherhood, when women often find their body less appealing than it used to be. Combined with the natural aging process, this may make them feel ashamed of their sexual needs and emotional desires.

Women often feel ashamed of the emotional needs of their "inner little girl:" educated by their mothers to care for others, they do not dare ask to be taken care of.[22] Coupled with women's veiled emotional and sexual neediness, these experiences may sustain shame and internalized disgust. As holding oneself to an ideal has shame as a permanent possibility, a society which emphasizes the ideal of self-reliability and invulnerability can make us ashamed of our emotional and physical needs.

The immediate family is a powerful agent in the development of shame, whether healthy or unhealthy. But the surrounding society is another. If we bear in mind that immediate family members are also conditioned by socially induced emotions, we have a strong case for women's potential shame and disgust at themselves being a consequence of socialization. Even if human beings share similar capacities for feeling and a common social and cultural world, feminists feel that significant differences of status, power, recognition, and responsibility in that social world prompt individuals to learn patterns of feeling and patterns of expressing feeling that make sense to those individuals and to their social position in the world.[23] As emotions within and between persons share an intense synergy, feminists prefer social theories of emotions. Thus, Margaret Walker insists that "we need to ask whose gazes we have learned to live under and what we have come to expect, fear, or need flows back toward us in the emotional responses of particular others to our displays of feeling. Some emotional synergies between people will have destructive consequences, as in interpersonal spirals of shame and contempt."[24]

It is important to uncover, and if possible, to distance oneself from these socially induced emotions—shame and disgust—in order to choose more freely one's attitudes toward one's body and one's inner vulnerability.

Liberation from socially induced opinions and feelings has always been at the core of the philosophic agenda. The problem lies in our willingness and ability to recognize them, however, because the products of good socialization are assimilated within the self. There has been lacking in the philosophic corpus a *theory* of change for those who are not wholly rational—all of us—

and who therefore need more than a rational explanation in order to change. Since the inception of philosophy, however, the tool that enables change—humor—has been repeatedly used *in practice*, indeed more than in theory, for example, by Plato in his Socratic dialogues.[25] In the next section we will see the benefits of systematically practicing humor as a philosophic tool for fostering self-knowledge, acknowledging ambivalence, reducing painful emotions such as shame and disgust, enabling acceptance of self and others, living with irresolvable conflict, and alternatively, providing conflict-resolution through the adoption of a worldview that considers conflict as characterizing the human condition.

HUMOR

Self-directed intra-personal humor enacts an inner dialogue which is a highly efficient tool for gradual change. Usually not considered as radical or revolutionary, humor is a 'win-win' situation, a 'both-and' rather than an either-or' position. Its core is compassionate aggression, with both components being necessary for effective criticism, which is the only means to grow. Self-directed intra-personal humor enables to acknowledge feelings and thoughts, maintain ambivalence toward them, and live in a state of full awareness of internal conflicts and reduced tension from them. Furthermore, humor eventually helps to alter the balance that characterizes ambivalence in a gradual movement toward inner resolution of the intra-personal conflict.

The resolution I am alluding to involves self-acceptance and self-liberation, in this case from attitudes toward women that associate them with vulnerability, animal nature, and death, and which may be interiorized as shame and disgust toward their body and inner self's vulnerability. The working of internal self-referential humor begins by furthering the awareness of shame and disgust and the recognition of their interiorized messages. This kind of humor generates an ambivalent attitude toward these emotions, followed by a gradual distancing from them due to their reduced impact, which leads ultimately to replacing shame and disgust with self-acceptance. Self-acceptance is necessary for compassion and for social and emotional well-being. Let me explain these ideas by detailing various facets of the philosophic exercise of humor.

1. Self-Knowledge: Self-knowledge is a pre-requisite of effective deliberation, which, in turn, is imperative for deciding whether and how to solve a conflict. Awareness of internal conflict and familiarity with the conflict's components are important for self-knowledge. Self-referential humor facilitates self-knowledge by creating the distance necessary to observe one's self with the calmness that characterizes aesthetic contemplation. By suspending blind emotions, silencing shame and disgust, and incapacitating rash action, a

safe inward environment is created where hidden aspects of the self are encouraged to emerge under the impartiality of the humorous gaze.

Self-knowledge is a mode of reflection which involves judgment and whose aim is to make our character less fortuitous and more deliberate. This is the same process as that of increasing control, for what moves our character in the desired direction is that we control it so as to approximate more closely our conception of a good life. This desirable transformation proceeds through the evaluation of our desires, capacities, opportunities, values, and actions with a view to forming from them enduring patterns conducive to living a good life.[26] Similarly, self-knowledge, in the sense of knowing one's heart, true desires and leading passions, is needed as a first step for attaining to the ideal of authenticity or "being yourself" (Guignon 2005, 14).

Self-knowledge assumes the inner dialogue we are all familiar with and which has been explored by philosophers, anthropologists, and psychologists. There are two main models of inner dialogue, the reflexive model and the social model, and humor fits them both. The reflexive model takes speech to be the manifestation of reflection, that is, of the act by which I am able to think about the contents of my consciousness. I may, for example, possess a moral intuition of the virtue of justice, and live according to its principles; but in reflecting on it, I examine this content from some higher or more abstract perspective. Where the original level is merely 'lived' and relatively unexamined, the higher level is evaluative and critical. Since this evaluation requires conceptual analysis, I talk to myself when I reflect. I may compare the abstract perspective with the lived one. This procedure is common in character-building. If we follow Baruch Spinoza, who is exemplary here, we evaluate ourselves according to a correct principle of living which we apply constantly to the particular instances frequently encountered in life.[27] To fully accept the gap between the ideal and reality, humor is needed in order to help us cope effectively with shame and disgust, among other emotions.

Other accounts of inner speech invoke a more overtly dialogical structure. Among these is the idea that my inner conversation takes place among different *personae*; the roles of 'parent,' 'child,' 'teacher,' or 'victim' which I carry within myself might be adopted in their relations to one another. My self can in fact be seen largely as a set of such roles, determined to a significant extent by my social relationships. This model allows for humorous interactions between these inner parts that mirror the important role humor plays in social conflicts. A familiar model for Freudian (and later) psychotherapy has the rational, conscious, articulating ego confronting its powerlessness in the face of the emotional, unconscious, and nonverbal id. The role of humor here is to encourage hidden aspects of the personality to emerge as a consequence of the promise of impartiality and tolerance associated with humor.[28]

2. Acknowledging Ambivalence: Acknowledging ambivalence is necessary for understanding oneself, others, and human relations in general. Ambivalence, the state of simultaneous conflicting feelings, is experienced in thoughts and emotions of both positive and negative valence toward someone or something. Its opposite is a rigid intolerance for ambiguity, nuance, and paradox. A common example of ambivalence is feelings of both love and hate for a person. The term also refers to situations in which 'mixed feelings' of a more general sort are experienced, or when a person experiences uncertainty or indecisiveness concerning something. Because both positive and negative aspects of a subject are present in a person's mind at the same time, ambivalence is a psychologically unpleasant state that often leads to avoidance and procrastination, or to deliberate attempts to resolve the ambivalence. Ever since the Swiss psychiatrist Eugen Bleuler introduced the term early in the twentieth century,[29] ambivalence in human attitudes has been under continual investigation, especially by psychologists.

Long before the term was coined, the experience of ambivalence—being pulled in psychologically opposite directions—had been noted. In his treatment of the emotions in part III of his *Ethics*, Spinoza makes much of ambivalence, which he terms fluctuation or vacillation, the result of a transfer of emotions which he calls imitation (*imitatio*) (Props. 17 and 27). He also focuses on various instances of types of ambivalence. In general, no observer of the human condition can fail to note the existence of mixed feelings, mingled beliefs, and contradictory actions.

Psychoanalysis has associated the awareness of ambivalence mainly with pathology, but ambivalence is possible without an abnormal breakdown of reasoning, as the 'logic' of emotion allows for ambivalence. A key concept in normal psychology, ambivalence is also embedded in social functions and professions.[30]

This makes the recognition of ambivalence imperative. Although knowing one's feelings may seem simple, many ignore or try to sedate strong emotions like anger, sadness, and fear, and eschew ambivalence as threatening. But our ability to handle conflict depends on being connected to these feelings and on tolerating ambivalence enough in order to let it emerge. Acknowledging hateful feelings in ourselves as well as in others might be necessary for true loving.[31]

Humor brings forth ambivalence, because in the humorous mode of thinking, contrary to rational thinking, a thing can be both X and not-X at the same time.[32] In Arthur Koestler's original view, 'bisociation,' or ongoing incongruity, creates a humorous effect, rather than its removal, as in the incongruity resolution model of humor. Michael Apter uses the notion of synergy to describe this cognitive process, in which two contradictory images or conceptions of the same object are held in one's mind at the same time. This produces the pleasurable sensation of having one's thoughts oscillate back and forth between two incompatible interpretations of a concept. Thus, in humor, we playfully manipulate ideas and activities so that they are simultaneously perceived in opposite ways, such as real and not real, important and trivial, threatening and safe.

The pleasure we derive from ambivalence through humor enables us to feel simultaneous contradictory emotions about the same idea, event, or person. It is the most fundamental skill required for handling both internal and interpersonal conflict. Unfortunately, throughout history we have tended to interpret conflict, whether internal or interpersonal, as traumatic, something that cannot be tolerated and must be avoided or stopped, rather than coping with it as a challenge.

3. Reducing Shame and Disgust: Humor is equipped to reduce shame and disgust. Humor is helpful because it provides us with a new perspective that transcends the current uncomfortable perspective. Adopting another perspective is contrary to the partial nature of emotions and is thus incompatible with an intense emotional state. Consequently, laughing at ourselves serves to distance us from a shameful situation as we join others (imagined or real) in taking a fresh perspective on it. The new vantage point humor provides thus helps to reduce the significance of a shameful situation.[33]

Humor can also reduce disgust, as the move from shame to disgust tracks the move from public to private, from external to internal, from child to adult, from repulsive to repressive. In *The Anatomy of Disgust*, William Miller argues that the comic and the disgusting share significant points of contact, and that there is an intimate connection between some styles of contempt, disgust, and the comic.[34] The experience of disgust can be more entertaining to us as is commonly the case in comedy when it is elicited by another's shamelessness or ineptitude. Through the distancing from ourselves that humor affords, our own ascribed inaptitude can also be a source of pleasure. If the comic and the disgusting share significant points of contact, the comic may be actively used in self-referential humor to discharge disgust.

The role of fear or disgust in laughter is such that the fear or disgust stimulus retains its function even when promoted to laughter-stimulus, but is bisociated with a positive emotion. Contemporary research on Amerindian clowns shows that in the clown the stimuli of fear and disgust are often indistinguishable from each other. In the light of the theory of bisociation, laughter itself is marked by ambivalence, the negative and distressing effects of fear and disgust being neutralized by their exalted place in the ritual. If laughter is used internally and self-referentially, the feeling of disgust is joined with laughter, enabling thus at least an ambivalent attitude toward disgust, which points toward its eventual eradication.

4. Acceptance of Self and Others: By gradually replacing feelings of shame and disgust, as well as other emotions, with sympathy and compassion, humor encourages self-acceptance and tolerance "of self and others."

Empathy may teach us something about humor, especially since both concepts seem to be elements of wisdom.[35] Empathy is obstructed when we project the parts of ourselves we reject unto others. In distancing ourselves from problematic feelings like shame and disgust, however, we can re-experience them in the sympathy we feel when they are someone else's. Instead of impeding compassion by projecting the rejected parts of the self onto others, this sympathetic distancing from self brings one closer to others. Acceptance of our vulnerability, finitude, and 'softness,' is necessary for compassion, and for our personal and social well-being.

5. Living with Conflict: As the incongruity theory of humor explains, the contradictions and incongruities contained in self-referential humor can help in living with conflict. Indeed, it feeds on them and replaces discomfort with pleasure.[36]

It may be that this is all that we can achieve, if it is true that we (both men and women) cannot fully accept our humanity. This has been noticed by various authors, such as Sigmund Freud and Friedrich Nietzsche, and more recently by Martha Nussbaum. She notes that Walt Whitman, the poet of democracy, asks of us in the final poem of *Leaves of Grass* to have a simple relationship to our own mortality and its bodily realization which frees us to truly pursue liberty and equality: without fear or loathing, we are to embrace the decay and brevity of our lives. Nussbaum objects to this ideal:

> But to ask of humans that they not have any shrinking from decay or any loathing of death is to ask them to be other than, possibly even less than, human. Human life is a strange mystery, a combination of aspiration with limitation, of strength with terrible frailty. To become a being who didn't find that mysterious or weird or terrifying would be to overcome some kind of subhuman or inhuman being, and it would also be to forfeit, very likely, some of the value and beauty of human life. At least we don't see clearly that it would not have this effect. If, however, the complex struggle we currently wage with mortality has disgust as its corollary, we should not expect to dismiss disgust utterly from our lives.[37]

In contradistinction to guilt, which is related to an action and whose antidote is forgiveness, shame is related to the whole personality, and consequently tends to seek the healing response of acceptance of the self despite its weaknesses, defects, and failures.[38]

Nussbaum and Morrison describe a movement toward health where the self is increasingly understood, and accepted, as human, incomplete, and partial, rather than as grandiose and demanding completeness. Yet, the idea that most people can come to accept their incompleteness, lack of control, and mortality is far too optimistic, Nussbaum believes.[39] However, I have recently shown how a systematic use of humor can result in a redemptive acceptance of our own humanity. I call the new worldview that obtains through such a transcendent acceptance, '*Homo risibilis*,' or the Ridiculous Human Being. This theory may be for the few, but because humor makes self-knowledge intrinsically pleasurable, I believe it has more chances of being successfully implemented than most philosophic theories.[40]

Even if keeping shame and disgust at bay through internal self-referential humor is all most of us can achieve, this lesser goal is worth attempting. This is a viable goal, because it uses humor in order to successfully live with internal conflict. Humor has been repeatedly recognized by sociologists and psychologists as an exceptional tool for living with (internal) conflict; and, contrary to common opinion, humor can be taught and learnt. I believe that success in achieving the more modest goal of maintaining shame and disgust at bay through the use of humor is guaranteed.

This goal is desirable, as no happiness is possible with internalized disgust, and shame is an important impediment to self-satisfaction. False views of the self, built on dissociating its desirable from less desirable aspects, cannot hold steady in the face of reality. In order to be stable, and thus deserve its name, well-being needs to be based on reality. Thus, developing a taste for reality through humor is a worthy goal, both in itself, and for its beneficial outcomes.[41]

NOTES

1. On humor's importance for philosophy, see Lydia B. Amir, "Humor in Philosophy—Theory and Practice," *Philosophical Practice* 7 (2012): 3, 1015–29; Lydia B. Amir, *Humor and the Good Life in Modern Philosophy: Shaftesbury, Hamann, Kierkegaard* (Albany, NY: SUNY Press, 2014).

2. This quote is taken from Frances Gray, *Women and Laughter* (Charlottesville, VA: The Macmillan Press, 1994).

3. For the history of humors as fluids to the modern comical sense of humor, see Barry Sanders, *Sudden Glory: Laughter as Subversive History* (Boston, MA: Beacon Press, 1995).

4. William Congreve, "A Letter to John Dennis Concerning Humor in Comedy," 10 July 1695, in John Hodges, *William Congreve: Letters and Documents*. London: Macmillan, 1964.

5. Gray, *Women and Laughter*, 6–7.

6. Arthur Schopenhauer, *The World as Will and Representation*, translated by E. F. J. Payne (New York, NY: Dover Publications, 1969). Kierkegaard is an exception to nineteenth-century thought on women's humor. See Amir, *Humor and the Good Life*; Lydia B. Amir "Kierkegaard and the Philosophical Traditions of the Comic," *Kierkegaard Studies Yearbook* (2013): 377–401.

7. Regina Barreca, *Last Laughs: Perspectives on Women and Comedy* (New York, NY: Gordon and Breach, 1988).

8. Audrey Bilger, *Laughing Feminism: Subversive Comedy in Frances Burney, Maria Edgeworth, and Jane Austen* (Detroit, MI: Wayne State University Press, 1998), 10–50.

9. Barreca, *Last Laughs*, 15.

10. Hélène Cixous's "The Laugh of the Medusa" (1976) has been reprinted in an anthology of post-modern ethics (Calarco and Atterton 2003). John Parkin devotes the last chapter of his *Humor Theorists of the Twentieth Century* to Cixous as representative of feminist laughter. See John Parkin, *Humor Theorists of the Twentieth Century* (Lewiston, NY: Edwin Mellen Press, 1997), 230–77.

11. Pierre Salesne, "'Cixous, Hélène' ou *l'art de l'innocence*," translated by M. Hanrahan, in *Writing Differences: Readings from the Seminar of Hélène Cixous* (Milton Keynes: Open University Press, 1988), 113.
12. Hélène Cixous, *Préparatifs de noces au-delà de l'abîme* (Paris: Des femmes, 1978), 276.
13. Cixous, "The Laugh of the Medusa," translated by Keith Cohen and Paula Cohen, *Signs: Journal of Women in Culture and Society* 1(1976): 4, 875–93. [Le rire de la Méduse. *L'Arc* 61: 39–54, 1975], 184.
14. Cixous, "The Laughter of the Medusa," *The Continental Ethics Reader*, edited by Matthew Calarco and Peter Atterton (New York, NY: Routledge, 2003), 282.
15. Martha C. Nussbaum, *Hiding from Humanity: Disgust, Shame, and the Law* (Princeton and Oxford: Princeton University Press, 2004), 107.
16. Plato, *Symposium* 189c–193e.
17. Max Scheler, "Über Scham und Schamgefuhl," in *Schriften aus dem Nachlass*. Band 1: *Zur Ethik und Erkenntnislehre*, 55–148 (Bern: Francke, 1957).
18. Nussbaum, *Upheavals of Thought: A Theory of the Emotions* (Cambridge: Cambridge University Press, 2001), 196–200, 342–7.
19. Elizabeth Young-Bruehl, *The Anatomy of Prejudice* (Cambridge, MA: Harvard University Press, 1996), 132.
20. Nussbaum, *Upheavals of Thought*, 346. See Klaus Theweleit, *Male Fantasies*, 2 vols., translated by Stephen Conway (Minneapolis, MI: University of Minnesota Press, 1987, 1989).
21. Andrew P. Morrison, *The Culture of Shame* (London and Northvale, NJ: Jason Aronson, 1986), 19, 86–9.
22. Eichenbaum and Orbach 1983.
23. Margaret Urban Walker, "Moral Psychology," in *The Blackwell Guide to Feminist Philosophy*, edited by Linda Martín Alcoff and Eva Feder Kittay (Malden, MA: Blackwell Publishing, 2007), 103–4.
24. Ibidem, 112; see also Cheshire Calhoun, "Responsibility and Reproach," *Ethics* 99 (1989): 389–406.
25. In Plato's *Laws*, the justification of the use of the comic is intellectual: the serious cannot be taught without the ridiculous (*Laws* VII, 816d–e); in the *Philebus*, however, the proper aim of comedy is to unmask ignorance and pretension, making it thus an important tool for furthering the moral aim of self-knowledge (*Philebus*, 48a–50b). See Amir "Kierkegaard and the Philosophical Traditions of the Comic;" Lydia B. Amir, "Taking the History of Philosophy on Humor and Laughter Seriously," *The Israeli Journal of Humor Research: An International Journal* 5 (2014): 43–87, 2014.
26. John Kekes, *Moral Wisdom and Good Lives* (Ithaca, NY: Cornell University Press, 1995), 127–8.
27. Spinoza, *Ethics*, Proposition 10 Scholium.
28. Since Plato, who equates thinking with inner dialogue in *Theaetetus* (189e), various philosophers emphasized the importance of inner dialogue. For references, see Amir "Taking the History of Philosophy on Humor and Laughter Seriously;" Hubert Hermans and Agnieszka Hermans-Konopka, *Dialogical Self Theory: Positioning and Counter-Positioning in a Globalizing Society* (Cambridge: Cambridge University Press, 2010).
29. Eugen Bleuler, *Dementia praecox*, translated by Joseph Zinkin (New York, NY: International Universities Press, 1952 [1911]).
30. For the ambivalence involved in normal emotions, see Patricia S. Greenspan, "A Case of Mixed Feelings: Ambivalence and the Logic of Emotion," in *Explaining Emotions* ed. Amélie Rorty, 223–50 (Berkeley, CA: University of California Press, 1980). For the sociology of ambivalence, see Zygmunt Bauman, *Modernity and Ambivalence* (Cambridge, UK: Polity Press, 1991); William I. Miller, *The Anatomy of Disgust* (Cambridge, MA: Harvard University Press, 1997).
31. Paola Valerio, "Love and Hate: A Fusion of Opposites—A Window to the Soul," in *Love and Hate—Psychoanalytic Perspectives*, ed. David Mann (Hove, East Sussex: Brunner-Routledge, 2002), 264.
32. Michael Joseph Mulkay, *On Humour* (Cambridge: Polity Press, 1988).
33. See Michael Lewis, *Shame* (New York, NY: Free Press, 1992), 127–37.

34. Miller, *The Anatomy of Disgust*, ix, 116.
35. Orwoll and Perlmutter 1990.
36. Amir, *Humor and the Good Life*, 219–86.
37. Nussbaum, *Hiding from Humanity*, 121–22.
38. Andrew P. Morrison, *Essential Papers on Narcissism* (New York and London: New York University Press, 1986), 370.
39. Nussbaum, *Hiding from Humanity*, 188.
40. See Amir, *Humor and the Good Life*, 219–86.
41. Part of this chapter has been read as a paper entitled, "Humor in Feminists' Inquiry and Ways of Life," at the 23rd World Congress of Philosophy in Athens, Greece (2013).

BIBLIOGRAPHY

Amir, Lydia B. "Humor in Philosophy—Theory and Practice." *Philosophical Practice* 7/3 (2012): 1015–29.
———. "Philosophy's Attitude towards the Comic. A Reevaluation." *European Journal of Humor Research* 1/1(2013): 6–21.
———. "Kierkegaard and the Philosophical Traditions of the Comic." *Kierkegaard Studies Yearbook* (2013): 377–401, 2013a.
———. "Humor in Feminists' Inquiry and Ways of Life." Paper read at the Roundtable "Feminism: Perceptions from East and West," the 23rd World Congress of Philosophy. Athens 2013b.
———. *Humor and the Good Life in Modern Philosophy: Shaftesbury, Hamann, Kierkegaard.* Albany, NY: SUNY Press, 2014.
———. "Taking the History of Philosophy on Humor and Laughter Seriously." *The Israeli Journal of Humor Research: An International Journal* 5 (2014): 43–87, 2014a.
Apter, Michael. *The Experience of Motivation: The Theory of Psychological Reversals*. London: Academic Press, 1982.
Barreca, Regina. *Last Laughs: Perspectives on Women and Comedy*. New York, NY: Gordon and Breach, 1988.
Bauman, Zygmunt. *Modernity and Ambivalence*. Cambridge: Polity Press, 1991.
Bilger, Audrey. *Laughing Feminism: Subversive Comedy in Frances Burney, Maria Edgeworth, and Jane Austen*. Detroit, MI: Wayne State University Press, 1998.
Bleuler, Eugen. *Dementia praecox*. Translated by Joseph Zinkin. New York, NY: International Universities Press, 1952 [1911].
Blyth, Reginald H. *Humour in English Literature: A Chronological Anthology*. Folcroft, PA: Folcroft Press, 1959.
Calhoun, Cheshire. "Responsibility and Reproach." *Ethics* 99 (1989): 389–406.
Cixous, Hélène. "The Laughter of the Medusa." In *The Continental Ethics Reader*, edited by Matthew Calarco and Peter Atterton, 276–284. New York, NY: Routledge, 2003.
———. *Préparatifs de noces au-delà de l'abîme*. Paris: Des femmes, 1978.
———. "The Laugh of the Medusa." Translated by Keith Cohen and Paula Cohen. *Signs: Journal of Women in Culture and Society* 1(1976): 4, 875–93. [Le rire de la Méduse. *L'Arc* 61: 39–54, 1975].
———. and Catherine Clément. *Jeune née*. Paris: 10/18, 1975.
Gray, Frances. *Women and Laughter*. Charlottesville, VA: The Macmillan Press, 1994.
Greenspan, Patricia S. "A Case of Mixed Feelings: Ambivalence and the Logic of Emotion." In *Explaining Emotions*, edited by Amélie Rorty, 223–50. Berkeley, CA: University of California Press, 1980.
Guignon, Charles B. *On Being Authentic*. London and New York: Routledge, 2005.
Hermans, Hubert, and Agnieszka Hermans-Konopka. *Dialogical Self Theory: Positioning and Counter-Positioning in a Globalizing Society*, Cambridge: Cambridge University Press, 2010.
Hodges, John. *William Congreve: Letters and Documents*. London: Macmillan, 1964.
Irigaray, Luce. *Sexes et Parentés*. Paris: Minuit, 1987.

Kekes, John. *Moral Wisdom and Good Lives*. Ithaca, NY: Cornell University Press, 1995.
Koestler, Arthur. *The Act of Creation*. London: Pan Books, 1964.
Lewis, Michael. *Shame*. New York, NY: Free Press, 1992.
Miller, William I. *The Anatomy of Disgust*. Cambridge, MA: Harvard University Press, 1997.
———. *Faking It*. Cambridge: Cambridge University Press. 2005.
Morrison, Andrew P. *The Culture of Shame*. London and Northvale, NJ: Jason Aronson, 1986.
———, ed., *Essential Papers on Narcissism*. New York and London: New York University Press, 1986a.
Mulkay, Michael Joseph. *On Humour*. Cambridge: Polity Press, 1988.
Nussbaum, Martha C. *Upheavals of Thought: A Theory of the Emotions*. Cambridge: Cambridge University Press, 2001.
———. *Hiding from Humanity: Disgust, Shame, and the Law*. Princeton and Oxford: Princeton University Press, 2004.
Parkin, John. *Humor Theorists of the Twentieth Century*. Lewiston, NY: Edwin Mellen Press, 1997.
Plato. *Works*. Translated by Benjamin Jowett, 4th Edition. New York, NY: Oxford University Press, 1953.
Salesne, Pierre. "Cixous, Hélène" ou *l'art de l'innocence*. Translated by M. Hanrahan, in *Writing Differences: Readings from the Seminar of Hélène Cixous*, 113–26. Milton Keynes: Open University Press, 1988.
Sanders, Barry. *Sudden Glory: Laughter as Subversive History*. Boston, MA: Beacon Press, 1995.
Scheler, Max. "Über Scham und Schamgefuhl." *Schriften aus dem Nachlass*. Band 1: *Zur Ethik und Erkenntnislehre*, 55–148. Bern: Francke, 1957.
Schopenhauer, Arthur. *The World as Will and Representation*, translated by E. F. J. Payne. New York, NY: Dover Publications, 1969.
Spinoza, Baruch. *The Collected Works of Spinoza*, vol. 1, edited and translated by Edwin M. Curley. Princeton, NJ: Princeton University Press, 1985.
Theweleit, Klaus. *Male Fantasies*, 2 vol., translated by Stephen Conway. Minneapolis, MI: University of Minnesota Press, 1987, 1989.
Valerio, Paola. "Love and Hate: A Fusion of Opposites—A Window to the Soul.' In *Love and Hate—Psychoanalytic Perspectives*, edited by David Mann, 251–64. Hove, East Sussex: Brunner-Routledge, 2002.
Walker, Margaret Urban. "Moral Psychology." In *The Blackwell Guide to Feminist Philosophy*, edited by Linda Martín Alcoff and Eva Feder Kittay, 102–15. Malden, MA: Blackwell Publishing, 2007.
Whitman, Walt. *Leaves of Grass*. Norton Critical Edition, edited by Scolley Bradley and Harold W. Blodgett. New York, NY: W.W. Norton, 1973.
Young-Bruehl, Elizabeth. *The Anatomy of Prejudice*. Cambridge, MA: Harvard University Press, 1996.
Ziv, Avner. *Personality and Sense of Humor*. New York, NY: Springer, 1984.

Chapter Seven

The Need to Be Needed

Ora Gruengard

An associative journey between different cases in my practice suggested the possibility that women need to be needed more than men. I started to explore the meaning of that impression, and its possible implications for counseling, by asking a clinical psychologist whether she had a similar impression. At first she said that she did not, but when we discussed our examples it became clear that she had in mind the *emotional* need to *feel* needed, for example, being important or meaningful to someone, while for me 'being needed' meant a *reason.* Psychologists are often interested in *explanations,* and from that perspective 'a need,' whether as an objective state of which the subject is not necessarily aware and whether as a subjective motive, is an ingredient in the *explanation* of his or her beliefs, attitudes, and behavior. As psychologists are oriented toward *changing* the patient's 'dysfunctional' beliefs, attitude, and/or behavior, they tend to think of them in terms of causes-effects or means-ends relations. I, as a *philosophical* counselor, am not an expert in inducing changes. From my perspective the beliefs, attitudes, and behaviors of the counselee are consequences of her *judgments* even when she is not aware of her judging activity, and her judgments are not necessarily rational. My philosophical expertise is the examination of judgments, and my job is to enable the counselee to make judgments that are more rational or less arbitrary. I do it by inviting her to explore her philosophical presuppositions and examine possible alternatives. We do it together, but it is up to her to judge whether her initial beliefs, attitudes, or behaviors should be changed, and decide what to do about it.[1] I am interested accordingly in the ways in which counselees *justify* their beliefs, attitudes, and behavior, and in such a context 'a need' is neither emotional nor biological, but rather *logical.*

When a counselee says to me "I would have chosen otherwise, but he needed me at his side," or "I am doing that just because he needs it," she is not necessarily *explaining* her behavior, but she is clearly trying to *justify* it. When I say that she seems to *need* to be needed, I may mean that she needs the 'being needed' either as the *true reason* for her behavior or as a *pretext* for an action that is actually done for other reasons and an *excuse* for not doing something else. The 'being needed' justification belongs, therefore, to the domain of the *moral*.

The impression that women use it more often than men evokes the unsettled debate about 'feminine' versus 'virile' morality. Limitations of space prevent me, however, from dealing with that issue in the present chapter.[2] I deal instead with a more limited question, which arises from the cases that are described in the chapter: Why women that are proud of their ability to think in the 'virile' terms of Kantian principles, contractual agreements and legalist rules, and prefer, moreover, occupations that are not involved with caring, are using the 'feminine' terms of benevolent caring as a pretext or excuse. I suggest that it reflects a moral confusion that is due to the fact that both 'virile' and 'feminine' moralities are insufficient and flawed. Both the presupposition of contractual arrangements between abstract or virtual rational partners (which underlies the 'virile' approach) and the belief in the existence of 'sympathy' for the 'similar' and/or the 'close' and a wish to reduce his suffering (which underlies the 'feminine' one) fail to provide modern persons with adequate tools for dealing morally with the concrete problems of interpersonal and familial that might bother them. Their actual behavior is confused, but they look for excuses in the ready-made arsenal of traditional roles that they do not really accept.

My practical conclusion is that philosophical counselors should create a space for dealing with question of morality that is neither 'virile' nor 'feminine' and more relevant than either to issues that bother modern persons in their everyday life.

I invite you to join me in the associative journey, consider my reflections, and share with me a space for debate and cooperation.

THE UNNEEDED CHILD

The first person that comes to my mind is T, a woman in her late twenties, diagnosed as a "negativist" (i.e. non-cooperative) schizophrenic in remission, hospitalized on and off since childhood. T comes from an immigrant family of Iranian origin, the seventh of twelve children.

When I asked her how it felt to be part of such a big family, she told me that her mother says that if she could, she would have aborted each of her last six embryos. I do not know whether T's mother cares for or about T, but I assume that T has got the message that she was neither needed nor wanted. She was, perhaps, needed, or rather used, by other members of her family:

following one of her relapses into a state of frightening delusions she tried to regain peace by hypnosis and a non-certified hypnotist "time-regressed" her, to "one of her previous lives" (T, herself, inspired by Hinduism, believes in metempsychosis). That treatment worsened her state and she was hospitalized. When I asked what she was at that "previous life" she said that she "remembered" being an "American Indian woman," and as such she "was being assaulted and raped." I spoke with her former certified therapists, who were aware of her "chronic" anger: they did not ask her about the non-certified hypnosis, and did not know whether sexual abuse had preceded her early hospitalizations. But they had also never asked her about the experience of being one of twelve children, did not hear about her 'would-have-aborted-you' mother, nor joked with her about her delusions. I choose to tell her that some psychologists would interpret her "regression to former lives" as the evocation of memory traces of forgotten events in her childhood, asked her whether the "gas balloons" that were about to explode "in the bus" of her hallucinations had taps, and suggested to open those taps a little bit when they threatening bus reappears. She laughed. Later she told me that those hallucinations had stopped and she missed them.

Unfortunately, my conversations with T, a loner and the only one in my sample that did not speak about family problems nor seem to need being needed or care about moral justifications, were interrupted by institutional changes. I therefore did not have the chance to learn whether she eventually found less frightening needs than having the previous life of a raped female and visions of exploding buses.[3]

THE NEEDED CHILD

T's case should be compared with that of A, a man at the same clinic, also from an immigrant Iranian family, who believes like her in metempsychosis (but his version is Cabalistic). A, who was complaining of depression, came with a long list of his good deeds: his father, who had been a respectable violinist in Teheran, was reduced in Israel to a street player and became addicted to drugs. When A was a child the father used to take him to the streets, as a beggar. A was eventually picked up by a welfare worker and sent to a youth group in a kibbutz. Later, as an educated adult, he took care of his aging parents and his less lucky siblings, but was very unhappy and lonely. A few years before our conversations he had "returned from the bad way," for example, adopted the Jewish religious way of life and he lives in an ultra-orthodox community. Yet joining that community did not alleviate his feeling of loneliness. I expressed my appreciation for his power to overcome his childhood experiences and his generosity and skills, but that did not seem to impress him. So I asked him whether the "returning" had made any difference.

My question changed completely his expression and tone and he said that the difference was enormous. It had enabled him to "understand that his suffering had a meaning:" "it is a punishment." At that time I was still too little acquainted with some of the Cabalistic beliefs that are prevalent among some groups of Orthodox Jews, and realized only gradually that the sinner was neither he nor any of his ancestors, but "his soul" in one of its "previous lives." I did not know then that being a "reincarnation of the soul of one of the defunct Just" and suffering the punishment that the latter "merited" (but had not had the occasion to repent before his death), is considered as "having been granted a privileged chance to do something good" and "correct" the "defect" in the "higher worlds." I believed mistakenly that what mattered was the very fact that the suffering became intelligible when he understood its cause and purpose. So, despite my atheist perspective and moral views, I was not even tempted to challenge that theodicy. I simply discussed with him issues of responsibility, and thanked him for teaching me things that I did not know. I believe that it enabled him to trust me, and tell me, in the next conversation, that he had "bad blood." That was his way of expressing the fear that he had inherited the "badness" of his father. The rest was a very effective dialogue.

A was, willy-nilly, needed by many persons and souls: an addict father, a helpless mother, neglected siblings, wandering souls, and higher worlds. But *he* did not care about being *needed*; he cared about being *good*.

THE OVERLY NEEDED MAN

This story leads me to the case of M, at the same clinic. We did not have the necessary time for the wished-for results, but our few meetings illustrate my point. M was presented to me by a psychiatrist who was convinced, unlike the psychiatrists depicted by Raabe[4] that M's suffering was due to difficult external conditions. He was concerned about the addiction of "that good man" to Valium. My first meeting with M began with mutual mistrust: he was suspicious and hostile and I was somewhat scared. He declared that he was a bad man who "does not care." A little opening was provided by . . . Saddam Hussein. The conversation took place just after the end of the first Gulf War, during which Israel was occasionally bombarded with Iraqi Scud missiles, so I asked him whether he had looked for a shelter when the Scuds were falling in his region. He mumbled that he did not care. I tried to change his mood by evoking childhood memories, and as he himself was born in Iraq, I asked him whether he remembered that country and whether its bombardment by the Coalition's forces mattered to him. I do not know who was more surprised: he by my unexpected question or I was by his answer. He said he cared very much, for the Iraqis "are good people." I told him that he lied to me when he said that he was a bad person, for he did care even about the "enemies," while many Israelis (and Americans et al.) that pretend to care about people ignore suffering in the other side.

In the next conversation M was much more trusting. He told me that people in his neighborhood were asking him to pray for them "as he is a good man" (God "listens to the prayers of the Just"). We started to discuss the terrible conditions under which M was living (a sick wife, a delinquent son, his intelligent and reliable daughter, who had recently been injured in a car accident, is paralyzed, and he himself, addict to soothing Valium and alcohol, losing the capacity to run his deteriorating business). We gradually started to sort out possibilities for his assistance. Our dialogues were interrupted just as we were planning to invite the daughter to join our consultations.

M was *needed* to an extent that was way beyond his capacities But what he cared about was being *good* and being *recognized as such.*

THE COMPASSIONLESS COMPASSIONATE KANTIAN

S is a very educated person, who had never experienced the ordeals of immigration, nor been a psychiatric patient. Yet she has spent a lot of time and money on personal, couple, and group therapies. She had married B a few years earlier, after a long period of cohabitation. Her former husband had died a short time after their divorce, at the end of a very long and troublesome process of separation: "he could not live without her." We started to talk when she was in her sixties and B in his late seventies. Both have memories and enduring fantasies of a better lover. Their alliance is not really romantic, yet it is far from being a *marriage de raison.* She prevents his *tête à tête* meeting with his former female acquaintances, and never leaves him alone in the evenings. According to her description, he "has never had satisfying intercourse," but still believes that "closeness could be experienced only through true orgasm." He "is neither able to get what *he* wishes nor satisfy *her* desires." Moreover, in contrast to her "sexy, athletic, and daring" former spouse, he is "an anxious" professor and, unlike a former lover from her youth who is still sending her love poems, he is "an intellectual" even in his "narrow-minded" love for music and literature. He is "very selfish and egocentric," as "a result of his dire childhood experiences:" both his parents got sick and died when his fugitive family, recently liberated from a prisoners' camp in Siberia, arrived at a refugee camp in an epidemic-ridden town in central Asia. The six-year-old child was cared for by his older brother instead of "being spoiled" by a mother "who had loved him erotically." The wandering orphans found eventually a home in an Israeli kibbutz. And ever since "he finds girls and women that take care of him," and "spread for him the jam on the bread."

The greatest contrast is, however, between B and herself. She was verbally, intellectually, and artistically a "*Wunderkind*," the idol of her father, to the resentment of his "unfaithful spouse" and his younger kids, who still envy and resent her." When the hands of her piano teacher began, so to say, to wander, she stopped at once her "promising musical career," and took the moral decision not to explain her reasons: she prevented the "teacher's murder and the father's heart attack." She got married very young and had two children and worked as schoolteacher. After the father's sudden death, she took charge of her "ungrateful" younger sister. Then she met a lover, a married man who was her "father substitute," but when she finally got divorced, the lover "failed to keep his promise to do the same." Years later she studied and then taught philosophy. She met B, a scientist "with philosophical pretensions," at the faculty while she was struggling with her "formerly admiring" supervisor over the final grade for her MA thesis. She shares with B some common philosophical and political interests as well as love for music and literature, but has reservations about his "limited understanding" of philosophical issues and "fixated tastes" in artistic matters: in literature "he is fascinated by books that describe the decadent world of the early twentieth century and remind him of his mother."

I have reasons to believe that her intolerance for his literary taste is a rejection of the irony of his favorite authors and the ambivalence and moral ambiguity of their protagonists She insists that "good books" should have a "clear moral message." When we discuss books my suggestions to listen not only to the "voice" that seems to express the author's "clear message" but also to his other voices are dismissed by her: I am "missing the point." She also refuses to listen to 'subtexts' and 'countertexts' in real-life conversations. It seems to be in agreement with her *declared* moral philosophy, according to which there are no true *moral* dilemmas, only moral choices that follow univocally from the application of the Kantian categorical imperative.[5] All other considerations "do not belong to the moral order." Questions that cannot be dealt with using the Kantian tools are accordingly therefore beyond moral discussion. But one's *declared* philosophy is not necessarily *presupposed* or *practically relevant* to one's life.

Her dilemma at the beginning of our conversation seemed to be a matter of timing. She wanted, on the one hand, to separate from B as she "actually had nothing, not even offspring, in common with him," and with the frustrating lack of "real intimacy" their "frequent disputes are unbearable." On the other, his health is precarious and she "cannot leave him precisely when he is going to be operated on." She conceived it as a clash between "her desires and interests" and "his needs." However, as "it follows from Kant's third version of the categorical imperative" that one's moral decision should not take into account one's own well-being, but should take into consideration the well-being of others, she decided to postpone the separation, and leave B only when he would have completely recovered. Whether that decision really followed from Kantian principle and whether the benevolence was due to their improvement by ideas of Hutcheson,[6] it sounded altruistic. But it seemed less altruistic when she refused, despite her constant complaints during that would do me a favor and to sleep with passionlessly rehabilitation period about his "unsupportable behavior" to try to understand his difficulties or else let him be cared for by more patient others. When he had more or less recovered she stopped to refer to him as a Kantian "end in itself," and started to plan the separation. During this period, which lasted several years and was dotted with recurrent health problems, she spoke more and more intensively about their frustrating sex life and the still more frustrating advice of sex therapists. Yet she was hesitant, a hesitation which is best summarized by the story of her aunt: this aunt, who was in her youth the beloved of "the famous poet" X, told her that many years after that, when he was already a moribund old man, she paid him a visit and he asked her to sleep with him in memory of the good old days, but she refused. Yet "she (the aunt) keeps asking me: 'what would have I lost if I had fulfilled his wish?' And indeed, what would she have lost?" I admit that I was tempted to answer "certainly not your modesty," meaning the two senses and the two women. I thought that I myself would have been insulted by the idea that somebody, with or without any sense of losing something, would have done me a favor and slept with me passionlessly. I think that I would not have cared whether the favor would have followed from his compassionate benevolence or his ability to consider me as an "end in myself." I also thought that I would but would have been very offended by his sharing his hesitations with a third party. I spared S the details of those reflections, but challenged her declared altruism toward B. Despite my conviction that such dilemmas were somehow beyond the horizon of Kant,[7] I tried to fit myself to her and stick to her admired philosopher,[8] and (with some help from Nietzsche) suggested to consider whether the pitiful "compassion" for the dying man might not be overruled by a more benevolent duty to respect other people.

As her true dilemma seemed to me a little more complicated than "following egotistically *my preferences* versus altruistic caring for *his needs*," I tried to enhance her awareness of other tones that could be heard in her avowals. It could have enabled her to be more honest about her other (occasionally expressed) considerations, and better connected to feelings and needs that she was apparently trying to hide. My aim was neither to increase her sincerity nor improve her consistency, but rather, in accordance with her declared Kantianism, foster her autonomy, with or without B. But it did not work.

S eventually decided to live separately and their common apartment was sold. She was staying at a friend's house, her new flat was being renovated, and that friend tried, like me, to support her on her new path. She, however, continued to meet with B daily, each time under a different pretext. Several years have passed. They are still living separately, although he tirelessly insists that they should return to living together. He still comes to her every afternoon and spends the evenings with her, they continue to quarrel about spoiled intimacy, tell their life stories to therapists, and explain to each other why their respective therapeutic conversations miss the point. Their 'tacit contract' has not changed: while his respect for her taste, attitudes, and opinions is much greater than her (declared) appreciation for his, she totally adapts herself to the latter. She is still not ready to find an occasion for going without him to a performance in which only she is interested, still annoyed with him, and would have left "if it were not for *his needs*."

S is eager to be—and sound—*morally good*. But her rigid Kantianism prevents her from asking with which of her husband's alleged needs she is *not* morally obliged to comply. Although she is far from being as loving, pious, or naïve as Bess in Lars Von Trier's 1996 movie *Breaking the Waves,* she complies, devotedly yet grudgingly, with his intimate wishes. Moreover, when he seems ready to give up, she sort of tempts him to try to get what he desires, although it is against her own (declared) wishes. It seems that she is still trying, in vain and with disgust, to be the only one who is able to "donate" him the experience that he has "never really had." She is still competing with the other women that might "spread for him the jam on the bread."

Her insistence that she is behaving in this way *because* it is *morally* good seems to me self-deceptive. What she badly needs is to *be needed* in order to *justify decisions* that are, perhaps, motivated by other wishes and anxieties, and thus hide from her pride her 'degrading' state of *being needing*.

THE ETERNALLY NEEDED

U is very different than the "eternal mothers" of her parents' generation. When I speak of such "eternal mothers" I have in mind two old housewives who, like many other women of their generation, gave up their professional dreams for the sake of their husbands' careers and accepted the traditional role of motherhood. Both these women have a "very sensitive" son who is "intellectually brilliant" but "emotionally delicate" and "socially maladaptive." Although the two are very different from each other, they both were over-protective since the "vulnerable" son's childhood. The sons themselves already have their own grown-up children, but the mothers are still convinced that without their continuous caring their "child would not cope."

They filter negative feedback as much as they can and prevent their 'protégés' from learning by experience and find spontaneously better ways to deal with their own personal and interpersonal difficulties. They believe that as housewives and mothers, everything in the family should always be under *their* control, and irritate anybody else in the family by their constant attempt to engage them in the protective project. The prize for such motherhood is, perhaps, the chance of securing 'forever' their role a 'needed mother.' The cost, besides the familial conflicts that are caused by the behavior of the privileged son, is the arrest of their own development. It is not clear whether these mothers are aware of their own *need to be needed* or understand their contribution to their sons' condition, but it is obvious that their conception of womanhood and motherhood as constituting limitless control and responsibility is mixed with a disguised *shame* for having an 'imperfect family' and *fear* of its disintegration. But unlike the "eternally needed mothers" of U's generation, they do not attempt to reconcile their biased caring with objective moral principles.

U belongs to a different generation, which is better acquainted with psychological theories, and more aware of the costs of fostering 'vulnerable' kids. U is also aware of the discrepancies between her behavior and her principles. She became pregnant without being married at a relatively late age, at the peak of her professional career. Like others who chose to be a single parent, she has gone through a whole series of unhappy relationships with men and is confused by the tension between her individualistic ideals and romantic dreams. She has not been indifferent to the nagging of her own mother to "compromise" and get married to an "available man" who should nevertheless be both "worthy" of her and a "reliable provider," but she has "managed" to get always involved with either "inadequate" or "unattainable" mates, and as she never wished to be a "good housewife," she preferred celibacy. She is, however eager to have "stable connections" and always had "steady girlfriends," and some acquaintances suspect that those ties are lesbian. Her attitude to some "irritating women," with whom she is befriended since childhood and without whom "she would be totally alone," is rather servile, although she is relentlessly critical, and her (declared) principles are rather rigid. Her behavior is, on the other hand rather inconsistent Her attitude to the son is similar.

U is not over-protective in the style of the older women; her grown-up, gifted but "eccentric, egotist, and anti-social" son needed, to my mind, protection against her harsh comments. According to her explanation she actually "stole the sperm" (of a divorced man) who "was totally disinterested in an additional child" in order to "get his good genes." But she has later realized that the man is a kind of drop-out, and she is afraid that the son might inherit that tendency. She sometimes seems to regret the whole mothering adventure. The "ungrateful and unpleasant" son sounds angry for not having a father, and tends to "punish" her for his own faults and failure. He sometimes claims that he "owes her nothing," as he never "asked her to give him birth:" U, however, takes care of all his material needs, and defends her dedication to him with explanations like "he will starve himself to death" if she does not cook him the food he likes, and would "commit suicide" if she suggests that he rent his own apartment. She acknowledges her fear that he will "disappear completely" from her life, and sometimes admits that she enjoys caring for him. She seems to believe that the loyalty of her girlfriends is not really reliable, and her friendless and economically dependent son is her only candidate for a reliable alliance.

U is more ready than S to admit her motives and acknowledge her contradictions, but prefers, like her, the present conflict-ridden situation to more harmonious alternatives. She needs to be needed by her son in order to justify the behavior that makes her feel guilt, but provides her security.

THE WOMAN NEEDS TO BE "NEEDED BY EVERYONE"

E, a lawyer, like U and unlike S, is ready to admit (off the record) her ambivalence, the ambiguity of her wishes and feelings, her weaknesses, her responsibility for flawed relationships with others, her doubts, contradictions, regrets. She is also ready to expose those of others, as long as it is *she* who is reading their thoughts, sometimes with a great deal of compassion, and doing their analysis: she believes that they need her in order to be understood and understand themselves. She likes to be challenged by alternative opinions, which she tends to appropriate as if they were always her own, and use them eloquently. Those tendencies seem to help her do a good job, her professional career is very successful and although she has accumulated quite a number of enemies, she is highly appreciated by her colleagues,

Her personal life is more problematic: twice divorced and separated from subsequent mates, she insists that she really loved and respected only the second husband, and, despite the crisis that caused their separation and the mutual loss of trust, declares that she still cares for him. She also declares concern for all the children that those men made with former and later spouses, an attitude that is in most cases neither trusted nor reciprocated. She was much more involved than the respective fathers in the parenting of her own children. She still supports her grown-up offspring emotionally as well as financially much more the fathers, who are nowadays, at least in non-traditionalist circles, no less confused than mothers about their roles, rights, obligations, and responsibilities with regards to relatives, but practically less committed. The supported children are, nevertheless, often angry with her. The "exes," each with their own excuses for themselves and reasons for grudge against her, ascribe it to her "strong personality," careerism, greed . . .

and the impact of her "horrible mother." And indeed, her *need to be needed* by her *"horrible mother"* lurks behind the need of that woman, clever advisor as well as a tough "ex" and reckless rival, to be needed as a wise, generous and a caring friend, mate, and mother.

A 'problematic mother' is, unfortunately, shared by many modern women. (Former generations dared to acknowledge problems only with stepmothers and mothers-in-law . . .). But E's mother was "intensely horrible:" Her childhood story begins with "she told me that I *wanted* to kill her! She accused me of her difficult childbirth!" and the story of her mother's last days ends with "she decided that we (E and her brother) did not deserve her inheritance." The mother did indeed write a will according to which her property should be donated to a certain institute. The angry E did what she always does in cases of conflict of interests: avoid legal processes as far as possible, but argues eloquently that moral as well as legal justice is on her side. She succeeded in dissuading the directors of the institute from making any claims, threatening to "expose the fact that their fund raisers were persuading 'semi-senile persons' to write wills in its favor." The inheritance was retrieved, but E's pain was not relieved. She always told, jokingly, anecdotes about the mother who was, to her mind, responsible for her "constant feelings of emptiness and loneliness;" but after the mother's death she did it obsessively and painfully.

E had more chances than her mother to realize her dreams, and their realization could perhaps be a way of caring for the frustrated mother, although the latter, an immigrant at troubled times, to whom things "just happened" against her plans, was never ready to accept that her "murderous" daughter should realize *her* dream. Yet E tends to identify herself with her more than she is ready to admit. Her style of living and mothering is apparently very different than that of her mother, but her kids accuse her nevertheless with "imitation of her mother;" for example, in her ways of "allocation of funds" to her children and selected "exes," or in the desire to keep others under her control: "They are not responsible enough to be left alone." She looks down on, in the same way as her mother, all her partners, irrespective of their academic level and professional status. She is disappointed with the "failure" of her "talented children" to "fully realize their potential," and "live wisely." Most of them are, to her mind, also "failed parents." They need her, and she, somehow, seems to need their anger. She is dedicated to her grandchildren, but also needs to be needed by them.

THE NEED TO BE RESPONSIBLE FOR POST-MORTAL EXISTENCE

The only thing that seems to have contributed to E's liberation from the ordeal of her obsessive preoccupation with the mother's memory was neither philosophical insight nor psychological self-understanding, but rather "by proxy," through the experience of another person, Z. I told her Z's story in an attempt to exemplify that a change of attitude is possible even in stubborn cases of double-binding.

The death of Z's aunt, the last witness to Z's troubled infancy and youth, created in her a new kind of feeling: The continued existence of her dead relatives "now depended only on her," for they "could exist only as people she remembered," as she was "the only survivor" who had witnessed their behavior. She could not, however, provide a "decent" existence for them in her memory, for "the traces of bad experiences were much stronger than those of moments of grace." In particular, she could not get over her conflict-ridden attitude to her father, a peace-loving and compliant person whom she had always protected against the aggressiveness of the other members of the family. He, however, always "betrayed" her by "failing" to protect her from the same "abrasive" people and showed more concern for her "problematic" brother. She did not know whether his declared stoicism, with which he used to explain (or defend) his placidity (or passivity), "was a sign of strength or renunciation" and whether his avoidance of any close contact "was a sign of gentleness or defensive rejection." She knew that psychologists, who understood him as little as she did, would love to have diagnosed his behavior as "passive-aggressive," but she did not agree with such a "judgmental" verdict. She could not tell whether the difference between her ethos and his was a matter of cultural difference (he was an immigrant who failed [or refused] to adapt to the environment in which she felt at home). She did not know why an "intelligent, industrious, and reliable" man like him, who did not like his job and loathed his employer, never looked seriously for a better job. She was angry with the aggressiveness of the other members of her family, but her obsessive thoughts were about her father's *ambiguity* and her own *ambivalence* toward him. She did not dare to be angry with this "parented parent," but was annoyed by people whose behavior reminded her of his "betrayals."

When Z, informed by a friend, arrived at the "Clinique of the Siberian self-made commonsensical therapist," she was motivated by curiosity rather than an interest to be treated. She brought up her obsession in order to understand the approach of the "strange healer." The "Siberian," in contrast, took her job very seriously and asked Z to explain her father's behavior. She dismissed Z's offered explanation and asked her to try another one, dismissed it, encouraged her to try once more, and so on. The process stopped only when Z did not find any further "pro-active" motives for her father's behavior, and the "commonsensical therapist" suggested that "he simply wanted to survive" under the oppressive conditions of his life. At that stage Z felt that she should "just let him be," for there was no point in being angry with such a helpless and exhausted person, or being frustrated with his "inability" to be decisive, assertive, and supportive. Z still felt that "there was something wrong in the process," but she actually got rid of her obsession.

The very description of Z's experience helped E and some other persons who had been entangled in the confusing game of 'parenting a parent' while expecting to be 'parented' by that person. Perceiving the frustrating parent (or parental figure) as simply a helpless "survivor" can indeed be liberating. Perhaps the *story* of another person who has experienced such a change can have such a great effect because it reinforces the listener's feeling of superiority without the fear of an actual realization that one's idealized angel and demon was just a 'miserable' human being. However, as we can see from Z's further experience, such a process does not necessarily enable one to feel toward the de-idealized 'parent' a 'feminine' *moral compassion.* Z felt, that, in a more 'virile' way, that the price of her liberation was the *dignity* of her late father as an *autonomous person* that had chosen to live according to the rules, values, and ideals that she herself failed to understand, and for which she herself was not responsible. E and the others' lesson is therefore just the *beginning* of a process, in which one should learn to distinguish *morally* between oneself and the 'problem-causing' other.

As Z has later learned, that is not the process of separation of a child from her mother (with which it is allegedly in initial symbiosis) her "individuation" as an independent adult,[9] but a philosophical process, in which the *moral* aspects of shame, guilt, obligations, and responsibilities are clarified. It is also a psychological process in which one learns that being needed is neither a guarantee for being loved nor a satisfying substitute. It took Z years to change her philosophical perspective—to call into question the residues of her 'subject-centric' phenomenological formation as well as the impact of the Jewish tradition that sees the descendant as the keeper of the name and memory of his ancestors.[10] She also needed to reflect on her other experiences of frustration in 'parenting-the-parent' (and in-laws, supervisors, and employers in a parent-figure role), and analyze the related issues of moral responsibility.

I do not know whether Z's father and her other '*protégés*' really needed her protection; she was angry with them because she believed that they did. The *experience* of recognizing their "miserable" inabilities helped her to get rid of the anger. But only the philosophical understanding that one is finally *unable* to know the 'correct explanation' for the behavior of another person helped her to get rid of the disrespectful pity toward her father, the disquieting residue of the "Siberian commonsensical—or manipulative—treatment." Under the impact of Levinas's approach to morality (Levinas, 1994) she was able to liberate herself from unjustified pity, assume responsibility for her shame and disrespect for a father who did not correspond to her childish interpretation of conventional ideals in her ideological environment, and liberate herself from the illusion that *she needed to be responsible* for her father's deeds, faults, memory, or reputation. She also had to become aware, despite her modern, secular, and liberal worldview, that she had a hidden dilemma between the loud voice that demanded an appraisal of anybody by "universal criteria" (and implied the possibility of rejecting her parents' way of life), and the quieter but persistent traditional voice whispering "respect thy father and mother" (and implied the possibility of self-abnegation).[11]

A PARTIAL ANALYSIS

Z, whose awareness of herself as "the responsible adult" was perhaps just a subjective feeling, does not seem to need her 'being needed' *as a justification or excuse*. But while Z still feels she is needed by some people and sometimes accepts it with joy, I have met others who reject it altogether. One of them does not need 'being needed' because she was always being needed, ad nauseam, by a hypochondriac mother; another, whose constant role as an admired '*Wunderkind*' has never been challenged by a jealous parent or envious siblings, is accustomed to the role of a 'star,' which is incompatible with any commitment or pretense of caring. A third declares that she does not need any contact: her parents "did not really care for her," she "does not want to care for others." In brief, some women do not want to be needed, others need it beyond the needs of others and against their interests, some are needed but do not like it, while others accept and enjoy it. Finally, some conflict-ridden women need to be needed in order to *use* the 'being needed' as a *justification* for behavior that betrays other needs.

I will spare the reader the detailed evidence for my conviction that S needs her present husband emotionally, financially, as well as socially, is afraid of failing to please him (let alone being abandoned by him) and intolerant to threats to her so-called 'narcissistic pride.' I will also omit the explanation for my belief that E and U are motivated by a 'will to power' that betrays self-deceptions, anxieties, and dependencies. My impressions with regards to the psychological issues of these people are irrelevant to the question that intrigues me as a philosophical counselor: why such women, intelligent and apparently non-conventional, *justify* their decisions by pretending to fulfill a stereotypical, traditional female role?

I do not believe that the need to be 'the caring one' is a female instinct that lurks behind modern claims for equality and freedom of choice. Nor do I share the conviction that women learn to be compassionate in the process of their socialization. The experiences of the women I know (myself included) testify that *many* environmental voices, different and incoherent, try to 'socialize' us. We often hear voices that try to control our assumed instincts or minds and direct our aspirations to conventional gender-roles. However, also we hear nowadays voices that encourage us, women of the modern world, to develop our 'non-feminine' sides, support our claims for justice, fairness, freedom, or equality, foster our 'self-realization,' 'will to power,' and competitiveness, and spend less time in caring for the well-being of our family members.

As a philosopher I am not supposed to judge which biological, psychological, or social factors determine which voices are, empirically, the most influential, and which conditions favor their dominance. My role is to engage in critical dialogues with all the voices that I happen to hear. As a philosophical counselor, however, I have to be aware no less than empirical scientists of the possibility that the voices that are echoed in the loud and 'trendy' *declarations* of my counselees are not necessarily more influential than the whispers of allegedly natural demands, traditional dictates, or ideals. Philosophical counselors who ignore them, believing that discerning contradictions between *explicit* statements or else proposing an alternative to a *declared* worldview are sufficient for inducing a real change, do not know enough about people. They also fail to understand the nature and contribution of philosophy.

All the women described here still hear whispered messages that are not necessarily in accord with the worldview that is dominant in their social *milieu,* but are still transmitted non-reflectively from one generation to the next. Those whispers say rather loudly that "a woman is *needed* by her husband/children/aging parents and *should give it a priority*."

But they also say the apparent contrary: a woman "*needs* a husband, and is appreciated by *his* virtues and achievements (and those of her children)," "she should help her parents nurture her brothers and prepare them for their roles as men," "enable her husband to fulfill his manly duties, comply with her husband's demands" and, last but not least, (as "the woman is responsible for matrimonial harmony"), "she should adapt herself to her husband's sexual needs—or caprices." They still hear what Mill says, in his book *The Subjection of Women*, "All men, except the most brutish, desire to have, in the woman most nearly connected with them, not a forced slave but a willing one, not a slave merely, but a favorite." (Mill, 1869, 17). Mill, however, did not take into account the fact that the oppressive "socializing agents" are often women, who also teach each other how to bypass those "oughts" by manipulation or hypocrisy. In this respect traditional women have an advantage over modern ones: A woman's compliance may indeed be considered a religious commandment and a moral virtue, and women are sometimes told that they should be *proud* of the *privilege* of having all those duties—but precisely because of that obedience to the rule avoidable: one can find a religious commandment or moral virtue that overrules it. When the traditional rules are abandoned and modern liberal ideals are incompatible with the whispers that are still heard, it is not clear whether one feels morally freer;

under conditions of ambiguity and ambivalence one feels rather more confused.

Moreover, in face of the enormous changes that have occurred on the level of interpersonal relations that formerly belonged to the domain of the family, both the new ideals and the conservative whispers do not provide satisfactory guidance. Almost all the people I have described come from either 'dysfunctional' families in the old sense, or non-legal alliances and short-term relations that were not taken into account by traditional thinkers, and most often would be considered by them, classical philosophers as well as religious authorities and conservative judges, sinful, immoral, and forbidden. Kant or Hegel, for whom the "animal" in us, that is, sexual acts and their consequences, is transformed into something "human" only when it is willingly subsumed under the "law" (Kant, 1997) and constitutes an "institution" (Hegel, 1896), actually reformulated the Augustinian or Thomist interpretation of Saint Paul's dictates, and they would have accused almost all the women that I described here, along with their mothers, aunts, and daughters, and, of course, mates with 'bestiality' for their extra-marital sex or pregnancy. Even Hume, who was less eager to translate religious dogma into secular terms, and believed that the family is basically just a useful custom, shared the conception that the family's function, just like that of "legitimate" sex, is procreation and the strengthening of the bond between parents in order to enable children to grow under secure and stable conditions. Later philosophers who were opposed to marriage for its alleged incompatibility with 'true love' seem to be irrelevant to women who seek stability and security, while socialist philosophers, who criticized the institute for being dysfunctional, oppressive, or hypocritical, and were perhaps acquainted with the phenomenon of women abandoned by the fathers of their children, would never dream of women preferring "stolen" or "donated" sperm to shared parenthood with the father.[12] Some of them had indeed visions of communities, where children would be cared for by the community while the parents enjoy 'free love,' but they did not guess the social and emotional problems in such communities. Even Mill, who was living "in sin" with a married woman and was probably alone in remembering that there are also families without children, did not consider the possibility of a second, third, or fourth short-term cohabitation of people beyond the age of procreation, surrounded by all kinds of "exes," with offspring from different sources, divided feelings, clashing financial interests and, with growing longevity, different rates of diminishing potency. . . . None of them thought of families being created or disintegrating under conditions of exile and immigration, where wives look down on their "inferior" or "non-adaptable" husbands, children are ashamed of their parents, mothers do not know how to cope and regret having children, or, lonely and insecure, arrest their children's growth with their ceaseless over-protection and endless reproaches and demands. Not one of them even imagined the possibilities not represented in my non-systematic sample, cf same-sex marriages and non-formal alliances, with or without children which can be had through the 'donations of eggs' and 'hiring' of wombs. None of them could have guessed what kind of moral questions would intrigue people across new networks of interpersonal connections. Sociologists describe such a state, where the old norms do not apply to new situations, as "anomie" (cf. Durkheim, 2006), and compete with psychologists with their explanations for depression, suicide, delinquency, or familial dysfunction. But whether people under such conditions fall into those states or whether they do not they often live in conflict and are more often confused: They often want to make morally right decisions, or morally justify those decision, while they do not know which criteria to apply.

The women who need to be needed in order to justify their decisions to comply with the needs of others although they are just like the men A and M: They wish to be as good as they can, or at least to be considered as such. They are not more caring than these men. And they are, just like them, like men and women in general nowadays, confused with regards to the limits of their familial obligations and responsibilities: parents with regards to children, children with regards to parents, and spouses with regards to each other and their own or the other's siblings, "exes," and so on . . . they are even more confusing if they belong to new kinds of families, with or without marriage, children, or spouses. They are also confused with regards to themselves: What do they deserve? To what extent they should they care for their own interests? Should they strive for their own happiness, comfort, security, liberty, peace of mind, self-realization, growth, a place in a mundane society, in the pantheon of cultural heroes, the world-to-come, the other world, the memory of decedents, or wherever?

Some people are not bothered by ambiguity. Some seek like A and M comfort in religion or like T—in esoteric fantasies. Some have patience and seek, philosophically, a rational and coherent solution, although they know that it will be partial and fallible. Some, like S, E, and U, seem to be intolerant for ambiguity, and despite their declared "virile" moral rule, which they conceive of as 'progressive,' justify their actual decision by a "regression" to traditional gender duties, such as, the 'feminine' morality of caring. There is a great difference between this 'regression' and the pretensions of traditional women to have more important duties and roles or aims; for they do not manipulate or cheat other people in order to attain their aim; they rather deceive themselves and prevent better relations with others.

THE ROLE OF PHILOSOPHY AND PHILOSOPHICAL COUNSELING

Thinking about women in my practice has brought me to issues that were not formerly themes of my philosophical reflections. The ethic of interpersonal relations on the level that traditionally belongs to the family is one of them. It is not an ethics of women or for women; it is ethic that is relevant from the perspectives of modern women, for whom fulfilling traditional roles is no longer taken for granted. Similar problems seem to bother men (not necessarily gays or transgender) that do not accept their traditional gender roles within traditional frames.

Philosophical counselors cannot find ready-made approaches in the philosophical arsenal. Past philosophers, whose moral theories were oriented by their political concerns with regards to the *polis* or the *state*, considered interpersonal relations as relations between *abstract citizens*, and did not develop an ethical discourse on the family level. They tended to leave such questions in the hands of custom, religious instruction, or civil law. But these regulations, which were sometimes the fruits of semi-philosophical debates between ancient (male) sages, are not only incompatible with an egalitarian attitude to women and minorities, they are also too detailed, restrictive, conservative, and worse of all—authoritative—to be bearable in secular, more or less liberal, circles. Moreover, much of the contemporary philosophical debate on this level is inspired by philosophers of law and was dedicated to questions of the *moral* permissibility of legally or conventionally forbidden activities (such as homosexuality, prostitution, pornography, sadomasochism, adultery, abortion, or euthanasia) and the *justifiability* of state intervention in the protection of the of the *rights* of those that might be hurt by such actions. The discussion of possible moral *duties* and *obligations*, especially between spouses or sex partners, was largely left in the hands of explicit or tacit 'voluntary contracts' between spouses or sexual partners. The philosophical contribution is supposed to be limited to the definition of *criteria* for *really free consent* and the *fairness* of contracts.

There are, indeed, women, mostly widows, that think in a businesslike manner and decide in advance, with or without their new partner's knowledge and consent, to leave him when his health deteriorates, his business runs into trouble, or his children's demands get on their nerves. It is understandable: that they do not want such a burden, and they are free to set their own conditions. But, despite the analogy to a commercial agreement, the explicit conditions of an alliance, whatever they are, cannot cover all the unexpected events and situations that might occur in a couple's life. The disparity between expectations and reality is, of course, still greater when the couple is young, less experienced and perhaps more romantic: Priests, rabbis, and so on may speak of an alliance for they assume the divine wisdom and human experience provide them with ready-made formulas that cover a wide range of marital eventualities. But how can a philosopher describe as a contract a relation into which one enters willingly but *rather blindly*? Perhaps one does it less blindly than the above-mentioned Bess, but one is as unable as she to predict the spouse's behavior under unexpected conditions. Can we speak here of a *fair* contract?

I have met, anyway, other kinds of widows: some would *not* look for a new partner because they did not want an unexpected burden and believed it was *immoral* to forsake a partner when he was in trouble; some *did not leave* the partner, but did not stop to wonder why they were staying with him; some, finally, were ready to leave before the partner became a burden, but they decide to stay, *because* the partner has got into trouble, and that has changed their perspective. Three of the four groups deal with moral responsibility toward a partner, independently of any consent with him. It shows, I believe, not only that the question about the *fairness* of a contract is different than the question about its *morality*, but also that in such context it is inadequate to speak of a contract. It is, as Hegel has already suggested, an alliance of a different nature. It is needless to add that other family relations—parenthood, siblings, in-laws, and so on—are not even a matter of non-mutual agreement. I do not remember where I read the opinion that parents are obliged to their small children because they created them without their consent, and for that reason children have no moral obligations to parents. I believe that most people do not agree with that, and ask themselves not *whether* there are inter-familial obligations, but *what is their limit*.

I do not think that the role of philosophical counseling is to preach morality or provide moral education, and certainly do not think that sexuality *per se* is immoral. But if our counselee says that she wants to behave morally, or we see that she is confused about what she ought to do and her feelings of guilt, shame, regret, anger, resentment, envy, and so on may involve confused moral judgments, it is our moral duty to enable her to examine with us moral perspectives and options in a way that is relevant to her specific problem situation.

In order to do that we need a morality that goes beyond the dichotomy of rule or caring moralities. I personally believe that we should think of human relations in terms of *friendship*. Such an approach should allow for a discourse on obligations which takes into account different degrees of closeness, and different degrees of emotional involvement, and it should be guided by moral criteria rather than psychological tendencies and conventional norms, with respect for the rights of other people that might be affected. It is neither a morality of abstract principles nor that of sentimental caring, but rather of concern, respect, and responsibility. Considerations of justice and mercy may be relevant in specific situations, but in others the analogies to the 'perfect state' or "ideal love" are irrelevant.

I am speaking, of course, of a space and perspective for moral debates, not of an ethical code, which to my mind is an impediment to moral thinking.

NOTES

1. Such examinations usually show that some presuppositions are false or at least not true and therefore corrigible or replaceable, and it may lead to changes of specific beliefs, attitudes, or behaviors. But it can be beneficial even if it does not, because a well-led dialogue offers new perspectives and therefore widens the horizon of possibilities and enhance the level of rational choices among them.
2. It is not an excuse; I have done it, lengthily, in a former draft, but was asked to shorten it.
3. I do not pretend to have found the cure for schizophrenic symptoms. Yet I believe that in our philosophically oriented conversations, where I expressed interest in her beliefs, respect for the ways in which she described them, and exemplified unexpected reactions and interpretations, I succeeded to give her some chance to experience being a worthy and rewarding person. I suspect that the psychiatric treatments given at the hospital and the "Have-you-brushed-your-teeth-today?" nagging of social workers at the control clinic did not foster in her the feeling that they or anybody body else did or would ever need her inspiring company.
4. Peter Raabe, *Philosophy's Role in Counseling and Psychotherapy* (Lanham, Maryland: Jason Aronson, 2014).
5. According to my interpretation, one should not abnegate one's preferences but rather apply to oneself as to others the duty to respect being "an end and not just a means." Cf. Stacey (2012).
6. Francis Hutcheson, *An Inquiry into the Original of Our Ideas of Beauty and Virtue in Two Treatises* (Indianapolis: Liberty Fund, Inc., 2004).
7. I discovered only later how obsolete are his opinions on sexuality and marriage. See Immanuel Kant, *Lectures on Ethics*, translated by Peter Heath (Cambridge: Cambridge University Press, 1997).
8. Immanuel Kant, *Groundwork of the Metaphysic of Morals* (New York: Harper and Row Publishers, Inc., 1964).
9. I refer to the psychoanalytic theories of Mahler (1967) and Bowlby (1969).
10. Like in other patriarchal traditions, the relevant descendants in the Jewish tradition are male. (In Hebrew the word for male and the word for remembering have a common radical). But Z never identified herself as a "non-male," and for that reason was also unaware of the possibility that the father's concern about the brother had to do with his being "the male descendent" rather than his being the "preferred child." Girls that grow up, as she did, with a declared egalitarian ideology, do not know even unconsciously that they are supposed to suffer from 'penis-envy.'
11. As her father was an immigrant who did not want to (or could not) adapt to a society that aspired to be a "melting pot," her experience is relevant to many Israelis (and immigrants in general). But I am afraid that the angry second or third generation of 'non-adaptable' immigrants needs even a deeper change of perspective in order to be able not only to fight, politically, for a better status for their origin group, but also accept their personal responsibility for their own shame and disrespect.
12. For an interesting analysis of their positions see Weikart, 1994.

BIBLIOGRAPHY

Bowlby, John. *Attachment and Loss, vol. 1: Attachment*. New York: Basic Books, 1969.
Durkheim, Émile. *On Suicide*. Translated by Robin Buss. London: Penguin Books, 2006.
Guyer, Paul. *Kant,* London: Routledge, 2006.
Gilligan, Carol. *In a Different Voice*. Cambridge, Mass: Harvard University Press , 1982

Hegel, Georg Wilhelm Friedrich. *The Philosophy of Right*. Translated by S. W. Dyde. London: George Bell and Son, 1896

Hume, David. *A Treatise of Human Nature*. Edited by David Fate Norton and Mary J. Norton, Oxford: Clarendon Press, 2000.

Hutcheson, Francis. *An Inquiry into the Original of Our Ideas of Beauty and Virtue in Two Treatises*. Indianapolis: Liberty Fund, Inc., 2004.

Kant, Immanuel. *Groundwork of the Metaphysic of Morals*. New York: Harper and Row Publishers, Inc., 1964.

Kant, Immanuel. *Lectures on Ethics*. Translated by Peter Heath. Cambridge: Cambridge University Press, 1997.

Levinas, Emmanuel. *Nine Talmudic Readings*. Translated by Annette Aronowicz. Bloomington: Indiana University Press, 1994.

Mill, John Stewart. *The Subjection of Women*. London: Longmans, Green & Dyer, 1869.

Raabe, Peter. *Philosophy's Role in Counseling and Psychotherapy*. Lanham, Maryland: Jason Aronson, 2014.

Stacy, Matthew. "Kant on Sex and Marriage: What Kant Should Have Said," A thesis submitted for the degree of MA in the Dept. of Philosophy at the University of Victoria http://dspace.library.uvic.ca:8080/bitstream/handle/1828/4158, 2012

Weikart, Richard. "Marx, Engels, and the Abolition of the Family" in *History of European Ideas,* Vol. 18, No. 5, 1994, 657–672.

Chapter Eight

Sex, Dating, and Love: Differences between Men and Women

Roxana Kreimer

Recent years have highlighted the value of different types of intelligence. It came the turn of mating intelligence, which consists of the entire set of psychological abilities for courtship as well as to form, maintain, coordinate, and terminate relationships. These types of skills are influenced by biological, psychological, and social factors, and it is important to avoid the reductionism of our analysis to only one of these three areas.

During the twentieth century there has been a lot of research related to the social and psychological patterns in our ways of living, sex, and love, but only recently there have been significant advances in the field of biological influences.

Scientific research has provided valuable evidence about several irrational sources that influence mate choice. In reviewing this evidence, philosophical counseling can lead us to more fulfilling choices. In this chapter I will start by differentiating the biological factors that influence the way men and women relate to sex and love as reflected in current scientific evidence. I will point out a number of the problems that these influences pose for the development of a proper mating intelligence for men and women, given that courtship and the development of a relationship require a great deal of cognitive work. I will illustrate the analysis with cases taken from my practice of philosophical counseling. My perspective in this chapter is that love can be understood as an art, as something we learn and improve on, not just something that 'happens' to us.

BIOLOGICAL INFLUENCES IN MATING INTELLIGENCE OF MEN

Courtship strategies were developed as an evolutionary drive for generational increase of offspring. An increase in the number of partners does not lead to more offspring for women, whereas it definitely does for men. When evolutionists talk about these strategies, they are referring to patterns of behavior that are unconscious.

The biological differences between men and women in their sex and love lives can be understood as differences in parental investment. In most species, females invest more than males, in the sense that men do not have to pay the physiological cost of pregnancy, while for women this is a commitment of her entire body. Across a wide range of age groups and continents there is a vast body of evidence which suggests that on average males have a greater investment in sexual variety than females. In forty-eight nations across the globe, men are reported as being more interested in having a large selection of partners throughout their life-span than women.[1] Although there are socio-sexual factors which influence differences across the sexes, culture itself does not affect differences in sex drive. Men select more partners in a speed-dating context and want to have sex earlier than women, and give more reasons for having sex than women. Their motives include knowledge ("I wanted to increase the numbers of partners I had experienced"), opportunity ("The person was available"), physical pleasure ("I was horny"), utilitarian reasons ("to improve my sexual skills"), and social status ("I wanted to look good"). Men are more likely than women to have sex outside a relationship and to indulge in short-term mating strategies.

In some ways men and women are more similar than dissimilar. Both prefer a sexual relationship based on love and commitment and value generosity, mutual love, humor, and intelligence. Despite their highly contextualized strategies, there are nevertheless very important differences which adversely affect a number of their selections. Both want to fall in love, and infatuation lasts an average of three to four years, a strategy on the part of nature to ensure that the male stays with the female during the early years of parenting. There are systems for long-lasting couples with high parental investment in other species. One example among birds: the European Robins (*Erithacus rubecula*), most commonly known in Anglophone Europe simply as the Robin. The male remains with the female and the breeding is not autonomous.

Humans are characterized by a strategy for long-term relationships, even if the model of couples who last for a lifetime is in crisis (long-term relationships are not necessarily equivalent to 'a whole life'). For many evolutionists this explains that women, being more vulnerable, are more selective, a strategy that also characterizes females of other species. Clark and Hatfield's study found that men who approached women for casual sex were perceived as less desirable by women, while women who approached men for casual sex were not perceived as less desirable by men. Women perceived men who approached women for casual sex as more physically dangerous and less likely to provide sexual satisfaction, and as having lower social status. Familiarity with men reduced the force of these perceptions (e.g., if the woman knew the man before, or if he was famous). From the point of view of adaptation, this familiarity would represent a lower risk for women. In the same study, women were much more likely to agree to have sex with a famous actor than with a complete stranger, whereas men were only slightly more likely to agree to have sex with Angelina Jolie than a complete stranger. We are not suggesting that men on average do not emphasize the need to have an affinity with their partners, just that it is not the most predominant requirement.

Men put an emphasis on beauty over other attributes in maintaining a stable relationship. As we have seen above, this is not a prerequisite for casual sex. Evolutionary psychologists suggest that this may be due to biology, since men on average feel more attracted to women who are of childbearing age, increasing the chances of fatherhood. Society reinforces this requirement by associating the idea of female beauty with youth.

Men who have casual sex or who form stable couples with other men also favor beauty and its association with youth over other attributes, while this preference does not seem so prevalent among lesbian couples.

These biological influences are unconscious, and can negatively affect men's choices, leading them to favor beauty far above other relevant traits—for example, ethical values, or cultural affinities, and making them suffer in the future all the negative consequences related to the incompatibility of characters and the lack of affinities. Men often leave their partners because they are no longer young and they no longer feel physically attracted to them in order to start a new couple with a younger woman. Even if he has children from a previous marriage and does not want to have more, he does so to please his new partner, assuming in many cases a host of economic and care responsibilities he would have preferred to avoid, even putting his health at risk where those responsibilities require more work than he can handle.

The fact is that men transgress sexual exclusivity pacts more than women, which often leads them to transgress ethical codes, such as lying to their partner, although they often love them.

Juan attended a philosophical counseling session when he was in the process of separating from his second wife. He had left his first wife when he fell in love with Laura, an attractive twenty-five-year-old who worked as a secretary in the office where he was manager. He had two sons from his previous marriage, of twenty-two and twenty-four years old, and a little child of five from his new one. His young wife used to react very aggressively to small mistakes. For example, if he promised to fetch their son from a birthday party, and he was a little late, she accused him of not taking care of their child, she screamed to him in the middle of the street and told him to sleep outside the house that night. She had a very bad relationship with the two sons from his previous relationship, criticizing them for no apparent reason and not even allowing them go out with their younger son under the pretext that they did not take good care of him. If Juan tried to defend his other sons, she accused him of being against her.

In the session we worked around some communication tools for assertiveness and suggested he could consider other female attributes in his choice of a future mate. For example, we worked around the empathic assertiveness, the idea that it is useful for communication to start a sentence empathizing (for example, "I understand that you can be upset by my late arrival to the birthday party. Nevertheless, this does not mean that I am not taking care of our child. I promise to fetch him in time in the future"), progressive assertiveness: (if the other does not respond satisfactorily to empathic assertiveness and continues to violate rights, insist more firmly but without aggressiveness), positive-assertiveness (expressing appreciation and affection for the other person), match point (find a limited point of agreement), broken record (repeat one's claims in a friendly and courteous tone whenever one encounters a not legitimate resistance).

David Buss and his colleagues have provided evidence which suggests that, compared with women; men are particularly astute at detecting signs of a female partner engaging in sexual infidelity.[2] Men remember more details regarding sexual infidelity than women do. Buss argues that men's astuteness regarding this issue is an evolutionarily shaped adaptation. Men in our evolutionary past were faced with the problem of paternal certainty—unlike females, who are always sure that their offspring are their genetic kin. As males are never completely sure that their offspring are their own, evolution may have favored them in providing cognitive abilities that helped to reduce the likelihood of a mate's sexual infidelity. They probably have a mechanism that helps them predict whether a female will have sex with another man. This is one of the many psychological processes that taken together represent mating intelligence, although this particular bias favors male jealousy, one of the starting points of the violence which leads to the death of many women all over world.

Another common bias in men is the tendency to overestimate the significance of the signals women give to show sexual interest. In terms of adaption this could be an advantage in encouraging men to court.[3]

BIOLOGICAL INFLUENCES IN MATING INTELLIGENCE OF WOMAN

Some studies reveal that women also have biases with regard to courtship.[4] They are commitment skeptics. This means that they are more likely than men to be skeptical of statements of commitment. As women are at risk for getting stuck with the cost of raising offspring without other parental help, they tend to be skeptical about men's commitment. The cost of this bias is minor compared with its major evolutionary benefit, which is to reduce the likelihood of mating with an unreliable partner.

Let's see an example from a philosophical counseling session. Martha is a thirty-seven-year-old who met a man in the house of mutual friends. They liked each other and two days later they met by chance in the street, and Martha invited him to go to a concert that night.

> "Did you go out together?" I asked.
> "No" said Martha, "he said he was sorry but he couldn't go."
> "What exactly did he say?"
> "That he had a sore throat and wasn't feeling well."
> "Did you invite him for some other time?"
> "No, it was obvious he was making an excuse."
> "How did you notice that?"
> "Just by what he said, that he wasn't feeling well.
> "Couldn't it have been true?"
> "Yes, but one more day passed and he has not phoned me yet."
> "He might in the future."
> "Maybe."

That weekend he phoned and since then they have been seeing each other every day and now plan to move in together to the same apartment.

What other unaware biological influences can affect women's mate strategies? On the one hand, in various animal species, females are more selective than males because, as we have seen, the copula has more consequences for females than for males. On the other hand, also in various animal species the female chooses the dominant male. In social animals, the alpha is the individual with the highest rank. Male alphas may gain preferential access to sex or mates. Common chimpanzees show deference to the alpha of the community through ritualized gestures such as bowing, allowing the alpha to walk first in a procession, or standing aside when the alpha challenges them.

When they can choose, women in general also feel more attracted toward men with power. When I refer to 'power' I mean material resources, creativity, sense of humor, fame, prestige within a given group, or a specific talent that stands out from the average.[5] The expectation that men should be taller and older than their female partner may also be related to this power issue.

Since men in positions of power tend to be a select few, it implies that these 'alphas' are seduced by several women in competition with each other. This situation does not favor women, because if they have mated an "alpha" man they risk being abandoned, and if they have fallen in love with a married 'alpha' and have initiated a relationship with him, there's a greater chance that their investment will not fulfill their expectations. Moreover, competition among women can lead to weight loss far beyond what it is recommended for good health.

Paula attended a session of philosophical counseling after she got pregnant by a professor of the university where she had started teaching. She was thirty-two years old and he said he was not happy with his marriage. As often happens, Paula thought that he would abandon his wife and they would raise their son together. But he had no intention of leaving his wife, and he finished his relationship with Paula. A year later, he told her that he had divorced his wife because he had fallen in love with a student and they were very happy. A better informed choice (knowing, for example, the disadvantages of being attracted to an alpha male) could have led Paula to choose otherwise.

In a study, Martie Haselton and Geoffrey Miller found that during ovulation women prefer short-term relationships with men who appear to have good genes (e.g., men who have more sense of humor, creativity, intelligence, and physical attractiveness), while during the rest of the month, they give priority to men's status and other indications such as the ability and willingness to invest in protection, provisioning, and care of potential offspring.[6] Some women can mate with a man who has both characteristics (good genes and good dad potential), but most women will end up with a partner who is not ideal at all levels. Fertility did not have an impact on preferences in long-term mating.

There is a very low probability that these preferences are conscious. Women's preferences cannot only be explained by cultural conditioning, as it is unlikely that culture causes women to favor creativity on high fertility days but not on low fertility days.

Humor may also have greater appeal for women depending on their fertility cycle.[7] In a study 206 female participants read storyboards about potential male mates with different levels of humor. Men who were described as being funnier were rated by women participants as significantly more socially sensitive, adaptable, extroverted, exciting, happy, and able to play with kids, as well as more intelligent, kind, tall, healthy, masculine, and muscular. In the imagination of women, men who are funny promise all sorts of features and virtues!

Research suggests that while both men and women say they like a good sense of humor in a potential mate, they differ in what they mean by this phrase. Women tend to prefer men who make them laugh, whereas men tend to prefer women who laugh at their jokes.[8]

In another study, Jennifer Hay found that males produce humor in courtship much more often than females. More than twice as many women as men seek a sense of humor or someone who will make them laugh.[9] Women tend to seek humor more than they offer it, whereas men are more likely to offer a sense of humor than to seek it. Funny women can be immensely sexy, and many men do value humor in women. But taken together, these results suggest that females, on average, prefer men who are funny. The problem is that in choosing a man for his sense of humor over other attributes women can cause problems for themselves because men, on average, make jokes that many women find too aggressive. Hay's study suggests that in most happy couples that last over time, women are more active in producing jokes, and men are more disposed to enjoy women's jokes.

Alice came to a session of philosophical counseling when she began to have problems with her boyfriend, a stand-up comedian who criticized her with sarcasm, and when she asked him to talk to her without being aggressive, he told her: "Darling, it's just a joke! Don't you have a sense of humor?"

Psychologists in Britain found that professional artists and poets have more partners than other people. Daniel Nettle, a psychologist at Newcastle University's School of Biology, and his colleague Helen Clegg, asked 425 British men and women, including professional artists, poets, and schizophrenic patients, about their creative activity, sexual encounters, and mental health characteristics.[10] Although creative people have long been associated with active sex lives, the researchers believe their study is the first to support this claim with empirical evidence. They found that professional artists and poets had between four and ten sexual partners, while less creative people had an average of three. The study also showed that the average number of sexual partners increased as the creative output went up. What the artists produce draws attention to them, which seems to enhance their sexual allure. *"It could be that very creative types lead a bohemian lifestyle and tend to act more on sexual impulses and opportunities, often purely for experience's sake, than the average person would"* said Nettle. According to the researchers, the active sex lives of artists are often tolerated even by long-term partners, who are less likely to expect loyalty and fidelity from them. But if a woman does not want an open couple relationship, this could be another trap related to the way she chooses a partner. She may feel more attracted to artists, but her chances of being abandoned or of living in triangular relationships could increase.

We said before those in different animal species females are more selective than males because sex has more consequences for females than for men. This can be seen, for example, in speed dating and in websites for online dating. On the other hand, we know that we can fall in love with the person of our dreams but remain with the one who pays attention to us. Nevertheless, we could ask ourselves if this extreme selectivity does not harm women's mate choice. John Townsend suggests that some feminists are wrong when they argue that men choose women who do not want to compete with them for intellectual status.[11] His hypothesis is that men are less selective: unlike women, they do not require a superior status to their partner, so the number of women that can be chosen increases. Are women who want to have a partner being damaged by their high selectivity?

Another trap into which women may fall is to seek a long-term relationship but feel attracted to more seductive men, who on average are oriented to short-term relationships.[12] This is particularly evident in speed dating, because here both women and men declare what they are looking for, and we can assess whether they achieve their goals or not. The chances are low: in a study of speed dating done in Germany by Jens Asendorpt, 6 percent succeeded in their search for casual sex and 4 percent succeeded in their search for long-term relationships. Men who wanted a committed relationship had a higher probability of success, while the majority of women who wanted a committed relationship ended in a short-term relationship because they felt more attracted to more seductive men. The study followed participants for a whole year and, many more women than men seeking stable couple relationships did not achieve their goal.

CONCLUSIONS

Schools not only should include sex education but also mating intelligence skills. Human intelligence for matchmaking is extremely complicated. Men and women are often 'deceived,' not by their partner but by unconscious biological, psychological, and social factors that influence their choice. In my book, *Falacias del amor* ('Love Fallacies'), I studied some social influences that link love to suffering, and I identified several fallacies that derive from a conception of love that has been characteristic of Western culture.[13] In this chapter I have reflected on unconscious genetic influences that may not favor the selection of the best partner. I think it is important to encourage philosophical counseling to interact with recent scientific studies, and not only with the insights of philosophers.

Love is an art: we can learn it, improve it, and teach it. It is something that we make, not that only 'happens' to us. It is the result, and not the cause of a relationship. Therefore, it is important for us to know some of the potential influences that can spoil our decisions, because this knowledge might allow us to make more conscious and responsible choices.

NOTES

1. See David P. Schmitt, "Sociosexuality from Argentina to Zimbabwe: a 48-Nation Study of Sex, Culture, and Strategies of Human Mating," *Behavioral and Brain Sciences*, 28 (2005): 247–275.

2. See David Buss and Martie G. Haselton, "The Evolution of Jelousy," *Trends in Cognitive Sciences*, 9 (2005): 11, 506–507.

3. See Glenn Geher and Scott Barry Kaufman, *Mating Intelligence Unleashed: The Role of the Mind in Sex, Dating, and Love* (Oxford: Oxford University Press, 2013).

4. Ibid.

5. See John Marshall Townsend, *What Women Want—What Men Want: Why the Sexes still See Love and Commitment so differently* (Oxford: Oxford University Press 1998).

6. See Martie G. Haselton and Geoffrey L. Miller, "Women's Fertility across the Cycle Increases the Short-Term Attractivness of Creative Intelligence," *Human Nature*,17 (2006): 1, 50–73.

7. See Scott Barry Kaufman, Aaron Kozbelt, Melanie L. Bromley and Geoffrey L. Miller, "The Role of Creativity and Humor in Human Mate Selection," in *Mating Intelligence: Sex, Relationships, and the Mind's Reproductive System*, ed. Glenn Geher and Geoffrey Miller (Hove: Psychology Press 2007), 227–262.

8. See Matthew M. Hurley, Daniel C. Dennett, and Reginald B. Adams, *Inside Jokes: Using Humor to Reverse-Engeneer the Mind* (Cambridge MA: MIT Press 2011).

9. Ibid.

10. See Daniel Nettle and Helen Clegg, "Personality, Mating Strategies, and Mating Intelligence," in *Mating Intelligence: Sex, Relationships, and the Mind's Reproductive System*, 121–135.

11. See Townsend, *What Women Want—What Men Want.*

12. See Jens B. Asendorpf, Lars Penke, and Back Mitja D., "From Dating to Mating and Relating: Predictors of Initial and Long-Term Outcomes of Speed-Dating in a Community Sample," *European Journal of Personality*, 25(2011): 1, 16–30.

13. See Roxana Kreimer, *Falacias del Amor, ¿Por qué anudamos Amor Y Sufrimiento?* (Buenos Aires: Paidós 2005).

BIBLIOGRAPHY

Asendorpf, Jens B., Penke Lars, and Back Mitja D. "From Dating to Mating and Relating: Predictors of Initial and Long-Term Outcomes of Speed-Dating in a Community Sample." *European Journal of Personality*, 25(2011): 1, 16–30.

Buss David, and Haselton Martie G. "The Evolution of Jelousy." *Trends in Cognitive Sciences*, 9 (2005): 11, 506–507.

Clark, Russell D., and Hatfield, Elaine. "Gender Differences in Receptivity to Sexual Offers." *Journal of Psychology & Human Sexuality* 2 (1989): 139–55.

Geher, Glenn, and Kaufman, Scott Barry. *Mating Intelligence Unleashed: The Role of the Mind in Sex, Dating, and Love.* Oxford: Oxford University Press, 2013 .

Geher, Glenn, and Miller, Geoffrey. *Mating Intelligence: Sex, Relationships, and the Mind's Reproductive System*. Hove: Psychology Press, 2007.

Haselton, Martie G., and Miller, Geoffrey L. "Women's Fertility across the Cycle Increases the Short-Term Attractiveness of Creative Intelligence." *Human Nature* 17 (2006): 1, 50–73.

Hurley, Matthew M., Dennett, Daniel C. and Adams, Reginald B. *Inside Jokes. Using Humor to Reverse-Engeneer the Mind.* Cambridge, Mass: MIT Press, 2011.

Kreimer, Roxana. *Falacias del Amor, ¿Por qué anudamos Amor Y Sufrimiento?*. Buenos Aires: Paidós 2005.

Nettle, Daniel and Clegg, Helen. "Personality, Mating Strategies, and Mating Intelligence," in *Mating Intelligence: Sex, Relationships, and the Mind's Reproductive System*, 121–135.

Schmitt, David P. "Sociosexuality from Argentina to Zimbabwe. A 48-nation Study of Sex, Culture, and Strategies of Human Mating." *Behavioral and Brain Sciences*, 28 (2005): 247–275.

Townsend, John Marshall. *What Women Want—What Men Want: Why the Sexes Still See Love and Commitment So Differently*. Oxford: Oxford University Press, 1998.

III

Thinking Emotions

Chapter Nine

Rational Emotions in Philosophical Counseling

Marianne Vahl

In this chapter I emphasize the importance of emotions in philosophical counseling, and explore whether rational emotions are relevant emotions in philosophical reflections and dialogue. I focus on two different rational emotions: respect and empathy. I then explain in what sense I find these two to be rational emotions. Furthermore, my ambition is to establish the relevance of these emotions to philosophical counseling. My investigation of rational emotions is based upon skepticism concerning what is commonly understood as a dualism between emotions and rationality.

I take as my starting point Carla Bagnoli's Kantian arguments for respect as being relational and, as such, being a moral attitude based upon mutual recognition. This view emphasizes one's own as well as other peoples' autonomy and authority over moral claims. In this view the concept of respect is intimately connected to the idea of rational agency and as such provides an interesting starting point when answering the question of whether or not the emotion of respect can be viewed as a rational emotion.

When exploring the emotion of empathy, I take into account the common distinction made between affective and cognitive empathy. Affective empathy often refers to the capacity of being able to feel other peoples' feelings, while cognitive empathy deals with understanding another person's mental state. I question whether these apparently different kinds of empathy may be considered rational.

RATIONALITY AND EMOTIONS FROM A HISTORICAL POINT OF VIEW

Several parallel dualisms have been proposed in philosophy, such as mind and matter, body and soul, and reason and emotions. Emotions have for long been seen as irrational while rationality has been associated with reason, thinking, and logic. Traditionally, emotions have also commonly been associated with women and reason with men, a view that supports the idea of the sovereignty of the intellectual activities of men over those of women.

This trend may be taken to originate in Plato's metaphysics and theory of the ideas and the distinction between body and soul. Plato is also often referred to as saying that emotions are like wild horses that need to be tamed by the intellect. However, Plato can be read differently and less dogmatically as one of the most important dialogue philosophers, in that he both wrote about dialogues and used a dialogical form of writing.[1] Maieutics is a method Plato originated where the aim was to reveal latent truth in a person's mind through questioning. In his dialogues about Socrates, Plato lets Socrates stimulate critical thinking through questioning and provocation. To participate in these dialogues, one did not need to be an expert or have any particular qualifications. The dialogues concerned challenges from the participant's own life. Philosophical counseling today is based upon these old practices of dialogue. Ancient maieutics and philosophical dialogues aimed at a kind of thought, λόγος (*logos*), that included the whole human being. So the rationality of dialogues in this tradition may very well include emotions, as I see it.

Did the strict division between emotions and rationality perhaps originate rather in theories of rationality associated with René Descartes and his *cogito ergo sum*, or from Immanuel Kant interpreted as neglecting the role of emotions in rational choice and agency? This interpretation is often opposed to David Hume's sentimentalism and belief that moral reasons originate from emotions and not from a categorical and autonomous source. Autonomy in this traditional understanding of Kant is based on the idea of a strong and independent I, different from Bagnoli's more modern social reading of Kant. On standard rationalist models, Bagnoli says that moral reasons bind all rational agents "with categorical authority because they are intrinsically normative facts, whose authority does not depend on anything contingent, such as our conventions, beliefs, and emotions."[2] In this view, emotions do not have the same authority as reasons, and as such they are not to be taken as rational.

The study of emotions has been neglected in the field of cognitive science as well. Only in recent years have emotions been given some attention as being important to the mind. In his book *The Emotional Brain*, Joseph LeDoux criticises this lack of attention, arguing that "cognitive science is really a science of only a part of the mind, the part having to do with thinking, reasoning, and intellect. It leaves emotions out. And minds without emotions are not really minds at all."[3] He contends furthermore that both emotional and cognitive processing are often unconscious and that emotions may thus very well be a kind of cognition.

In his Nobel Lecture "Maps of Bounded Rationality," Daniel Kahneman reflects over his works with Amos Tversky in economics and cognitive psychology.[4] Kahneman and Tversky combined what had commonly been studied separately, namely, the study of the psychology of our judgement and the psychology of our choices with emphasis on framing processes or our perspectives of a situation. Their research explored the distinction between our intuitions and reasoning, where intuitions were understood as preferences, intentions, judgements, and thoughts which come to mind easily and without deep reflection, analogous to perceptions, and in contrast to the slower processes of deliberate thought. In his essay Kahneman argues that our cognitive functioning is twofold: a slow and deliberate mode and an automatic and fast mode. When judging and choosing, we most commonly use our intuitions, but they may be modified by deliberate operations. This insight into how we may make judgements and choices challenges the idea of perfect rational choices based upon calculations, pure reasoning, and logic, an ideal implying that one has all the information and time needed when making choices and judgements. That emotions are now accepted as playing a role in actual decision making in fields like economics suggests not only that emotions are not irrational, but also that humans are incapable of making perfect rational choices. What I find must be revised is what we mean by rational.

Nevertheless, even though emotions are getting more attention in several disciplines and are increasingly being considered as not always irrational, but as neutral or "non-rational"—and are sometimes even deemed necessary for rational decisions—this does not fully recover their reputation. The idea that emotions are often rational does not appear to be the dominant view or even considered a possibility by many scholars.

RATIONAL EMOTIONS

Rationality is a concept commonly understood as denoting something positive about human beings. But can it really be understood as such without including emotions? If being considered rational is to be understood as being well-functioning in some situations, do not emotions then play a vital role? Robert C. Solomon argues along these lines in his book *The Passions*: "'Rational' does not mean reflective; 'rationality' signifies intelligent purposive activity, whether reflective and fully articulated or not. Contrary to their usual image, the emotions are paradigmatic of such activities."[5]

But when are emotions rational? In his paper "On the Rationality of Emotions," Klaus R. Scherer tries to answer this question.[6] To define rational emotions, he first investigates the term 'rational' by means of common understanding and several definitions spanning a diversity of fields of research. He ends up distinguishing between three kinds of rationality that are meant to include many of the well-known notions of rationality. Scherer associates the first type, functional/purposeful rationality, with something like Aristotle's idea of a practical reason φρόνησις (*phronesis*), that is, the faculty to deal in an optimal manner with volitional mean/end choices; he also mentions Max Weber's concept of *Zweckrationaliät*, that is, choices to find appropriate means to reach a wanted end. The second type is the intellectual or inferential sort of rationality, including logical argumentation and the ability to theorize and abstract; this analytically cognitive rationality has traditionally had no place for emotions. The third type is reasoning and consensus-based rationality, similar to Kant's notion of reason and to the idea of intersubjective consensus when deciding to conform to an opinion or to a norm. For an emotion to be rational, Scherer argues, one of these three types of rationality must be met. But what do we mean by an emotion? In his paper Scherer answers this question by referring to functional views on emotions agreed on by many scholars. He concludes that emotions can be characterised as being motivational, and by claiming priority and action-readiness, they engage the whole person and have to do with the organism reacting to something considered as relevant.[7] Further, Scherer argues that we need a theory detailed enough to evaluate whether emotions are rational. He calls the theory he proposes an "appraisal theory." Such appraisal theories see emotions as a process and study the connection between the different perspectives that people have to a situation and that lead to different reactions. This implies seeing the diversity of emotional responses. Appraisals are sometimes deliberate but are more often automatic evaluations or estimates of an event causing a reaction. I find appraisal theories relevant for philosophical practice because of their level of sophistication in their view of emotions, a level of sophistication that is necessary for describing both what goes on and what should go on in the complex endeavor of a dialogue.

When judging if an emotion is rational, Scherer proposes that one can consider components of emotions, including cognition, and check whether they fulfill at least one of the criteria for rationality. He takes into account "the three aggregated emotion components of appraisal, response (bodily symptoms, action tendencies, and expression), and regulation."[8] Emotion regulation is an important function in controlling and regulating our emotions in order for them to be appropriate. Emotion needs to be functional, or seen as reasonable by others, to be rational. We must be capable of "appropriate reflection and integration of all emotion components" and of finding a "balanced conscious and unconscious processing."[9]

In this rational sense I find emotions to be of great importance for philosophical practitioners. Training and improving emotional skills and emotion regulations would be very useful for philosophers. This is opposed to the not so uncommon idea of philosophical dialogues as a purely intellectual activity where emotions have no place. Scherer's concept of rational emotions challenges such a view by claiming that emotions may have a rational impact, even in the case of intellectual rationality. In the intellectual or inferential sense, emotions are rational because of intellectual appraisal in the meaning of "cognitive evaluation and inference."[10] Scherer claims that intellectual appraisals vary in their level of consciousness and deliberation with the aim of optimizing the cognitive inference and evaluation in responding to an event. This may include evaluating one's own coping abilities and reflecting on various implications, activities that I consider very important to philosophical practitioners.

RESPECT UNDERSTOOD AS A RATIONAL EMOTION

Philosophical counseling may be said to differ from other forms of counseling, such as psychological counseling, in that it gives more authority to the guest or client. In many disciplines the counselor is the expert, diagnosing illness and aiming at curing a problem. In philosophical dialogues the guest is considered an expert of themselves and their own life. One of the philosopher's main tasks through dialogue is to stimulate the guest's own reflections. The underlying attitude is one of respect for the other person's autonomy. The idea I will now explore is whether respect can be said to be a rational emotion, one that is important or even necessary to secure the rationality of a philosophical dialogue.

To help me in achieving this, I will use some of Carla Bagnoli's Kantian arguments. In the anthology *Morality and the Emotions*, Bagnoli supports a dialogical interpretation of respect, understood as mutual recognition, which focuses on the relational and practical aspects of the concept.[11] Bagnoli bridges the gap between emotions and reason by taking a practical standpoint, where "respect as the emotional aspect of practical reason avoids the dilemma between the rationalist views of objective demands of morality that have no grip on us and a sentimentalist view of moral reasons that denies their categorical authority."[12] What is a reason for us is also a reason for others.

According to Bagnoli, respect is a moral emotional attitude which has to do with the recognition of other people's autonomy and hence with seeing others as rational agents. This recognition can be painful, since it tells us about how our desires limit us as rational beings, and since we realize that our desires do not always have priority over others. On the positive side, the feeling of respect can give improved self-esteem when we overcome desires by recognising others. The emotion of respect is thus complex and is experienced in many ways, both as being free and at the same time as being bound through the recognition of others. It is hence not a feeling in the sense of being an awareness of something, something passively received. Respect is rather a moral motive, a practical attitude and force serving as an incentive for action; in this sense, pure reason can be practical. Bagnoli refers to Kant as describing respect as a feeling not based on our sensibilities but grounded in the idea of lawful activity. Respect has both a normative and a relational nature and is in Bagnoli's view both a quality of the will and something we practice in relations with others. Respect has to do with how we should be, by loving and taking care of others and supporting their choices and pursuits. It is more than merely an attitude, Bagnoli says, it is an emotion that guides us in how to act with other people. Respect is an emotion with a relational nature.

In the context of dialogues, I find this understanding of the emotion of respect as satisfying Scherer's criteria of being a rational emotion because it is important for the purpose of a dialogue, it is socially reasonable, and it is vital for securing relevant inferential activities.

I find that Bagnoli's dual approach, both practical and normative, points at a stronger claim to rationality than the ones Scherer proposes. So regardless of stimuli and outer events, Bagnoli claims that emotions in the guise of respect may serve as normative reasons.

I find this conception of respect as a rational emotion to be a mode of thinking that philosophical counselors should aim for. One expression of this mode is by viewing the guest as the expert of their own lives and meeting them as autonomous agents, a perspective I was trained to take while studying to become a philosophical practitioner in Oslo.

Bagnoli provides us with Kantian arguments that bridge the gap between reason and emotion, claiming that practical reason is also an emotional capacity. This means that even in the traditional rationalistic view, emotions can be argued as being vital for rational activities. However, her approach is limited to one emotion with supposed rational content, namely, the emotion of respect. Hence, Bagnoli does not go as far as Scherer in this respect.

Scherer also contends that the dualism between emotions and reason originate in Plato's concept of the tripartite soul, which distinguishes between cognition, motivation, and emotions. In this regard, Scherer notes the following:

> Strangely enough, the old Platonic notion of separate systems is resurrected by modern neuroscience. . . . The "dual-systems" notion claiming the existence of

> two separate processing systems, an automatic (emotion driven) and a controlled (cognition driven) one, which plays a major role in current neuroeconomic accounts of behavioral choices (Loewenstein, Rick, and Cohen, 2008; Rustichini, 2008), leans towards Plato and tends to see activity of the so-called controlled system (mostly conscious cognition) as a sine qua non condition for rationality.[13]

This kind of evidence from science, insinuating that there is a duality between emotion/passion and cognition/rationality, is interesting but does not need to conflict with the idea of cognition and emotions understood as aspects or perspectives of rational emotions. As LeDoux points out, there are different emotional systems mediating different emotions.[14] I also find this view of the diversity of our emotional brain allows for the possibility of rational emotions.

Scherer meets the evidence from science insinuating a duality between emotion and cognition by showing when emotions are rational. I do not think this is enough. One major challenge is the common association of rationality with cognition to the point where they are considered synonymous. In judging rationality Scherer asks, "When are emotions rational?" I believe it is equally important to ask, when is our reasoning rational? When are our inferences rational? When is the use of logic rational? And which emotions are involved in these processes in order for them to be rational? One answer could be that we have rationality when our cognitive functions work appropriately with our emotional functions. In this respect my suggestion is to view the concepts of cognition and rationality separately, with cognition understood here in the traditional sense as dealing with thinking, logic, reasoning, and intellect (leaving emotions out). Let's change how we think of the relationship between rationality and cognition. With rationality I therefore suggest that we mean the capability of integrating or finding a good balance between emotions and cognition, where the attitude of rational emotions is significant of such a mode.

Similar ideas are to be found in the writings of the psychiatrist Carl Gustav Jung. In order to become whole and in balance, one needs to integrate the opposite pairs of the conscious and the unconscious, anima and animus, the feminine and the masculine. According to Jung, "our rational philosophy does not bother itself with whether the other person in us, pejoratively described as the 'shadow,' is in sympathy with our conscious plans and intentions."[15] Rational philosophy is in this sense a view of rationality as something out of balance. A question in this spirit could be, can rational emotions be seen as the feminine tilt to rationality ensuring such a balance? Rather than seeing rational emotions as a feminine tilt or shadow to masculine rationality, I prefer a more equal approach that views rational emotions as where the masculine meets the feminine, as an intersection creating the desired balance.

RELEVANCE

But from a practical point of view, how does one accomplish or judge this balance or mode? How can one proceed in a dialogue in order to find the required balance between cognition and emotions relevant for dealing with a given situation? I believe one needs to have some guiding principles. In my reading, a common feature of both the requirements for the cognitive aspects of rationality and for emotions (when rational in Scherer's sense) is the one of relevance. As Scherer has argued, emotions when appropriate make it possible for us to make good decisions, reflections, and judgements. This is because of the capability of our emotions to react to what is relevant in our changing environments.[16]

Since the emotions' capability of rapidly finding out what is relevant in a given situation is something they have in common with our cognitive features, I would like to supply Scherer's theory of rational emotions with knowledge concerning relevance and cognition understood more traditionally. Since my concern is dialogue I will pay attention to research and ideas presented by the philosopher and linguist Deirdre Wilson on verbal communication. Wilson explains that her relevance theory, a theoretic approach to pragmatics she co-developed with Dan Sperber concerning how to maximise relevance, spans from finding the relevant perceptual and conceptual inputs to the relevant background knowledge and coming to the best conclusions.[17] According to Wilson, the claim of relevance theory is that the guiding principle both in cognition and in communication is the search for relevance.

Relevance theory is based upon two descriptive, not normative, principles: the cognitive principle of relevance, that is, that "human cognition tends to be geared to the maximisation of relevance;" and the communicative principle of relevance, that is, that "every act of overt communication conveys a presumption of its own optimal relevance."[18] With cognition, Wilson means "to include at least the mechanisms for perception, memory and inference."[19] To most easily get the highest cognitive effect, the cognitive system will focus on what appears as relevant, true and worthy of your attention. Many of these processes are automatic, Wilson claims, and both perceptual and inferential mechanisms will automatically try to find the most relevant input and come to the most relevant conclusions. Moreover, Wilson contends that the comprehension system monitors for contradictions between knowledge and interpretation, so that if the listener does not quickly hear any contradictions, she will assume the hypothesis to be correct. The system thus looks for the best available interpretations quickly and does not go into depth. This is analogous to Scherer's view that emotions are rational because of their capability to quickly decide what the relevant or appropriate reaction to something is. Rational emotions are in Scherer's sense (though not in Bagnoli's sense) situational, and their rationality is due to their ability to respond quickly and accurately. This is as opposed to more traditional theories of rationality and to ideas of perfect rationality, where expectations are high concerning the level of information available and our abilities to process this information perfectly.

All in all, Wilson's reflections concerning how our cognition functions due to the principle of relevance, I find to go well with Scherer's theory of rational emotions as being appropriate and relevant responses to events. This supports my suggestion that rationality in dialogues may have to do with finding a relevant balance between emotions and cognition. For as Wilson contends, a rational listener will look for the relevance in what a speaker is saying in order to grasp the speaker's intentions. Further, Wilson claims that a rational speaker needs to meet the listener's expectation of relevance, or otherwise she will lose the listener's attention. I believe this suggests that when a philosopher facilitates a dialogue, she must aim at appearing relevant to the guest and be able to find what is relevant in what the guest says. Typically, a philosopher will ask questions, often open-ended ones, which do not obviously point at any particular answer. But how should one communicate the relevance of such questions to the guest? Indeed, how does a philosopher proceed in order to ask relevant questions? What is a good question? These are situations where I believe it is important that the philosopher is empathic, that she is able to take the other person's perspective and imagine what would be a relevant question to ask that person.

IS EMPATHY A RATIONAL EMOTION?

As a student of philosophy, I attended a seminar with Joseph Raz at the University of Oslo. In the ensuing discussion, the question of whether empathy could be said to be a rational emotion was raised. The idea was that empathy could be seen as a provider of knowledge. No conclusions were made at the seminar, but the question has intrigued me ever since. After getting into philosophical counseling, the importance of empathy in such dialogues has been striking to me.

Analogous to the dualism of rationality and emotions in philosophy, the research into empathy in the field of psychology/social theory has centered on an assumed duality between cognitive/intellectual empathy and affective/instinctive/emotional empathy, where cognitive empathy has to do with intellectually taking another person's perspective and where affective empathy often refers to feeling what another person feels.

Historically empathy originates from two different traditions, both from the concept of sympathy in David Hume's and Adam Smith's philosophies, and from German aesthetics and the term *Einfühlung*. Smith introduced the idea of sympathy or "fellow-feeling," that is, the ability to share feelings, like joy or pity, with the aim of matching another person's emotional state. This experience of a fellow-feeling is in this reading not only a result of our senses but also of our imagination, by placing ourselves in the other person's situation. Traditionally, however, the term sympathy often refers to a passive way of feeling what someone else feels, where empathy as originating from *Einfühlung* points at a more active process to understand intellectually the mental state of another person. This has led to empathy being seen as two "distinctly separate phenomena, cognitive role taking and affective reactivity to others."[20]

More recent research, however, has shown that a more integrated view better explains what is really happening. In his book *Empathy*, Mark H. Davies presents the concept of empathic concern as a concept with both affective and cognitive content. For affective empathy Davies uses the term parallel effect, and for cognitive empathy his focus is on the ability of perspective-taking or role-taking. Altruistic motives, such as non-egoistic helping, are due to the interaction of the two capacities of parallel effect and perspective-taking. Davies claims this interaction gives rise to the feeling of empathic concern. In philosophical dialogue I believe empathic concern could be viewed as a feeling or an awareness of a rational emotion. This is so both because of the affective and cognitive content of empathic concern, and because it satisfies Scherer's criteria of being purposeful and reasonable in ways relevant to dialogue. However, with rational emotion I have something more active in mind than just a feeling or an awareness of something.

To be able to understand how another person feels, I believe it is important to be able to share the feeling. Sharing a feeling provides you with vital information; it is an experience that is not purely accessible in an intellectual manner. Too much emotion in a dialogue is not appropriate, however, and it needs to be relevant to the given situation in order to be rational. On the other hand, not enough emotion may lead to manipulative and egoistic behavior. Egocentric affective empathy may occur when fellow-feeling causes distress.[21] In the context of philosophical dialogue, I guess this is the case when the philosopher loses focus on the guest in order to comfort his or her own distress. Empathy I find to be an emotion or attitude that makes it possible for a philosopher to maneuver in an open and free philosophical landscape, to care for and understand what is being said, to make good predictions concerning the guest's reactions to the conversation, and to be able to ask good questions relevant to the guest and her life.

Davies, like Scherer, presents a multifaceted model to meet the complexity of what he wants to explain. Is this kind of approach perhaps necessary because of the fuzzy and dynamic nature of the concepts of empathy and respect and of rational emotions in general? One challenge with this descriptive approach is that one easily ends up with the dualism one intended to avoid. The concept of empathic concern has a bridging quality that implies dualism. In my opinion this does not have to be a problem if the dualism implied is not substantial but rather an expression of different perspectives or aspects of the same. I prefer to use the word empathy for the rational emotion instead of empathic concern, in order to avoid dualism as the most likely or only implication communicated, and to make a point of empathy as an active dialogical mode for action. Another way of avoiding dualism when investigating rational emotions may be to consider their more structural properties.

The ancient word λόγος (*logos*) refers to something more than abstract intellect, and philosophical dialogue (διά-λόγος *dia-logos*) in this tradition should aim at fulfilling this broader understanding. Smith's idea of sympathy as an emotion that makes individuals limit themselves in order to regulate egoism is similar to Bagnoli's idea of respect understood as something that simultaneously limits our autonomous sovereignty and makes us larger by relating us to others and otherness. The etymology of the word 'respect,' from Latin *respīcĕre*, points to its relational features, as meaning to look again and again at someone, refusing to fix the person looked at within a static, unchangeable, inanimate, and therefore objectified identity. It has as such a lot in common with Smith's understanding of sympathy as a "fellow-feeling," and more generally in common with the idea of empathic perspective-taking. Both respect and empathy have to do with the willingness to see the other person again from new perspectives. Empathy and respect are, in this sense, related concepts, concepts transcending the dualism originating from the idea of a solitary I. So the emotions of respect and empathy can be said to fulfill the very nature or purpose of dialogue as relational, and as such being rational emotions in the context of dialogue.

CONCLUSION

What I have aimed at showing is that it makes sense to talk of rational emotions, and that the emotions of respect and empathy exemplify such rational emotions vital to philosophical counseling. The arguments given are based on a dual approach, both normative and descriptive, in order to sketch a model of rationality capable of encompassing both how things are and how things ought to be. This approach suggests that both deliberate, active thinking and what has traditionally been thought of as feminine, passive mental activities play an equally important part when it comes to rationality. What is important is to find a good balance between our faculties when facilitating a dialogue, a balance that can be found in many different ways and still is considered rational. In judging rationality I consider it important to value and respect both others' and my own judgements. This implies a dialogical approach based upon mutual recognition and respect in evaluating and judging rationality, where rationality is seen as a matter of diversity.

I have argued against common assumptions that emotions are unruly elements that negatively interfere with rational thinking and behavior. Instead, I suggest that as philosophical practitioners we must focus on how to understand the emotions of both others and ourselves just as much as being concerned about logical inferences and abstract analysis. This includes focusing on improving our emotion regulation skills and ability to monitor our own emotions in dialogues. In improving these abilities we will be more able to operate in a mode of rational emotions when facilitating a dialogue.

So instead of seeing emotions as at best the feminine tilt to rationality, I argue for seeing emotions and cognition as being equally important in terms of rationality. My aim has thus been to rehabilitate the reputation not only of emotions but also of rationality as being something of high value.

NOTES

1. Helge Svare, *Den gode samtalen: Kunsten å skape dialog* (Oslo: Pax, 2008), 239–41.
2. Carla Bagnoli, "Emotions and the Categorical Authority of Moral Reasons," in *Morality and the Emotions*, edited by Carla Bagnoli (Oxford: Oxford University Press, 2011), 62–81, at 62.
3. Joseph LeDoux, *The Emotional Brain: The Mysterious Underpinnings of Emotional Life* (New York: Simon & Schuster, 1996), 25.
4. Daniel Kahneman, "Maps of Bounded Rationality: A Perspective on Intuitive Judgment and Choice," Nobel Prize Lecture, 8 December 2002 (available at http://www.nobelprize.org/nobel_prizes/economic-sciences/laureates/2002/kahnemann-lecture.pdf).
5. Robert C. Solomon, *The Passions: Emotions and the Meaning of Life* (Indianapolis, IN: Hackett, 1993), 183.
6. Klaus R. Scherer, "On the Rationality of Emotions: or, When are Emotions Rational?," *Social Science Information* 50 (2011), no. 3–4: 330–50 (doi: 10.1177/0539018411411018).
7. Ibid, 338.
8. Ibid, 337.
9. Ibid, 337.
10. Ibid, 333.
11. Bagnoli, "Emotions and the Categorical Authority of Moral Reasons," Bagnoli, "Introduction," in *Morality and the Emotions*, edited by Carla Bagnoli (Oxford: Oxford University Press, 2011), 1–36.
12. Bagnoli, "Emotions and the Categorical Authority of Moral Reasons," 78.
13. Scherer, "On the Rationality of Emotions," 332.
14. LeDoux, *The Emotional Brain,* 106.
15. Carl Gustav Jung, *The Undiscovered Self,* translated by R. F. C. Hull (New York: Penguin, 2206), 81.
16. Scherer, "On the Rationality of Emotions," 330.
17. Cathrine Felix, and Marianne Vahl, "What Goes On in the Head is Not Magic," interview with Deirdre Wilson, *Filosofisk Supplement* 1(2008) 47–54 (available at http://foreninger.uio.no/filosofisk-supplement/numre/konflikt.pdf).

18. Dan Sperber and Deirdre Wilson, *Meaning and Relevance* (Cambridge: Cambridge University Press, 2012), 6; cf. Dan Sperber and Deirdre Wilson, *Relevance: Communication and Cognition* (Oxford: Blackwell, 1995), 260–72.
19. Felix and Vahl, 2008.
20. Marc H. Davies, *Empathy: A Social Psychological Approach* [Social Psychology Series] (Oxford: Westview Press, 1996), 9.
21. Ibid, 23–45.

BIBLIOGRAPHY

Bagnoli, Carla. "Emotions and the Categorical Authority of Moral Reasons." In *Morality and the Emotions*, edited by Carla Bagnoli, 62–81. Oxford: Oxford University Press, 2011.

———. "Introduction." In *Morality and the Emotions*, edited by Carla Bagnoli, 1–36. Oxford: Oxford University Press, 2011.

Davies, Mark H. *Empathy: A Social Psychological Approach* [Social Psychology Series]. Oxford: Westview Press, 1996.

Felix, Cathrine, and Marianne Vahl. "What Goes On in the Head is Not Magic." Interview with Deirdre Wilson. *Filosofisk Supplement* 1(2008), 47–54. http://foreninger.uio.no/filosofisk-supplement/numre/konflikt.pdf.

Jung, Carl Gustav. *The Undiscovered Self.* Translated by R. F. C. Hull. New York: Penguin, 2006.

Kahneman, Daniel. "Maps of Bounded Rationality: A Perspective on Intuitive Judgment and Choice." Nobel Prize Lecture, 8 December 2002. http://www.nobelprize.org/nobel_prizes/economicsciences/laureates/2002/kahneman-lecture.pdf.

LeDoux, Joseph. *The Emotional Brain: The Mysterious Underpinnings of Emotional Life.* New York: Simon & Schuster, 1996.

Scherer, Klaus R. "On the Rationality of Emotions: or, When are Emotions Rational?" *Social Science Information* 50 (2011), no. 3–4: 330–50. doi: 10.1177/0539018411411018.

Solomon, Robert C. 1993. *The Passions: Emotions and the Meaning of Life.* Indianapolis, IN: Hackett.

Sperber, Dan, and Deirdre Wilson. *Relevance: Communication and Cognition.* Oxford: Blackwell, 1995.

———. *Meaning and Relevance*. Cambridge: Cambridge University Press, 2012.

Svare, Helge. 2008. *Den gode samtalen: Kunsten å skape dialog*. Oslo: Pax.

Chapter Ten

The Awakening of Φρόνεσις: Philosophical Practice and the Call for Traditional Female Values

Camilla Angeltun

Philosophical practice wishes to invite guests into philosophical dialogues, with the guests' lives and challenges as its point of departure. We invite guests to something more than just talking about philosophical themes or listening to a lecture on Kant. We train to develop context sensitivity and to really listen and investigate the guests' experienced situations, moral dilemmas, relationships, feelings, and thoughts. From this context sensitivity we search for relevant philosophical thoughts from our educational background that can shed some light or challenge the guests' perspectives. This opens up a new field for the uses of philosophy, philosophy as practice. Or rather, it reawakens an ancient way of looking at philosophy. Not only does philosophical practice challenge the way we think about philosophy today, it also brings philosophy and dialogue together. This calls for another set of values, and, in my opinion, for another goal.

Philosophical practice calls for the awakening of the Aristotelian virtue of practical wisdom or *phronesis*, which in the original ancient Greek is φρόνεσις.[1]

Values like empathy, listening, feeling, and intuition are traditionally associated with the feminine, and they are surely necessary and important for engaging in a dialogue. My question is how to bridge the gap between important values for engaging in a philosophical dialogue and the core values often emphasized in traditional philosophy. Being a woman and working as a philosophical practitioner, I have experienced several deep-rooted and difficult questions that need to be addressed in order to answer this question. In my experience of both the curriculum and the educational system at the University of Oslo, values which have traditionally been relegated to the masculine like objectivity, rationality, rhetoric, and discussions are much more emphasized than values which have traditionally been relegated to the feminine. The curriculum is also, not surprisingly, dominated by male philosophers, just as the history of philosophy is dominated by male philosophers. As the Norwegian philosopher Tove Pettersen points out: When we look for values that are protected by ethics and moral philosophy, we find, for example, that autonomy and independence are considered more valuable than relations and dependence. Rationality is considered more valuable than feelings. The public sphere has been seen as much more important than the private, and when it comes to moral deliberations, the emphasis is on impartial decision-making rather than decision-making situated in a relational context. As a consequence, traditional female values have been marginalized.[2] So, how should female practitioners deal with the fact that ethics and moral philosophy are, and have been, mainly produced by men? How should practitioners relate to, and avoid being confused by, the fact that our educational philosophical background is unbalanced, with its heavy emphasis on traditional masculine values?

I admit to having felt a great deal of confusion when trying to answer these questions and it doesn't help that they are seldom addressed in university settings or among practitioners. This confusion has created many either/ors in my thought system that at times seemed impossible to unite. Self/other, objectivism/relativism, mind/body, thoughts/feelings, and independent/dependent are just some of the dichotomies of Western thinking that have confused me. Because my own life experiences, and experiences in dialogues with others, do not fit such either/or thinking, I wanted to move beyond this by trying to unite the traditional dichotomies in a way that seemed more in accordance with the way I experienced life. I believe that the most important point in Carol Gilligan and feminist ethics is not to take a stance in an either/or fashion, as in male or female, feelings or rationality. We should instead lift the perspective to a both/and stance.[3] It is the being-there in the situation that gives us clues to what tools are needed to solve the particular challenge in question. It is both feelings and rationality, both your perspective and the openness to go into dialogues with others that bring forth good solutions. In connection with this I see something profound in the Aristotelian virtue of *phronesis*. Φρόνεσις *(phronesis)* demands, in my opinion, a both/and perspective which balances traditional masculine and feminine values, according to what is needed in the particular situation. However, my objective in this essay is not to say that this both/and perspective is *the* female voice, or to exclude the male voice. Instead, I want to argue for that I will label *the human voice*. This is the voice which aims at a human flourishing for both men and women, as it considers this as a more profound goal than objective truths and pure reason. In this awakening of φρόνεσις (*phronesis*), I believe female practitioners to be of great importance, both in questioning thinking in dichotomies and by exploring new paths, useful in practice, which include values that have traditionally been relegated to the feminine. This chapter is inspired by this thought. Its main focus is to search for important perspectives, useful in philosophical practice, that include traditional female values and point to a direction that is beyond thinking in dichotomies. This inspiration guided me to Heidegger's readings of the Aristotelian φρόνεσις and to see this in connection to Gilligan's *mature care.*[4]

THE ARISTOTELIAN ΦΡΌΝΕΣΙΣ AND HEIDEGGER'S CARING

To Aristotle the ultimate goal for humans is not to gain objective truths or to be wealthy. He points to the importance of a continual human flourishing and an active tension toward improvement as fundamental and irreplaceable prerequisites for the pursuit of happiness. Humans strive for εὐδαιμονία (*eudaimonia,* 'happiness,' or 'good *daimon*'), and Aristotle tells us in his *Nicomachean ethics* that we feel happy when we have the freedom to develop our opportunities and when we realize our possibilities. What characterizes human progress is a harmony between our thinking and our striving. Important factors for this striving are moral virtue, relationships with others, and morally good people to look up to in our society. We find this goal of human flourishing and this relational ontology also in Heidegger's philosophy and in the ethics of care. I believe these two basic beliefs to also be important for philosophical practice. First, as I will explore further in this chapter, these two basic beliefs challenge philosophical practitioners to move beyond thinking in dichotomies. Second, guests have different reasons for coming to philosophical dialogues, but one common goal for most guests is the wish to succeed as a human being, together with other human beings.

To Aristotle the individuals who qualify as model persons are the ones who have acquired practical wisdom (φρόνεσις, *phronesis*). An individual with well-developed practical wisdom is what Aristotle calls a φρόνιμος (*phronimos*). Reasoning is at its best when it's controlled by this intellectual virtue, which he calls φρόνεσις. This also means that good reasoning is controlled by ethics. As φρόνεσις controls human action, this means that it also controls πρᾶξις (*praxis,* right/moral action). So, φρόνεσις is an intellectual virtue we can develop, which gives us direction when it comes to handling situations in a morally good way (practical thinking). Life always requires action, so practical wisdom is what control life as a whole. Aristotle mentions two intellectual virtues, σοφία (*sophia*, 'wisdom,' in a more detached, non-participative, theoretical sense) that which maintains ἐπιστήμη (*episteme*, knowledge or science) and φρόνεσις (practical wisdom) which maintains πρᾶξις (*praxis,* moral action). He distinguishes between σοφία (*sophia*) and φρόνεσις (*phronesis*) in the following manner: "Σοφία involves reasoning concerning universal truths, while φρόνεσις includes a capability for rational thinking."[5] Aristotle also points out "nor is intelligence about universals only. It must also come to know particulars, since it is concerned with action and action is about particulars."[6] In other words, what Aristotle emphasizes is that it is necessary, but not sufficient, for the practically wise to know what, for example, courage is, you also have to know how to apply courage at the right time and for the right reasons. One situation might call for the use of empathy, another for the use of theory, and so on. The φρόνιμος (*phronimos*) have the ability to figure out what is right to do in any given situation. The key to developing φρόνεσις is experience, both in the sense of being present in your experiences and learning from your experiences. What I am curious to investigate further is what this context sensitivity consists of. What is needed to be present in situations and how do we learn from our experiences? How can we enhance this in philosophical practice? Can we invite guests to philosophical dialogues that can both explore the guests' *praxis* and develop their φρόνεσις? I believe we can, and that Heidegger's reading of the Aristotelian φρόνεσις sheds a challenging and intriguing light on this issue.

Martin Heidegger showed a great deal of admiration for the Aristotelian notion of φρόνεσις, which became a basic thought in developing his concept of *Dasein* (being-there) and *In-der-Welt-sein* (being-in-the-world), in his central work *Being and Time.*[7] When we look at Heidegger's concept being-in-the-world, we can analyze it in two important ways. The first one is to emphasize *being-in.* The question here is what is it for a human being to be-there, or to be "open" to the situation? The second one is to analyze the disclosure of the world itself, which for Heidegger can discloses itself for us in moments. Being-in always presupposes a determinate but contingent world where there is an important potential for developing practical wisdom (φρόνεσις, *phronesis*) in these moments of being-in-the-disclosures-of-the-world.

I would like to explore this point further by looking at an early essay from Heidegger called *Phenomenological Interpretations with Respect to Aristotle.*[8] This essay provides us with some interesting thoughts on Aristotle in connection with Heidegger's own thinking. In this essay Heidegger seeks to establish "factical life," which in his later work became being-in-the-world. Being-in-the-world is what Heidegger wants to establish as the proper starting point of philosophical inquiry, and what he criticizes Western philosophy for having lost sight of. He tells us that the basic sense of the movement of *factical* life is caring and describes caring as "being-out-toward-something." He points out that caring is a basic structure of being-in-the-world, and it is the proper starting point for understanding a human (*Dasein*). This fundamental movement of life is the movement of the repeated actualization of *Dasein*'s fundamental potential. In other words, it tells us more about the striving Aristotle points out to be important in human life. Humans are happy when they feel *openness* to being out toward and meaningfully involved with the world.[9] And this kind of being is first and foremost in our everydayness.

Heidegger points out that: "So far as *Dasein* is at all, it has Being-with-one-another as its kind of Being."[10] Another aspect of worldliness is being-with others, or in Heidegger's terms *mitsein. Dasein* is essentially being-with. Following in Husserl's footsteps, Heidegger was one of the first great representatives of Western philosophy to shift the focus from the individual to the relational. When he changes the ideal of an eternal *cogito* closed in on itself to a dizzying openness to the world, he commits philosophy to a rediscovery and reevaluation of those values traditionally relegated to the private and feminine sphere. Values that earlier had been regarded as not worthy of dignified thought become important in Heidegger's understanding of what it is to be-there or to be *open* to the situation. Furthermore, when the human is essentially being-with, what naturally becomes important is speech. Daniel L. Smith points out, in his essay *Intensifying Phronesis: Heidegger, Aristotle, and Rhetorical Culture*[11] that "disclosive movements of discourse might be better thought of as movements that articulate relations that open 'spaces' where phenomena may be disclosed and encountered."[12] Discourse, writes Heidegger, "which belongs to the essential constitution of *Dasein*, and also constitutes its dis-closedness, has the possibility of becoming idle talk, and as such of not really keeping being-in-the-world open," as well as, "hold(ing) any new questions and discussions at a distance."[13] Heidegger's point of view is that discourse is more than self-expression, signification, predication, and propositions. What is more important for him is the discourse's fundamental movement toward disclosure. In other words, an important source for developing φρόνεσις is the opening of "spaces" through discourse where the *Dasein* can explore and encounter new connections to the world. I believe an important question for philosophical practice to investigate is how to avoid offering idle talk and make sure that our dialogues offer this quality of keeping being-in-the-world-open.

But what is this "disclosure" and what does Heidegger mean when he uses the words "keeping-being-in-the-world-open?" Heidegger traces the idea of truth back to the ancient word ἀλήθεια (*aletheia,* 'truth'), which is the derivative combination of the verb λανθάνω (*lanthano,* 'to stay hidden' and 'to forget') plus the privative alpha, 'ἀ.' In this way, Heidegger reminds us that the origin of the 'truth' concept is the human attitude to stay open to the revelation of reality by nature itself. Heidegger shows another way of looking at the concept of truth, as un-concealment or disclosure as such, rather than the more common notion of truth as correct perception. This conception of truth as un-concealment is at the heart of Heidegger's philosophy and denotes the stance that an entity can show itself forth to *Dasein* in terms of a particular possibility. Something is *brought* out of concealment by and into the light of human understanding. This conception of truth is one of the hidden treasures Heidegger wants to reawaken from the ancient world. Let us investigate this conception of truth and connect it to the Aristotelian virtue φρόνεσις (*phronesis*).

Heidegger refers to two basic modes of coming to see and know the world. The first one attends to what is unchanging and eternal, the second to what may be otherwise. The first mode corresponds to the intellectual virtues ἐπιστήμη (*episteme,* science) and σοφία (*sophia,* 'wisdom' in a more detached, non-participative, theoretical sense), while the second mode corresponds to the intellectual virtues τέχνη (*techne*, technical 'know how,' producing) and φρόνεσις (circumspection/insight). Furthermore, Heidegger describes πρᾶξις (*praxis*) and ποίησις (*poiesis*)[14] as the first ways of carrying out this disclosing of the world(s). It is in these human activities we find the most profound moments of possibilities for removing the world from concealed-ness and covered-ness. This is also to say that τέχνη (*techne*) and φρόνεσις—expressions of ποίησις and πρᾶξις—'precede' ἐπιστήμη (*episteme,* science) and σοφία *(sophia)* as modalities of disclosure.[15] To connect this to philosophical practice we could say that when we explore τέχνη in our dialogues, we are involved with securing techniques that can become routine and are aimed at the mastery of presence. Φρόνεσις, on the other hand, remains in an openness that must be responsive to the happening (un-concealment) of presence. A happening that always exceeds its control. A famous saying from Heidegger underlines this point: "World never is but "worlds." In other words, this happening of the world comes forth in an event-like manner. As a practitioner I am fascinated by this thought and strive to give space for this openness to "the happening of presence" in my dialogues. To me this is of great importance, and I believe this to be one of the main factors that make philosophical practice different from interventions we may label as therapy or coaching.

What makes φρόνεσις (and *mature care* as I will argue for later) so important for philosophical practice is that this intellectual virtue attends to the particular circumstance in which *Dasein* acts. This is to say that it is a disposition that seeks to disclose the circumstances of a situation without losing sight of relevant (to the situation) theoretical and practical knowledge. This virtue pays attention to technique and theory, but cannot be reduced to it. This also means that φρόνεσις cannot be systematized like τέχνη (*techne*, or technical and productive know-how). To engage a world '*phronetically*' is, therefore, an attempt to understand its possibilities for relations and action as it "happens." According to Heidegger, φρόνεσις in Aristotle's work discloses "the right and proper way to be *Dasein*." Living a good life requires a mode of seeing and knowing that is neither the know-how of τέχνη nor the modes of theoretical seeing.[16] Even if a purely contemplative life is a major goal in Aristotle's philosophy and in Western philosophy after Aristotle, this alone cannot disclose what is the right desire since it is disconnected from practical life. What is needed is a mode of "uncovering the truth" that sees and takes account of both aspects of human life, and their connections with everyday life and theoretical understanding. That mode of discovering the truth is φρόνεσις. In a way we can say that φρόνεσις is the 'golden mean' between *poiesis* (*techne*) and θεωρία (*theoria)*: ἐπιστήμη (*episteme*) and σοφία (*sophia*). Φρόνεσις guards against the potential excesses of both. In considering and combining desire and intellect, φρόνεσις attends to *Dasein* in its wholeness as a being, it strives against *Dasein's* tendency to "cover" its wholeness through technical and theoretical excesses. This is what authenticity really means in Heidegger's philosophy. In other words, authenticity means φρόνεσις' disclosing movement away from 'losing sight' of *Dasein's* whole true nature.[17] In my opinion thinking in dichotomies, which marginalizes values traditionally attached to women, has lost sight of *Dasein's* whole true nature. I believe the 'essence' of 'I' is not a 'substance,' but existence. So, 'worlds' and 'existence' can be seen as two sides of the same coin, and to get to know your "existence," you must stop investigating and searching for it. Instead be-there when 'I' (worlds) happen. The important question to ask yourself is; what do you find in these moments of being-there? Can you separate your feelings from your rationality, your mind from your body, the masculine values from the feminine, and so on? To me the technical and abstract way of looking at the individual and human experiences, handed down to me from the university, felt unwhole, constructed, and confusing. It is not the moments of either feelings or rationality, masculine values or feminine values, independence or dependence I am longing for, it is the moments of integration.[18]

To connect Heidegger's disclosures with the Aristotelian virtue *phronesis* in a more practical manner, I believe that what Smith calls "*phronetic* disruptions" is a keyword for philosophical practice. The disruptions coming from the reality outside us, the disclosures that often make us uncomfortable and confused, are golden opportunities to change and develop more practical wisdom. This tension and confusion comes as a natural reaction to the confrontation with the limits of our wisdom. I vividly remember one of my biggest "*phronetic* disruptions" in the beginning of my training to become a philosophical practitioner. I eagerly read my books before classes and held my hand up high every time something came to my mind. This was, in my experience, 'how to be a good student.' Suddenly one of my teachers turned to me and told me that these were classes for learning how to do dialogues where the main point was to train/follow rules and show trust in the wisdom of the group. This happening confused me and I must admit that I felt a little hurt inside. I had trouble finding words for what had just happened. What was this tension I felt inside? This was something I had never experienced before, my student strategies had been working just fine in the past. After reflecting and talking about it with a friend, I suddenly realized something new and important. I understood that while I was eager to show what a good student I am, I was only listening to myself and I had no serious interest in others. I realized that what this wise teacher had showed me was that I needed to start to listen. In that moment of realization I changed and I created a new and important connection to the world around me. This insight depended on a *process* involving feelings and rationality, both a dialogue with myself and others. This insight needed something outside me to disrupt my usual habits, the courage to be-there in my tension and openness to investigate.

CAROL GILLIGAN AND MATURE CARE

Gilligan listened to the experiences, concerns, deliberations, and observed the developments of ordinary women facing real life challenges. Contrary to much of mainstream philosophy, she worked from a Heideggerian 'method' used for investigating the everydayness of *Dasein*. She discovered an important voice and developed a moral perspective hitherto ignored by traditional ethics and moral philosophy. This voice is of great importance for philosophical practice because we as practitioners are reminded that the dominant ethical theories, with their gender blindness and emphasis on rights and justice, fail to see how care and context sensitivity is an indispensable part of moral life. These failures weaken their credibility as adequate, universal ethical theories. Pettersen writes in her book *Comprehending Care*: "Traditional moral philosophy, in my view, has failed to take up the challenge of Gilligan's findings and claims. Mainstream moral discussions continue to ignore the importance of care and to prolong centuries of insensitivity towards gender."[19] This needs to be challenged, and I believe that the core values in philosophical practice, with its emphasis on philosophical dialogues and context sensitivity, are taking up this challenge.

Gilligan's main theme in her book *In a Different Voice*[20] is differences in deliberation between men and women. Her research shows that women tend to deliberate from context sensitivity and from a care perspective, while men tend to deliberate from principles and from a justice perspective. She argues that the traditional way women deliberate should not be regarded as less moral and less mature than the dominant moral philosophical way of making moral resolutions. Gilligan's work has paved the way for the development of alternative concepts and new analytical categories in moral philosophy and ethics which are in accordance with the goals of feminism in ethics.[21] She gives us a more complex model for a moral actor, and challenges the traditional ontology that has laid the foundations for mainstream ethics and moral philosophy. As a backdrop of her project, I see important insights from both Aristotle and Heidegger, which are rediscovered and formulated in new and important ways.

Gilligan emphasizes that moral maturity consists in the ability to think "both/and." It is a type of thinking "which flows back and forth connecting self and other, mind and body, past and present, consciousness and culture."[22] The ethics of care can be regarded as relationship "code" based on a guiding principle that protects against harm and promotes well-being and human flourishing, and as a theory encourages the development of a particular attitude.[23] Historically, culturally, politically, and economically, care is linked to women. Care is a value and virtue associated with women`s work, with their nature and purpose in life. Aristotle, Augustine, Thomas Aquinas, Rousseau, Kant, and Hume have all contributed to such a view.[24] In my opinion care is a valuable virtue for both men and women, because care is not an attribute of being, but rather a fundamental structure constitutive of its very existence. In the work of Gilligan, the notion of care and its developmental process towardsa moral perspective can be found at three levels. In her book, Pettersen reflects on these levels with the notions of selfish care, selflessness care, and mature care.[25] I find the concept of mature care of great importance and I believe that it is an interesting extension of the Aristotelian concept of practical wisdom (φρόνεσις) and Heidegger's concept of *mitsein* 'being-with.'

Gilligan was concerned with understanding moral development and how people make moral judgments, and in her research on this subject she discovered three levels. The first is all about survival, a stage where it is important to learn to take care of yourself. Care is looked at as self-care, primarily understood as to protecting the self against harm. The transition to the next level is due to an awareness of one's "attachment or connections" to others, where it is important for us to give care to others related to us. We shift from making decisions based on self-interest to taking social norms and other people's expectations into consideration. This stage can be termed altruistic, and there is a danger at this level, of self-extinction. At the highest level the individual starts to reflect upon the relationship between self and others. Questions like "is it egoistic or responsible, moral or immoral to include my own needs within the compass of care and concern?" and "how can I unite the care for myself and the care for others?" are important for developing mature care.[26]

We see that the concept of mature care balances altruistic and egoistical motives, including both emotion and cognition. It is also context sensitive by making the decision depend on the situation. Mature care is realized where the concern for self and others are harmonized, depending on the situation. A person with the capacity to engage in mature care has a very important ideal, which is not to do harm to either to themselves or to anyone else.[27] He or she is sensitive to the situation (is mentally present in the situation) and learns from both good and bad experiences. He or she investigates the situation thoroughly before making decisions and sees it as important to have a dialogue with all people involved in order to obtain different perspectives on the matter in question. Mature care is not either/or, but the ability to know what the right action is in the right situation at the right time. Thus we are back to the Aristotelian virtue of φρόνεσις.

Gilligan challenges deontological, utilitarian, and liberal theory's ways of presenting how moral deliberations are carried out. An ethical choice is often presented as a resolution taken by a single actor. This actor is calculating, counting his or her reasons for and against making a choice and in the end making the best choice for what to do (or not to do). As I see it, this model is not very close to real life. That is because choices are seldom taken in isolation, but within the actor's relations and dialogues with other people. The choices we take in daily life often involve and have consequences for others related to us. This main focus on rationality as a source for moral counseling is also criticized by Gilligan and in feminist ethics. Kant and Utilitarianism have furnished us with abstract principles as guiding stars for solving moral issues, with feelings considered as a factor that undermines rationality and disturbs good moral decisions. Apart from not being very close to real life, I would say this excludes the being-in-the-world dimension that Heidegger points out to us and we lose the awareness and openness needed to open spaces for disclosures. Traditional feminine values like care, empathy, compassion, and trust are of great importance for moral decisions, values which help to point the way toward good moral decisions and are important for our understanding of which situations we need to handle in the first place. To develop as a mature caregiver it is important to pay attention to the psychological tensions and the implications which follow when emotions and actions are at odds. This is not to say that it is about either feelings or rationality, but to say that both feelings and rationality need to be taken into account if we are to be moral human beings. Feelings and rationality are not opposed to each other, mature care involves both emotion and cognition and humans are both interdependent and autonomous. A recurrent topic in Gilligan's moral philosophy and the ethics of care is this way of not thinking in dichotomies, important for philosophical practice as it seeks to disclose the circumstances of real human experience. This way of thinking includes "*phronetic* disruptions" that break with the ideal of the continuity of the Cartesian *cogito*, which has served as the dominant model of thought over the centuries and that still serves as model for scientific thought. The Aristotelian φρόνεσις, Smith's disruptions, Heidegger's caring, and Gilligan's mature care provide a backdrop for rethinking thought in a framework more comprehensive, dialectical, and dynamic, as well as less rigid and male-dominated.

CONCLUDING REMARKS

In this chapter I have explored what I believe are important perspectives, useful in philosophical practice, which include traditional female values and point to a direction that is beyond thinking in dichotomies. Heidegger's readings of the Aristotelian φρόνεσις inspire me as a philosophical practitioner to "open spaces for disclosure" and to be sensitive to the happening of the 'world' or 'I' in my dialogues. The experience (both in its happening and on reflection afterward) of these 'open spaces' is of great importance for developing practical wisdom (φρόνεσις). How to open these spaces is not clear or easily understood by reading a book. It is something you develop in your character and in your craft as a practitioner and it needs experience and practice, as well as openness, awareness, dialogical skills, care, curiosity, and courage. I also believe it needs female philosophical practitioners, proud of being women, philosophers, and practitioners who dare to fight for the important feminine values needed for opening spaces of disclosure, disclosures which are not necessarily connected to gender and other dichotomies in the ways we have been used to thinking throughout our philosophical upbringing. The challenge is to bring forth a both/and perspective, with the capacity to tune in to the situations before using abstract, principle-guided theories and methods. In other words, we need to develop our own practical wisdom (φρόνεσις, *phronesis*).

I also believe it is important to explore the '*phronetic* disruptions' together with our guests, where the guests' habits and ways of being in his or her everydayness have been challenged by an important and disruptive disclosure. We can be-there with the guest in the confusion and tension that these disclosures can bring forth and encourage the guest to explore this tension, dare to take risks or to go outside the general rules so that he or she can learn to tune in to the situation—in short: learn to do what the rules cannot tell you to do, learn to become authentic. Important disclosures are often expressed in the 'real' questions, which you can sense from the guest's body language, in the intensity and silence the question brings forth. The guest does not have an answer to this question. The power of the guest's curiosity to understand what the answer could be, the search for new words and tools and the intensity of his or her wondering, is a kind of philosophizing that creates cracks in everydayness. I believe Leonard Cohen when he sings: "There's a crack in everything, that's where the light gets in." Isn't this what the difference between learning philosophy and to philosophize really is?

NOTES

1. Aristotle, "Nicomachean Ethics," *Readings in Ancient Greek Philosophy: From Thales to Aristotle, third edition,* ed. S. Marc Cohen, Patricia Curd, and C. D. C. Reeve (Indianapolis/Cambridge: Hackett, 2005), 869–875.

2. Tove Pettersen, "Feminist Ethics," *Norsk Filosofisk Tidsskrift* 4 (Oslo: Universitetsforlaget, 2007), 245. (My translation).

3. Pettersen, *Comprehending Care. Problems and Possibilities in the Ethics of Care* (Lanham: Rowman & Littlefield, 2008), 54; 100–101.

4. Ibid., 13–14.

5. Aristotle, "Nicomachean Ethics."

6. Ibid., 872.

7. Martin Heidegger, *Being and Time*, trans. John Macquarrie and Edward Robinson (New York: Harper Perennial Modern Thought, 1962).

8. Heidegger, "Phenomenological Interpretations with Respect to Aristotle," trans. Michael Baur, *Man and World* 25:355–93 (Netherlands: Kluwer Academic Publishers, 1992).

9. Ibid., 361–362.

10. Heidegger, *Being and Time*, 163.

11. Daniel L. Smith, "Intensifying Phronesis: Heidegger, Aristotle and Rhetorical Culture," *Philosophy and Rhetoric* Vol. 36, No.1 (Pennsylvania: State University, University Park, PA, 2003).

12. Ibid., 82.

13. Smith, "Intensifying Phronesis," 94–95.

14. Heidegger developed *poiesis* further in his later works, where art became an important source for the unconcealment of truth.

15. Smith, "Intensifying Phronesis," 83.

16. Ibid., 87.

17. Ibid., 88.

18. I understand Heidegger's being-there (Dasein) to implicate an experience of the integrating total being.

19. Pettersen, *Comprehending Care*, x.

20. Carol Gilligan, *In a Different Voice: Psychological Theory and Women's Development.* (Cambridge Mass.: Harvard University Press, 1982).

21. Pettersen, *Comprehending Care*, 27.

22. Ibid., 100–101.

23. Ibid., 166.

24. Ibid., 24.

25. Ibid., 13–14.

26. Ibid., 13.

27. Include humans, animals, and nature.

BIBLIOGRAPHY

Aristotle."Nicomachean ethics." *Readings in Ancient Greek Philosophy: From Thales to Aristotle, third edition,* edited by S. Marc Cohen, Patricia Curd, and C. D. C. Reeve. Indianapolis/Cambridge: Hackett, 2005.

Gilligan, Carol. *In a Different Voice: Psychological Theory and Women's Development*. Cambridge Mass.: Harvard University Press, 1982.

Heidegger, Martin. *Being and Time*. Translated by John Macquarrie and Edward Robinson. New York: Harper Perennial, 1962.

Heidegger, Martin."Phenomenological Interpretations with Respect to Aristotle." Translated by Michael Baur. *Man and World* 25:355–93. Netherlands: Kluwer Academic Publishers, 1992.

Pettersen, Tove. *Comprehending Care: Problems and Possibilities in the Ethics of Care.* Lanham: Rowman & Littlefield, 2008.
———. Feminist Ethics. *Norsk Filosofisk Tidsskrift* 4 (2007): 242–258. Oslo: Universitetsforlaget, 2007.
Smith, Daniel L. "Intensifying Phronesis: Heidegger, Aristotle and Rhetorical Culture." *Philosophy and Rhetoric,* Vol. 36, No. 1. Pennsylvania: State University, University Park, PA, 2003.

IV

Sharing Insights

Chapter Eleven

He Comes to My Practice: Sharing Sensibilities

Rayda Guzmán González

> The same emotional effects in men and women have, nonetheless, a different tempo. That's the reason men and women do not cease misunderstanding each other.
> —Nietzsche, *Beyond Good and Evil*, #85

Everybody describes their job as a series of tasks which follow one another in order to reach a desired result. As a matter of fact, philosophical counseling is not an exception, but the problem is that philosophy itself is difficult to explain. Things can be more complex when someone is asked to write about their professional field taking into consideration their gender, but it can only happen to a woman! A man will never be asked to do it. Instead of considering this a prejudice against women, I will state that the reflection on the relationship between gender and philosophical practice is absolutely feminine.

By saying this, I suggest that the problem of thinking about gender is feminine as opposed to masculine, which should be understood as related to a patriarchal structure that for centuries colonized knowledge through the power exercised by men. The founding myths of procreative goddesses gave way to patriarchal religions in which women were necessarily the mother. Although some daring male gods did give birth to creatures by breaking their own heads, like Athena-Minerva, goddess of wisdom and symbol of philosophy. Knowledge whose symbol is a female creature that has not been given birth by a woman should draw our attention!

For years, in a veiled way, academia has required women to have a position on the issue of gender, where they feel obliged to answer the typical query "what am I doing here?" which stigmatizes them as a 'woman.' Whatever the answers or the personal circumstances of each of the women who have dedicated themselves to philosophy are, they are all connected by this sensation: I am a woman therefore I am a philosopher or *vice versa*. This is very odd!

I want to make clear that what distinguishes female philosophical thought from professional academic thought is that the first is forced to ask authentic existential questions of the kind *how is my Dasein,* as Heidegger would say. I would pose such questions differently: how is it possible that my *in-der-Welt-sein* (being in the world) is conditioned by my gender? Am I different precisely because of this question?

As proof of what I say, most of the women engaged in academic philosophy have no choice but to ask themselves these things, even though they serve no purpose. If one bears this in mind, I consider it as producing a particular way of thinking. I will illustrate this with an anecdote. One day a young candidate for a bachelor's degree in philosophy expounded her thesis on the relationship between the body and its interpretation in Nietzsche's thought. After finishing her dissertation a teacher asked her the following question: *How can you discuss this in an author, who steadfastly repudiates women, where is your female body in this approach?* She was extremely surprised because she thought she would be asked about her research, but never imagined she would be judged as a woman for dealing with this issue. She replied quickly: *my female body is right here, underneath this miniskirt.* Having personally witnessed the scene, I can tell that because of her response, she got a lower mark than she deserved.

The answer of the young woman was impetuous; maybe she should have gone into detail about the relationship between male and female as it appears in the thought of Nietzsche, but that would have forced her to think about a problem which was not the main subject of her research. She just wanted to do philosophy without having to deal with the standard objection to the misogyny of Nietzsche as an obstacle to her research. The jury was confronted with its own veiled male chauvinism while gazing at the red miniskirt she was wearing. Inadvertently they assumed all the paragraphs against women by Nietzsche as a given, but could not understand that in the midst of his misogynist language Nietzsche was also mocking the patriarchy.[1]

In *Beyond Good and Evil*, we can find any amount of material which suggests Nietzsche was a misogynist. To judge by his own philosophical and methodological approach to knowledge as interpretation, this would be a very poor reading. It should be read as a sign of great cynicism, which I would consider highly appropriate to its stance as cultural criticism. In number 237 (*bis*) we read: "Woman has hitherto been treated by men like birds, which, losing their way, have come down among them from an elevation: as something delicate, fragile, wild, strange, sweet, and animating—but as something also which must be cooped up to prevent it flying away." It would be absurd to think that Nietzsche defends the idea that women must stay at home, as many of his detractors claim. Nietzsche is setting up a popular belief that denigrates women by labeling them as strange creatures, but, in what sense? Why should they be cooped up to prevent them from flying away? What does this freedom imply for men? I would suggest that the idea of strangeness, of different beings who should be treated differently is something that is part of a masculine way of conceiving of the world (which is not exclusive to men; many women think in the same way). These creatures treated as caged birds may symbolize the feelings of all those men and women who assume a feminine vision of the world. Translated into a more conventional language, this position (which I call feminine) is reflected by an open vision of reality which understands differences of gender as a cultural phenomenon, but rejects the masculine view of discourse as reflected in universal expressions which deny differences and singularities If a male philosopher questions how his gender affects his thinking, shouldn't we suspect that he is showing a different perspective which could have justified the desire of old-fashioned philosophers to coop him up to prevent him from flying away?

Let us imagine our story of the young girl, but this time we are talking about a young man. He is exposing his research on Simone de Beauvoir to a jury composed exclusively of women. One of them asks where his male body is in his reading of *The Second Sex*. He feels offended by doubts cast on the legitimacy of his intellectual curiosity due to his gender. The boy impetuously answers that his body is there, under his pants, thereafter that answer is taken as an obscenity for that sensitive female jury which had interpreted it as an attack on women. Welcome to the world of thought! Being female or male does not depend on the genre, it is an attitude. I think Nietzsche is one of the first to notice it.

In *Beyond Good and Evil*, paragraph 144, he says: "When a woman has scholarly inclinations there is generally something wrong with her sexual nature. Barrenness itself conduces to a certain virility of taste; man, indeed, if I may say so, is "the barren animal." We should notice that for Nietzsche this taste for science is a symptom of a sterility which should make it odd for women due to their reproductive capacity as Beauvoir recognizes in the preface to *The Second Sex.*[2] In that sense Nietzsche is describing a male image of knowledge characterized by being merely imitative or repetitive, as reflected in some squared-away academy. This claim appears in other texts, such as *The Untimely Meditations*,[3] but also in a particular approach to the Greek world.[4] This kind of sterile knowledge can be imitated or practiced by anyone (man or woman) who seems to have a problem with feminine nature. This cannot then be used to accuse the scholarly women of being sexually problematic, because it would be like accusing Eisenstein of mistreating children due to the famous scene in *Battleship Potemkin.* I would propose this interpretation: the practice of science by someone who understands the feminine nature of knowledge must be fruitful and creative in order to avoid falling into the sterility and repetitiveness that is characteristic of some strait-laced academics.

One of my favourite paragraphs, number eighty-four in *Beyond Good and Evil*, says: "Woman learns how to hate in proportion as she forgets how to charm."[5] When I read this for the first time, I rejected it, yet was very curious. Then, I came across the study on seduction by Baudrillard,[6] which made me reinterpret this paragraph and apply it to philosophy. Guided by Nietzsche himself, I came across the preface to the same book, where he begins by saying: "Supposing that Truth is a woman—what then? Is there not ground for suspecting that all philosophers, in so far as they have been dogmatists, have failed to understand women—that the terrible seriousness and clumsy importunity with which they have usually paid their addresses to Truth, have been unskilled and unseemly methods for winning a woman?"[7] If Nietzsche was a misogynist it would make no sense to preface the book in this way. Actually, Deleuze's[8] suggestion on this fact is to understand Nietzsche's thought as a transmutation of values, as a result of a reinterpretation of knowledge in a liberating sense: "Nietzsche presents the purpose of his philosophy to free the thought of nihilism in all its ways. And this implies a new way of thinking, a shock to the basis of thought, a reinstatement of the genealogical principle itself, a transmutation."[9]

This is how we should address the odious combination of woman and philosopher, not as a gender issue, but as a proof that the academic exercise of philosophy as we know it so far has been sterile because it has forgotten to charm and it is not able to seduce as it is excessively masculine.

In particular, when someone asks me about this matter (gender plus philosophy) and links it to my practice of philosophy with regard to the care of people, I like to emphasize that my practice regains for philosophy its legacy of use for the public good, a vocation it should be proud of. Just as no one would suggest the demolition of the Parthenon because it is in ruins, philosophy is not a wreck; both are legacies of our history and our identity. The preservation of feminine action while rejecting patriarchal attitudes toward novelty is a characteristic of progress.

At this point, I stand up for Nietzsche and his consideration on women. In paragraph eighty-six from *Beyond Good and Evil*, he says, "In the background of all their personal vanity women themselves have still their impersonal scorn—for 'woman.'"[10] It means that we have to reject a picture of woman which does not express her potential but is rather a caricature. Because of the use of this image we are dealing with a concept emptied out of reality and nothing is more accurate than calling it vanity. Vanity is part of the set of masks for seduction, but it must be consistent, as it is logical to reject any label that undermines a complete identity. Moreover, both female and male have nothing to do with generalizations or universal concepts such as *the* man and *the* woman. If we interpret this paragraph beyond the obvious, as Nietzsche always insisted we should, we can understand it as a complaint against the universal abstract concepts of idealism. If we reject the tag *the* woman, we do it because we do not want to be stigmatized. We can find a sense in here for justifying the use of Nietzschean misogyny in order to ridicule any woman philosopher dedicated to understanding and interpretation, as in this case she should be able to answer: Yes, he is misogynistic, but against what kind of woman?

This approach is pivotal for my practice because it makes me conceive of the human being I have in front of me beyond his gender or sexual choice. Everyone needs to locate their thought in order to generate new spaces for thinking. This localization allows my client to give birth to new truths and solve conflicts caused by their old beliefs.

My practice therefore depends on withdrawing from a rigid masculine academic model of thinking, keeping the spirit that distinguishes philosophy from any other intellectual discipline. When I work with people I follow a path pointed out by Gadamer in *The Enigma of Health*:[11] the basis of any treatment is to show respect and always talk in a way that does not force or pressure people toward a concrete point of view, and that *does* invest in difference as the only means to guide the consultant toward finding their own path. In other contexts, this would be called an 'hermeneutic effort.'

I insist on difference not to strengthen it but to play with it, as difference can generate productive situations only if we make it more flexible and understandable. To treat is to treat well, and by recognizing difference I am able to work with inspiration, creativity, and seduction.

Generally speaking, I have always rejected sticking to methods because they have been represented to me as a rigid, masculine, doctrinaire way of thinking, so I prefer to use the concept of *strategy* to explain the way I work. It means that I take my time in explaining how the matter is going to be treated, while at the same time I am looking for harmony with my client, taking into account our differences, be they personal, social, cultural, ideological, whatever. What follows explains how my client and I came to share sensitivities. As a man, he came with a lot of questions related to the meaning of difference between men and women, with a rooted belief that this was the cause of his problems.

When I started working with my client, I tried first to prepare him for dealing with the feminine in the way I have already explained. I brought to his attention this text from Deleuze: "As terrible mothers, terrible sisters and wives, femininity represents the spirit of revenge and the resentment which animates man himself. But Ariadne, abandoned by Theseus, senses the coming of a transmutation which is specific to her: the feminine power emancipated, become beneficent and affirmative, the Anima."[12]

I will explain how the transmutation of the values of my client occurred under *the* feminine vision of the world and how a man with all his rigidity could embrace a more comprehensive and less authoritarian way of thinking. The understanding of everything that was happening to him came by leading him on a different path, introducing him to laughter and play.

I use a lot of techniques in my practice related to humour, irony, and games; these are perhaps feminine traits of thinking, and are opposed to calculated, regulated, predictable phenomena as tools of pure science.

HE CAME TO MY PRACTICE:
SHARING SENSIBILITIES (THE CASE)

Introduction

To the dismay of my client, a friend suggested that he should read Marinoff's *More Plato Less Prozac*.[13] The book suggested that not all human problems are psychological. After an Internet search he found there was a philosophical counsellor near by, so he visited my website and my profile convinced him I was the professional he was looking for. His primary motivation was the rejection of the idea that psychiatric treatment was sufficient to relieve his discomfort. Even though he was aware that he needed pharmaceutical aid, he realized that was not to be the real solution to his problem. Jack needed to talk to someone. He had visited a psychologist who did not want to get involved with someone already treated and medicated by a psychiatrist. The psychologist told him that if he could not wait until his medication kicked in, he should go back and talk to his psychiatrist.

Jack felt abandoned; maybe he could not express clearly what he felt. He did not want to create a conflict between two different specialists, but wanted to discuss what would be best for him. He had been suffering from anxiety and panic attacks for a long time and did not know the cause. But he was not interested in resolving this; he was anxious about something else. He returned to tell his doctor that the medication was affecting him too much, that he felt passive, unwilling, and had difficulties getting his day started. He was very depressed and lethargic most of the time. As a response, his psychiatrist suggested antidepressants, but Jack refused. It was then that the psychiatrist invited him to seek a second opinion, someone to make him understand that taking medication was a personal decision related to the way he chose to live.

Following his psychiatrist's advice, Jack came to my practice. As he had found when he browsed my website, my professional objective is to clarify problems by facilitating different points of view and helping to gain perspectives relevant to the whole consultant and their overall well-being.

The interviews

It is Monday morning about 10 a.m. We had already exchanged some impressions by phone, where he explained to me some psychopharmacological decision he had to take. I had told him we could meet to assess the dilemma and work on decision making. I had insisted I had no authority to prescribe or advise against taking of any medication.

He arrives on time, a young man of around thirty, casually but fashionably dressed, very thin, with a shy look and a melancholy air. He carries a bag as if he were a student. These clues are very important for the first contact. Body language tells me how I should direct what I am going to say, gives me cultural references, and helps with my questions.

The interview started by introducing myself to him as I tried to pose the classical deontological questions: what do you expect from me and what do you think I can do for you? What do you expect from me and what I cannot do? What can I do for you and you do not expect from me? This is the moment where I test the level of empathy and the ability of my client to compromise. I usually mix this introduction with some joke to evaluate their sense of humor and willingness to engage in dialogue. Jack is receptive, but I notice he is not very accessible, so I interrupt myself with questions such as: am I being clear? I notice he takes his time in answering. I realize that he is a prudent and reserved man.

Jack is the youngest of three children and still lives with his parents. He is a musician; he plays the piano (apparently his job) and has recently been on a U.S. tour. He feels insecure, physically ill; he cannot overcome the end of a relationship and feels an anxiety.

He feels frustrated by the fact that he has gone to a psychologist and psychiatrist and it has not worked out so far. I think about how philosophy could help him. I have a section from my notes where I set out four options, like this:

Philosophical support will go toward:

a. change of attitude
b. revision of values
c. examined life
d. philosophy of life

I choose 'a.'

Then I described my impressions to him and we started discussing my strategy. First I proposed we take care of his health, as those inner conflicts which do not reveal themselves are expressed through physical symptoms. Second, we reviewed the circumstances which were causing his anxiety and depression. I argued that any situation cannot be conceived without a frame in which it becomes relevant, and I insisted on the importance of consistency in philosophy and life. Finally, we got into the matter of couples breaking up, because when we separate from the one we love it becomes a time in our lives when we have to examine many of the doubts which surround us as individuals. This process always involves looking into the concepts of guilt and possession.

A distinctive feature of the thought that I have called *the* feminine that it is not seduced by the logic of an immediate resolution of the most obvious problems—in this case the mourning caused by the break up and its accompanying jealousy. I chose instead to take care of the physical body, which was experiencing symptoms inhibiting him from seeing himself as an intelligent, sensitive, and healthy young man. My gaze was that of a woman who asks herself: what's wrong with this man?

We proposed and explained the strategy that I would have applied, and he agreed to it, at least insofar as I could isolate each of the parts of his concerns which he had chosen to start with as the most urgent for him, because to attend to *the* man was the priority. Thus, we spent several sessions on the subject of his disease, as he insisted on calling himself a hypochondriac. A concept needed to be clarified here. I told him that hypochondria should be understood as the concealment of a more serious problem by inventing an illness which it was convenient to assume, that in fact, none of his health problems existed. He reacted to this by showing me the red spots of his eczema on his skin. "These cannot be invented," he said, "they persist even though I am following a treatment." We talked for a long time about the issue of health and its relation to philosophy. I brought the *Paideia* of Jaeger[14] into my arguments, also a couple of statements by Nietzsche and Gadamer on health. We were trying to get to some common ground on health and illness. I brought to the discussion the epicurean idea of the health of the soul. He laughed when I went even further and said that the only disease philosophers can diagnose is κενοδοξία (*kenodoxia*), understood as having empty opinions, that in this respect he seemed perfectly healthy to me. I had suggested some ideas from Rüdiger Dahlke's book,[15] so I went to my library and read to him the part where eczema is interpreted as a symptom of an internal conflict. Eczema, Dahlke says, evokes borders (they are very well-defined spots), that these are barriers against the outside world, and at the same time is the manifestation of an internal injury, struggling to emerge, to cry out, and to be attended to. His healing in this case would come when he brought to his attention his inward conflicts, working them out. It was a crucial moment for both of us. He had shown a wounded body to a woman who had given back to him a vision himself as a human being, without gender, just human. She now understood him from the common ground that unites all human beings: hope. I think it was very important to him because he left behind his masculine role ("I shouldn't show my wounds to any woman") and allowed himself entry into a space in which men and women can engage in a dialogue base on true equality and authentic reciprocity.

Each session started with a kind of health report. Mornings were very hard for him because he had really rough bouts of anxiety. He had decided to continue his treatment with the psychiatrist, who had accepted his refusal to take antidepressants and agreed to adjust the high dosage of anti-anxiety meds as their strength had had such negative effects. His treatment for eczema seemed to be paying off, although he had lately begun to suffer from a kind of ringing in his ears, the cause of which was unknown.

– Can't you see? I am a hypochondriac! I'll never feel good!

– Never is a long time. Let's be more precise. On which days and at which times don't you feel well?—He looked at me as if I was making fun of him, but I continued,—I am being serious, sometimes it helps to know when the malaise starts and when it ends, how long it lasts, and all the details of its duration, because health is a condition that develops over a period of time, which can be measured.

– Yes, but that's not the problem.

– What is it then?

– That I never feel good, both physically and spiritually . . .

– I know, but don't you think that, as you make the connection, there is a direct relationship between them and is so close that it generates that feeling of 'eternity?' Let me continue, what I mean is that health is a global state, you have gone through a very painful time, you've lost the person you loved, you torture yourself when you see her happy with another man while you are trying to rebuild your life. You get up in the morning without courage and go to work and things are not getting any better, your music is being affected because you're not happy . . . And you still don't understand what's wrong? Therefore it is important to find that moment in your day when you do not feel bad, because that's the moment which will show us a way to follow . . . When do you feel good?

– Mid-morning when I have a coffee and see the sun.

– Do you enjoy it?

– Yes, I feel relaxed. I am not worried, of course I have taken my medicine in the morning . . . –said with sarcasm.

– Umm . . . –to follow on in the same sarcastic tone, I added–is that when you hear the ringing noise?

– No, it's always at night, but the doctor cannot find the cause.

He was very serious. My own sarcasm has also been a strategy to see if the rest of his symptoms were still present. I continued:

– Have you ever thought the cause could just be stress, for example? Are you relaxed at night?

– Are you kidding me? The nights are the worst; it is really hard to accept . . .

– . . . the end of the relationship with Marianne?

– Yes and no. Actually I mostly think about my friends and how they already have wives, some have children, a career and a good job, and I . . . I think I have nothing but my suffering for a woman who never loved me . . .

The change in the dialogue's focus from illness and suffering to solitude and frustration was part of the strategy, and showed him the close relation between them.

– So, you have something, even if you have forgotten about your music, but we will get into that later. If you are suffering for a woman who does not love you, it means that you've been able to love. Let's go slowly: why do you compare yourself to others? Imagine that one of your friends. He is thinking: "I'll bet Jack's very happy every night because he's single, he can do what he wants: compose music, go on tour, work in a music store where his boss understands and supports him and lets him do these kinds of things." He also thinks you are lucky to live so well and have such a good relationship with your parents. He saw you yesterday relaxing at a coffee shop, enjoying the beautiful morning while he had to be in his office at the bank with a stack of papers and later has to leave in a hurry to be on time to pick up the kids at school.

He laughed.

– That guy doesn't exist! –

– Maybe not but . . . what if he does?

– That would be an attack on my claim that I'm unhappy! – He said wryly.

The fact that he could have another point of view about his masculine social role was one of the keys to understanding what was happening to his male body. We had already devoted several sessions to the subject of humor and irony, and he had learned to laugh at himself. The fact that he took the initiative in doing so, at this time, was very important. It was not just a matter of avoiding comparisons with the ready-made images of success society sells to us, but of understanding the difference between gender (man/woman), and attitudes (masculine/feminine). We discussed what the sense was of being a man and what the sense was of being a woman, and the meaning behind what we call 'feminine' or (rather than and) 'masculine.'

– So, I'm a feminine man . . . can women fall in love with a man like me?

– Have you ever fallen in love with a masculine woman?

– I really think I don't know . . . really! –

– Yes, you do! A dominant woman who controls you, who wants you to obey her and never really talks things over because there is only one indisputable truth: hers . . .

He laughed and added . . .

–Have you ever met Marianne? That's just like her! Now that you mention it, I was the one that always brought tenderness, illusion, music, to the relationship. All she did was make plans for the future, criticize my ideas and my job, meanwhile she would tell me I was wasting my time and should be doing something else. It was when I invested in that business that failed because I just couldn't get my head around it. That's when she really made me feel totally useless . . .

– . . . so she left you for a more handsome man who earned more money, was professionally stable . . . need I say more?

– How do you know all this?

– I have seen a lot of soap operas. – I laughed.

We then explored in depth the matter of 'being,' and examined the meaning of authenticity in Heidegger.[16] Heidegger says that human beings are unique because they can pose questions about themselves and are conscious of their finiteness, as well as able to project themselves into the future. What does this mean for us? How can we use this notion? Proposing questions like this I tried to uncover real concerns to show how the social roles determine our behavior and most of the time do not give us the alternative of developing all our potentialities.

A sensitive man is a problem for a society in which sensitivity is a sign of weakness; a sensitive woman is also a problem because *the* feminine has to be understood as a way towards authenticity, a way of questioning roles and automatic habits. Seduction, for example, is used as a resource to gain power over the other and has become a kind of competitive game, where the number of beings seduced is directly proportional to a person's dominance. This is why loving in terms of equality needs a touch of seduction, charm, enthusiasm, friendship, and complicity: it implies a constant shift between roles. This type of dynamic love requires the masculine and feminine polarities remain in constant flux, with both willing to take any attitude necessary for the development of a proper life project both as individuals and are willing to take any attitude as necessary to the development of the life project as individuals and as a couple. Even without a partner, we need to understand this tension, as one sometimes has to alternatively assume male and female roles to allow for a certain plasticity, which is crucial to broadening one's understanding. We can say that this plasticity facilitates much more assertiveness.

To the extent that the sessions continued, Jack was bringing more and more questions about how he had lived so far. He defined himself as apprehensive, and tender, and believed this was at the root of his problems.

– Maybe I'm too affectionate. I like taking care of my partner, being attentive, cuddly. I like to plan things we can do together. I think this is nice, but maybe it is the cause of break ups and reproaches. I don't understand anything! You are a woman, how do you see it? If your partner calls you, wants to take care of you, would you think that he just wanted to control you? Would you take it the wrong way?

– No, but remember that we move between *the* masculine and *the* feminine. Personally, since you ask me, not really. Thank you for taking me into account. My personal life is not really the issue here, so I can use it like any other story, as another text.

– But have you ever broken up with someone for this reason?

– Yes, of course! –

He was surprised at my wry reply.

– Why? I don't understand, too feminine for your taste?

– Listen to this. Once I had a boyfriend who was very attentive to me. One day he came to visit me with some beautiful flowers, but on precisely that day I had already decided to break up with him because I didn't feel anything special for him. I knew I didn't love him. I imagine he had the same question: "why doesn't she love me when I love her and deserve her love? And why do I love someone who does not deserve my love?"

– Yes! Why?

– Why do you think? – I wanted him to make a quick deduction.

– I know. You didn't love him and you used it as an excuse that he brought you flowers, right? – he said with sarcasm and we laughed . . .

No, you're crazy! I said laughing. – I just told him I didn't love him and that he shouldn't waste him time on this relationship. I recognized that he was a very sweet, tender, and a beautiful man who needed to find a woman to love him.

– And how did he take it? – He was curious.

I had been conducting the dialogue just to get to this reaction. His curiosity was a sign of his involvement in a process of thinking about a problem at a distance from it, one of the conditions of hermeneutical focus.

– Badly, really badly. No one, whether they are a man or a woman, can feel happy about being rejected. It's unbearable because it's as if a part of us had been erased. We have given the other an image; we are waiting for a positive feedback, which is the starting point for love between a couple. We decide to engage one with the other a result of this seductive and narcissistic play of images.

– A little selfish, isn't it?

– Yes.

– But . . . I always believed that love was surrender, caring for one another, sharing. The pain comes because you cannot have that anymore, right?

– You said the right thing when you said 'have;' a person is not a possession. Perhaps we should re-read Erich Fromm,[17] who makes the distinction between 'to have' and 'to love.' In his understanding, although this dilemma focuses on a vision which can be misunderstood as selfish, but it leads to a conception of the being, being oneself as a love gift. Maybe this is the essence of surrender and unconditional love, but he doesn't go so far as to say that love is based on the need to be reflected in the other. For a better understanding of this we could perhaps turn to Sartre.[18] Anyway, I think it's a very poetic idea which is shared by contemporary philosophers such as Levinas, or Gadamer, both of whom explain how the presence of another human being is crucial to becoming conscious of ourselves. This isn't a philosophy seminar, of course, but the idea is that we are what we are because there is another, not as constricting our desire but, as an extension of what we have in common, humanity. When you look at me and I look at you, there is something that unites us. I recognize you as Jack and give you this feedback, through my gestures and my answers I am building an image of you that makes you feel good. If we could not communicate in this friendly way, perhaps you wouldn't be here sharing impressions.

– I see, I had offered something to a woman and she rejects me because she didn't love me . . .

– Yes . . .

. . . and, then I got so sad because her rejection confirmed that the image she had of me was not what I wanted her to have . . .

– What else?

– By this mechanism, she had the power to erase your presence (the image you wanted to project, the one with which you feel comfortable), which can be seen as a violent action. So, not being able to express the violence against her, you decided to express it against yourself.

– Are you sure? In what way?

– I don't know if I should really be saying this, but experience has shown me how someone can transform inner suffering into physical symptoms. For example: torturing oneself at night with invidious comparisons, accidentally on purpose bumping into her just to see her with her new boyfriend and maintain a bond that speaks to you of her and her happiness . . . all that makes you suffer . . . oh, and I missed something! A kind of self-laceration which causes all those red marks on your skin!–His face showed surprise, the kind when someone feels liberated despite having just discovered an undesirable and uncomfortable truth. It was an intense and useful session which showed us a way of differentiating women in how they live love in relation to men. I could then draw on my own experience to discuss how one evolves toward mature love. We laughed a lot as we spent some time reminiscing on first loves whose names we could not remember. I told him some true and fictionalized stories of other experiences, trying to give him the opportunity to get a wider perspective on love, one that insisted on the possibility of a love story free from guilt and sadness.

One day he came to my practice with news. He had had an intense anxiety attack. I asked him to tell me all the details as precisely as he could: when it started, how long it lasted, et cetera. Together we noted how he felt pressure whenever a situation was out of his control.

On that particular day he was going to take a plane and was anticipating the moment when the plane would take off, and he felt this fear of flying. It was a big problem because he had just received another invitation to a concert abroad. We agreed to the following: over the next week he was to identify when this anxiety appeared, down to the subtlest symptom in any given situation. What we needed to know was whether he would be able to anticipate it from any recognizable physical signs. He could do it by memory or direct experimentation, which was not difficult because he often suffered from such attacks. My intention was to target his conscious awareness of this problem, to familiarize himself with it, and accept it as part of his personality. At the same time, we needed to have an accurate description of the situation if it was going to be treated by his psychiatrist. Once he had it clear in his mind, he could speak to him to see if it would be appropriate to get some medication.

– I'd take anything not to feel it . . .

– Why?

– Because I feel really bad, really uncomfortable . . .

– Why?

– Because it's not a nice feeling . . .

– Does it last long?

– No, only about fifteen minutes . . .

– Then what?

– Little by little I get over it and I start to relax . . .

– Could we say that anxiety is so bad because it only lasts fifteen minutes?

– No, it's because I just don't like the feeling . . .

This last statement leads us on to discuss the concept of anxiety, where I drew on Kierkegaard[19] and Freud.[20] According to Freud, anguish should be understood first of all as a sign of life. At the same time, it can be viewed as uncertainty and a warning: the anguish of being cornered and compelled to find a solution, anguish as fear. Distrust as counsel and fear as a companion. We got on to the subject of prudence as a kind of measure and practical wisdom, in the sense of the ancient φρόνεσις (*phronesis*). I gave its classical definition to show how anguish can be related not only to the very basic, naked life, but also to the wisdom of life, which is tension toward a fuller and fully humane existence. He began to understand.

– So, anxiety can be positive, is that it?

– Yes. We all suffer from it in a lesser or greater degree, there are personalities that are more vulnerable than others, but in any case it is a consequence of a vision of life. After this explanation you haven't shown any discomfort because you are starting to assume that anguish is part of your life just as it is for everybody else. We cannot live without it.

– The point is to learn to live with it . . .

– Exactly! Can you imagine your music without your anguish? . . . His gaze was fixed on the horizon as one who remembers some endearing moment, intimate, loved. There was a smile on his face and his eyes lit up.

– That's impossible! When I compose to feel calmed! I forget about the world. It's just me and my music. It conveys what I want people to know of me and my experiences. I express myself through its minimalism. I want to evoke states of stillness, serenity, meditation . . .

– Can't you see? To the extent that anxiety is not treated as a problem, you can invite it into a convivial relationship; you can leave a decent place for it in your life. I don't think you have to use punish this conviviality with pills.

Jack talked to his psychiatrist who approved medicine just for his anxiety attacks. As he managed to control his anxiety, invitations to Germany, England, France, and Holland followed. Not only had he learned to trust himself, but even the pilot off the plane! With his new perspective on love and gender, he threw away his antidepressants and broke off definitively with his ex-girlfriend. It was important that he could be thankful and at peace with her ex-girlfriend and with himself. There was a conversation between them where she wanted to blame him for the failure of their relationship and humiliated him, while he insisted that they should at least be respectful of all they had lived through together, as they were equally responsible for what had happened and both still deserved to find happiness . . .

– Jack, letting her go was a great act of love. I have found that if I hate the person who has rejected me, I hate a part of my own life and I'm not willing to do that. My love will always be with me and I am free to give it to those who deserve it and I will remove it from those who don't. That has to be learned. In this business of love there is no blame, no one is guilty. Sartre spoke of the importance of commitment and its relation to liability. We are responsible for what happened, everything, good and bad. We always have to think that at that time we did our best, but we did not warrant success.

Jack carried on with his story. Marianne insisted on blaming him for not measuring up her expectations. She felt cheated and was convinced there were a lot of men better than Jack. He remembered how much he had suffered because the way she thought of him, probably using his new-found logic, self-confidence, and sense of irony. He told me that when she dared to compare him with other men he suddenly felt a surge of anger.

– What did you say? – I asked.

– I said, "Yes Marianne, there are better men than me, but there's only one like me." Rayda, she was so astonished she did not even know what to say. She started insulting me and began to cry. I was tempted to embrace her; it was my big chance, but . . .

– Why didn't you do it?

– Because she seemed so pathetic, she didn't really interest me at all. I felt she wasn't the person I had suffered so much for. But I cannot understand it really: how could I have changed in this way? How did it happen?

– I think I know. You reacted to her violence with equal violence. After all the nights you suffered her insulting you finally responded with indifference. It was spontaneous. A philosopher who advocates dialogue says that one of the most violent actions we can commit against another human being is not to let them talk, not to answer them, not to give him a chance to explain. She insults you with the comparisons, one of the things you have suffered for so many nights, and you responded with indifference. You tried to talk to her in one language, looking for reconciliation, and she replied to you in another, making clear she wasn't interested in what you were saying. She chose to understand your relationship as a mistake, as something she will never assume responsibility for.

– You're right. It felt violent to me when I was indifferent to her tears, but she deserved it. She showed that she had never understood the man who loved her; she didn't understand my way of loving.

– Or maybe it wasn't the way she needed to be loved . . .

– I've got more news for you.

– Don't you want to talk about this matter?

– No, I've decided there's a girl out there who wants to be loved they way I know, one who is willing to fluctuate between *the* feminine and *the* masculine. The news is I'm dating a girl and I think we're in love . . .

–That's great! – I was happy to see him so confident and fragile, so clear, so human.

– And there's something else!

– Another concert?

– No – he lifted his shirt and his eczema was gone, only a few tiny marks left to witness the battle. – I didn't say anything because I thought it was temporary and would probably return, but it turned out it had been months since it disappeared.

– Did you go to a dermatologist?

– No, it wasn't a dermatologist. This time some credit has to go to the practice of philosophy.

In our closing session, we laughed at the most difficult times he had been through and remembered with affection the most important. I made a list of concepts and gave him a number of tips for emergency situations such as:

1. Assume what belongs to you; give no credit to pieces of imposture.
2. Allow yourself to commit to what you have chosen.
3. Live with defects and virtues as if it were no difference between them.
4. Care for your health if it allows you to live better.
5. Compose music whenever you need to.

And . . . these were crucial:

1. Facing pointless tears is pointless.
2. Beware of hysterical amphetamine addicted girls. (a private joke)
3. Beware of the distressed and disoriented girls.

I think the visit to a counselor gave this man a view of himself that brought him out of a spiral of self-destruction, violent in nature and, in that sense—without prejudices—very masculine. The fact that his eczema had disappeared was confirmation of how conflicts are expressed by our body. Its disappearance meant the healing of past wounds and that he had learned to stay away from the things which were damaging him: comparisons, jealousy, and complacency.

CONCLUSIONS

This text suffers from inevitable space limitations. I would like to make clear that this is not an apology for *the* feminine against *the* masculine, or an assertion of the benefits of one attitude over another. Finding a balance between these forces and the discovery of how we can profit from them in creating a more comfortable and desirable way of life should be our goal. In this regard I would recommend a re-reading of Nietzsche's Deleuzian interpretation.

In line with my philosophy I would say that as human beings we have to make this world a habitable, comfortable place to live in. Taking place as a metaphor, we know that it can allow us to move more freely, but can also impose limits, which is what makes it interesting. In order to avoid obstacles and find alternative routes we must recover a sense of spatial thinking, taking into account our temporality and a proper sense of our own history

Bearing in mind Gadamer and Ricoeur, I believe we inhabit the world by means of the word.[21] An inhabited world is one where we can say something meaningful to and for everyone. What is lived has to be narrated, told to others in an exchange of spatial arrangements. Masculine and feminine are simply subjects which lie behind all stories, where the story itself is not what counts, but which forms the basis for a narrative, a baseline argument for added details. Without this understanding, the philosopher's words are in vain and we are all doomed to κενοδοξία (*kenodoxia*).

NOTES

1. Heidi Hartmann defines patriarchy "as a set of social relations between men who have a material base, and though hierarchical, establish or create interdependence and solidarity among them that enable them to dominate women." See Heidi Harmann "The Unhappy Mar-

riage of Marxism and Feminism: Towards a More Progressive Union," in *Feminist Theory Reader: Local and Global Perspectives,* ed. Carole R. McCann (New York: Routledge, 2003).

2. Simone de Beauvoir, *The Second Sex* (1st American ed. New York: Knopf, 1953).

3. Friedrich Wilhelm Nietzsche, *Untimely Meditations* (Cambridge: Cambridge University Press, 1997).

4. We should examine the claim of Wilamowitz-Moellendorff against "The birth of Tragedy."

5. Nietzsche, Friedrich Wilhelm, *Beyond Good and Evil: Prelude to a Philosophy of the Future* (New York: Oxford University Press, 1998).

6. "Un destin ineffaçable pése sur la séduction. Pour la religión, elle fut la stratégie du diable. Qu'elle fût sorcière ou amoreuse. La séduction est toujours celle du mal. Ou celle du monde. C'est l'*artifice* du monde. Cette malédiction s'est mantenue inchangée à travers de la moral et la philosophie (. . .)" Jean Baudrillard, *De la Séduction* (Paris: Denöel 1988), 9. [Eng. trans. Brian Singer: "A fixed destiny weighs on seduction. For religion seduction was a strategy of the devil, whether in the guise of witchcraft or love. It is always the seduction of evil—or of the world. It is the very artifice of the world. Its malediction has been unchanged in ethics and philosophy (. . .)" Montréal: New World Perspectives, 1990), 1].

7. Retrived from: http://www.fullbooks.com/Beyond-Good-and-Evil1.html.

8. Gilles Deleuze, "Dionysus and Zarathustra," in *Nietzsche and Philosophy.* London: Continuum, 1992.

9. Ibid., p. 21.

10. Retrived from: http://www.fullbooks.com/Beyond-Good-and-Evil2.html.

11. Hans Gadamer, *The Enigma of Health: The Art of Healing in a Scientific Age* (Stanford: Stanford University Press, 1996).

12. Gilles Deleuze, "Dionysus and Zarathustra."

13. Lou Marinoff, *Plato, not Prozac!: Applying Philosophy to Everyday Problems* (New York: HarperCollins, 1999).

14. Werner Jaeger, *Paideia: The Ideals of Greek Culture* (Oxford: Blackwell, 1944).

15. Rüdiger Dahlke, *Disease as a Symbol: Psychosomatics—The Messages Behind Your Symptoms* (Altkirchen: M-TEC Verl., 2011).

16. Martin Heidegger, *Being and Time* (New York: Harper, 1962).

17. Erich Fromm, *The Art of Loving* (1st ed. New York: Harper & Row, 1956).

18. Jean-Paul Sartre, *Existentialism and Humanism* (Brooklyn: Haskell House, 1977).

19. Søren Kierkegaard, *The Concept of Anxiety: a Simple Psychologically Orienting Deliberation on the Dogmatic Issue of Hereditary Sin* (Princeton, N.J.: Princeton University Press, 1980).

20. Sigmund Freud, *The Psychopathology of Everyday Life*. (New York: Norton,1965).

21. Paul Ricoeur, *A Ricoeur Reader: Reflection and Imagination* (Toronto: University of Toronto Press, 1991).

BIBLIOGRAPHY

Baudrillard, Jean. *Seduction.* Translated by Brian Singer. Montreal: New World Perspectives, 1990.

Beauvoir, Simone de. *The Second Sex*. 1st American ed. New York: Knopf, 1953.

Critchley, Simon. *The Cambridge Companion to Levinas*. Cambridge: Cambridge University Press, 2002.

Dahlke, Rüdiger. *Disease as a Symbol: Psychosomatics—The Messages Behind Your Symptoms*. Altkirchen: M-TEC Verl., 2011.

Deleuze, Gilles. "Dionysus and Zarathustra." In *Nietzsche and Philosophy*. London: Continuum, 1992.

Freud, Sigmund. *The Psychopathology of Everyday Life*. Translated by James Strachey. New York: Norton, 1965.

Fromm, Erich. *The Art of Loving*. 1st ed. New York: Harper & Row, 1956.

Gadamer, Hans. *The Gadamer Reader: A Bouquet of the Later Writings*. Edited by Richard E. Palmer. Evanston, Ill.: Northwestern University Press, 2007.

———. *The Enigma of Health: The Art of Healing in a Scientific Age*. Stanford: Stanford University Press, 1996.

Guzmán, Rayda. *La Mujer Serena*. Barcelona: Sirpus, 2007.

Hartmann, Heidi. "The Unhappy Marriage of Marxism and Feminism: Towards a More Progressive Union." In *Feminist Theory Reader: Local and Global Perspectives*, edited by Carole R. McCann, New York: Routledge, 2003.

Heidegger, Martin. *Being and Time*. New York: Harper, 1962.

Jaeger, Werner. *Paideia: the Ideals of Greek Culture.* Oxford: Blackwell, 1944.

Kierkegaard, Søren. *The Concept of Anxiety: A Simple Psychologically Orienting Deliberation on the Dogmatic Issue of Hereditary Sin.* Edited by Reidar Thomte and Albert B. Anderson. Princeton, N.J.: Princeton University Press, 1980.

Marinoff, Lou. *Plato, not Prozac!: Applying Philosophy to Everyday Problems*. New York: HarperCollins, 1999.

Nietzsche, Friedrich Wilhelm. *Beyond Good and Evil: Prelude to a Philosophy of the Future*. Translated by Marion Faber. New York: Oxford University Press, 1998.

———. *Untimely Meditations*. Translated by R. J. Hollingdale. Cambridge: Cambridge University Press, 1997.

Ricoeur, Paul. *A Ricoeur Reader: Reflection and Imagination*. Edited by Mario J. Valdes. Toronto: University of Toronto Press, 1991.

Sartre, Jean-Paul. *Existentialism and Humanism*. Brooklyn: Haskell House, 1977.

Chapter Twelve

How Might Philosophical Counseling Be in Garments From Simone de Beauvoir's Armoire, *The Second Sex*?

Narelle Arcidiacono

Simone de Beauvoir's *The Second Sex* is a story of epic proportions. Her meticulous attention to what it is to be a woman was unprecedented at its time of publication in 1949. Over the past sixty-five years it has seeped into communal consciousness to the point that to speak of the rights of woman is almost seen as *passé*, and to grant Beauvoir the status of major change agent an old-fashioned notion. These views fail to recognize the enormity of her project and its historical and practical significance. It is for reasons of historical perspectives that I have chosen to use the original French to English translation by H. M. Parshley for this chapter. While I acknowledge wholeheartedly the great worth of the 2009 French to English translation by Borde and Malvany-Chevallier,[1] at this point (2014) Parshley's translation, with all its shortcomings (for example his consistent use of fraternal language) is the one that has had most influence to date. What is of greater relevance here is the question that Luce Irigaray examines within the title of her paper "Is the Subject of Science Sexed?" In other words, is there, within the logical and syntactic/semantic framework of existing discourse, an opening or a degree of freedom that allow the expression of sexual difference? It is, then, a question of analyzing the laws (including those not articulated as such) that determine the acceptability of language and discourse in order to interpret their connection to a sexed logic. This analysis can be pursued from a number of perspectives.[2]

My perspective is that Beauvoir was an immensely courageous and creative woman who produced a body of work highly valued when written, and increasingly valued again today, having been through a time in the philosophical and feminist wilderness. It is also is worth noting that I do not consider myself an apologist for Beauvoir but someone who values her worth, frailties and all. I am aware, for example, that Beauvoir confessed to "political indifference and ignorance during the early 1930s when she and Sartre initially underestimated the importance of the Nazis' rise to power."[3] This however does not diminish her overall contribution. In her paper "The Reinvention of the Couple," Julia Kristeva writes of Beauvoir. "I think she is a woman who had the audacity and the courage to get burnt by what she says and what she cannot say, and that she makes communicable the truth of desire. That is one of the essential contributions of existentialism, in her form anyway, to today's culture."[4]

I endorse Julia Kristeva's statement and consider it all the more powerful for the flaws she implies. Kristeva supports Beauvoir without elevating her to mystic status, something that would not sit well with the existential position. Freedom, authenticity, and bad faith, as garments from Beauvoir's armoire *The Second Sex,* are measured herein and the particular needs, rights and desires of women in philosophical counseling are tested for fit. My claim: the current clothing of philosophical counseling must be recut, redesigned, and restructured in order that the constricting corset of current practice that binds woman's communication can be released, facilitating breath.

WHAT DOES BEAUVOIR BRING TO PHILOSOPHICAL COUNSELING?

On my first reading of *The Second Sex* in 1972, Beauvoir's existential notion of freedom as something that must be fully exercised in order to live authentically held great value for me; it continues to do so. That this freedom must come without cost to others is compelling, and her view that a project falls into one in bad faith if one's own or another's freedom is compromised is commanding. Beauvoir explores the links between freedom and the expression of freedom that is authenticity, and how the existent can best ensure a life that is a project illustrative of, but not dependent on, these factors. This distinction between dependency and illustration is of paramount importance to philosophical counseling because dependency undermines freedom and authenticity and renders a project as one in bad faith; whereas illustration represents freedom in action as it greets mutuality as a fertile space unencumbered by method restriction. On the other hand, philosophical counseling that demands fidelity and dependency to a particular method, regardless of individual style, restricts the power of the client to engage authentically.

Philosophical counseling values a vital illustration of freedom and an active eradication of dependency; it does not provide answers to questions, a tactic that amounts to an assault on freedom, but instead a fertile environment for co-construction. Furthermore, philosophical practice does not threaten the principal component of existentialism, that is self-generation through the complete accomplishment of one's own freedom without ever encroaching on that of others or the Other, as it is the counselee who seeks an external eye not in a quest to be transformed by the practitioner but by philosophizing with the practitioner. It is not a relationship like psychiatry or psychology that is a response to a particular pathology, but a very deliberate temporal act committed with full agency and exercised as a deliberate and individual choice. This echo of personal responsibility is not, however, like the cry of the libertarian whose quest for freedom comes at the cost of others. Nor does it imply forfeiture on the part of the counselee or counselor, for to forfeit would be to deny, to both participants, access to freedom just as an authoritative approach restricts.

The more meticulous the application of existential attributes to the process of philosophical counseling the greater the growth of freedom will be, as opposed to a field of practice plagued by the pestilence of authoritarianism. The following questions asked by Beauvoir in *The Second Sex* hold considerable weight in the practice of philosophical counseling: "Can one rely on one's own heart? Can one have confidence in others?"[5] The existentialist ethics that Beauvoir pioneered have at their core the mutuality of freedom, a form that maps well with a philosophical counseling model that avoids domination. A *Just Story*, when used in conjunction with the ethics of existentialism, is a device (analyzed later in the chapter) that encourages liberty, creativity and intellectual rigor. It privileges innovation alongside reasoned argument rather than static point of view; it is philosophizing in action, visceral and instinctive, guided by a sense of wonder and grounded in the expertise of the qualified counselor and the agency of the counselee.

WOMAN

My first contact with the practice of philosophical counseling was exhilarating, and the influence of that experience of immense value. However, when I tried to emulate the style of my teacher I only managed to appear and/or be aggressive. Wearing the comforting cloak of the devotee I was so masculine as I prostrated at the feet of the guru and cast myself in his play, comforted by the anonymity of the chorus. Beauvoir warns of settling for this space. "And, actually, it is not by increasing her worth as a human being that she will gain value in men's eyes; it is rather by modeling herself upon their dreams. When still inexperienced, she is not always aware of this fact. She may be as aggressive as the boys; she may try to make their conquest with a rough authority, a proud frankness; but this attitude almost surely dooms her to failure. All girls, from the most servile to the haughtiest, learn in time that to please they must abdicate."[6]

Fortunately for me this condition was not terminal and as the poultice of reason took hold and, with some trepidation I reverted to woman, I began to question domination and its value. In her paper "The Practice of Sartre's Philosophy in Philosophical Counseling and Existentialist Psychotherapy," Shlomit Schuster questions the authoritative approach: "If the personal, dominant convictions of the philosophical practitioner are authoritative and deny the counselee the freedom of developing his or her own views, such influence is to be rejected since it obstructs the development of authentic thought."[7]

Philosophical practice must support and nurture freedom of expression and value woman's way of being if it is to realize its own authenticity, as denying the sensibilities of the group called woman translates to distortion, thereby falling short of authenticity. A dramatic question hangs in the air: does the imposition of didactic hard-line tactics simply impose another straitjacket on the voice of woman? Hélène Cixous emphasizes in *The Laugh of the Medusa* the imprisonment of woman's voice: "Every woman has known the torment of getting up to speak. Her heart racing, at times lost for words, ground, and language slipping away-that's how daring a feat, how great a transgression it is for a woman to speak-even just to open her mouth-in public. A double distress, for even as she transgresses, her words fall almost away upon the deaf male ear, which hears in language only that which speaks in the masculine."[8]

The quest for freedom and authenticity in philosophical counseling will be compromised if the manipulation of power is manifest in the relationship between counselor and counselee. Participants committed to notions of freedom and authenticity have a greater opportunity of ensuring that dialogue and the *project* of self-reflection does not descend into a *project* in bad faith, that is; they do not become codependent nor restrictive, domineering nor manipulative but remain committed to the mutual application of liberty and a mutual interest in seeking an authentic self through the affirmation and demonstration of freedom. This mutual application of freedom is vital to the integrity of the counselor/counselee relationship because if the actions and expressions of the philosophical counselor are simply an expression of group doctrine, or an echo of the voice of the most dominant; the authentic voice of the individual fails to be heard. Beauvoir considers such forms as inauthentic and thereby not advancing toward freedom; they are projects in bad faith.

In viewing second sex status it is essential to recognize that a problem does exist and to acknowledge that many of the difficulties illuminated by Simone de Beauvoir in *The Second Sex* are still manifest and vigilance is required in addressing them. It is inaccurate to say that the struggles of woman have been won, for everywhere in all societies, social classes, industry and employment, economic enclaves, political and spiritual practice; clearly they have not. Negative discrimination toward woman is not a superficial phenomenon but a systemic non-application of symmetry. It is woman who lacks. It is woman who is defective in some manner. It is woman who must define herself by what she is not rather than by what she is. It is woman who is the Other, claims Beauvoir, and it is this Otherness that confirms a duality. "To decline to be the Other, to refuse to be a party to the deal—this would be to renounce all the advantages conferred upon them by their alliance with the superior caste."[9]

An uncomfortable example of this is the brutality residing within the soothing tone of the word 'domestic' in the term 'domestic violence.' This belies the ferocious nature of the actions of the self-anointed 'superior class' that is man, for it is this superior caste that describes and defines the broad environment. Woman as 'domestic' goddess creates 'domestic' bliss whilst invoking the 'domestic' brutality of the Gods of self-love, for it is man who writes the script and edits and re-writes the play at will. Members of this superior caste are constantly cast in lead roles while woman is restricted to the position of 'extra;' she will rarely appear in anything but crowd scenes; there are few lead roles for her. The advantage of this 'extra' work is that woman will always be required; she will always have a place albeit one conferred on her by where and how she places her allegiance. If she seeks to assert her own creativity, write her own script, edit her own life, renounce the position allotted to her, and break free from the crowd she will feel the consequences. Not only will the serious man (for woman is frivolous) interrogate her, but also it is possible that the crowd will turn on her for daring freedom.

The use of the 'interrogatory consultation' in philosophical counseling is to be avoided, for it limits the growth of personal freedom and thereby the quest for authenticity. According to Beauvoir. "Such interrogations put in question the very meaning of life, the life of each and of all. The so-called serious man is really futile, because he accepts ready-made justifications for his life: whereas a passionate and profound woman revises established values from moment to moment. She knows the constant tension of unsupported freedom; it puts her in constant danger; she can win or lose in an instant."[10] It is the anxiety and strain of escape from the enforced position of the Other, that woman must overcome in pursuit of freedom. This is no simple task for she must expel interrogation as a tool of the superior caste and install her own platform; one that no longer jolts from under her until she is lifeless, hanged once more for daring to speak as woman. Her own platform will support creativity, deliberation, rigor, desire; casting off the strictures of the repressive environment of the superior class. Michèle le Doeuff[11] warns of the prison of permissiveness, fidelity, and amateurism, the trifecta toward a project in bad faith. Le Doeuff claims the institution that is philosophy offers woman, through smiles and wiles, a place; she is permitted into the practice; she accepts with such gratitude for rarely is she permitted into the inner stable of the superior caste. However, she will never be the trainer just the apprentice to the master to whom she is so grateful: Her appreciation knows no bounds. The master offers a horse for practice, it may be Hegel; it may be Heidegger; and she pledges fidelity. There she remains straddled by the yoke of amateurism, choked, never to realize a stable of her own. There is no room for her, and no room to move.

Constrictive structures such as the hardline didactic model of philosophical counseling must be questioned particularly with regards to the sensibilities of woman. To fully incorporate woman, philosophical counseling must locate and develop a space between and inclusive of, rationality and emotion, feminism and poetry, images and metaphor, theatre and story, myth, legend, and desire, in the pursuit of freedom. With infectious laughter woman will fling open the shutters of the academy and scale independence and freedom. Julia Kristeva in her paper "The Reinvention of the Couple" writes of the most infectious causes of freedom. "And so the theme of freedom was conjugated and interpreted in very many ways, and also the mode of direction which, in my view, is finally what remains and is the most infectious: the imaginative mode of expression, literature, as an indicator of that presence of the private both in being in the world and in time."[12]

The story that is *The Second Sex* is both an example of and testimony to Beauvoir's existential ethics in practice, through which she undertakes an exhaustive biological examination of women: "But I deny that they establish for her a fixed and inevitable destiny. They are insufficient for setting up a hierarchy of the sexes; they fail to explain why woman is the Other; they do not condemn her to remain in this subordinate role for ever."[13]

A JUST STORY

Beauvoir's existentialist ethics are antidotes for a philosophical counseling that is propelled only by strict adherence to group doctrine; in contrast to the device of a *Just Story* that relies on transparency and grace, joy and wonder. A *Just Story* will illuminate the vital signs of authenticity, freedom, and bad faith focusing on client-directed desires and needs rather than the joust of the practice. Creating and sharing a *Just Story* is literature and thought in action; a temporal space for open dialogue that allows for the sensibilities of the individual. For a story to be justified for inclusion into a philosophical counseling session it will enlighten and enliven the narrative of the session while representing personal power in action, exploring never dominating. In this context the professional philosopher practitioner, in concert with the client, will explore the existential requirements of a just story that are necessary in the pursuit of freedom: for example for a story to be 'just' its content must apportion no blame to others or the Other. The counselor engages with the client in a deep inquiry of the links between freedom and the expression of freedom that is authenticity and reflects with the client on the question: How can the existent best ensure a life that is a project illustrative of, but not dependent on, these factors? Beauvoir illuminates the distinction between dependency and illustration and the critical importance of eradicating dependency that undermines freedom and authenticity and renders a project in bad faith, but supports illustration that represents freedom in action.

Three elements are required in tandem to constitute a *Just Story*. First, the story is one told by its teller for the purposes of self-reflection, self-understanding, and the furthering of self-knowledge. That is, the timbre of the story is justified by a significant motivation for enquiry rather than being just a story told for conversational purposes or to fulfill one's reciprocal verbal commitments. Secondly, a *Just Story* will present its teller in the most transparent way possible at the moment of telling. This does not imply or command self-derision, but a commitment to stripping away superfluous detail in the pursuit of freedom. And thirdly, it will provoke, as a consequence of the interaction between the teller and the receiver, thoughtfulness about the notion of freedom, the value of freedom, and the relationship these perspectives have to self-accomplishment.

With regards to the choice of a story, my view is that from whatever experiential realm a story comes it will necessarily suffer from observational constriction due to the impossibility of universal coverage of the subject of existence. This does not mean however, that stories lack value. What is of paramount importance is the motivation of the storyteller, which is to manifest their own freedom and not restrict the freedom of others. Motivation is vital because it exists without the help or hindrance of methodology, translation, or talent, and if considered allows for a less than perfectly or overtly expressed intention to be understood as authentic. Explicitly, I am thinking about asylum seekers with whom I have worked, who flee their homelands in the most desperate of circumstances. Occasionally they may not have the skills to read and/or write in their first language, nor speak in the language of the 'ruling class,' but there is no mistaking their intentions with regards to their application of and commitment to freedom and authenticity. Presenting the gift of a *Just Story* to a philosophical counseling session provides space for advancing collaboration while celebrating the ethics of authenticity as the worth of the counseled is honored and explored with intellectual rigor without domination. A *Just Story*, in concert with just dialogue, neither limits one's own freedom nor exploits another's but assists in the very personal task of pursuing self-fulfillment and preserving vitality. These stories and dialogues best provide rich terrain for enquiry and the edification of vital signs when guests are guided by the philosophical counselor, without projection, to the philosophical questions within the story. Practitioners will be ever mindful that to impose their own will or manner on the guest amounts to a restriction of liberty, which plunges the project into one in bad faith.

MOTIVATION

Diary entries made by Beauvoir in one of her autobiographical works *The Prime of Life* provide some insight into a philosophical space inhabited by Sartre and Beauvoir and raise questions regarding motivation, dependency, and the journey toward authenticity. "3 November 1940: Simone offers Jean-Paul her diary to read. He responds: Jean-Paul: You should expand your analysis of yourself. Simone: I would like to do so. I feel that my character has now set into a well-defined mould [sic]: I shall soon be thirty-two, and feel myself a mature woman—but what *sort* of woman? I wish I knew. For instance, in what way am I typically 'feminine,' and in what ways not? Generally speaking, what do I ask of life today, what expectations do I have of my intellect, where do I stand with regard to the world at large? If time permits, I shall study such problems in this notebook. Jean-Paul: . . . 5 November 1940, Simone: I've decided not to undertake the task of self-analysis we discussed two days ago. I want to finish my novel. Feel the need to live actively, not sit down and take stock of myself. Jean-Paul: (He vanishes into the night)."[14]

In the dialogue above Beauvoir offers what might be interpreted as a *Just Story*, which includes appropriate questions for a philosophical counseling session. Furthermore, the dialogue serves as a stimulus for reflection on procedural elements of a consult such as: What qualities, if any, of a *Just Story* does the dialogue display? How, if at all, is attention to the notions of freedom and authenticity demonstrated in this dialogue? What, if any, is the evidence of bad faith in this interchange? What elements, if any, indicate an authoritative approach? How is generosity expressed in this dialogue? What motivates the interlocutors?

In *The Second Sex*, Beauvoir engages in a detailed examination of the motivation of five storytellers, Montherlant, D. H. Lawrence, Claudel, Breton, and Stendhal, with all failing to be given the Beauvoir stamp of authenticity. "When he describes woman, each writer describes his general ethics and the special idea he has of himself; and in her he often betrays also the gap between his worldview and his egotistical dreams."[15] It is these 'egotistical dreams' that cause Stendhal, the frontrunner of the five for the place of good faith merchant, to lose ground and for his project to ultimately be declared in bad faith. Stendhal is a great lover of woman; what he loves most about her is her authenticity. He supports and nurtures this joyous love in his writing and actively pursues notions of liberty, freedom and, ultimately, transcendence. Beauvoir writes of Stendhal's devotion: "These women are, quite simply, alive; they know that the source of true values is not in external things but in human hearts. This gives its charm to the world they live in: they banish *ennui* by the simple fact of their presence, with their dreams, their desires, their pleasures, their emotions, their ingenuities."[16]

The defining factor that undermines the purity of Stendhal's quest for freedom is his dependence on woman for his own transcendence. He looks to her beauty, her pure motivation, her authenticity, and freedom to help drive his *ennui* away. He is not able and/or willing to define his own freedom. His dependency limits the growth of his freedom as well as that of woman caught in the cycle of escape and capture, caves and shadows.

CONCLUSION

The integrity of philosophical counseling is consolidated when practiced in accordance with its primary element, philosophy, and is cognizant of the sensibilities of woman, resisting bondage and exploitation. The existentialism of Simone de Beauvoir as represented in *The Second Sex* provides powerful tools in this quest. The necessity for participants to seek an authentic self through the affirmation of freedom is paramount and the application of freedom is vital to the integrity of the counselor/counselee relationship. In creating a practical device, a *Just Story*, I have provided a structure that enables the relationship between existentialism, philosophical counseling, and the discourse of woman to flourish. I have asserted that for a story to be identified as a *Just Story* it must meet three requirements. The first requirement is that it must stimulate self-reflection, self-knowledge, and enquiry. Secondly, it must value and display transparency as a vehicle toward freedom and authenticity: and finally it must engage the teller and receiver in an interactive process of thoughtfulness about freedom, the value of freedom, and their connection with self-accomplishment. Furthermore, I have applied Beauvoir's search for clarity and understanding of what it is to be a woman to the practice of philosophical counseling, concluding that practitioners in this field must be ever mindful of her position. The philosophical counseling environment must recognize the nature of woman's discourse, and value varying forms of expressive and receptive language and communication. In questioning a didactic approach to philosophical counseling I do not censure but draw attention to the limitations of conformity to just one particular mode of practice and provide insights into styling possibilities for a philosophical counseling outfitted, without constriction, in garments from Simone de Beauvoir's armoire. In consideration of the knowledge that her armoire is not so much an armoire, as a warehouse brimming with the greatest range of threads, the choice of existential garments has been limited to freedom, authenticity, and bad faith. In dressing philosophical counseling in Beauvoir's garments I have made judgments about fit and style and in so doing explored possibilities for future development and conclude that the existentialist ethics of Beauvoir as expressed in her epic story *The Second Sex* are a good fit for philosophical counseling and that a *Just Story* can assist in the illumination of the vital signs of authenticity, freedom, and bad faith.

Wearing her strength, she rests softly, nesting light with fire. She has a thousand stories, endless stories to share. So often displaced, discarded as an empty vessel impaled and distorted, the sand washes over her. She tries to breathe with all the energy she can muster, to tell her story, but she is worn down by the waves: silenced once more.

NOTES

1. Simone de Beauvoir, *The Second Sex,* trans. Constance Borde and Sheila Malovany-Chevellier (London: Jonathan Cape, 2009).
2. Luce Irigaray, "Is the Subject of Science Sexed?" trans. Carol Mastrangelo Bové, *Hypatia* 2 (1987):3, 80.
3. Ursula Tidd, *Simone de Beauvoir: Gender and Testimony* (Cambridge: Cambridge University Press, 1999), 171.
4. Julia Kristeva, "The Reinvention of the Couple," *Diogenes* 54 (2007): 216, 31.
5. de Beauvoir, *The Second Sex*, 253.
6. Ibid., 333.
7. Shlomit C. Schuster, "The Practice of Sartre's Philosophy in Philosophical Counseling and Existential Psychotherapy," *The Jerusalem Philosophical Quarterly* 44 (1995):1, 101.
8. Hélène Cixous, *The Laugh of the Medusa,* trans. Keith Cohen and Paula Cohen, 876.
9. de Beauvoir, *The Second Sex*, 253.
10. Ibid.
11. Michèle Le Doeuff, *Hipparchia's Choice: An Essay Concerning Woman's Philosophy etc.* Trans. Trista Selous (Oxford: SUNY Press, 1994).
12. Kristeva, *The Reinvention of the Couple*, 216.
13. Simone de Beauvoir, *The Second Sex*. Trans. H. M. Parshley. 1953, 60.
14. Simone de Beauvoir, *The Prime of Life*. Trans. Peter Green. Penguin, Middlesex 2001, 34.
15. de Beauvoir, *The Second Sex*. 1953, 259.
16. Ibid., 249.

BIBLIOGRAPHY

de Beauvoir, Simone. *The Second Sex.* Translated by Constance Borde and Sheila Malovany-Chevellier. London: Jonathan Cape, 2009.

de Beauvoir, Simone. *The Prime of Life*. Translated by Peter Green. Middlesex: Penguin, 2001.

Cixous, Helene. *The Laugh of the Medusa.* Translated by Keith Cohen and Paula Cohen. Chicago: The University of Chicago Press, 2009.

Irigaray, Luce. *Is the Subject of Science Sexed?* Translated by Carol Mastrangelo Bové. *Hypatia*, Vol. 2 (1987): 3.

Kristeva, Julia. "The Reinvention of the Couple." *Diogenes* 54 (2007): 216, 29-–34.

Le Doeuff, Michèle. *Hipparchia's Choice: An Essay Concerning Woman's Philosophy etc.* Translated by Trista Selous. Oxford: SUNY Press,1994.

Schuster, Shlomit C. "The Practice of Sartre's Philosophy in Philosophical Counseling and Existential Psychotherapy," *The Jerusalem Philosophical Quarterly* 44 (1995):1, 99–114.

Tidd, Ursula. *Simone de Beauvoir: Gender and Testimony*. Cambridge: Cambridge University Press, 1999.

Chapter Thirteen

Young Women and the Strengthening of One's Moral Character

Marie-France Lebouc

Peter is a young European man.[1] As our interview progresses, he strikes me as different, saying things that I find myself surprised to hear. The last piece of a teaching assignment that will be described here, this one-on-one interview dating back to May 2013 became a turning point for me. Thanks to it, I realized that, in reaction to an assignment I gave students in my business ethics and international aid ethics classes over the years, I had come to expect some topics and discourses as typical from men and others as typical from women.

This immediately calls for two remarks. First, I do not pretend that what I am about to discuss here are the only topics or types of discourse for which men and women's approach to ethical self-discovery differ. Those are merely the topics for which I was able to see that they do. Second, I do not wish to suggest that there is any sort of essential feminine/masculine divide that would explain the differences I observed. Rather, I usually hear one type of discourse on the part of young women and another one on the part of young men, with notable exceptions to both, such as Peter. It is these exceptions that helped me realize that there was such a thing as what had become, to my ears, a normal gendered discourse. At the same time, these exceptions are also the elements that point to my own expectations as an educator and as a highly educated and privileged middle-aged woman in arguably the most gender-equal part of North America. Hence, what follows constitutes a narrative of my own discovery of women's moral voices as well as a narrative of the discovery of my own voice.

I teach applied ethics in a business school where we train students in the management of private businesses, public organizations, not-for-profit organizations, social enterprises, and non-governmental organizations working in international development and humanitarian aid. Our programs put a strong emphasis on social responsibility. In the ethics courses I provide, I see it as my responsibility to help students work on strengthening their moral character. Indeed, while they may learn how to write a code of ethics or how to implement a compliance program within their organizations, it is only a strong moral backbone that will help them resist the many slippery slopes of the workplace and face difficult moral dilemmas. Such as life is, we know that morally demanding times do come, and I want students to be strong enough to stand their moral ground and be the person they wish to be when faced with ethical challenges.

To do so, I have designed a teaching assignment aimed at helping students work on strengthening their moral character. In presenting the assignment to students, I try to not differentiate between male and female students. I ask students of both genders to do exactly the same thing. However, an experience of several years has shown me that male and female students react differently. It is this difference that I will try to explore here.

I will first explain what the assignment consists of. I will then describe the school of ethics it is rooted in. Finally, I will explain how female students react to the assignment and how they differ from their male counterparts.

AN EXERCISE IN DISCOVERING ONE'S MORAL CHARACTER

Conventionally conceived, ethics is mainly a matter of principled reflection, with Kantian (or deontological) deliberation, and Utilitarian (or consequence-oriented) deliberation being the two main models of thinking. The former is centered on the moral duties that need to be enacted, whereas the latter focuses on finding the action that will optimize consequences.

However, as Gilligan has been in a position to show, principled reasoning is not superior to other forms of moral thinking.[2] The problem outlined by several authors, especially in the field of ethics of care, is that principled reasoning does not guarantee superior results.[3] On the contrary, it serves to separate morality from emotions and imagination.[4]

Centuries before ethics of care, Greek philosophers put forward the role of virtue in ethics. While principled ethics is about finding the right action or behavior in a particular situation, virtue ethics is about the agent becoming a better person through solving this situation and all the situations that follow. In virtue ethics, the good life (εὐδαιμονία, *eudemonia*) is not equivalent to the decontextualized application of moral principles. Rather, it emerges from the repetitive search for moral balance in every situation. That is why, in the

Nicomachean Ethics, Aristotle compares virtue to spring: "For one swallow does not make a summer, nor does one day; and so too one day, or a short time, does not make a man blessed and happy."[5]

Aristotle depicts what we call "moral character" as moral excellence or moral virtue. He writes that "moral virtue comes about as a result of habit, whence also its name (ethics) is one that is formed by a slight variation from the word ἦθος (*ethos*, 'habit')."[6] Simply learning about philosophical concepts, for instance, has little if anything to do with developing character or virtue. He even mocks those who think that the mere accumulation of concepts will make them good persons. Character or virtue only comes through the practice of good and just actions. To Aristotle, the person with a virtuous or strong moral character is the person who does virtuous actions and, symmetrically, the person who does virtuous actions becomes a person with virtuous or strong moral character.

I deem this view of ethics critical to the presence of morally strong and virtuous persons in the workplace. To encourage such thought, I introduce students to a tough question: Where are you at in terms of virtue or character and where do you want to be or go?

To do so, back in 2007, I developed an individual exercise based on introspection and dialogue around the students' moral values. It is an experiment in self-discovery, designed for students with no prior knowledge of ethics and with little interest in anything philosophical. As mentioned earlier, the instructions are identical and presented in a strictly similar manner to male and female students.[7]

The rules are as follows: over the fifteen-week semester, students must keep a log of various situations they are involved in that present ethical issues. These may range from simply giving up their seat for an elderly person on the bus to more existential choices. For example, one female student chose to record her deliberations on whether or not to apply for an interesting marketing job at a tobacco factory. As most students discover over the course of the semester, small and apparently unimportant situations hold ethical challenges that help them understand their moral character just as well as big decisions. Therefore, they needn't wait until something critical happens in their lives; everyday events are just as interesting as crises.

As per the instructions I give, the situations they choose to describe can be work-related or not. I do not make it a requirement that what they record be strictly something that happened in their workplace. Here again, the rationale behind this is to let them find and explore any situation that lends itself to learning and increasing self-awareness. As I will explain below, there is a difference in the interpretation male and female students give to this particular instruction.

I prefer students to be able to work on current situations. The constant scrutiny of their present daily lives enhances their ethical awareness, that is, their capacity to detect ethical problems in situations as they unfold. However, over the years, many students have asked permission to work on past situations that, in some respect, they felt were still unresolved. So, as long as they also included current situations, I have accepted past situations.

Students are asked to start their logs as early as possible—during the first or second week of the semester—and must write at least twice a week. Therefore, they have to keep these logbooks during at least thirteen weeks. The semester ends with a mandatory one-on-one meeting with me where I help each person unravel what they have learned about themselves. It offers us an opportunity to revisit every conceptual notion presented in class and in the assigned readings, and actively use them to describe and understand the student's moral character. It is important to note that I do not ask to read students' logs. They bring them to our meetings so as to be able to discuss the entries they choose to share with me.[8] Through dialogue, I help them review the items they analyzed as shown in the list below.

Each log entry must contain two types of information. First, students must write a paragraph simply describing the situation; this is for memory purposes only, and will be used during our one-on-one conversation that will take place several weeks later. They then write a half-page analysis of that situation. The analysis must be centered on themselves and tackle some of the following elements:

- personal moral values they think were involved (or moral duties or principles);
- personal values they enacted in the situation;
- if they are aware of having used a form of moral reasoning, what type of reasoning it was;
- the degree to which they could put their ethical decision into action or, if there was no formal decision made, the degree to which their actions (including discourse) in this situation were in line with the moral image they project (or their espoused values);
- other elements such as whether they were immediately aware of ethical issues, any kind of ethical competencies they displayed (picked from a list studied in class), and other notions seen in class.

Of course, analyses in log entries made during weeks one or two are far less complex than what students are able to write in the last part of the semester. Many students ask for interim meetings or send me questions via email, as they want to make sure they understand what I expect from them. Indeed, it is a very unusual type of assignment for a business school. Many students express their discomfort at having to place themselves at the center of their preoccupations.

METHODOLOGY

What I present below is a reflection over a teaching experiment that began in September 2007. Ever since, I have supervised at least one undergraduate group and one graduate group per year, on some years two undergraduate courses and two graduate ones. The number of students per class can vary greatly from fifteen to forty-five. Over the years, the composition of the groups has evolved in favor of women, as in many other academic courses. Whereas in 2007, men and women were on average equally represented, women now outnumber men in the ethics courses I deliver by a proportion of about two-thirds. Participants are usually in their twenties, early twenties for the undergraduate students, late twenties, sometimes early thirties for graduate students. A few students are older, up to their forties and fifties and, of course, their reactions to the assignment are clearly marked by this longer life experience. Here, I will focus on the young men and women I have met.

To stay relevant over the years, I have adapted and changed nearly all aspects of the ethics courses I deliver based on student feedback. Yet, to my own surprise, the moral character log has remained. In their course reviews, a majority of students declared it to be a good way to learn about themselves—although not necessarily always a pleasant or easy experience [9] The following sections are taken from the notes I have made over the years when rethinking about how the classes had gone and what needed to be changed.

I will not quote any verbatim transcripts of the interviews I had with students. In order to allow students to feel comfortable enough to choose and analyze *any* situation they consider productive to further the knowledge of their own moral character, I give them a written assurance that everything they will write and say, and everything I will read, hear, or deduct from our conversations will be treated with the strictest confidentiality. Therefore, I have never collected transcripts. Indeed, when I started this teaching experiment, I had no intention of making it the basis for an empirical study. I did not suspect how much one day I would want to discuss the results of this experience. My personal life history—that of a white woman growing up in a well-off and well-educated family in a very gender-equitable country—certainly explains how I could initially be unconscious of a phenomenon that I gradually became aware of: a difference in the way young women and young men react to the assignment I give them and go about completing it. Thus, what I present below is the product of multiple observations and unsystematic notes I made about that phenomenon.

FINDINGS

Private and Professional Selves

It has been shown by Gilligan that, when we listen to girls, we discover that instead of thinking of moral dilemmas exclusively in terms of principled reasoning, it is possible to conceive of them in terms of relationships to be preserved.[10] The young women I have guided in this exercise did not see themselves as isolated beings confronted with a moral problem. On the contrary, they based their analyses of themselves on what Gilligan calls "a central insight, that self and other are interdependent."[11] I think that this fundamental understanding finds a corollary in the way young women tackle the discovery of their moral character.

Young men I have interviewed usually preferred to focus on professional or academic situations. Yet, as mentioned above, they are not required to limit their examination to work-related situations; they may include examples or situations from any sphere of their lives. Occasionally, they may have chosen to analyze a personal or private situation: a negotiation with their landlord, an argument in the shared kitchens at the students' residences, and so on. However, in the examples that I have heard, these young men often presented an account in which they occupied a central position and stood in opposition to someone else.

Young women take the instruction about private life more literally. It would be very difficult to give an exhaustive account of all the types of situations I have heard young women report for this assignment. Many of them draw from their personal lives first, sometimes even choosing to not talk about work during the final interview. Their families, life partners, and friends form the central topics, not their jobs.

It would be erroneous to conclude that women's lives revolve first around the private sphere. The young women I meet have strong professional ambitions and they work hard so that these ambitions can come true. Rarely do they sound worried about the possibility of carrying through with both a professional career and a meaningful private life. They have a good sense of what they like and what they want to achieve professionally. They will have a career; they know.

That is where the corollary to interdependency appears. Most of the young women I've worked with on this assignment seem to embrace the notion that we are a unique moral or ethical person, in the sense that we hold the same set of values and beliefs, and show some moral character across the various spheres of our lives. The private sphere and the strong relationships found in it form the roots of this unique and consistent moral character. Therefore, instead of focusing on who they are at work, young women prefer to examine who they are without restrictions.

I am left with questions as to why young men do not make the same choice. Is it because they are shyer and see the barriers between private and work lives as a way to preserve an intimacy they do not wish to share with me? Is it because they think that work-related situations are the most relevant in the business-school context and will thus offer the best opportunity for self-discovery?

The ethnic and cultural background of the few male students who talked about their families may give a hint that culture could be a factor to consider. With the notable exception of Peter, the student I talked about in the introduction, the others were of Black African, North African, or Middle Eastern descent. These are cultures where interdependency is stressed and valued; so it should not be surprising to hear some young male students integrate it into their understanding of who they are and what their moral character is.

Bringing the Body into the Discourse

Another topic on which young men and women I interviewed tend to differ is the mention of their own bodies.

Few young men actually talked about their bodies. When they did, most of them restricted their remarks to training, gaining muscular mass, sometimes losing weight, seldom if ever losing fat. The situations they chose to analyze were used to discuss their experiences with self-discipline, be it in a positive or a negative way, for instance a lack of willpower to attend the gym three times weekly as they wished they could. Whenever they talked about their body, they gave the impression that they maintained it because it helped them do things. For instance, one young man explained how his rather small body frame was balanced by surprising agility, allowing him to have the upper hand in a fight with another student. Overall, I got the notion that, to some extent, they did objectify their own bodies. I did not sense the same kind of intense, even conflicting, relationship that I and so many other women seem to have with their own bodies. I do not wish to convey by that remark that young men are in any way more satisfied and less critical of their bodies than women are. However, I hardly know from this teaching assignment whether they are or not. From what I have been in a position to hear over the years, if and when they talk about their bodies, they do not do it in the same fashion women do.

A large proportion of the women I interviewed talk about their body, even if not all of them do. The most striking element however is not the number of women who addressed that topic but what they said and how. It would be a platitude to state that young women objectify their bodies and that many think poorly of themselves in terms of their looks. Nevertheless, surprisingly few young women focused on that aspect of their body for their moral character log. The majority of women who talked about their body did it in relation to other topics.

The first, although somewhat obvious, issues many young women talked about were pregnancy and children. Some of them mentioned the approximate time of their lives when they wanted to have children ("very young," "when I get my degree," "when I get my first real job," "before I'm 40," even "never," etc.). It is something I have seldom heard a young man express. Usually, the young men who talked about having children were already fathers or were about to become one. A regular discussion of parenthood by these young men would focus on a concern clearly expressed by a young father last semester: he was wondering how he ought to act to present his son with a good role model. I also met a very small although extremely interesting sample of young men who chose to spend time writing and talking about fatherhood. They did so in connection to specific cultural factors. Most of them were from Northern Africa, the Middle East, or sub-Saharan Africa. These boys wanted to have children; they strongly desired to become fathers and were quite certain they would be good ones. Yet they voiced concerns that they could perhaps not become the fathers they wanted to be, since in their birth country, society, and even their close relatives may not let them be as present for their child as they would like. One African student stated that his views on parenting were better accepted in Canada than in his native country and was wondering how he could go back to the traditional role set for him once his studies were over. The interesting element is that their analyses about fatherhood were centered on care for the children as a series of concrete actions such as feeding, changing diapers, or rocking a baby in one's arms—not simply caring psychologically, but using one's body to provide care for a child. However, out of the dozens of students I have had the opportunity to interview, less than ten male students have decided to speak about trespassing gender roles in parenthood to talk about it in the terms I have just described.[12]

On the contrary, parenthood, giving birth, pregnancy, miscarriage, or abortion were very much part of women's reflections on their moral character. Mothers spoke about their children and mothers-to-be spoke about their children-to-be. An extreme example was provided by a female student in her early twenties who, due to a particular medical condition, was given by her doctors a maximum of two years to have a child before she was to undergo a hysterectomy. The academic assignment became an opportunity for her to reflect on existential choices: Did she want to be a mother? If yes, did she want to be a biological mother? And what about a father? These existential questions made up the whole of her log and of the subsequent interview.

A few female students—an annual average of two or three—chose to talk about their decision to have an abortion, either in the recent weeks or months before our final interview, or sometimes a few years back. Their motives for putting an end to their pregnancy may have varied, but bad timing is certainly the most frequently cited. These young women reported how they carried on a long and complex deliberation prior to making their decision, even if the decision was made at a time when they did not know the names or characteristics of the type of moral reasoning they conducted; they reported having taken into consideration consequences, moral principles, as well as what kind of person and mother they wanted to be.

Talking about abortion is always a very sensitive moment in an interview. My role is limited to helping the young woman facing me use this experience as a way to know more about herself and her moral character. I confess it has been so overwhelming sometimes that I took refuge behind questions about the deliberation process, about what her gut feeling at the time was telling her, and so on. At times, it has been challenging for me to do so because my own understanding of what would have been the right decision to make in that situation may have differed from the student's own choice. However, since those have always been retrospective discussions, I believe I have always done my best not to lead these young women to doubt that the choice they made was right for them at that time, and not to throw them into moral and psychological turmoil. From what I heard, none of these young women had made this decision lightly; they all reported heavy existential self-questioning, sometimes with their partner and sometimes even with their relatives (often their mother). Even when the abortion had taken place years before, some still wished to take advantage of this assignment to reflect upon it. Just as Gilligan has noted, the young women I have listened to tried to make sure they acted responsibly.[13] Of course if a woman was taking it lightly, I suppose she would not mention it in her log. Those who chose to mention it saw abortion as a critical moment in their lives, a moment worth re-examining in order to understand their present moral character.

It is with very discernible regret that I say I am still waiting for a male student to explain that and to what extent his girlfriend having an abortion was a defining moment for his moral character.

Other female students, having grown up in war zones, reported having lived very difficult experiences like harassment or even rape. One day, one girl in her late twenties explained that although unacceptable, these things that happened to her during wartime were to be expected. They were part of what had been 'normal' at that time of her life. I was struck by her use of the word as, given my own life experience, I cannot conceive of the 'normalcy' of rape and violence. Living through these dreadful episodes as well as others such as the loss of family members and responsibility of taking care of their relatives at a very young age, of course, made these women the moral individuals they are now. Even when not recorded in writing in their logs, these experiences were shared with me during the interview to contextualize a different situation or decision they had chosen to analyze. These particular young women showed a tremendous amount of resilience, and it should come as no surprise that it is without anger or self-pity that these episodes were mentioned. Instead, they were milestones in a life that made them who they are.

In comparison, only once has a male student explained to me that he had grown up in a difficult situation—in this instance, in a refugee camp—and briefly touched on the hardships of his youth. Others, whom I knew came from places where they were confronted with war and violence, held a more political discourse, sharing much less of their personal ordeal.

Other female students discussed illnesses that had temporarily or definitively transformed their lives. In one instance, it was a congenital kidney condition that limited her options in life such as her ability to travel to certain countries. In several other instances, students reported problems of mental health such as burnouts or depression.[14] In another example, the student decided to talk about her eating disorder and how the assignment had brought her to realize she urgently needed to seek professional help, which she had secured by the final interview. I have met with male students who were living with or had previously suffered from medical conditions and mentioned it in informal conversations. However, none of them chose to discuss their condition or its impact on their life within the context of this academic assignment. So, in the case of many young women I met, once again, taking their body into consideration seemed a natural or normal path to learn more about their moral character.

Expressing Doubt, Accepting Equivocity

There is a third aspect in which I have found young men and young women to differ: the way they face and express doubt and ambivalence, what I will describe below as equivocity.

During the one-on-one interview, many young women, and even older ones for that matter, expressed doubt. They did not seem embarrassed to confess not knowing immediately what to do or what to think about a situation. I am not suggesting that ambivalence was not difficult for them, but rather that they considered it within the realms of possibility and not necessarily as unproductive. There was an almost palpable anxiety when they wanted to arrive at a decision that may affect others or when they commented on a decision that did affect others. In an odd way, it was Peter's discourse—the young man I mentioned in the introduction—which highlighted the importance of that element of ambivalence.

When listening to Peter, I suddenly became aware that his voice was not in tune with other men's voices I had grown used to hearing. He did not claim to know right away what to do, but rather agreed that he would have to deliberate, ponder things, ask his conscience, his best friends, and so on. I have been equally surprised to hear a few young women very convinced and positive that they knew immediately what was to be done in situations that I thought were complex. I soon came to realize that this attitude really annoyed me, as I thought them less self-confident than cocksure and questionless. For instance, one girl in her early twenties astonished me when asserting that, in case of a conflict, the right thing to do was always to confront the other or, were she the only witness to a conflict, to force a confrontation between the parties. She insisted on the "always," explaining that it was what her parents had taught her, and ignoring what she had been told in conflict resolution classes. A few moments later, she insisted that intellectual superiority was a moral value and that, therefore, the higher the university degree a person held, the worthier that person and their opinions would be. Again, she told me that was what her parents had taught her. I was deeply irritated by the fact that she would not question what she had been taught; she would not be ambivalent and withstand doubt. She would have an immediate and decontextualized knowledge of what to do and jump directly from there to action. Yet, as underlined by Arendt, the capacity to raise questions is absolutely fundamental to the capacity to make moral decisions.[15]

The young female student I have referred to in the above paragraph made me understand that equivocity is different than doubt. Contrary to the latter, that carries negative connotations, equivocity is a positive phenomenon. It means that several voices coexist and therefore several stories may be told and several accounts may be given of a situation. Which one can be said to be legitimate? It seems as if, contrary to what Weick claims, not all individuals rush to solve this question.[16] I have become accustomed to men trying to move rapidly through it, hence my surprise when listening to Peter. Young women, for their part, seem to be able to face equivocity for a longer moment. The ones I interviewed normally took a moment to consider it. I see that capacity as a net gain rather than a loss: as they are socialized to take others into account and preserve relationships, women gain the ability to perceive the coexistence of several voices and weigh the legitimacy of each one, even at the risk of lingering before making a decision, and seeming timid and irresolute.

Do men doubt less? Are they simply shyer when it comes to expressing ambivalence? Is it possible that they perceive equivocation as only negative? Unfortunately, I do not have an answer to those questions.

CONCLUSION

Feminist researchers in ethics have established that women oftentimes understand the world in terms of relationships to be preserved and do not resort to *only* principled reasoning as the way to go about ethical situations. The main finding of the teaching experiment I report here is a confirmation that this "network view" has a deep impact on the way young women approach work on their own moral character. When placing themselves in the spotlight for the purpose of knowing themselves better, many of them do not erase and ignore the bonds that tie them to others, especially dear ones. On the contrary, their virtue, or moral character, grows out of these bonds. It is also discernible when they talk about their body, although maybe in a less obvious manner. They do not refer to their body as a physical extension of their selves. More accurately, they present their body as the mediator for a number of relationships, be it with a baby or with an aggressor. Again, when expressing their own doubts, women do so because they take into account the points of view of others.

In the *Nicomachean Ethics*, Aristotle explains the role of true friendship (φιλία, *philia*) and then of true friendship for oneself (φιλαυτία, *philautia*) in the strengthening of one's moral character. Although scholars do not unanimously agree on definitions of these notions, in class I do not delve into the debates surrounding *philia* and *philautia.* Rather, I try to give students an idea of friendship that would show them a practical way to strengthen their character. Therefore I settled on using Konstan's definition: "Philia [. . .] has two uses. In one sense, it coincides with philein and refers to an altruistic wish for the good of the other; in another, it names the state of affairs that obtains between philoi, which requires that each philos have the corresponding wish for the other."[17]

Here, altruism and reciprocity are of the essence. We must add that the building of such a bond takes time and there is no φιλία (*philia*) or friendship that is not inscribed in duration. Finally, as Aristotle puts it: "the friendship of good men is good, being augmented by their companionship; and they are thought to become better too by their activities and by improving each other."[18] This means that friendship results in the betterment of friends and the reciprocal strengthening of their moral characters.

As already mentioned, in the *Nicomachean Ethics*, Aristotle uses φιλία as the model for another critical form of friendship: φιλαυτία (*philautia*)[19] or friendship for oneself. Learning to be a friend for another teaches one to be a good friend for oneself. Aristotle writes:

> Now each of these [qualities and products of friendship] is true of the good man's relation to himself. [. . .] And such a man wishes to live with himself; for he does so with pleasure, since the memories of his past acts are delightful and his hopes for the future are good, and therefore pleasant.[20]

Friendship for oneself brings about self-betterment and the strengthening of one's moral character, in a manner identical to friendship for another. It allows one to walk a thin line between self-leniency and self-condemnation, the line of self-acceptance.

Presented thus, φιλαυτία is a form of care for oneself, a relationship where one is concerned with providing that which is good for oneself. It is a mindset that would seem to come easily to most women, given their skills at envisioning the world as a net of relationships.

Nevertheless, young women I interviewed showed difficulties, sometimes tremendous ones, in being friends with themselves. Whereas they could spontaneously see the importance of others in their lives and how strong bonds to others helped them build a resilient moral character, the importance of their own selves and the necessity to wish themselves the same good they wished others did not seem easy to achieve. As a result, common conduct for many of these young women was to forget about themselves and put others first. I have met others with diametrically opposed behaviors, who confused attending to the superficial needs fostered in contemporary Western society (pleasure or short-term gratifications in particular) with care for oneself. Gilligan explained that women's moral posture seems to always fluctuate between abnegation or responsibility for others and what they fear may be considered as egotism, which is, putting a positive focus on themselves.[21] Therefore, although they have all the key elements in hand to become true friends with themselves, they may still find it extremely difficult. It could be hypothesized that this is the case because they do not seem to be taught how to deeply care for themselves in the way they learn to care for others. It could also be that their moral character is not strong enough yet, because they are young and not sufficiently aware of themselves. Therefore, strengthening their moral character could be the key to enabling them to dare to be their best friends and better care for themselves.

The good I think this course assignment does is to show young women how they are holding all the cards. The thirteen-week log and the final one-on-one interview help them understand how empowering it is to be able to put one's good deeds and the not so good ones in perspective. It amounts to giving oneself another chance, something a best friend would do. Another chance is a chance to do better and, since virtue is a *habitus*, strengthening one's moral character implies, as Aristotle suggests, trying again and again.

NOTES

1. His name has been changed.
2. Carol Gilligan, *In a Different Voice: Psychological Theory and Women's Development* (Cambridge, Mass.: Harvard University Press, 1982).
3. Gilligan, *In a Different Voice*; Nel Noddings, *Caring, a Feminine Approach to Ethics & Moral Education* (Berkeley: University of California Press, 1984); and Patricia Benner, *Expertise in Nursing Practice: Caring, Clinical Judgment, and Ethics* (New York: Springer, 1996).

4. See in particular Randy S. Parker, "Nurses' stories: The search for a relational ethics of care," *Advances in Nursing Science* 13(1990):1, 31–40.

5. Aristotle, *Nicomachean Ethics*, ed. William David Ross (Kitchener, ON: Batoche Books, 1999), Book I,7.

6. Ibid., Book II, 1.

7. Some students can opt out of this assignment for mental health reasons since more and more students present mental health problems such as burnouts, depression, or strong anxiety. An introspective assignment such as this can clearly enhance these problems and, in some cases, I only accept the participation of a student with an authorization from a mental health specialist who has known the student for some time. In one case, a student has chosen to go along with the assignment and she and her therapist included it in her therapy.

8. The interview is based upon my commitment to discuss only what the student in front of me is willing or comfortable enough to discuss, and upon my pledge to respect confidentiality (which they have in writing since the beginning of the semester). Of course not all the students regularly write in their logs twice a week for thirteen weeks as asked. Some do far less and yet are able to find some sort of benefit from the little they have done. Only once in seven years have I had to ask to see one student's logbook because I suspected, and turned out to be right in doing so, that that person had not kept a log at all and was inventing situations for the interview.

9. Consequently, in August 2009, I have decided to attend a workshop of the American Philosophical Practitioners Association (APPA) to learn about better ways to guide and support students in this exercise through philosophical counseling.

10. Gilligan, *In a Different Voice.*

11. Ibid., 74.

12. There is an interesting parallel to draw with the fact that it is male students of the same cultural origin that spoke about their relationships to their families as stated in the previous section. Although, this time, rather than using traditional values, they confronted them.

13. Gilligan, *In a Different Voice.*

14. Those were students who had ceased medical and psychological treatment over twelve months prior to the beginning of the semester. As mentioned in note 4 above, in one instance, the student and her psychotherapist used the assignment as a therapeutic aid.

15. Hannah Arendt, *Eichmann in Jerusalem: a Report on the Banality of Evil* (New York: Viking Press, 1963).

16. Karl Weick, *Sensemaking in Organizations*. Thousand Oaks: Sage Publications, 1995.

17. David Konstan, "Aristotle on Love and Friendship." *Schole: Ancient Philosophy and the Classical Tradition* 2(2008): 2, 212.

18. Aristotle, *Nic. Ethics*, Book IX, 12.

19. θιλαυτία (*philautía*) is the compound of φιλία (*philía*) and αὐτός (*auotós*, 'one's own').

20. Ibid., Book IX, 4.

21. Gilligan, *In a Different Voice*.

BIBLIOGRAPHY

Arendt, Hannah. *Eichmann in Jerusalem: A Report on the Banality of Evil*. New York: Viking Press, 1963.

Aristotle. *Nicomachean Ethics*. Translated by William David Ross. Kitchener, ON: Batoche Books, 1999.

Benner, Patricia. *Expertise in Nursing Practice: Caring, Clinical Judgment, and Ethics*. New York: Springer, 1996.

Gilligan, Carol. *In a Different Voice: Psychological Theory and Women's Development*. Cambridge, Mass.: Harvard University Press, 1982.

Konstan, David. "Aristotle on Love and Friendship." *Schole: Ancient Philosophy and the Classical Tradition* 2(2008): 2, 207–212.

Noddings, Nel. *Caring, a Feminine Approach to Ethics & Moral Education*. Berkeley: University of California Press, 1984.

Parker, Randy S. "Nurses' stories: The search for a relational ethics of care." *Advances in Nursing Science* 13(1990):1, 31–40.
Weick, Karl. *Sensemaking in Organizations*. Thousand Oaks: Sage Publications, 1995.

Chapter Fourteen

Conversations with Women

M. G. Piety

PSYCHOTHERAPY AND PHILOSOPHY

"The talking cure" was an expression coined by Bertha Pappenheim (better known by the pseudonym Anna O.) for her therapy with Joseph Breuer, one of the founders of modern psychoanalytic theory. She gave it this name because it centered on conversation. The mere act of discussing her neurotic symptoms with Breuer, she discovered, had a therapeutic effect. Freud liked Pappenheim's expression and hence also occasionally used it to refer to his own method of psychoanalysis. Unfortunately, Breuer's treatment of Pappenheim was not nearly as successful as both he and Freud claimed.[1] Pappenheim was actually institutionalized *after* Breuer had purportedly cured her. Fortunately, she eventually recovered and became a distinguished social worker and advocate of women's rights.

What went wrong with Pappenheim's 'treatment?' Was it that talking was not actually so therapeutic as she had, at first, supposed? Or could the problem have been the nature of her "conversations" with Breuer? Breuer, like Freud, was a physician. That is, he was a man trained in the method of the natural sciences, a method that assumes a strong, law-like relationship between 'effects' and their purported causes, a method that denies human freedom any substantive role in a person's psychological and emotional life. Moreover, he was a man of his time, authoritarian both in his attitude as a physician toward his patients and in his attitude as a man toward women. Perhaps the problem with Pappenheim's 'conversations' with Breuer was that they were not really genuine conversations, that they were not marked by the mutual respect that is essential in all genuinely productive dialogues.[2]

"We live in a world," writes John Launer, "that is unified, if at all, by the idea that talking does indeed cure. Whether as doctors or therapists, our daily experience is that letting people talk does make a difference (Launer, 466). Recognition of the psychotherapeutic potential of conversation and attempts to harness this power so that it could be used to improve people's lives are as old as philosophy itself, or at least as old as Plato. "Socratic conversation," observes the philosopher and psychoanalyst Jonathan Lear, "had a therapeutic intent."[3]

The general public has been very slow, however, in recognizing the therapeutic potential of philosophy. Philosophers are often told that they live too much in their heads, too much in the world of ideas, that they deny too much of their humanity by placing too much emphasis on thought. Many people argue that thought is a kind of flight from the present and that to think too much is to fail to live in the present and thus to miss what makes life truly valuable and meaningful. There is support for such a view in the philosophical tradition itself. Plato often speaks as if he sees thought as a kind of flight from concrete reality. Socrates famously describes philosophy in *The Phaedo* as preparation for death. The body, he points out, and its needs are a constant distraction, an irritation to the philosopher who would prefer to be rid of them. The senses deceive, and attending to physical needs takes time away from contemplation of the eternal, unchanging truth.

Kierkegaard also talks about thought as a kind of withdrawal from concrete reality. There is undoubtedly some truth to this perspective. Yet there is also a sense in which reflection is ineluctably part of the present, a part of the whole person and his or her experiences. This, I take it, is what lies behind the debate concerning whether it is actually possible to live as the Pyrrhonist skeptics advocate one should.[4] That is, the debate concerns whether it is possible to live without beliefs, which is the same thing, really, as asking whether it is possible to live without reflecting on experience.

Maybe it is possible for animals to live without reflecting on their experience. It does not appear possible, however, for human beings to do this. Intellectual pleasures are as much a part of the present for us as are sensual or emotional ones. Human beings are thinking creatures, in the broadest sense of the term 'thinking.'[5] They like thinking. Yes, thought would appear, at least, to have practical value. But that isn't the only reason engage in it. They do this because it is intrinsically valuable. Human beings like knowing things; they like understanding things. Knowledge and understanding are necessary for a fully satisfying human life, even for the least intellectual among us.

Human beings have an inherent need to reflect on their experiences, to make some kind of sense of them. They want an account of existence that will connect all the disparate temporal pieces of their lives into some sort of meaningful whole, something that will give an overarching meaning not merely to an individual life, but to a larger whole of which an individual life is only a part. And, of course, there are better and worse ways of doing this.

People don't want any old overarching account of the meaning of life. They want a coherent one. They want one that makes sense of their experience. They want one that will survive the tests of new experiences; one that will withstand scrutiny. Moreover, to the extent that people feel their lives are at least partially a result of choices over which they have some control, they want an account of existence that will enable them to exercise this control positively, or in ways that will help them to live happy and fulfilling lives. The production of such an account of the meaning of life requires a great deal of reflection, rigorous analysis, and even imagination.

An account of the meaning of life is, one could argue, the main purpose of philosophical reflection. We may never actually finish the project of producing such an account, but the activity of its production, no matter how large or how small a portion of our waking life it consumes (and it will consume greater or lesser amounts of people's lives depending on how reflective they are by nature), is crucial to a satisfying human life.

THE ESSENCE OF PHILOSOPHY

All philosophy is, in this sense, therapeutic. The ancients, particularly during the Hellenistic period, understood this.[6] Now, finally, we are beginning to rediscover the therapeutic potential of philosophy. A person doesn't have to be a scholar to tap that potential. Anyone can do philosophy, even someone who's had little to no exposure to academic philosophy. There is no 'beginning' philosophy and no 'advanced' philosophy. You can't do philosophy at all without jumping right in the deep end of the very same questions all philosophers have wrestled with since the time of Plato, questions such as what it means to be happy, or whether people really have free will.

I have my students read John Searle's *Mind: A Brief Introduction* (Oxford, 2004) in my philosophy of mind class. One of the most interesting chapters of this book is on free will. You don't have to be a professional philosopher to be interested in the question of whether human beings have free will. Almost everyone is interested in this question because, it makes an enormous difference in the quality of a person's life if he feels his actions are, or are not, under his control.

But how can we know whether any of our actions are free? "The first thing to notice," Searle asserts, when examining such concepts as "psychological determinism" and "voluntary action," "is that our understanding of these concepts rests on an awareness of a contrast between the cases in which we are genuinely subject to psychological compulsion and those in which we are not" (Searle,156).

"What do you think of that statement?" I asked my students. "Is there anything wrong with it?"

"It's begging the question," responded one of them matter-of-factly.

"Yes, that's right," I said smiling. "Searle is BEGGING THE QUESTION!" Mr. Big deal famous philosopher, John Searle, whose book was published by Oxford University Press, commits a fallacy that is easily identified by an undergraduate student who is not even a philosophy major. That is, the issue Searle examines in that chapter is whether we have free will. He even acknowledges that we sometimes think our actions are free when they clearly are not (the example he gives is of someone acting on a post-hypnotic suggestion, but other examples would be easy enough to produce).

But if we can be mistaken about whether a given action is free, how do we know that any of our actions are free? We assume that at least some of them are free because it sometimes seems to us that our actions are free and other times that they are compelled. But to say that it sometimes *seems* to us that our actions are free is a very different sort of observation from Searle's that we are sometimes *aware* that we are not, in fact, subject to psychological compulsion.

Searle distinguishes, however, between "psychological compulsion," which he associates with the conscious experience of compulsion, and what he calls "neurobiological determinism," which he asserts compels action just as effectively as the former, but which is never "experienced" consciously at all. So a charitable reading of the passage above might incline one to the view that Searle was not actually begging the question in that an awareness of an absence of psychological compulsion does not constitute and awareness of freedom.

But alas, Searle has to restate his position in the very next page in a manner that is even more conspicuously question begging. "We understand all of these cases [i.e., various cases of unfree action]," he asserts, "by contrasting them with the standard cases in which we *do* have free voluntary action" (Searle, 158; emphasis added). You can't get more question begging than that. The whole point is whether any human action is ever really free or voluntary.

THE ROLE OF WOMEN IN PHILOSOPHICAL CONVERSATION

Professional philosophers can be incredibly obtuse, and ordinary people, even today, with the right sort of help and encouragement, can expose that obtuseness. This is one of the primary joys of philosophy—intellectual problem solving. All inherently pleasurable activities, even intellectual ones, are therapeutic in that they are among the things that make life worth living.

The therapeutic potential of philosophy is not exhausted, however, by this sort of pleasure. Human beings cannot help but reflect on their experience and *how* they reflect on their experience is an important constituent of that experience. The skeptics were right about that. Thinking, for example, that an experience is bad, while it may not actually make the experience bad, will more than likely make it worse than if one could refrain from such reflections.

Philosophical reflection has obvious practical value. Things often do not turn out as we hope. We are thus continually forced to dig new channels into which to redirect our desires. This work, over time, can be exhausting. Reflecting on our experiences can help to make that labor more productive, can help us to conserve our energies.

Really to do philosophy, however, is not simply to think. Human beings are not merely intellectual creatures, they are also social ones. They need conversation. They need more than ordinary conversation, however, in order to develop fully their thoughts and insights. They need what Jonathan Lear referred to as "Socratic conversation." That is, they need conversation with someone practiced in philosophical reflection, someone who can gently help to direct their thoughts into productive channels.

When people think of philosophers, they typically think of men. This is undoubtedly part of the reason that men still greatly outnumber women in the ranks of professional philosophers. Western concepts of gender identity make it easier, however, for both men and women to engage in the kind of soul-searching exchanges that are essential to realizing the therapeutic potential of conversation when their interlocutors are women rather than men. This insight was alluded to in Socrates's own account in *The Symposium* of how it was a woman, Diotima, who taught him to be a philosopher. It seems Socrates had not himself developed the method of conversation that is now widely referred to as 'Socratic,' the method whereby a person's own assertions and arguments are used against him, or as one would say nowadays, are used to deconstruct his position.[7] Socrates learned this method of directed questioning from Diotima.

That Socrates should have learned his method of conversation from a woman should not be surprising. Women have long been acknowledged as particularly adept at conversation. It was primarily women who lay behind the eighteenth- and nineteenth-century phenomenon of the literary "salon" where philosophy was often discussed and where conversation was raised to the status of an art.[8] The role of women in the phenomenon of the "salon" is widely recognized. If Whitehead is correct, however, in his assertion that the entire history of Western philosophy can be characterized as a series of footnotes to Plato,[9] then all of Western philosophy is ultimately traceable back to a woman.

What one could call the "feminine roots" of Western philosophy should, again, not be surprising. The kind of deep probing that is characteristic of philosophical conversation requires a certain vulnerability, a willingness to examine one's most firmly held and treasured beliefs. Vulnerability of that sort is something women, at least in Western culture, are generally more comfortable with than are men. Moreover, men are generally more comfortable in exposing their vulnerability to women than they are in exposing it to other men. Women are, to a certain extent, socialized to be nurturing and this makes people in general more comfortable making themselves vulnerable to women than to men. Women are widely perceived to be less threatening, more supportive, more encouraging.

Anglo-American philosophy is among the most confrontational and combative of academic disciplines and this has made it a particularly difficult discipline for women. Sometimes this is because women, in Western culture, are not socialized to enjoy conflict the way men are and so the environment of academic philosophy can occasionally seem hostile to them. Other times stereotypes of femininity work against women who in fact thrive in such environments. Colleagues may condemn such women as 'overly aggressive' when, in fact, they are no more aggressive than their male counterparts.

There is one area of philosophy, however, for which enduring gender stereotypes make women better suited than men: philosophical counseling. Women are the ideal partners in the Socratic conversation the aim of which is teach what one could call the 'method of philosophy' for revealing the essential components of the "good life." Female philosophical counselors are modern-day Diotimas teaching their interlocutors the joys of the life of the mind and the instrumental value of philosophical thought. And, indeed, many women, such as those in this volume, have played leading roles in this developing practice.

Socrates argued that he was no more knowledgeable than any of his contemporaries, or that if he did possess what one could call an epistemic advantage relative to them, it consisted merely in the fact that while everyone appeared to him to be equally ignorant, he alone was aware of his ignorance. Socratic conversation, at least genuinely Socratic conversation, does not involve leading people to predetermined conclusions. Such one-sidedness was very likely part of the reason that Pappenheim did not benefit from her 'conversations' with Breuer to the extent that both Breuer and Freud claimed that she did. "Socratic conversation," writes Jonathan Lear, was meant to motivate a person to care about his soul."[10] This is done by gently encouraging people to examine their lives and their beliefs, and in this way to come to their own conclusions about how best to live, to develop their own overarching accounts of the meaning of life.

The female philosophical counselor gently teaches her client to think in, again, the most holistic sense of that term. She teaches her client to examine his or her life in a way not generally encouraged in our fiercely anti-intellectual culture.[11] What can be a disadvantage to female philosophers—for instance, that they are sometimes not perceived to speak with the same authority as are men—is actually an advantage to the philosophical counselor. A good philosophical counselor does not lecture. She engages her client in life-changing conversation, introduces that person to the joys of the life of the mind and to the potential of philosophical reflection to improve the quality of a person's life.

CONCLUSION

Thought never disappoints. The more faithful you are to it, the more faithful it is to you. The more time you devote to it, the more it rewards you. It is unfailing that way. Thought is not like the capricious lover, happy one day, impossible to please the next. Thought is patient and always responsive to the one who attends to it. It always waits for you and always receives you warmly on your return. And it is full of friends: Plato and Aristotle, Epictetus and Kant, all wait there like Aspasia (another woman well-versed in the art of conversation) ready to engage, to challenge, to stimulate.

Let's return now to the example with which I began this paper, the chapter from John Searle's *Mind: A Brief Introduction* that dealt with the question of whether human beings have free will. I did not tell my student that Searle's argument begged the question. I opened up space in the conversation for him to come to that insight on his own.

Do human beings have free will? It certainly seems like they do. Isaiah Berlin argues in his essay *Historical Inevitability* that it doesn't really matter whether we can prove that human beings have free will because we cannot rid ourselves of the impression that we do.[12] That we cannot escape the impression that it is possible for us to shape, at least to some extent, the course of our lives means that we similarly cannot escape the impression that we need to devote at least some thought to how best to do that.

What better way, what more effective way is there to work out one's thoughts than through conversation? And what better conversational partners can one find than women, than modern-day Diotimas gently helping people to discover the good life for themselves?

NOTES

1. See, for example, John Launer, "Anna O. and the 'talking cure,'" *QJM: An International Journal of Medicine* 98 (2005): 465–466.

2. I do not mean by this to suggest that Breuer had no respect for Pappenheim. He described her as "markedly intelligent, with an astonishingly quick grasp of things and penetrating intuition" (John Launer "Anna O. and the 'talking cure.'" *QJM: An International Journal of Medicine* 98 [2005]: 465). My point here is simply to remark that Breuer would not have considered a patient and, in particular, a female patient, to be on an equal footing with himself so far as discussions of that patient's illness were concerned.

3. "The Socratic Method and Psychoanalysis," *A Companion to Socrates*, ed. Sara Ahbel-Rappe and Rachana Kamtekar (Wiley-Blackwell, 209), 442.

4. See M. F. Burnyeat, "Can the Skeptic Live his Skepticism?" in *Explorations in Ancient and Modern Philosophy* (Cambridge: Cambridge University Press, 2012), 205–235.

5. When I say "broadest sense of the term 'thinking'" I am explicitly distancing myself from that portion of the philosophical tradition that professes belief in the possibility of purely objective, or 'pure thought,' divorced from the emotional life and subjective experience of the thinker.

6. See Susan Suavé Meyer, *Ancient Ethics* (London: Routledge, 2008).

7. See *Plato's Symposium*, ed. and trans. Alexander Nehamas and Paul Woodruff (Indianapolis: Hackett, 1989) 201e–203b. See also Jonathan Lear, "The Ironic Creativity of Socratic Doubt," *MLN* vol. 128 no. 5, 1007.

8. See Dena Goodman, "Enlightenment Salons: The Convergence of Female and Philosophic Ambitions," *Eighteenth-Century Studies* 22, 3 (1989): 338.

9. Alfred North Whitehead, *Process and Reality* (New York: Free Press, 1979) 39.

10. Lear, "The Socratic Method of Psychoanalysis," 442.

11. See Richard Hofstadter, *Anti-Intellectualism in American Life* (Vintage, 1966).

12. Isaiah Berlin, "Historical Inevitability," *The Proper Study of Mankind: An Anthology of Essays* (Farrar, Straus and Giroux, 1997) 119–190. I am indebted to my father, Harold Russell Piety, for his generous gift to me of this volume.

BIBLIOGRAPHY

Berlin, Isaiah. "Historical Inevitability." In *The Proper Study of Mankind: An Anthology of Essays,* edited by Henry Hardy and Roger Hausheer. New York: Farrar, Straus, and Giroux, 1997.

Burnyeat, M. F. "Can the Skeptic Live his Skepticism?" In *Explorations in Ancient and Modern Philosophy.* Cambridge: Cambridge University Press, 2012, 205–235.

Goodman, Dena. "Enlightenment Salons: The Convergence of Female and Philosophic Ambitions." *Eighteenth-Century Studies* 22, 3 (1989): 329–50.

Hofstadter, Richard. *Anti-Intellectualism in American Life.* New York: Vintage, 1966.

Launer, John. "Anna O. and the 'talking cure.'" *QJM: An International Journal of Medicine* 98 (2005): 465–466.

Lear, Jonathan. "The Socratic Method and Psychoanalysis." In *A Companion to Socrates,* edited by Sara Ahbel-Rappe and Rachana Kamtekar. Hoboken: Wiley-Blackwell, 2009.

———. "The Ironic Creativity of Socratic Doubt." *Modern Language Notes* 128 (2013) 5.

Meyer, Susan Suavé. *Ancient Ethics.* London: Routledge, 2008.

Plato. *Plato's Symposium.* Edited and translated by Alexander Nehamas and Paul Woodruff. Indianapolis: Hackett, 1989.

Whitehead, Alfred North. *Process and Reality.* New York: Free Press, 1979.

V

Acting to Change

Chapter Fifteen

Woman as Healer

Dena Hurst

Initially when approached with the idea of contributing to a work dedicated to the work of women in philosophical counseling, I was excited to participate. I deemed adding to the growing body of research in philosophical counseling as a worthwhile and much needed cause. In writing this chapter, I struggled greatly, primarily because I am a reluctant feminist at best. While I advocate for the values shared by contemporary feminists, including equality, caring, collectivity, and justice for all people, I find that the baggage of early feminism can be a heavy burden to carry. There are, I believe, more common human problems than gender-specific problems, and thus there are roles for all philosophical counselors to play, roles that are shaped more by life experiences that include sex and gender than by sex and gender alone.

I agree with the feminist claim that both sex and gender influence how we are perceived by others and how we perceive ourselves and the world. I agree with the feminist claim that there are individuals who suffer unfair treatment based on their sex or gender. I believe that women therapists face unique challenges in their work due to the perceptions of men and women alike. A concern that has weighed on my thinking throughout the many draft forms this chapter has taken is that in emphasizing women as unique, whether as counselors or potential clients, we run the risk of furthering gender divisions by gendering problems and the approaches philosophical counselors take in the therapy process.

In other words, though there is a rich history related to women, it is not my intent to leave readers with the idea that the role of women in philosophical counseling is more important or superior in any way to the role of men. As I agree with performative gender theories, making gender a choice and not a biological or social mandate, the conclusions reached here can apply to anyone with who identifies with women, sex, or gender aside. It is with a conflicted heart that I champion the power of that archetype, in awe of the strength it promotes and hesitant that it may continue inequities resulting from sex- and gender-based bias.

While our language is limited to man and woman, male and female, these terms do not adequately capture biological characteristics or notions of individual identity with regard to sex or gender. This is one benefit that archetypes offer, and why I refer to the archetype of Woman as healer and not to healing women. It is the qualities and the work of women healers that is the focus.

A LONG HISTORY

There is a long and rich history of women as healers, arising out of their traditional responsibilities as caretakers and life givers. This history has crossed time and societal boundaries; women in the role of healer can be found in nearly every culture. This history is documented by written and oral records, including case stories and descriptions of medical techniques and treatments, as well as in the stories handed down through generations.

Many tribal cultures have been gynocratic, despite the emphasis (in the West, at least) on the 'medicine man.' Women healers learned their skills from their mothers, other community members, and, depending on the tribal belief system, from spirits or a creator. The medicine woman in tribal cultures was a holistic healer, a healer who united mind, body, and soul. They were viewed as having a connection to a spirit world or some sort of unique spiritual knowledge. Their healing power was seen as a natural ability, a gift bestowed on them, but not as an ability present in all women. These medicine women had a deep faith in the healing process, viewing themselves as a conduit for healing power, rather than as the source. In many traditional or tribal societies (North and South America, Africa, China, Korea, and others countries), women still fulfill this role.

Beyond tribal practices, women in medicine can be found in other societies. In ancient Egypt, there were female medical students in Heliopolis (1500 BCE). In Greek mythology, all of Aesculapius' (son of Apollo) daughters were destined to healing work. Aspasia, long-term companion of Pericles, left a journal detailing her surgical techniques.

Women in ancient Europe practiced healing in their homes, tending to ailing family members. Some women developed specialties, such as herbalism, the ancient equivalent of pharmacy, or midwifery. The role of women practicing medicine in European societies declined sharply during the Middle Ages due to a number of forces, and interestingly paralleling the modernization of Western society and transitions in economic systems.

Historically, women were prevented from seeking formal education, most especially in the form of university learning. Beginning in the fourteenth century, as science and knowledge progressed and as universities began offering medical programs, women were denied access to any kind of academic training. Those who persisted in practicing medicine outside their own homes risked severe punishment. As the Middle Ages advanced, women healers were branded as witches and as such were hunted at the behest of church and civil authorities.[1]

Though the witch hysteria eventually died down, the institutions that supported it did not. Increasingly, medical knowledge was consolidated in universities, and entry was granted to wealthy white males and the occasional female (also generally white and from a prominent family). The peasant and working classes continued to rely on local healing women as they could not afford to pay for the services of trained doctors.

Medicine continued to become professionalized in the West, and the traditional medicine practiced by healing women was discouraged and ridiculed by the professionals. As centuries passed and women gained greater access to university education, they fought to take their place alongside their male colleagues and to be treated as equals. The goal of preserving the rights of women as healers capable of providing affordable and accessible care gave way to the larger goal of attaining equal social and political rights, specifically, the right to vote.[2]

Women have made tremendous strides in healthcare, and now gain entry to medical programs and have a range of specialization options in many Western(alized) countries. There are still professional inequities as female healthcare providers, like women in other professions, must balance house and family with work demands and remain the primary care providers in the home. In many countries, however, women still lack access to educational opportunities and continue to bear the majority of caretaking responsibilities.

As the role of women was evolving, medical care itself was undergoing a change. When healing women were the primary source of care, they did their best to treat all ailments, physical and mental, and to educate patients and families. As medicine shifted to being the purview of the trained elite, specializations gradually became the norm. Not only was treatment of the physical body parsed among different fields of study, treatment of mind and body became widely separated.

In recent years, research in to patient outcomes is slowly reversing this sharp division of knowledge within medicine. Patient outcomes in methods that emphasize treating the whole patient and integrating traditional and contemporary healing practices are being studied. The biopscyhosocial model—a model that encourages evaluating patient issues in terms of their biological, psychological and social/environmental aspects—has been in practice for more than thirty years (though it is falling out of favor). William Osler's work in medical humanism is regaining popularity. The number of people (in Western countries) turning to organic foods, naturopathic and homeopathic preventives and treatments, and spiritual belief systems is also evidence of wider interest in a more holistic approach to healthcare.

Philosophical counseling holds the promise of reviving the almost lost roles for women as healers and doing so in a way that empowers women as well as those they seek to help. Philosophical counseling allows women to embrace the archetypal: as medicine woman, as priestess, as Socratic midwife embodied, as wounded healer.

WOMEN AS THERAPISTS

In addition to their work as healers, women have also served as advisors and confidantes. Part of the role of women as healers was to answer questions about health issues, particularly issues that were seen as taboo, such as questions about women's sexual health. They have also provided counseling to families regarding potential mates for their children and to younger generations on the protocols of courting, marriage, and family planning. They helped individuals through the grieving process when a loved one died, and they offered advice on moral dilemmas. In this role as counselor, women have traditionally relied on their life experiences as well as the collective memory of the society passed down to them by earlier generations.

This role is still alive and well. In many Native American tribes, women play the dominant leadership role. They are the preservers of tribal history and they are valued for their insights on a range of personal and social issues. In some African and South American communities, wise women are often thought to have a type of clairvoyance; individuals will seek their advice on major life decisions or to attempt to understand why an illness or tragedy has befallen them.

In Senegal, a study of women traders revealed that part of their work involved counseling family members, friends, and others by answering questions and sharing knowledge on everything "from cooking and self-fashioning to marital issues, familial conflict mediation, and sexuality."[3] The Senegalese women rely on their own experiences as well as what they have observed during their work in the marketplace. "A few invoke their long genealogy, drawing from a repository of knowledge inherited from their parents and family genealogy."[4] These trader women recognize that trials are part of the human condition. Everyone has issues to overcome in order to create the life that is desired.

In Western countries, women are entering the professions of psychology and psychiatry; in both fields in the United States, women completing doctoral programs (psychology) or medical residences (psychiatry) outnumber men. There are no data definitely explaining why women are pursuing these two career fields, but there are some documented characteristics of female psychiatrists that might provide insight. One characteristic is "a personal or family history with psychiatric disorders," supporting the wounded healer archetype.[5] Female psychiatrists also report higher career satisfaction than female physicians in other specialties, and they have a higher rate of belief in their ability to make a difference through their work.[6]

It is a mistake to assume that women are natural caregivers or that women prefer careers in which they can nurture and care for others. It is rewarding, though, that psychology and psychiatry are fields where women are actively represented, at least in some parts of the world. This shows that the barriers to women presented by professionalizing and segmenting healthcare have to some degree been overcome, and that a path for more women to participate has been cleared.

Further, stereotypes associated with female therapists—that they work better with women or that men do not want a female therapist or that men may seek out a female therapist to understand how women think—are slowly being eroded. Though much has been written on the sex and gender of therapists and counselors and the various relationship benefits and pitfalls, there are few data that support the claim that one sex or gender is better for a particular patient.[7] What the data are showing is that a successful therapist-patient relationship rests more on the connection of the two as individuals; it is the lived experiences of the therapist that influences how he or she is perceived by the patient.

That women are active in the mental health, and specifically counseling/therapy, field provides an opportunity for philosophical counseling to be a means of drawing women into philosophy programs. While personally I do not think this is a goal desirable in itself, more women for the sake of having more women, there are ample research studies in the disciplines of education, sociology, and business that demonstrate the value of diversity in any learning and collaborative environment.[8] Women do not carry with them a universal experience as a woman; but like any human being, women have equally varied and unique lived experiences that can enrich any academic program.

The presence of woman in therapy roles, professional and informal, also provides philosophical counseling with the opportunity to expand not only the scope of counseling in general, but also to transform the therapist-patient relationship. The role of therapist that many women fulfill, through both formal and informal societal structures, helps support the idea that "knowing thyself" often takes the wisdom of others to help process the individual lived experience, that each person's journey of becoming is unique, but not one that is taken alone. The qualities of the archetypal Woman can be developed in order to foster a bond of care, compassion, and equality.

WOMEN AS PHILOSOPHICAL COUNSELORS: NEW OPPORTUNITIES

The history of healing women offers new paths beyond the accepted clinical interactions for the philosophical counselor to offer services to individuals and families in their homes, to specific marginalized groups through support and advocacy programs, even to entire communities and governments that have institutionalized oppression, segregation, and violence. This work would not be limited to helping individuals cope or find personal meaning in such environments, but would also seek to transform the community. If the goal of philosophical counselors could be stated as helping individuals fulfill their purpose, then they must live in a society that enables individuals to do so. Aristotle provides philosophical counselors with the framework for reframing societies to foster the ends of the individual.[9] Rousseau can provide a vision of what a 're-natured' society, one devoid of the corrupting influences, might be like.[10] Women as healers, though in many societies powerless to make grand social changes, have long sought to provide a safe space in which individuals could come to know themselves. The influence of society on the development of the individual should not be accepted as the boundaries of philosophical counseling. Philosophical counselors can learn from the history of healing women that the role of therapist may also mean assuming the role of champion or change agent.

This approach borrows from the social constructivism of Humberto Maturana and Kenneth Gurgen. While their views take the extreme form of denying that there is anything beyond the socially constructed individual, there are more moderate ways of applying a social constructivist perspective. To some extent it is found in the literature emphasizing culturally competent care, care that is aware of, and respectful of, the patient's cultural teachings and belief systems. In addition, a social constructivist approach will attempt to identify cultural influences that have shaped the individual's choices and the issues the individual wishes to resolve.[11] Women as healers have traditionally understood the social context in which they worked, and often suffered the same concerns as those they were helping.

Being part of the social context is one quality that the philosophical counselor should have, and there are key reasons for this requirement. In part, it connects to the concept of the archetypal wounded healer. This archetype is expressed in the Greek myth of Chiron:

1) The wounded healer is kind, gentle, and intelligent, 2) He is a gifted man of medicine, 3) He is a teacher to many students of medicine, 4) His wounds are arbitrary and meaningless; they occur accidentally, 5) He does not welcome his suffering, and does not embrace pain voluntarily; the tradition of martyrdom is thus ruled out from the Wounded Healer narrative, 6) His suffering is endless and hopeless; although a great healer, he cannot cure

himself; he is immortal, so he cannot wish for death to end his suffering, 7) He keeps healing and teaching others despite his suffering, and 8) The end of the healer's suffering endows it with meaning, and involves saving the life of someone else (Prometheus) and achieving his own freedom from agony.[12]

Healing, particularly a healing of the mind or spirit, can best be provided by someone who understands the needs of the patient. This would require a person who has similar lived experiences, including lived experience of the patient's societal influences. It is only when we have endured a pain or trauma ourselves that we can feel true compassion for others in the same situations,[13] and it is compassion for the patient that drives the healing process. Without having the shared experience, the best the counselor can hope to provide is insight based on a secondary understanding gained from reading the accounts of or talking to others who have had the experience the patient describes. The counselor can imagine what he or she would feel in that situation. But the counselor could not know, indeed could only poorly imagine, what the patient is thinking and feeling. The counselor may be able to feel sympathy for the patient, but not genuine compassion. Sympathy comes from a position of power; compassion comes from a position of equality.

Being part of the social context also allows the counselor to rely on qualitative methods in research and practice. As mentioned prior, this fits neatly with the concept of culturally competent care. It also pulls from phenomenology, ethnography, and narratology. It values the lived experiences of both the patient and the philosophical counselor, and encourages the counselor to use shared experiences to strengthen the healing process.

By emphasizing the patient's social context and lived experiences, philosophical counseling can expand on the foundation laid by feminist theory. Heretofore, feminist theory has been the primary framework through which to understand how the individual is influenced by power structures, how to describe oppression and its effects, and how to talk about gender as part of the social context. Feminist theory, in short, has been the only way to talk about what gender means, gender roles, the role of women in philosophy and in healing, and the intersections of race, religion, class, and gender. It has been the only way for non-white, non-privileged, non-heterosexual, and transwomen to have a voice. Employing the archetype of Woman as healer allows for the lived experiences of women to be shared with other women. It also offers a perspective for anyone with the lived experiences of archetypal Woman to share those experiences.

The connection between the healer and patient must be genuine if the healing is to be successful. This is a lesson from the history of women as healers. While the biological sex of the patient or therapist itself is not a determining factor, research shows that a misalignment of shared experiences can have a negative impact on the patient's outcome. For example, "counselors with less egalitarian gender-role attitudes exhibited significantly more stereotypical behaviors than did counselors with more egalitarian attitudes did. Additionally, rigid European White male gender roles may interfere with counselors' therapeutic skills and prevent counselors from providing culturally sensitive therapy."[14] This misalignment can arise whether the therapist is, or identifies as, male or female, again highlighting the importance of lived experiences over sex or gender alone. "When counselors work from the assumption that their clients have the same needs, desires, values, and perspectives as they do, they are likely to make errors based on differences in culture and context. Counselors with multicultural competence take the time to co-develop goals with clients and their communities that prioritize the clients' values, culture, and context."[15]

Practicing therapy as women healers have done, within a social context and with a desire to resolve social inequalities, will require a change in the qualities desirable in a philosophical counselor. Though there is some variation in the listing of these qualities, standard ones seem to be: "empathetic listening, objectification (taking a step back), logical reasoning, conceptual analysis, critical and creative thinking, synthesizing particulars, and seeing things in perspective."[16] Logical reasoning, critical and creative thinking, conceptual analysis, and seeing things in perspective are all part of the woman as healer tradition. Empathetic listening is as well, though as explained, the empathy comes from the lived experiences shared with the patient and is distinct from sympathy or pity. One key difference in the approach of healing women is that objectivity is not specifically sought. There is much research on the problems of entanglement or projection between therapist and patient, and indeed, some boundary does need to be maintained to prevent the philosophical counselor being pulled too deeply into the lives of those seeking help. However, the very nature of using lived experiences to create a bond with the patient requires that the patient not be listened to or talked at, one separate individual to another. Healing women have long understood the interconnectedness of mind and body within an individual as well as between individuals as part of a larger social context.

There is a model for this approach that has had success in elder care in China. Women-run elder care homes have been on the rise since the early 2000s as a way to address poor living conditions for many elderly living in government-run homes. As China's economy has changed, young people leave home to work and so the traditional support system for the elderly is declining. What is unique about the approach taken in the women-run homes is that they purposefully set out to "blur the provider-client division of power imbalance by regarding the elders and themselves as equal members of an extended family."[17] The elderly residents in the homes come from all geographic regions in China and have varying levels of education, income, and health needs. However, the residents are generally known to the house owners in some way and are introduced through personal friends or family. "The owners explained that 'trust' is crucial to fulfilling their vision of intimacy, reciprocity, and mutual respect."[18]

While working with patients with psychological, emotional, or spiritual concerns is not the same as helping those with physical ailments, the idea of redefining the therapist-patient relationship is not all that radical a notion. Similar social justice models have been in employed in counseling, with the aim of providing individuals with an understanding of their problems and needs and the ability to better advocate for themselves specifically with regard to the injustices they experience.[19] This is merely an extension of work already being done by practicing philosophers. The philosophical framework has already been provided by the long tradition of women as healers and through existing theories and research methodologies.

CONCLUSION

Philosophical counseling offers many unique opportunities for women as counselors to continue work in a long tradition of healing women that goes beyond the typical therapist-patient relationship. Philosophical counseling can be a vehicle for building community, preserving and continuing histories, empowering the oppressed and marginalized, and fostering greater social justice.

Going beyond the therapist-patient relationship may overstep the bounds, fluid as they are, of what philosophical counseling is, but it is worthy of conversation to explore ways that this approach to healing can go beyond helping individuals cope in an unjust world toward making the world a place where individuals can flourish.

Author David Orr sums up what can become a goal of philosophical counseling:

> The plain fact is that the planet does not need more successful people. But it does desperately need more peacemakers, healers, restorers, storytellers, and lovers of every kind. It needs people who live well in their places. It needs people of moral courage willing to join the fight to make the world habitable and humane. And these qualities have little to do with success as we have defined it.[20]

Is this not what philosophers have sought to do since they first began to develop theories so many centuries ago?

NOTES

1. William L. Minkowski, "Public Health Then and Now: Women Healers of the Middle Ages: Selected Aspects of Their History," *American Journal of Public Health*. 82 (1992): 2.

Retrieved from http://www.ncbi.nlm.nih.gov/pmc/articles/PMC1694293/pdf/amjph00539-0138.pdf.

2. Barbara Ehrenreich, *Witches, Midwives, and Nurses: A History of Women Healers* (New York: The Feminist Press at CUNY, 1973). Retrieved from http://www.marxists.org/subject/women/authors/ehrenreich-barbara/witches.htm.

3. Marierne S. Lo, "Confidant Par Excellence, Advisors and Healers: Women Traders' Intersecting Identities and Roles in Senegal," *Culture, Health & Sexuality* 15 Suppl 4(sup4), 2013, S467-81.doi:10.1080/13691058.2013.793404.

4. Lo, "Confidant Par Excellence . . ."

5. Erica Frank, et al., "Characteristics of Female Psychiatrists," *American Journal of Psychiatry* 158 (2001): 205–212. doi:10.1176/appi.ajp.158.2.205.

6. Frank et al., "Characteristics of Female Psychiatrists."

7. See, for example, Daniel Bowman, Forrest Scogin, Mark Floyd, and Nancy McKendree-Smith, "Psychotherapy Length of Stay and Outcome: A Meta-analysis of the Effect of Therapist Sex," *Psychotherapy: Theory, Research, Practice, Training*, Vol 38(2001): 2, 142–148; National Registry of Evidence-Based Programs and Practices, Substance Abuse and Mental Health Services Administration, U.S. Government; *Evidence-Based Therapy Relationships*, Retrieved from http://www.nrepp.samhsa.gov/Norcross.aspx; and Kuldhir Singh Bhati, *Impact of Gender Matching on the Therapeutic Relationship: A Stage Analysis*, (Ann Arbor, MI: ProQuest, 2008). There are many other articles and books on the topic.

8. See, for example, American Council on Education and American Association of University Professors, "Does Diversity Make a Difference: Three Research Studies in Diversity in College Classrooms," 2000, Retrieved from http://www.aaup.org/NR/rdonlyres/97003B7B-055F-4318-B14A-5336321FB742/0/DIVREP.PDF; Patricia Gurin, Biren A. Nagda, Gretchen E. Lopez, "The Benefits of Diversity in Education for Democratic Citizenship," *Journal of Social Issues* January 2003, Retrieved from: http://www.personal.umich.edu/~pgurin/benefits.html; Evan Apfelbaum, "What's the Business Case for Diversity in the Workplace," MIT Sloan Management, February 27, 2013, Retrieved from: http://mitsloanexperts.mit.edu/diversity-in-the-workplace/; Forbes Insights, "Global Diversity and Inclusion: Fostering Innovation through a Diverse Workforce," 2013, Retrieved from: http://images.forbes.com/forbesinsights/StudyPDFs/Innovation_Through_Diversity.pdf. Many other resources are available on this topic.

9. See in particular Aristotle, "Nicomachean Ethics," *The Complete Works of Aristotle*, ed. Jonathan Barnes (Princeton, New Jersey: Princeton University Press, 1984), 1729–1867.

10. See in particular Jean-Jacques Rousseau, "Discourse on Inequality Among Men," *The Social Contract and the Discourses*, trans. G. D. H. Cole, ed. P. D. Jimack (London: Everyman, 1993), 31–126.

11. R. Rocco Cottone, "A Paradigm Shift in Counseling Philosophy," *Counseling Today* September 2013. Retrieved from http://ct.counseling.org/2013/09/a-paradigm-shift-in-counseling-philosophy/.

12. Ayesha Ahmad, Galia Benziman, & Ruth Kannai, "The Wounded Healer as Cultural Archetype," *CLCWeb: Comparative Literature and Culture*, 14(2012): 1. Accessed March 23, 2014.

13. See the Oxford English Dictionary for the etymology of "compassion," from the Latin *cum* (with) + *passio*, past participle of the deponent verb *patior*, meaning suffering, enduring, leaving, accepting. *Patior* is related to the Greek concept of πάθος (*páthos*), which is the etymon of passion but brings a much broader meaning, inclusive of the tragic dealing with fate, coping with sufferance, and, more generally, experiencing. The etymology of "sympathy" is from the Greek *syn* (together) and *páthos*, typically meaning having a fellow feeling or being affected by like feelings. Sympathy is feeling; compassion is action. The difference is perhaps best stated by Buddha, "Compassion is that which makes the heart of the good move at the pain of others. It crushes and destroys the pain of others; thus, it is called compassion. It is called compassion because it shelters and embraces the distressed." (Dhammapada-atthakatha, 193)

14. Ruth Chu-Lien Chao, "Racial/ethnic Identity, Gender-role Attitudes, and Multicultural Counseling Competence: The Role of Multicultural Counseling Training," *Journal of Counseling and Development*, 90(2012): 1, 35+. Retrieved from http://go.galegroup.com/ps/i.do?id=

GALE%7CA279261383&v=2.1&u=tall85761&it=r&p=AONE&sw=w&asid=3d72da1ecdc46c11eb9b7a9c7c94cde1.

15. Hugh C. Crethar and Carrie L. Winterowd, "Values and Social Justice in Counseling," *Counseling and Values*, *57*(1), 2012, 3+. Retrieved from http://go.galegroup.com/ps/i.do?id=GALE%7CA289620152&v=2.1&u=tall85761&it=r&p=AONE&sw=w&asid=0c1342ba567b103494b28349cfe16a5c.

16. Dirk Louw, "Defining Philosophical Counselling: An Overview," *South African Journal of Philosophy*, 32 (2013): 1, 60–70.

17. Haijing Dai, "To Build an Extended Family: Feminist Organizational Design and Its Dilemmas in Women-led Non-governmental Elder Homes in China," *Social Forces* 92 (2014): 3, 1115–1134. Oxford University Press. Retrieved from Project MUSE database.

18. Haijing Dai, "To Build an Extended Family . . ."

19. Crethar and Wintercrowd, "Values . . ."

20. David W. Orr, *Earth in Mind: On Education, Environment and the Human Prospect* (Washington, D.C.: Island Press, 2004.), 12.

BIBLIOGRAPHY

Ahmad, Ayesha; Benziman, Galia; and Kannai Ruth. "The Wounded Healer as Cultural Archetype." *CLCWeb: Comparative Literature and Culture* 14 (2012): 2. Retrieved from http://go.galegroup.com/ps/i.do?id=GALE%7CA286392440&v=2.1&u=tall85761&it=r&pAONE&sw=w&asid=1a5ade441717934dbac504c18b893e19.

Chao, Ruth Chu-Lien. "Racial/ethnic Identity, Gender-role Attitudes, and Multicultural Counseling Competence: The Role of Multicultural Counseling Training." *Journal of Counseling and Development* 90 (2012): 1, 35. Retrieved from http://go.galegroup.com/ps/i.do?id=GALE%7CA279261383&v=2.1&u=tall85761&it=r&p=AONE&sw=w&asid=3d72da1ecdc46c11eb9b7a9c7c94cde1.

Cottone, R. Rocco. "A Paradigm Shift in Counseling Philosophy." *Counseling Today* September 2013. Retrieved from http://ct.counseling.org/2013/09/a-paradigm-shift-in-counseling-philosophy/.

Crethar, Hugh C., and Winterowd, Carrie L. "Values and Social Justice in Counseling," *Counseling and Values*, *57*(2012): 1, 3. Retrieved from http://go.galegroup.com/ps/i.do?id=GALE%7CA289620152&v=2.1&u=tall85761&it=r&p=AONE&sw=w&asid=0c1342ba567b103494b28349cfe16a5c.

Dai, Haijing. "To Build an Extended Family: Feminist Organizational Design and Its Dilemmas in Women-led Non-governmental Elder Homes in China." *Social Forces* 92(2014): 3, 1115–1134. Oxford University Press. Retrieved from Project MUSE database.

Ehrenreich, Barbara. *Witches, Midwives, and Nurses: A History of Women Healers*, (New York: The Feminist Press at CUNY, 1973). Retrieved from http://www.marxists.org/subject/women/authors/ehrenreich-barbara/witches.htm.

Frank, Erica, Boswell, Lisa, Dickstein, Leah J., and Chapman, Daniel P. "Characteristics of Female Psychiatrists," *American Journal of Psychiatry* 158 (2001): 205–212. doi:10.1176/appi.ajp.158.2.205.

Lo, Marierne S. "Confidant Par Excellence, Advisors and Healers: Women Traders' Intersecting Identities and Roles in Senegal." *Culture, Health & Sexuality*, 15 Suppl 4(sup4), 2013, S467-81.doi:10.1080/13691058.2013.793404.

Louw, Dirk. "Defining Philosophical Counselling: An Overview." *South African Journal of Philosophy*, 32(2013): 1, 60–70.

Minkowski, William L. "Public Health Then and Now: Women Healers of the Middle Ages: Selected Aspects of Their History." *American Journal of Public Health.* 82(1992): 2. Retrieved from http://www.ncbi.nlm.nih.gov/pmc/articles/PMC1694293/pdf/amjph00539-0138.pdf.

Chapter Sixteen

Sexism and Gender Issues in Academic Philosophy: Philosophical Practice as a Balancing Act

Marleen Moors

Thinking begins only when we have come to know that reason, glorified for centuries, is the most stiff-necked adversary of thought.
—Martin Heidegger[1]

Years ago, as a graduate student in metaphysics at a well-known Dutch university, I held a book of great interest to me in my hands: *Heidegger and a Metaphysics of Feeling* (2008).[2] I proffered to one of my college professors that I deemed it a work of great scholarship and would like to write a paper on the same topic. Even though my professor was a kind man, he scoffed at the idea because of the title of the book. I later sensed that many topics that focused on a metaphysics or ontology of emotions, feelings, or interpersonal bonding did not get the same recognition as other topics that had a more 'masculine feel.' While attending a seminar for women in philosophy on gender issues and sexism in academia, I discovered that many women feel the same way but that it remains an individual experience rather than a collective one.

Current literature shows that many women don't feel comfortable in obtaining the higher ranks of academic philosophy or experience discrimination and sexism on the path of doing so.[3] Many women who enroll in graduate school either decide to forsake pursuing a PhD, don't finish it, or fail to apply for tenure on its completion. In "Changing the Ideology and Culture of Philosophy: Not by Reason (Alone),"[4] Sally Haslanger notes quite poignantly that a large reason why many female students opt out is discrimination toward women in philosophy departments. This experience that often remains tacit or inexplicit.

Even though the situation has much improved since the 1980s, from 2002–2007 the percentage of women publishing in *Mind* was only 6.38 percent. From 2008–2011 it was still only 9.5 percent.[5] Currently less than 20 percent of philosophy faculty in the United States are women.[6] Haslanger posits that subconscious gender/race schemas govern philosophy and that hostility to femininity is one aspect of it. Whereas this article does not treat explicit sexism or discrimination in academic philosophy, it acknowledges that implicit sexism or an unconscious bias toward a masculine ontology within academic philosophy may cause women and men to experience professional discomfort. The difficulty that women experience feeling at home in hypermasculine philosophy departments is closely related to feeling the need to repress several aspects of their self-image, such as interrelatedness, empathy, and cooperation. It is my contention that the current epistemology in philosophy departments in the West still privileges intellect, instrumental rationality, and non-situated thought over situated thought, practical philosophy, and abstract knowledge obtained and subtracted from real-life circumstances.[7] We seem to suffer from a 'hierarchy of thinking:' non-situated theoretical philosophy seems to be given priority over situated thought such as philosophy of emotions and feelings, philosophical dialogue, and the philosophical analysis of behavioral and psychological conflicts in society or interpersonal relationships.[8] In effect, the neutral posture, the objective viewpoint of the knower—the non-situated, distanced standpoint—is valued higher than the particular standpoint of the situated viewer who works 'in the field' and who obtains philosophical insight through communication and interpersonal dialogue. In other words: the universal trumps the particular and the written word trumps the spoken word.

The tendency to look down on feminist metaphysics or metaphysics of emotions as 'not real philosophy' reveals that the discomfort with nontraditional or noninstrumental reason and holistic epistemology is a systematic problem within Western philosophy. The hyper-masculine aspects of philosophy not only harm women but also harm men who do not identify with a hyper-masculine self. The professional discomfort that we refer to is not merely a male-female issue of gender and embodiment or a result of a bias toward women and their reasoning capacities, but is an inherent imbalance between masculine and feminine components of individuals. When masculinity is associated with '*not* being emotional, sensitive, inter-relational, and open' but with 'rigidity, discipline, rationality, and competition' one creates discomfort in academic employees whose self-image does not match these principles.

The current growth of philosophical practice in the Netherlands indicates an increasing interest in practical philosophy. Philosophical practice is booming. An increasing amount of young male and female academics leave academia to start their own practices. Does philosophical practice provide something to counselors and clients that academic philosophy omits or disregards? If so, what is the specific nature of philosophical praxis and in what sense is it philosophical? It is not the purpose of this chapter to rewrite the historical association of masculinity with reason or to offer a way to undo the male-female dichotomy still prevalent in Western culture. Rather, this paper addresses the nature of academic philosophy today as still predominantly ruled by the masculine principle, thereby creating a limited view about what valuable knowledge is. It is an investigation that seeks to understand why the epistemology that the philosophical counselor incorporates in philosophical dialogue in his/her practice is frequently considered inferior to academic epistemology. The preoccupation with abstract and clear thought, historically considered a specific masculine trait, often results in a common devaluation of other forms of philosophic knowing. This chapter uses its analysis of reason and masculinity to shine light on the unique nature of philosophizing in philosophical practice. It calls for an open dialogue, a sharing of feminine and masculine insights that can offer a possible escape from hierarchical dualisms. We seek to transcend the idea that there is one valid way of gaining 'proper' knowledge and propose that philosophical practice offers something unique to contemporary philosophy: a *locus* where the *event* of philosophizing can freely take place between equals.

MASCULINE ONTOLOGY AND ACADEMIC PHILOSOPHY

> When philosophy conceives the essence of being as Logos, it is already the Logos of domination—commanding, mastering, directing reason, to which man and nature are to be subjected.
>
> —Herbert Marcuse [9]

When I was a graduate student in philosophy, I had the recurring feeling that I was not a real philosopher. I associated true philosophy with mental rigidity, discipline, clarity of mind, and stoicism. In contrast, my mind was hungry, associative, playful, creative, and extremely restless. Because I could not match my feeling of being out of place with the cultural environment I was in, I thought there must be something wrong with me. In hindsight, I unthinkingly associated philosophy with masculinity. True philosophy was for men, not for women. It is surprising that a woman like me, who held an undergraduate in philosophy and religious studies with an above average grade point average and who committed herself to many years of studying philosophy, would have the implicit presupposition that philosophy is something masculine and thus not for me.[10]

At a recent conference for women in academic philosophy in the Netherlands the discussion about sexism and gender issues in academia was raised. Why are there so few female professors in philosophy in the Netherlands? Despite several reasons such as explicit sexism, department politics, a highly competitive environment, and practical problems such as child care responsibilities and less time for research, one other possible reason was overlooked during the discussion: implicit gender schemas. A gender schema is a cognitive process that provides a model for understanding unconscious bias. It creates small sex differences between men and women in their characteristics, evaluations, and behavior.[11]

"A schema is a mental construct that, as the name suggests, contains in a schematic or abbreviated form someone's concept about an individual or event, or a group of people or events. It includes the person's or group's main characteristics, from the perceiver's point of view, and the relationship among those features."[12]

When gender schemas are at play we color a social minority or an individual according to our prejudices. By the same token, they influence men and women's self-image because we start behaving according to the societal micro messages we receive about our race, gender, or sexual preferences. In philosophy, we may for instance presume that one is not good at logic because one is a woman and "logic and math are for boys," as one was told in high school. Or a man who wants to work on feminist philosophy denies himself this fulfillment because "feminist philosophy is for women" or emasculates men. Consequently, our biases prove valid because that is what we choose to see. As Haslanger indicates in "Changing the Ideology and Culture of Philosophy,"[13] the familiar dichotomies that are part of Anglophone philosophy such as the distinction between rational/emotional, subjective/objective, and mind/body also define gender dichotomies.[14] Even though she posits that these dichotomies are not explicitly gendered, experience confirms that male and female philosophers working in the area of feminist philosophy, emotions, inter-relational dialogue, or areas defined by nature and embodiment are often devalued as less serious or less rational philosophers. What this assessment likely discloses is a deeply rooted hegemony of masculinity within academic philosophy that rules out any other ontologies as valuable.

According to Michael Armato, associate professor of Sociology and Women's Studies at Northeastern Illinois University, "the academic enterprise creates the image of academic men as 'men of reason' in contrast to 'non academic men,' who are portrayed as governed by passions, insecurities, and the like, and all women, academic or otherwise."[15] He supports the idea that the more conservative areas of academic philosophy—such as metaphysics, logic, and epistemology—are entrenched with a masculine ontology about the nature of reality. Historically, rationality has been taken for granted for centuries as a masculine principle rather than as feminine *and* masculine or simply as gender neutral. In order to understand the occurrence and meaning of implicit gender schemas in academia, we must try to grasp the underlying epistemological presuppositions about what valuable knowledge exactly *is*.

Philosophy departments are often hyper-masculine due to a highly competitive, non-nurturing environment. Academic philosophic discourse is quite judgmental and oriented toward individual accomplishment rather than group accomplishment.[16] On the one hand, the focus on abstract reason as the presumed means of obtaining valid knowledge leaves out several aspects of human existence as objects of study, such as the metaphysics of emotions, non-dualistic and/or feminist metaphysics, philosophy as communication and/or dialogue, and other forms of interpersonal discourse. On the other, it devalues other modes of epistemology and knowledge accumulation such as the philosophical value of empathy and listening. It is not uncommon for academics that prefer to study feminist metaphysics or an academic study of the psychological aspects of human consciousness, that 'doing metaphysics' is less valued or is taken less seriously. Why is this so?

Dominant positivist epistemological assumptions may contribute to this tendency to associate reason with masculinity, as they are bound up with a specific notion of masculinity as rational and authoritative.[17] Both men and women in academia work in an environment that supports their cultivation of masculine gender identity.[18] Considering that the cultivation of masculine gender identity is the dominant ideology in academic philosophy, it often takes place subconsciously. As a result, it is unavoidable that the more practical, situated, emotive, and dialogical forms of philosophy that are not associated with values that are viewed as masculine, are colored 'feminine' or inferior to 'real philosophy.' Masculine ontology holds that correct knowledge is knowledge obtained by reasoning as a clear and pure process of the mind rather than holistic reasoning grounded in embodiment, interrelatedness, dialogue or—a word even more disliked—intuition. When associating reason with masculinity, we duly associate it with discipline, linearity, universality, objectivity, authority, specialism, and thoroughness. As a result, 'real philosophy' is frequently thought of in the same way.[19]

HEGEMONY OF THE MASCULINE

We should not confuse unconscious gender schemas with explicit discrimination or sexism of one party by the other. Women also develop prejudices about women and how they ought to behave and assume that certain capacities and modes of behavior are not feminine and thus not desirable or socially accepted. The same applies to men who suffer from the influence of masculine ontology as they experience it as the superimposed ideal of how a real man and a genuine philosopher ought to fell, behave, and work.

The 'hegemony of the masculine' is thus an ideology that applies to both genders. It is extends to far more than explicit gender bias. Because it is often subconscious, it influences one's own self-image and how one perceives oneself and one's capacities. It creates a personal horizon of limitations and possibilities. The conviction that certain attributes are 'masculine' and therefore superior to or more valuable than attributes that are traditionally considered feminine, such as connecting, authenticity, compassion, empathy, and 'collaborative and supportive work attitudes' harms both genders.[20]

Interestingly, the dominion of rationality in Western history can be traced back to Ancient philosophy itself where rational-scientific thought was related to the masculine, whereas narrative and nature were related to the feminine. Ross-Smith and Kornberger argue that maleness from the beginning of Western thought was symbolically associated with reason whereas femininity was associated with nature.[21] Because men were linked with the mind—the opposite of nature and matter—they started associating masculinity with rationalism.[22] Inasmuch as this distinction was placed in hierarchical order, whatever was deemed masculine was considered superior to anything associated with the feminine.[23] As a result, "Rational knowledge has been constructed as a transcending, transformation or control of natural forces; and the feminine has been associated with what rational knowledge transcends, dominates or simply leaves behind."[24] And what do we want more in life than control?

In *Cratylus,* Plato's seminal writing on etymology and sexuality, courage is indicated as something masculine. "I think we have not yet discussed courage . . . Of course it is clear that not the current opposed to every current is courage, but only that opposed to the current which is contrary to justice; for otherwise courage would not be praised. The words ἄρρην (*arren*, 'male') and ἀνήρ (*aner*, 'man') refer, like ἀνδρεία (*andreia,* 'virility, courage, highness of the soul'), to the ἀνά (*ana,* 'upward') current or flow. The word *gune* (γυνή, 'woman') seems to be much the same as *gone* (birth)."[25] As Todd Reeser claims in *Moderating Masculinity in Early Modern Culture*,[26] courage is a manly virtue since the masculine flows "up" or against "as does male ejaculation," whereas the "feminine flows down in menstruation and child birth."[27] Although both genders are defined by flow, they move in different directions, which define their masculinity or femininity.[28] Plato's disciple Aristotle viewed women as nothing less than "deformed male[s]," because they were devoid of semen, the only principle deemed active in conception."[29] In addition, woman is, among others, "more mischievous, less simple, more impulsive . . . [T]he male, on the other hand, is more spirited than the female . . . more savage . . . more simple . . . and less cunning" (ibid.). "[T]he fact is, the nature of man is the most rounded off and complete, and consequently in man the qualities or capacities mentioned above . . . are found in their perfection . . . Hence woman is [among others] . . . more compassionate [,] . . . more easily moved to tears [,] . . . more jealous, more querulous, more apt to scold and to strike [,] . . more deceptive . . ." and so on.[30] According to Barbara Parsons, emeritus professor at the University of Wisconsin–Platteville, Aristotle perceived the principle of life for woman, as for man, as a soul with capacities for both rational faculties (deliberation and decision) and irrational faculties (emotions and appetites); however, in the soul of woman, unlike that of man, the rational power is not strong enough to govern the irrational one.[31]

This distinction between the rational and non-rational is equally found in Plato's *Phaedrus*, where the philosopher distinguishes between form and matter as to the distinction between soul and body.[32] The active, rational, and thinking soul rules over the body and over the appetitive and the courageous.[33] The body—nature—must be constrained. Since reason was the measure of knowledge of God and the world for the Ancients, it expresses the real nature of the mind independent of the body. According to Genevieve Lloyd, Australian feminist and philosopher, "rationality has been conceived of as transcendence of the feminine itself: and the 'feminine' itself has been partly constituted by its occurrence within this structure."[34] Not surprisingly, "abstract thought, objective judgment, or general principles are seen as masculine characteristics, whereas subjectivity, emotions, and orientation towards the concrete are understood as female."[35] Non-scientific knowledge such as phenomenology, theories of embodiment, ethics, and feminist metaphysics can consequently be considered trivial to the results that logical positivism produces. All in all, intellectual rationality is considered non-situated whereas femininity is associated with situatedness.

To return to Ross-Smith and Kornberger, the ancient Greek association of femininity with embodiment or nature was consequently reinforced by Cartesian dualism and Bacon's empiricism in the eighteenth century.[36] Cartesian rationalism is founded in detachment, dispassion, and in mind/body dualism and is a dominant category "assigned to the masculine, whereas non-reason is subordinated and assigned to the feminine."[37] In Bacon's empiricist philosophy we clearly recognize the association of the feminine with nature and how it must be controlled: "the removal of the pursuit of knowledge from abstract definitions and deductive reasoning and focusing it on the ideas of unbiased analysis of concrete data, inductive reasoning, and empirically supported conclusions. . . . in Bacon's philosophy, nature maintains its femaleness but becomes knowable and controllable."[38] Bacon perceived the goal of science as a "chaste and lawful marriage between Mind and Nature that will bind [Nature] to [man's] servitude and make her [his] slave."[39] Nature is thus subservient to rationality. The mind, a powerful source, is considered the guiding source of human power and controls the human body and the external environment.

As we see, the association between instrumental reason and masculinity, whether applied to males or females, is a thorough one. It also extends to organizational discourse. The technologization of professional knowledge is thoroughly rooted in the metaphysical sensibilities of Western cultures.[40] A masculine ontology seeks to incorporate everything it encounters into a model of production, productivity, performance, and profit, exactly what we see happening at universities today. Despite appearing gender-neutral, organizational discourse is masculine in nature since instrumental rationality and masculinity are inextricably intertwined, despite appearing gender neutral.[41] Not surprisingly then, "masculine instrumentality has [already] chased out the *intimacy* through which such conformations from the 'Other' might be plausible, let alone sustained . . . Its discourse is highly instrumental and devoid of intimacy yet occupied with identity, and driven by rarely reflected upon corporate or bureaucratic goals that are presumed inviolable."[42] [Italics mine] If this is the nature of organizational discourse, what does that say about contemporary philosophy departments?

As long as academic philosophy privileges instrumental reason and disembodied transcendence over embodied, practical, situated knowledge, philosophical insights obtained through field experience or interpersonal dialogue remain undervalued in organizations and beyond. We are not disembodied pure intellects, but people who live with others. As a result of the dominion of instrumental thinking, Western civilization suffered for centuries from the consequences of oppressive dualism, treating intuition and the intellect as separate and conflicting faculties. This is a persistent yet devastating myth that limits us as individuals and as a culture and sustains a false moral division between situated knowledge and clear abstract rationality. Rather, instrumental thinking in the search for timeless truth drives us from the center of our lives—daily living—because it reduces experience to an abstraction. Philosophy should rather bracket truth, let us open ourselves up to alterity, uncertainty and the unexpected in the act of philosophizing. Anything less does philosophy a disservice.

PHILOSOPHICAL COUNSELING AS BALANCING ACT

> Logos is powerless without the power of eros . . .
> Philosophy is the translation of eros into logos
> —Byung-Chul Han [43]

In 2004, Daniel Duane remarked in The *New York Times Magazine* that "[A]mong *serious* academic philosophers—even those who address the so-called human-condition questions—there is an almost visceral revulsion at the very idea of philosophical counseling."[44] Note the word 'serious.' Are philosophical counselors in any way a lesser breed of philosophers? As long as disinterested inquiry is considered as morally superior to situated reasoning through dialogue, and as long as emotive life is perceived as irrational and as lacking in epistemic value, the practical life will be considered inferior to the contemplative life for a long time to come.[45] In his recent work, *Agonie des Eros,* German philosopher Byung-Chul Han connects a lack of Eros in our Western society to a lack of connection with others.[46] Data-driven positivistic science does not give us insight or truth since information is not the same as knowledge. Insight, rather, has a negative nature because it is exclusive, exquisite, and executive.[47] It is not something that can be commanded and exists outside of the dominion of instrumental reason. Rather, an insight that is preceded by experience can collapse everything that was, and give something totally different a new beginning.[48] Insight is an uncontrollable event. Thinking is based on the 'untrodden' path, on the desire for something that is unknown and one does not yet grasp.[49] Not everything must be understood and be made readily available. Insight is a happening in the same manner that Han's Eros is something that 'happens.' In a sense we are hit by Eros' wings when, philosophically speaking, we make an essential step into the unknown. For Han, contemporary thought is in agony because it lacks the risk of alterity, uncertainty and open in dealing with a different Other. Thinking, for example, deep existential thought, starts with Eros or longing. Without Eros—often considered the creative feminine force—philosophy loses its vigor, drive, and vitality and turns repetitive and reactive. The 'reason-as-virtue' paradigm places predominant value on instrumental reason as 'real philosophy' and does the act of philosophizing as an act where a spontaneous event of insight can take place a disservice. Practice applies thought to a real thing in the world upon which it acts. The phenomenology of practice 'grasps' the world rather than it merely 'thinks' it: it grasps the world 'pathically.'[50]

The philosophical practice is unique because the vitality, drive, and vigor that academic philosophy often lacks can come to full expression in the interpersonal, therapeutic relation between counselor and client. Every conversation is, in a sense, an untreated path or an atopic Other. In addition, the competence of practitioners is tied to *pathic* knowledge in the sense that practicing depends on the sense and sensuality of the body, personal presence, relational perceptiveness, tact for knowing what to say and do in contingent situations, thoughtful routines and practices, and other aspects of knowledge that are pre-reflective, pre-theoretic, and pre-linguistic[51] rather than on mere theoretical and/or instrumental knowledge.

Indeed, "it is much easier for us to teach concepts and informational knowledge than it is to bring about pathic understandings," as philosopher

Max van Manen indicates.[52] Philosophical practice thus offers both θεωρία (*theoria*), and πάθος (*pathos*), whereas academic philosophy, if we may say so, offers θεωρία alone. From a phenomenological point of view "[T]he practicality of phenomenology of practice should not be sought in instrumental action, efficiency, or technical efficacy"[53] because philosophy does something *to* us rather than us doing something *with* it. Or, as Wittgenstein contends, "philosophy is not a body of doctrine but an activity."[54]

Why *pathic* knowledge remains undervalued in academia is a mystery. We are foremost social beings. We cannot ignore the Other in his or her alterity. The client is a different person and therefore wholly Other to me, in the same way that the path of philosophizing is a mystery to me. Whereas Bacon sought certainty by means of instrumental reason, in philosophical counseling there is no such thing as timeless, absolute certainty or truth. The endeavor to philosophize freely without vast categories opens up the possibility to go the untrodden path. Philosophical dialogue aims for transformation. It is foremost, as Heidegger says, "our own human activity" and "we ourselves, the questioners . . . are placed into question."[55] The fundamental question in practice is not so much what truth is, but how insight discloses itself between two equals and which ontological presuppositions ground the client's personal reality. A regular philosophical concept or abstraction "only gives us an indication, a pointer to the fact that anyone who seeks to understand is called upon by this conceptual context to undertake a transformation of themselves into their *Dasein*."[56] When we want to balance out masculine principles in order to develop equilibrium between feminine and masculine principles, we must explore the patterns of emotional experience that organize the subjective life of the client rooted in debilitating assumptions concerning his or her own identity. The acknowledgement of the other (the client) as Other and different from oneself, and an openness toward discovering hidden depths of the other's lived experience as aspects of the philosophical practice contribute to a richer understanding of the philosophical life rather than impoverishing it.

NOTES

1. Martin Heidegger. *The Question Concerning Technology and Other Essays*, trans. William Lovitt (New York/London: Garland Publishing Inc., 1977), 112.
2. Sharin N. Elkholy. *Heidegger and a Metaphysics of Feeling: Angst and the Finitude of Being* (London: Continuum, 2008).
3. Sally Haslanger. "Changing the ideology and culture of philosophy: not by reason (alone)," *Hypatia,* 23:2 (2008): 210–223 and Michael Armato, "Wolves in Sheep's Clothing: Men's Enlightened Sexism and Hegemonic Masculinity in Academia," *Women's Studies: An Interdisciplinary Journal* 42:5 (2013): 578–598.
4. Haslanger, "Changing the Ideology."
5. Sally Haslanger, "Are we breaking the ivory ceiling? Women and minorities in philosophy," PowerPoint presentation, 2011. Research data: Co-citation study, Healy, 2013.

6. Sally Haslanger. "Breaking the ivory ceiling . . . Women and Minorities n Philosophy," OZSW conference. Rotterdam: November 15, 2013.

7. I am implying that a philosophical insight obtained from—for instance—a philosophical dialogue between two speakers that originates in an existential question of one of these speakers is considered less valuable by academia than a philosophical insight that is based on philosophical analysis of written language and is a result of solitary mental reflection.

8. I recognize that the way this paper treats rationality might not do justice to advanced feminist discussions and standpoints on the historical and cultural meanings of reason. Nowhere do I attempt to make my analysis of rationality into the final rationality of Western history.

9. Herbert Marcuse, *Eros and Civilization: A Philosophical Inquiry into Freud* (London: Routledge & Kegan Paul LtD, 1998), 125.

10. In hindsight, Genevieve Lloyd's assertion was an eye opener: "Philosophers have at different periods been churchmen, men of letters, university professors. But there is one thing they have had in common throughout the history of the activity: they have been predominantly male; and the absence of women from the philosophical tradition has meant that the conceptualization of Reason has been done exclusively by men. It is not surprising that the results should reflect their sense of Philosophy as a male activity." In: Genevieve Lloyd, *The Men of Reason: 'Male' & 'Female' in Western Philosophy* (Methuen & Co, 1984), 104

11. Haslanger, "Changing the Ideology," 3–4.

12. Virginia Valian, *Why so Slow? The Advancement of Women*, (MIT Press, 1998), 104.

13. Haslanger. "Changing the Ideology," 210–223.

14. Ibid., 3.

15. Michael Armato, "Wolves in Sheep's Clothing," 578–598.

16. Haslanger. "Breaking the ivory ceiling . . . Women and Minorities in Philosophy."

17. Armato, 2005

18. Armato, 2005, 582.

19. According to Lawrence Blum, professor of philosophy at the University of Massachusetts Boston, reason and rationality are at the center of the conception of the good or moral man for the moral rationalist. The defining qualities of a morally admirable man are described as: rationality, self-control, strength of will, consistency, acting from universal principles, and adherence to duty and obligation (Blum, 287–288). Interestingly, Blum states that to Kant and Hegel a further characteristic of a morally upstanding man is the *absence* of the following qualities: sympathy, compassion, kindness, caring for others, human concern, and emotional responsiveness. These qualities are closely bound up with emotions and the emotional aspects of being human, rather than with rationalism. An upstanding, moral man thus has qualities associated with reason and an absence of qualities associated with emotions. See: Lawrence Blum, "Kant's and Hegel's Moral Rationalism: Feminist Perspective," *Canadian Journal of Philosophy* 12:2 (1982): 287–288.

20. Valerie Fournier and Warren Smith. "Scripting Masculinity," *Ephemera* 6:2 (2006): 141–162.

21. Anne Ross-Smith and Martin Kornberger. "Gendered Rationality? A Genealogical Exploration of the Philosophical and Sociological Conceptions of Rationality, Masculinity and Organization," *Gender, Work & Organization* 11: 3 (2004): 280–305.

22. Ibid.

23. Ibid., 283.

24. Lloyd, *The Man of Reason*, 1.

25. Plato, *Cratylus,* trans. H. N. Fowler (Cambridge: Harvard University Press, 1977), 103–105.

26. Todd Reeser, *Moderating Masculinity in Early Modern Culture* (University of North Carolina, 2006).

27. Ibid., 153.

28. Ibid.

29. Barbara Parsons, "Aristotle on Women," in *Women's Studies Encyclopedia* (Westport: Greenwood Press, 1999), 110. Even though we cannot really blame Aristotle for his biological

determinism with the empirical evidence they had in those days, it is unfortunate that he extends his naturalism to psychology and politics.

30. Aristotle. "History of Animals" 608b. 1–14 (Book IX, Ch 1). In: *The Basic Works on Aristotle*. Ed. Richard McKeon (New York: The Modern Library) 2001, 637.

31. Parsons, "Aristotle on Women," 110.

32. Plato, "Phaedrus," in: *Plato: Complete Works*, ed. John M. Cooper (Indianapolis/Cambridge: Hackett Publishing Company, 1997), 524–525

33. Plato, *Phaedrus*, 246a6.

34. Lloyd, *The Man of Reason*, 104.

35. Ross-Smith and Kornberger, "Gendered Rationality?," 283

36. Ibid., 283–284.

37. Ibid., 284.

38. Ibid.

39. Benjamin Farrington, *Francis Bacon, Philosopher of Industrial Science* (London: Lawrence and Wishart, 1951), 187.

40. Max Van Manen, " Phenomenology & Practice," 1 (2007), 19.

41. Ross-Smith and Kornberger, "Gendered Rationality?" 282–287.

42. Fournier and Smith, "Scripting Masculinity," 152.

43. Byung-Chul Han, *Agonie des Eros* (Berlin: Matthes and Seitz, 2013), 62–63.

44. Daniel Duane. "The Socratic Shrink," *New York Times Magazine*, March 21, 2004, 34–37

45. As Hans Georg-Gadamer once said, "just as the individual who needs relevant knowledge, must constantly reintegrate knowledge into the practical knowledge of his everyday life, so also a culture based on science cannot survive unless rationalizing the apparatus of civilization is not an end in itself, but makes possible a life to one can say 'yes'" (Gadamer, 35–36). To put it differently, scientific thought must stand at the service of collective well being rather than that it is an end in itself; and theory must feed practice simultaneously.

46. Han, *Agonie des Eros.*

47. Ibid., 61.

48. Ibid.

49. Here, Han seems to be much inspired by Heidegger's later thought.

50. "The corporeal, relational, temporal, situational, and actional kinds of knowledge cannot necessarily be traced back to conceptualizations. These are the modes of knowing that adhere immediately to our lived experience, in our body, relationships, and the things around us, that they seem invisible." Van Manen, "Phenomenology and Practice."

51. Ibid., 21.

52. Ibid.

53. Ibid., 13.

54. Ludwig Wittgenstein, *Tractatus,* 4.112 (Dover Publications Inc., 1998 [1922]).

55. Robert D. Stolorow and Robert Eli Sanchez, "Philosophy as Therapy: The Case of Heidegger." *International Journal of Psychoanalytic Self Psychology*, 4:125–131, 2009, p. 126.

56. Martin Heidegger, *The Fundamental Concepts of Metaphysics: World, Finitude, Solitude,* trans. W. McNeill & N. Walker (Bloomington: Indiana University Press, 1997), 297.

BIBLIOGRAPHY

Aristotle. "History of Animals" (Book IX, Ch1). In *The Basic Works on Aristotle*, edited by Richard McKeon. New York: The Modern Library, 2001.

Armato, Michael. "Wolves in Sheep's Clothing: Men's Enlightened Sexism and Hegemonic Masculinity in Academia." *Women's Studies: An Interdisciplinary Journal* 42:5 (2013): 578–598.

Blum, Lawrence. "Kant's and Hegel's Moral Rationalism: Feminist Perspective." *Canadian Journal of Philosophy*, 12:2 (1982): 287–288.

Duane, Daniel. "The Socratic Shrink." *New York Times Magazine*, March 21, 2004.

Elkholy, Sharin N. *Heidegger and a Metaphysics of Feeling: Angst and the Finitude of Being.* London: Continuum, 2008.
Fournier, Valerie and Warren Smith. "Scripting Masculinity," *Ephemera* 6:2 (2006): 141–162.
Gadamer, Hans-Georg. *Praise of Theory.* New Haven: Yale University Press, 1998.
Han, Byung-Chul, *Agonie des Eros.* Berlin: Matthes and Seitz, 2013.
Haslanger, Sally. "Changing the Ideology and Culture of Philosophy: Not by Reason (Alone)." *Hypatia* 23:2 (2008): 210–223.
———. "Are We Breaking the Ivory Ceiling? Women and Minorities in Philosophy." PowerPoint presentation, 2011. Research data: Co-citation study, Kieran Healy, 2013.
———. "Breaking the ivory ceiling . . . Women and Minorities in Philosophy." OZSW conference. Rotterdam: November 15, 2013.
Heidegger, Martin. *The Fundamental Concepts of Metaphysics: World, Finitude, Solitude.* Translated by W. McNeill & N. Walker. Bloomington: Indiana University Press, 1997.
———. *The Question Concerning Technology and Other Essays.* Transletd by William Lovitt. New York/London: Garland Publishing Inc., 1977.
Lloyd, Genevieve. *The Man of Reason: 'Male' & 'Female' in Western Philosophy.* Methuen & Co, 1984.
Marcuse, Herbert. *Eros and Civilization: A Philosophical Inquiry into Freud.* Edited with a new preface by Marcuse. New York: Random House, Vintage Books, 1962.
Parsons, Barbara. "Aristotle on Women." *Women's Studies Encyclopedia.* Edited by Helen Tierney. Westport: Greenwood Press, 1999.
Plato, *Cratylus.* Translated by H. N. Fowler. Cambridge: Harvard University Press, 1977 .
Reeser, Todd. *Moderating Masculinity in Early Modern Culture.* University of North Carolina, 2006.
Ross-Smith, Anne, and Martin Kornberger. "Gendered Rationality? A Genealogical Exploration of the Philosophical and Sociological Conceptions of Rationality, Masculinity and Organization." *Gender, Work & Organization* 11: 3 (2004), 280–305.
Stolorow, Robert D., and Robert Eli Sanchez, "Philosophy as Therapy: The Case of Heidegger." *International Journal of Psychoanalytic Self Psychology* 4 (2009):125–131 2009.
Valian, Virginia. *Why So Slow? The Advancement of Women.* MIT Press, 1998.
Van Manen, Max. "Phenomenology & Practice," 1 (2007), 11–30.
Wittgenstein, Ludwig. *Tractatus Logico-Philosophicus.* Dover Publications Inc., 1998 [1922].

Chapter Seventeen

Relationship Violence: How Philosophical Counseling Can Help

Kate Mehuron

Before my practice as a philosophical counselor, I trained as a counselor for survivors of domestic violence in a government-funded agency and its shelter. I was involved in several roles, including answering the telephone crisis line, person-to-person counseling, and co-facilitating two support groups; one composed of heterosexual women over forty years of age and the other composed of lesbian and bisexual survivors of abuse by other women in their lives. This chapter identifies some philosophical counseling approaches that I would use in the present context, if I encountered similar cases that I experienced as a domestic violence counselor. The North American domestic violence counseling system, I argue, is largely constrained by a conceptual model of gender oppression that limits how domestic violence counseling is delivered and that excludes people who do not fit under that model; people who have experienced relationship violence and who would benefit from counseling approaches that are relieved of those constraints. Philosophical critique of the conceptual model of gender oppression shows its heterosexist limitations and can advance philosophical counseling approaches that offer counselors and clients more cognitive and emotional space for personal deliberation. This deliberation, in the philosophical counseling context, is freed of the gender oppression model's heterosexist assumptions. Some of these situations will be described for that purpose but all personal identifiers are changed for the complete anonymity of my clients. I will focus on my lesbian-bisexual clients, as there is little discussion in the philosophical counseling literature with this focus.[1]

As a philosophical counselor, I rely on the use of critical analysis and specific theoretical perspectives to gain some understanding of personal situations.[2] To understand this particular domestic violence shelter and its management's policies and discourse, it is important to grasp the conceptual model on which its normative structure is built. Philosophical critique can clarify the model's normative structure, and this critique highlights how the model articulates the intersection of sexuality, gender, and relationship violence. How people are spoken to, treated, and counseled reflects the agency's normative structure, or principles of practice. All of this provides information for a philosophical critical analysis with practical applications for counseling. Within the North American domestic violence movement, the predominant conceptual and normative framework is the sociological gender oppression model. Gender oppression is defined as "oppression associated with the gender norms, relations, and stratification of a given society." Modern norms of gender in Western societies consist of the dichotomous, mutually exclusive categories of masculinity and femininity.[3]

Most North American domestic violence agencies find that the vast majority of those harmed by the interpersonal power and control dynamics associated with domestic violence are women. So, agencies' discourse and services are developed with regard to supporting women, yet the services are presumed to apply to any person who is victimized in an intimate relationship, including lesbians and men (both heterosexual and gay). My agency asserts that most U.S. domestic violence laws also extend to protect men battered by women, and that most of them also protect lesbians and gay men. The gender oppression model is implicit in the agency's discourse: men and masculinity are the presumed perpetrator class in domestic violence discourse, and women and femininity are the presumed victim-survivor class. Other gender and sexuality groups are homogenized, in practice, within this gender oppression conceptual framework. During the five years that I was a peer counselor, lesbian-bisexual women were recruited by the shelter to participate in the specialized group that I facilitated. The agency used flyers posted at local gay and lesbian bars, bookstores, and university lesbian and gay program offices.

Presently, the domestic violence shelter in my community no longer offers specific services and outreach to lesbian and bisexual survivors. The majority of its clients are heterosexual women, and it continues to accept the gender oppression framework and its homogenization of the needs of non-heterosexual clients within that framework. The problem with the overall adoption of the gender oppression model by domestic violence survivor support agencies is that the implicit homogenization of non-heterosexual gender and sexual orientations can lead, in practice, to unexamined heterosexist attitudes and practices. By "heterosexist" is meant: discrimination or prejudice by heterosexuals against homosexuals.[4]

In most North American domestic violence agencies, the overall normative commitment is to foster the survivors' capacity for choice and autonomy. Counselor training sessions provide factual information about local social services, drug and substance abuse factors, and specific health and safety issues facing survivors and their families. The power-control wheel is the most prevalent didactic tool used by U.S. and Canadian domestic violence agencies. It was developed by Domestic Abuse Intervention Programs in Duluth, Minnesota, and has been widely adapted by agencies. The Programs website states "A batterer systematically uses threats, intimidation, and coercion to instill fear in his partner. These behaviors are the spokes of the wheel. Physical and sexual violence holds it all together—this violence is the rim of the wheel."

The Wheel is not gender neutral; it is a graphic representation of the gender oppression framework. The first hint of its non-neutrality was its ineffectiveness in the context of my efforts to use it as a tool to counsel non-heterosexual women. To understand the reasons for the Wheel's shortcomings, philosophical deconstruction of heterosexuality, presumed by this model to be the normal and normative framework of these women's social relations, is necessary. The Duluth site continues:

"The Power and Control Wheel represents the lived experience of women who live with a man who beats them. It does not attempt to give a broad understanding of all violence in the home or community but instead offers a more precise explanation of the tactics men use to batter women. We keep our focus on women's experience because the battering of women by men continues to be a significant social problem—men commit 86 to 97 percent of all criminal assaults and women are killed 3.5 times more often than men in domestic homicides."[5] The situational complexity of each lesbian-bisexual woman that I counseled did not always map well onto the power and control wheel. In my other support group of heterosexual women over forty, the wheel was a much more effective tool for their reflections on their experiences of interpersonal violence from men.

CLIENT STORIES

I struggled to use the wheel in my responses to the lesbian and bisexual experiences of abuse that were aired in my group. Tanya was in a physically abusive relationship with a woman who was financially dependent on her. Tanya herself was on an extended disability leave for a nerve disease affecting her mobility and manual dexterity. She also had two children of elementary school age. Liz arrived in the group disoriented after her roommate threw her against a wall and hit her, announcing that she (the roommate) had been diagnosed as a multiple personality in recovery. Liz's household consisted of this woman and another, her ex-lover. Both were verbally abusive, one physically abusive, and both were financially dependent on her. She was struggling to find a place that she and her teenage daughter could afford to live. Both Tanya and Liz physically fought back against the physical abuse. The financial dependency of the abusers, in Tanya's and Liz's situations, is one notable anomaly from the power and control wheel. In most heterosexual cases, the woman is financially dependent on the man; his male-dominant social status is depicted by the wheel. Researchers focused on same-sex battery have remarked on the implications of financial dependency in violent same-sex relationships, noting that intense dependency of batterers on their victims is a correlative factor of the violence, perhaps due to the social isolation incurred by cultural homophobia.[6]

Gina joined our group without a significant abuse history. She felt that her family of biological origin was psychologically abusive to her because she came out to them as a lesbian. She had not had a lover nor had she dated in several years. She had a three-year-old boy and worked full-time. She felt that her family was also emotionally abusive to her son. It was difficult to understand Gina's motives for joining the group. We wondered whether her family of origin's homophobic rejection and emotional abuse of her and her son was enough of a reason to participate in a lesbian survivors' support group. I posed this analytical question: if family homophobia itself is a form of domestic violence, then is there a boundary between lesbian "survivors," "assailants," and the rest of the non-heterosexual population who suffer the "insidious trauma" of a homophobic and heterosexist culture? The concept of insidious or cumulative trauma was developed by multicultural trauma theorists in the 1990s.[7] It has been productively applied to the cumulative psychological impact of experiences of oppression, such as heterosexism and homophobia, experiences that do not meet the diagnostic criteria for post-traumatic stress disorder (PTSD).[8] The concept of insidious trauma captured our intuitions regarding Gina's needs. We were pleased to accept Gina's participation because it provided a unique space for integrating her feelings stemming from her marginalized sex-gender status in the culture at large, and for coming to terms with ways to deal with the intergenerational homophobia in her family.

In these cases, the heterosexist meaning of "domestic" and associated terms ("intimate," "partner," "family") is rendered ambiguous by lesbian and bisexual relationships that require, in the context of support group conversation, constant interpretation. Sometimes in spite of the graphic guidelines of the power-control wheel used by the shelter, each woman tried to specifically name the abuses harming her and her chosen family. Each worked to disentangle the gender-based connotations of "assailant" so they could construct a useable index of batterer-like behaviors. Tanya and Liz worked through an emotional gamut of guilt over their own defensive physical violence, sense of disillusionment, betrayal, and feelings of retaliatory anger. Neither regarded themselves as powerless. Rather the dependency of their attackers on them was regarded by the group as a paradoxical aspect of their situation.

The question arose as to whether we need an entirely different way to articulate the experiences of abuse that ought to be included as situations meriting counseling by the domestic violence agency. Our struggle to find a descriptive and normative vocabulary for these experiences of abuse was typical, given the gender oppression framework within which we tried to evaluate this abuse. Cecil was the only participant in the group whose experiences more or less mapped onto the gender oppression framework and the power and control wheel, even though her abuser was a woman. She lived in an intimate relationship with this woman who was a police officer, owned a gun, and threatened her with it. The level of this woman's violence toward Cecil approached lethality. Due to the masculinized profession of Cecil's abuser and the direct lethality of the abuse, the power and control dynamics approximated the masculine and feminine dichotomized roles in the gender oppression model. Cecil's adaptation to the threat was stereotypically feminized insofar as she did not participate in defensive combat. She was passionately attached to her three dogs and struggled to find a place to live that would permit her dogs. She kept a full change of clothes and money in her car and often locked herself in her basement with a door accessing the garage, living in fear that her partner would kill her and her animals. She had reached a level of passive resistance to her partner's violence because she felt that fighting back could jeopardize her very life. The power-control wheel aptly captures heterosexual women's hesitation with respect to calling out their abusers who have highly visible, respected professions and prestigious social roles. But it could not represent the double closet that Cecil experienced as a lesbian woman who could not call out her abuser without exposing herself to homophobic ridicule or indifference.

My experience as group facilitator at the shelter illustrates many further points of conceptual ambiguity made by researchers on lesbian intimate violence. These are summarized in the following discussion.

CONCEPTUAL AND SEMANTIC AMBIGUITIES

My agency's choice of terms caused confusion among group participants and myself; why "lesbian and bisexual" survivors, to the exclusion of self-identified gay men, queer, transgender, or other self-identified non-heterosexual people? The inclusion by domestic violence agencies of lesbian and bisexual women who experience abuse was the result of lesbian feminist activism in the 1980s. Kerry Lobel's 1986 anthology *Naming the Violence: Speaking Out About Lesbian Battering*[9] broke new ground by documenting the forums held by the Lesbian Task Force of the National Coalition Against Domestic Violence. Contributors to this anthology critically address the lesbian feminist presuppositions and the gender oppression framework adopted by the domestic violence movement.

Lesbian feminism is recognized by the contributors to hold an uneasy alliance with the domestic violence movement, similar to lesbian feminism's uneasy early position in North American second-wave feminism of the 1960s and 1970s.[10] In the latter, lesbians were idealized as women-identified women who resist patriarchal gender norms by the very fact of their sexual, erotic, or affective practices with other women: the lesbian utopian ideal. In second-wave feminism, lesbians were subsumed under the category of 'woman;' gendered like heterosexual women as subordinate to men in a patriarchal culture. The lesbian difference from heterosexual women is attributed to their sexual-erotic resistance to this subordination, shared in common with all women whose gender identity is imposed by a misogynist cultural context.

Domestic violence has been recognized since 1994 by the United States federal government as a serious human rights violation; the federal Violence Against Women Act is touted as "a comprehensive approach to violence against women combined with tough new provisions to hold offenders accountable with programs to provide services for the victims of such violence."[11] My agency followed the discourse of the federal Violence Against Women Act in its volunteer training seminars and its operational vocabulary. The gender oppression framework as institutionalized by the domestic violence movement equates gender difference with the social and sexual subordination of women by men. The rigid gender binary that is implicit in this domestic violence discourse constitutes the 'assailant' or 'perpetrator' as 'male' and the 'victim' or 'survivor' as 'female.' This is rationalized by reference to the statistical prevalence of domestic violence perpetrators that are male.[12] This regulated vocabulary is intended to downplay attributions of passivity and subordination to those who participate in the services. It is also intended to downplay attributions of hierarchical authority and dominance to those who provide the services. But lesbian-bisexual practices appear, under the heterosexual gender oppression perspective, to imitate the coerciveness, dominance, or abusiveness of the male-female dynamic.

The 1980s Lesbian Task Force forums testify to the limitations and exclusions occasioned by this imitative position of the lesbian-bisexual woman in the domestic violence movement and the idealization of lesbian relationships in second-wave radical feminism. Contributors to the anthology *Naming the Violence* describe their deep disillusionment with the idealization of the lesbian as the embodiment of resistance to patriarchy. The voices of women abused by other women in intimate relationships disrupts this idealism, leaving a conceptual void filled with heterosexist stereotypes of lesbian-bisexual relationships: the lesbian perpetrator as a masculinized, male-identified butch and the lesbian victim as the feminized counterpart to her masculinized female abuser. This discourse erases the bisexual woman, whose putative gender and sexual identity confusion is invisible in domestic violence discourse.

By the mid-1980s, coalitional efforts between the U.S. gay and lesbian civil rights movement and the feminist domestic violence movement hinged on whether homophobia would be institutionally recognized as an axis of patriarchal oppression. This recognition would allow institutional space for serving lesbian and bisexual women, for they were viewed as women first, and secondly as lesbian-bisexuals who are coping with internalized and cultural homophobia. Patriarchal oppression, the key tenet of U.S. second-wave feminism, did not permit gay men or gender-nonconforming men in supportive institutional space. As men, they presumptively carry culturally ingrained misogyny. The evidence used to rationalize this presumption is the overwhelmingly disproportionate number of men who commit domestic violence against women. But the conflation of heterosexual men's behaviour patterns with non-heterosexual men's behavior patterns resulted in excluding gender-nonconforming men, as men, from domestic violence services. The gender oppression framework recognized the patriarchal, homophobic oppression of non-heterosexual men, but did not provide a rationale for why they ought or ought not to receive the services of a domestic violence agency. Many service providers believed that to offer the support services of their domestic violence agency to non-heterosexual men was tantamount to inviting men in general, hence abusers, to participate. This normative framework continues to receive critique in the social science research literature.[13] Our aforementioned confusion as to the reasons for the agency's exclusion of self-identified gay men, queer, transgender, or other self-identified non-heterosexual people is clarified by this elucidation of the bias of the agency's gender oppression framework. But to build alternatives to it, we need philosophical critiques of this framework and the constructive potential of philosophical counseling to overcome the limitations of this framework. Philosophical counseling can, with cognizance of this dominant framework, engage a client in dialogue that assists analytical, evaluative, and narrative reorientation toward the situation and effects of relationship violence.

QUESTIONING DOMESTIC VIOLENCE DISCOURSE

I have looked for community resources committed to serving gender-nonconforming people. These exist in my metropolitan area, but they are not directly affiliated with institutionalized domestic violence agencies or shelters. The reasons for this are discussed by social science researcher Janice Ristock in *No More Secrets: Violence in Lesbian Relationships*.[14] Ristock provides a discourse analysis of the service and counseling speech of domestic violence service providers, comparing this to the speech of lesbian and bisexual women survivors. Her research contribution is her discourse analysis of transcripts of her interviews with 102 lesbian and bisexual women and eight focus group sessions with a total of seventy feminist service providers.[15] She takes “lesbian” as an umbrella concept that includes women involved with women who may identify as gay, dyke, boyz, butch, femme, queer, bisexual, two-spirited, or transgender.[16] By “dominant discourses” Ristock means the social practices that construct the particular truths, experiences, subjectivities, power relations, and normative attitudes found in transcripts of domestic violence speech.[17]

Paying attention to the discourses of lesbian and bisexual women who have experienced intimate violence and the discourses of service providers, Ristock describes the material conditions revealed by their expressed subjective experiences and the beliefs implied by their responses to interpersonal violence. She finds a disjunctive relation between the educational materials and counseling vernaculars provided by domestic violence agencies and the verbal expressions of lesbian and bisexual survivors. Her interviews show that a wide range of contextual factors surround lesbian and bisexual intimate abuse. These contextual factors are not simple causal factors. Rather than create more typologies or correlates of lesbian-bisexual intimate abuse as positivist social science research tends to do, Ristock urges that we grapple with questions of motivation and intention within the specific contexts of abuse disclosed by these narratives.

For example, Ristock finds that patterns of abuse reported in the interviewees’ *first* lesbian relationships are not reported in other social science research, even in the widely known earlier research by Claire Renzetti.[18] *First* relationships, she finds, are a focal point of intense experiences of social vulnerability, outsider status, and the homosexual closet. Fear of social homophobia especially in small, rural locations is a factor that is more intense than the internalized homophobia much remarked by the dominant social science research. The experience of dislocation surfaced in many of the interviews: a factor minimized in most domestic violence research. Interviewees provided narratives of interpersonal and social violence in multiple contexts: personal histories of family and peer abuse; interlocking oppressions of racism or poverty; and drug and alcohol abuse. Within a lifetime of oppressive experiences, relationship violence becomes one part of a larger story wherein the simplistic lens of ‘perpetrator and survivor’ does not entirely resonate. Many of the interviews disclose fluctuating interpersonal power relations that resemble the notion of “cycles of violence” in the domestic violence literature.[19]

Yet the choreographies of violence between partners and family members frequently disrupt the power and control wheel paradigm. This oversimplifies the choreography of violence uncovered in these transcripts. Rather than add more categories of aggression to lesbian-bisexual schemas of domestic violence, Ristock recommends that counselors acknowledge the complex motivations shown in fighting back: the taste for revenge, the resiliency, strength, and agency of the survivor. Rather than accepting the legal label of 'mutual abuse' with the presumed equality of power and intention to harm, counselors need to listen to the nuances in motive and intention described in narratives of "fighting back." Ristock argues that effective responses to intimate violence necessitates that we grapple with such questions as "How do we assess acts of resistance or differing levels of intention within each partner when fighting continues?"[20]

This question dovetails with philosopher Claudia Card's articulation of the need for understanding and providing moral reparations in the aftermath of abusive relationships. Card, in *The Atrocity Paradigm: A Theory of Evil*, describes the moral remainders of interpersonal violence: the personal debts, unexplained wrongs, feelings of remorse, regret, or gratitude that present possibilities for repair of damages done.[21] Card's extensive description of the moral powers of victims and the moral burdens and obligations of perpetrators indicates a valuable direction for domestic violence counselors and by extension, philosophical counselors. We need to develop the capacity to see the moral powers, possibilities, burdens, and obligations of people who have participated in the choreography of violence and who have an interest in addressing the culpabilities and harms that overlap with the search for legal remedies. Moral reflection and ethical deliberation is an important supplement to the universalizing and didactic models wielded by domestic violence service providers. Just as supplements are not trivial but rather core remedies in health regimes, the supplement of moral reflection in Card's sense is key to evaluating the dynamics and consequences of domestic violence. This, in addition to critical analysis, is the realm within which philosophical counselors can be helpful to those who are coping with interpersonal violence in their lives. This dimension is fraught with moral nuances that need to be sorted out by the survivor with reference to evidence-based sources that detail the likelihood of repeated scenes of violence subsequent even to the batterer's show of remorse. Philosophical resources such as Card's analysis are an invaluable part of the philosophical counselor's toolbox for helping a client to carry out an evaluative re-orientation toward the effects of relationship violence.

For example, the gender oppression model assumes that the male perpetrator is incorrigible; his lethality and remorselessness excludes him from the bounds of counseling interventions. Ristock notes that the lesbian and bisexual perpetrator is typically constructed as an imitation of male badness. The consequence is that service providers are usually unwilling to work with lesbian and bisexual perpetrators, as well as male perpetrators. Ristock writes: "We need discursive possibilities that allow different narratives of subjectivities in which the whole person in all of her multiplicity can be considered within a larger context."[22] The context of misrecognition within which many lesbian-bisexual relationships are convened has its symptoms, described by social scientist Lori Girshick in *Women to Women Violence*: lack of social legitimacy, mutual over-dependency, closets within families of origin, mortal fear of being exposed by one's abuser.[23]

Girshick remarks that in some surveys, most survivors say they want services and treatment for abusers so their abusers stop hurting others, and they empathize with their abusers insofar as they share common struggles against racism, homophobia, and xenophobia. Service providers want to keep the dominant gender oppression discourse in order to hold perpetrators accountable. But a philosophical approach may uphold that there can be critical reflection for the sake of 'seeing' instances where an offender is capable of living up to obligations of reparation or restitution. Such instances, Claudia Card shows, are occasions for the survivor to exercise moral powers such as appropriate expressions of mercy or forgiveness.[24] By noting this, I do not wish to downplay the dangers associated with reparations made by abusers. A deep understanding of the potential lethality of the abuser must always be a key part of this moral deliberation.

Ristock criticizes the "necessary speech" of domestic violence shelters. Official speech is required to keep shelters funded. When the dynamics of woman-to-woman violence are public in the form of specific services, there is the danger of misogynist and homophobic groups using backlash tactics to downplay male violence. Unfortunately, service speech made intelligible by the power and control wheel obfuscates understanding woman-to-woman abuse and the motivational and intentional dimensions of fighting back.[25] But ethical deliberation concerning the meaning of power dynamics, of consent, and definitions of what constitute abuse ought to be a part of service provision rather than suspended as too dangerous for an agency to sponsor.

QUEER THEORY CHALLENGES TO THE GENDER OPPRESSION MODEL

Since the 1970s, the U.S. women's movement for equality and the lesbian and gay equality movement have increasingly influenced the legal landscape. For example, "sexual harassment" has become a legal term embedded in U.S. federal civil rights legislation,[26] the Supreme Court overturned the criminalization of homosexual sodomy[27] and declared federal law banning same-sex marriage as unconstitutional.[28] In the 1990s, queer theory, "an approach to literary and cultural study that rejects traditional categories of gender and sexuality,"[29] swept North American academia and catalyzed political voices to challenge the binaries implicit in the gender oppression model. The transgender rights movement, using queer theoretical formulations, energetically advocated to reform public spaces and institutional structures to accommodate transgender needs. This movement is gaining success on many issues.[30]

If the domestic violence movement integrates the queer theoretical insights reaped by these recent social movements, then unique services, community outreach initiatives, and counseling vernaculars would flourish on behalf of lesbian, gay, bisexual, and transgender survivors. The gender oppression framework and the North American clinical and professionalized infrastructure of domestic violence services would be productively challenged to grow in inclusive directions. The relevance of non-heterosexual men's situations to the gender-oppression model of the feminist domestic violence movement is only narrowly and prejudicially retained as 'male perpetrator.' So, much practical and theoretical work should be done with regard to gender-nonconforming male situations. As a result of systemic misrecognition, there is now even less research on gender-nonconforming male-to-male intimate relationship violence than on lesbian relationship violence.[31] Gender-nonconforming men should receive recognition as research subjects and recipients of specialized domestic violence support services. Despite the importance of this issue, for the narrower purpose of this chapter I will continue to focus on gender-nonconforming female situations, the legal implications of such, and the interpretive light that philosophical queer theory sheds on these situations.

Philosophers Cheshire Calhoun and Judith Butler challenge the gender-oppression model's insistence that the categories of gender and sex are produced solely by patriarchal heterosexual practices and norms. The possibilities of multiple genders and multiple sexualities are foreclosed by this narrow focus on dominant heterosexual norms. Calhoun observes that challenging lesbian and gay subordination and challenging women's oppression is not the same. She argues that the gender and sex difference between heterosexual women and lesbian-bisexual women is not represented in the gender oppression framework, because this framework cannot conceptually integrate the axis of heterosexist subordination. Calhoun describes this type of social subordination as displacement, wherein heterosexist social policies and norms function to construct the identities of non-heterosexual people as citizen-deviants and to systemically deny them access to a legitimate, protected private sphere. This axis of displacement subjects gender-nonconforming people to the stigma of being "family outlaws" and attributes to them inferior cultural stereotypes as people inherently morally untrustworthy, in violation of God, nature, and the state.

The axis of displacement, Calhoun argues, denies non-heterosexual people the liberty to publicly represent their sex and/or gender identity, to have access to a protected and legitimate private sphere, and to influence and sponsor future generations of non-heterosexual people. The axis of heterosexism supports cultural displacements that include: homophobic differentiation between 'real' women and 'pseudo-women' and the social construction of those who are stigmatized as non-women and unreal genders or sexes. Calhoun writes:

> If, instead, feminism is about women and the open spaces of possibilities between this binary 'woman/man,' then lesbians can be theorized within a feminist frame. But the cost of opening the feminist frame in this way is quite high. With the lesbian not-woman enter the gay man, the heterosexual and gay male transvestite, the male-to-female transsexual, the male lesbian and the like—this time not as men or imitation women, but as the third term between gender binaries.[32]

The queer theory alternative shows that the production of gender and sex binaries are historically linked to dominant heterosexuality. But queer theory insists that genders and sexualities are neither reducible to nor determined by this dominance. Butler calls for a new lexicon of genders and sexualities that can name the actual gender and sex constellation that disrupts heterosexist categories.[33] The question as to whether these groups of people can or should be included as subjects within a new paradigm is complicated by the pressing issue of legal definitions of gender and sex identity.

Legal advocates who would assist non-heterosexual clients to negotiate the court system are well aware of the harmful legal ambiguities that the axis of displacement reinforces. Queer theorists acknowledge the predicament of sex and gender definition presented by queer critique. Butler notes that we have to present ourselves as subjects before the law. Although our lives depend on protections, legal sanctions, and norms of recognition, it would be a mistake if we take legal definitions to be what we are in some essential sense. In addition to the need for legal recognition, the supportive legal interventions by domestic violence agencies require, to some extent, sex and gender classifications. In this regard, the stakes are high for domestic violence legal advocacy for non-heterosexual people.

Legal scholar Ruth Ann Robson places lesbian social survival at the center of her reasoning. Robson cautions against the sublimation of lesbianism into dual-gendered theories or into queer theory, both of which are vulnerable to the bias of male privilege. She states that "if the legal issue pertains specifically to lesbians, I will be influenced by my beliefs as to the existence of such essentialist creatures as lesbians who can be protected by antidiscrimination laws."[34] Putting lesbians at the center of her legal theory, she argues, necessitates a critical attitude toward the law, the concepts of which have colonized the lives of lesbians. Robson urges that domestic violence activists reflect whether the law is always appropriate or beneficial to lesbian survival. Robson observes that when lesbian domestic violence incidents receive the attention of the law, it is frequently the lesbianism that is punished rather than acts of interpersonal violence. Robson's observations are supported by Calhoun's analysis of how the heterosexist axis regulates lesbians as citizen-deviants. Robson provides several case examples that show the courts' interpretation of lesbian defendants' complaints to be preconditioned by a gender-oppression model of domestic violence. The more 'masculine' party is often prejudged to be the violent perpetrator. Robson argues that these cases show that gender-nonconformity itself becomes a presumed proof of violence in court. She notes that "ironically, the identification of violence with maleness, coupled with heterosexism and homophobia, domesticates us as lesbians when we attempt to avail ourselves of these concrete reforms. Such domestication interferes with the benefit any of the concrete reforms can have on our survival."[35]

Many contemporary judges and legal officials are educated on domestic violence issues. They recognize abuse stemming from dominant/submissive interpersonal relationships based on the dual-gender heterosexual framework. But when faced with domestic violence charges filed by lesbians or bisexual women, often they seem unable to apply these gendered distinctions. Even in U.S. states where restraining orders are statutorily available to lesbians, the courts may find "mutual combat" rather than domestic violence. The implication of the denial of a restraining order is that lesbian intimate violence is indistinguishable from the legal category of "assault." Or, a mutual restraining order apportions responsibility for the violence between the parties, adjudicating that "fighting" rather than "abuse" has occurred. A battered lesbian who pushes her partner in self-defense may violate a mutual restraining order. Both may be convicted of this violation with dire employment penalties such as disqualification from state employment, work in mental health facilities, child care facilities, alcohol and drug treatment facilities, nursing homes, youth services, and work with the mentally disabled.[36] The statutory definitions relevant to domestic violence vary from state to state, so a lesbian seeking a restraining order must mold herself and her assailant into the categories of the statute in their particular state. This is difficult at best. Some statutes that resort to broad definitions of the "family" will include lesbian defendants who can successfully analogize their relationship to the recognized legal categories of "family" or household."[37]

Heterosexism in the U.S. legal system is widespread. There is widespread denial of equal protection from domestic abuse under the law. Few U.S. states and the District of Columbia offer specific statutory protection for same-sex domestic violence. Only Vermont explicitly states that all laws related to heterosexual spouses extend to same-sex partners codified under civil union legislation. Girshick documents that nine states exclude lesbians, bisexuals, and gay men from domestic violence statutes by explicitly covering only male-to-female relationships or by stating that partners need to be married or formerly married. There is wide variability even within the same state for terms of eligibility to file criminal charges of battering or civil restraining orders. Within state law, the phrase "current or former household member" can allow lesbian and bisexual women access to legal protection, but such phrases are often mixed with other parts of state statutory language that refer to "persons of the opposite sex," and so on. Such inconsistent language obtains in eight states, where "personal relationship" is heterosexually defined. Twenty-five states stipulate that "living together" or "cohabitation" is the only status by which lesbian and bisexual women can gain access to legal protection. But definitions of "cohabitation" differ widely from state to state. In California, it means "unmarried man and woman." In Delaware it applies to same- and opposite-sex adults; in Virginia, it means "spouses" determined as opposite-sex couples.[38] These judicial semantic ambiguities abound in U.S. states that once had sodomy laws, prior to *Lawrence vs. Texas*, criminalizing lesbian and bisexual defendants. Admitting a lesbian relationship prejudices the courts, especially in states where former sodomy laws have created a climate wherein some sexual behaviors continue to be perceived as abnormal, immoral, or illegal.

These observations are illustrated in a unique way by Girshick's study of woman-to-woman sexual violence. Girshick's study included seventy self-identified lesbian or bisexual women who reported and described experiences of woman-to-woman sexual violence. She finds that statutory definitions of rape are most often framed by heterosexist assumptions regarding "sex" as penile-vaginal intercourse. The most common sexual violations reported in her study of woman-to-woman sexual abuse involved forced vaginal and anal finger penetration or penetration with the use of objects. At the time of her study, Pennsylvania was the only state that included this type of sexual abuse in its statutory definition of rape. If and when same-sex sexual abuse is brought to the attention of the law, it is most often categorized and trivialized as sexual battery: a misdemeanor. Girshick finds Washington State to provide an unusually concise and inclusive statutory model that should be emulated by the other U.S. states. "Sexual intercourse" has its usual meaning, but is extended to include a precise description of a wide range of sexual behaviors between same- or opposite-sex persons. Prosecutorial charges can derive from same-sex and opposite-sex rape, on a range of first to third degrees.[39] Because of the heterosexual subtext of rape that pervades the minds of legal professionals, the sexual violence that a woman may experience at the hands of another woman will not be handled as seriously as rape perpetrated by a man. Out of Girshick's study of seventy participants and ninety-one incidents of woman-to-woman sexual violence, many of which involved physical injury and forced restraint, only seventeen had police contact or used the courts.[40]

Girshick and Robson note that the pursuit of equal protection by the law can lead lesbians and bisexual women into complex legal problems that may be worse than the alternative of avoiding legal redress and resorting to friends and community resources. The high probability of legal problems facing lesbian and bisexual survivors who seek legal redress lends strong support to Calhoun's thesis that the equal marriage movement is vital to the interests of non-heterosexuals. Calhoun argues that the equal right to same-sex marriage will be an important counter-force to the legal displacements of lesbians, gays, bisexuals, and transgender people from same-sex domestic violence support. Now that the U.S. Supreme Court has declared unconstitutional the federal Defense of Marriage Act, the social experiment begins.

CONCLUSION

During the time that I wrote this chapter, a heterosexual acquaintance within my circle of friends decided to separate from her husband and file for divorce, due to the physical and verbal abuse she had suffered in her thirty-year marriage. Without hesitation, I recommended some contemporary resources for her to read, including Bancroft's *Why Does He Do That? Inside the Minds of Angry and Controlling Men.*[41] Increasingly, men are taking responsibility for men's role in relationship violence, as this resource attests. Some of the most effective resources for domestic violence intervention are those written and led by men willing to talk about the motivational factors underlying men's violence and in men's efforts to change their behavior. Male counselors and male service providers who are willing to hold male perpetrators accountable are also a reassuring resource to women who are finding their way through the confusion of intimate heterosexual violence. Most updated self-help books on divorce include relevant material on domestic violence.

My acquaintance had never read about domestic violence, called a domestic violence crisis hotline, or confided in anyone about her experiences. She didn't know the complex legal territory of filing for divorce nor the available legal options relevant to those who have experienced domestic violence within the marriage. These resources have become normalized as part of our North American culture. Her reading was the first step toward her autonomy. The resources that I gave her provided the needed new vocabulary, critical analysis, and evidence-based insight to motivate her, make decisions and even to influence her husband to seek help from other men in a domestic violence men's treatment group.

Although it is unclear how she will resolve her situation, in her case the gender-oppression model on which these resources are based once again showed its efficacy. She did not need to consult a psychiatrist or a clinical psychologist, because her situation is no longer pathologized by our culture as a mental health problem; the available resources are effective enough to be used by her to plan her own direction. Perhaps I functioned as a shadowy philosophical counselor in this case. I didn't announce myself as such; I was simply there as a supportive participant in her situation, In my own mind I was offering my previous counseling experiences, bibliotherapy as guidance through directed reading[42] and critical analysis to her.

In contrast, the most common sources of help for gender-nonconforming people are psychiatrists, clinical psychologists, psychotherapists, and friends. Shelter services still are viewed as biased toward heterosexual women coping with male perpetrators. As I have shown in this chapter, this perception is largely true. As dire as is the ongoing need for heterosexual women and men to seek help in domestic violence situations, the same holds true for gender-nonconforming people. There are not enough resources for the latter. Had my acquaintance been lesbian, bisexual, or transgender, I would not have had accessible self-help references ready at hand. My acquaintance would probably not have told her problem to this circle of friends due to the homophobic social invisibility of her personal life. She might have consulted a psychiatrist or clinical psychologist, only to receive a diagnosis and a pharmaceutical prescription; medical substitutes for informed self-care practices.[43]

Philosophical counselors can offer an alternative to clinical and social services if we are aware of the heterosexist presumptions of the dominant gender-oppression discourse of domestic violence. Ironically, the mainstream success of the domestic violence movement discourages it from the next level of self-transformation. The practical and moral burden lies on lesbian, gay, bisexual, transgender organizations to continue to develop counseling vernaculars, community outreach initiatives, educational materials, and legal advocacy that directly address the particular contexts within which non-heterosexual people experience relationship violence. These organizations work to open spaces of possibility as they challenge the axis of displacement that prohibits non-heterosexual people from access to legitimate protection in their private lives. On a positive note, the newly authorized 2013 Violence Against Women Act (VAWA) includes an historic provision. The U.S. Department of Justice states:

> For the first time in any federal funding statute, VAWA 2013 recognizes the civil rights of LGBT victims and survivors by explicitly prohibiting VAWA grantees from discriminating on the basis of sexual orientation or gender identity. This groundbreaking provision will ensure that LGBT victims of domestic violence, sexual assault, and dating violence and stalking are not denied, on the basis of sexual orientation or gender identity, access to the critical services that OVW supports.[44]

Given this federal provision, this is the best time for us to become aware of how our implicit beliefs about gender and sex categories influence our counseling practices.

Philosophical counselors can participate in this social transformation by sharing the moral burden of helping ourselves and others to envision social justice on the level of gender and sexuality. Philosophical applications are equally as vital as political activism: moral reflection, critical analysis, theoretical understanding of how groups of people are normatively and socially marginalized and the implications of this in people's lives. Within the contexts of relationship violence and trauma, philosophical counseling is complementary to the political activism necessitated by these contexts. Philosophical counseling is in itself an activist response to these situations, wherein parties to the violence are learning to critique the situation in order to change, or recover or extricate from it. The use of philosophical critique serves to open new possibilities of life. If philosophical insights and methods are not applied to the sphere of relationship violence, then lesbians, bisexual women, and gender-nonconforming men will continue to be assimilated to heterosexist standards and discourses in institutional support contexts.

Judith Butler eloquently says: "Possibility is not a luxury; it is as crucial as bread. I think we should not underestimate what the thought of the possible does for those for whom the very issue of survival is most urgent."[45] This is one of the core tasks of philosophical counseling itself: to apply critical analysis to social prejudice, clearing the way for the thought of the possible.

NOTES

1. Peter Raabe, "Sex and Logic," in *Issues in Philosophical Counseling* (Westport, CT: Praeger Publishers, 2001), 57–72.
2. Kate Mehuron, "Case Studies from Research at Eastern Michigan University," *Philosophical Practice*, 4:3 (2009): 492–501.
3. Vrushali Patil, "Gender Oppression," in *Blackwell Encyclopedia of Sociology*, ed. George Ritzer (Malden, MA: Blackwell Publishing, 2006).
4. "Heterosexism," s.v. *Merriam-Webster* Online, accessed March 22, 2014, http://www.merriam-webster.com/dictionary/heterosexism.
5. The Duluth Model. Social Change to End Violence Against Women, accessed March 22, 2014, http://www.theduluthmodel.org/training/wheels.html.
6. Claire M. Renzetti, *Violent Betrayal: Partner Abuse in Lesbian Relationships* (Newbury Park, CA: Sage, 1992).
7. Maria P. Root, "Women of Color and Traumatic Stress in 'Domestic Captivity': Gender and Race as Disempowering Statuses," in *Ethnocultural Aspects of Posttraumatic Stress Disorder: Issues, Research, and Clinical Applications,* eds. Anthony J. Marsella, Matthew J. Friedman, Ellen T. Gerrity, and Raymond M. Scurfield (Washington, D.C.: American Psychological Association, 1996), 363–387.
8. Dawn M. Szymanski and Kimberly F. Balsam, "Insidious Trauma: Examining the Relationship Between Heterosexism and Lesbians' PTSD Symptoms." *Traumatology*, 17:2 (2011): 4–13.
9. Kerry Lobel, *Naming the Violence: Speaking Out About Lesbian Battering* (Seattle: Seal Press, 1986).
10. Laura Brunell, "Feminism," s.v. in *Encyclopaedia Britannica* Online, last updated August 27, 2013, http://www.britannica.com/EBchecked/topic/724633/feminism/216008/The

-second-wave-of-feminism.

11. The White House, Factsheet: The Violence Against Women Act, accessed March 23, 2014, http://www.whitehouse.gov/sites/default/files/docs/vawa_factsheet.pdf.

12. U.S. Department of Justice, "Extent, Nature, and Consequences of Intimate Violence Against Women Research Report" (Office of Justice Programs, National Institute of Justice, 2000), https://www.ncjrs.gov/pdffiles1/nij/181867.pdf.

13. David Island and Patrick Letellier, *Men Who Beat Men Who Love Them: Battered Gay Men and Domestic Violence* (New York: Harrington Park Press, 1991).

14. Janice L. Ristock, *No More Secrets: Violence in Lesbian Relationships* (New York: Routledge, 2002).

15. Ibid., 32–34.

16. Ibid., 23.

17. Ibid., 39.

18. Claire Renzetti, *Violent Betrayal: Partner Abuse in Lesbian Relationships* (Thousand Oaks, CA: Sage Publications, 1992).

19. Tod W. Burke and Stephen S. Owen, "Same-Sex Domestic Violence: Is Anyone Listening?" *The Gay and Lesbian Review Worldwide XIII* 1:6 (2006).

20. Ristock, 76.

21. Claudia Card, *The Atrocity Paradigm: A Theory of Evil* (New York: Oxford University Press, 2002), 169.

22. Ristock, 127.

23. Lori B. Girshick, *Woman-to-Woman Sexual Violence: Does She Call It Rape?* (Boston, MA: Northeastern University Press, 2002),162.

24. Card, 178–179.

25. Ristock, 129.

26. U.S. Equal Employment Opportunity Commission, "Sexual Harrassment," accessed April 4, 2014, http://www.eeoc.gov/laws/types/sexual_harassment.cfm.

27. Laurence H. Tribe, "Lawrence v. Texas: The 'Fundamental Right' That Dare Not Speak Its Name," *Harvard Law Review*, 117:1894-95.

28. Supreme Court of the United States, "Filings in the Defense of Marriage Act and California's Proposition 8 Cases," accessed April 4, 2014, http://www.supremecourt.gov/docket/domprp8.aspx.

29. "Queer Theory," s.v. *Merriam-Webster* Online, accessed April 4, 2014, http://www.merriam-webster.com/dictionary/queer%20theory.

30. Transgender Advocacy Network, accessed April 4, 2014, http://transadvocacynetwork.org/.

31. Maya Shwayder, "A Same-Sex Domestic Violence Epidemic is Silent," *The Atlantic*, November 5, 2013, accessed April 4, 2014, http://www.theatlantic.com/health/archive/2013/11/a-same-sex-domestic-violence-epidemic-is-silent/281131/.

32. Cheshire Calhoun, *Feminism, the Family, and the Politics of the Closet: Lesbian and Gay Displacement* (London: Oxford University Press, 2000), 73.

33. Judith Butler, *Undoing Gender* (United Kingdom: Routledge, 2004).

34. Ruthann Robson, *Lesbian (Out)Law: Survival Under the Rule of Law* (Ithaca, New York: Firebrand Books, 1992), 17.

35. Ibid., 158.

36. Ibid., 162.

37. Ibid., 164.

38. Girshick, 137–138.

39. Girshick, 143.

40. Girshick, 146.

41. Lundy Bancroft, *Why Does He Do That? Inside the Minds of Angry and Controlling Men* (New York, NY: Berkely Books, Penguin Group, 2003).

42. Eileen Krauss, "Bibliotherapy,"*AHIL Quarterly*, Summer 1966: 18.

43. Kate Mehuron, "Encountering the Diagnosis in Philosophical Counseling Practice," in *Philosophical Practice*, 3:2 (2008): 277–284.

44. "Ensuring Access for LGBT Victims of Domestic Violence, Sexual Assault, Dating Violence and Stalking," U.S. Department of Justice Office On Violence Against Women Blog, September 30, 2013, accessed April 4, 2014, http://blogs.justice.gov/ovw/archives/2433.
45. Butler, 129.

BIBLIOGRAPHY

Bancroft, Lundy. *Why Does He Do That? Inside the Minds of Angry and Controlling Men*. New York, NY: Berkely Books, Penguin Group, 2003.

Brunell, Laura. "Feminism," s.v. in *Encyclopaedia Britannica* Online, last updated August 27, 2013. http://www.britannica.com/EBchecked/topic/724633/feminism/215008/The-second-wave-of-feminism .

Burke, Tod W., and Owen, Stephen S. "Same-Sex Domestic Violence: Is Anyone Listening?" *The Gay and Lesbian Review Worldwide XIII*, 1:6 (2006).

Butler, Judith. *Undoing Gender*. United Kingdom: Routledge, 2004.

Calhoun, Cheshire. *Feminism, the Family, and the Politics of the Closet: Lesbian and Gay Displacement*. London: Oxford University Press, 2000.

Card, Claudia. *The Atrocity Paradigm: A Theory of Evil*. New York: Oxford University Press, 2002.

The Duluth Model. Social Change to End Violence Against Women, accessed March 22, 2014. http://www.theduluthmodel.org/training/wheels.html .

Girshick, Lori B. *Woman-to-Woman Sexual Violence: Does She Call It Rape?* Boston, MA: Northeastern University Press, 2002.

"Heterosexism," s.v. Merriam-Webster Online. Accessed March 22, 2014. http://www.merriam-webster.com/dictionary/heterosexism.

Island, David and Letellier, Patrick. *Men Who Beat Men Who Love Them: Battered Gay Men and Domestic Violence*. New York: Harrington Park Press, 1991.

Krauss, Eileen. "Bibliotherapy."*AHIL Quarterly*, Summer 1966.

Lobel, Kerry. *Naming the Violence: Speaking Out About Lesbian Battering*. Seattle: Seal Press, 1986.

Marsella, Anthony, Friedman, Matthew J., Gerrity, Ellen T., and Scurfield, Raymond M., eds. *Ethnocultural Aspects of Post-traumatic Stress Disorder: Issues, Research, and Clinical Applications*. Washington, D.C.: American Psychological Association. 1996. Mehuron, Kate. "Case Studies from Research at Eastern Michigan University,"

Philosophical Practice. 4:3 (2009).

Mehuron, Kate. "Encountering the Diagnosis in Philosophical Counseling Practice," *Philosophical Practice*. 3:2 (2008).

Patil, Vrushali, "Gender Oppression." *Blackwell Encyclopedia of Sociology*. Edited by George Ritzer. Malden, MA: Blackwell Publishing, 2006. Queer Theory," s.v. Merriam-Webster Online. Accessed April 4, 2014. http://www.merriam-webster.com/dictionary/queer%20 theory.

Raabe, Peter. "Sex and Logic." *Issues in Philosophical Counseling*. Westport, CT: Praeger Publishers, 2001.

Renzetti, Claire M. *Violent Betrayal: Partner Abuse in Lesbian Relationships*. Newbury Park, CA: Sage, 1992.

Robson, Ruthann. *Lesbian (Out)Law: Survival Under the Rule of Law*. Ithaca, New York: Firebrand Books, 1992.

Shwayder, Maya. A Same-Sex Domestic Violence Epidemic is Silent." *The Atlantic*, November 5, 2013. Accessed April 4, 2014. http://www.theatlantic.com/health/archive/2013/11/a-same-sex-domestic-violence-epidemic-is-silent/281131/.

Supreme Court of the United States, "Filings in the Defense of Marriage Act and California's Proposition 8 Cases." Accessed April 4, 2014. http://www.supremecourt.gov/docket/domprp8.aspx.

Szymanski, Dawn M. and Balsam, Kimberly F. "Insidious Trauma: Examining the Relationship Between Heterosexism and Lesbians' PTSD Symptoms." *Traumatology*. 17:2 (2011).
Transgender Advocacy Network. Accessed April 4, 2014. http://transadvocacynetwork.org/.
Tribe, Laurence H. "Lawrence v. Texas: The 'Fundamental Right' That Dare Not Speak Its Name." *Harvard Law Review*. 117.
U.S. Department of Justice, "Extent, Nature, and Consequences of Intimate Violence Against Women Research Report." Office of Justice Programs, National Institute of Justice, 2000. https://www.ncjrs.gov/pdffiles1/nij/181867.pdf.
U.S. Department of Justice Office On Violence Against Women Blog, "Ensuring Access for LGBT Victims of Domestic Violence, Sexual Assault, Dating Violence and Stalking," September 30, 2013. Accessed April 4, 2014. http://blogs.justice.gov/ovw/archives/2433.
U.S. Equal Employment Opportunity Commission, "Sexual Harrassment." Accessed April 4, 2014. http://www.eeoc.gov/laws/types/sexual_harassment.cfm.
The White House, Factsheet: The Violence Against Women Act. Accessed March 23, 2014. http://www.whitehouse.gov/sites/default/files/docs/vawa_factsheet.pdf.

Chapter Eighteen

Giving Birth to Derrida's Mother: Philosophical Practice at the End of Philosophy

Helen Douglas

This room is not large. On the tile floor are two woven rugs, one eggshell green and one pale yellow with a green geometric design. There are four chairs, a couple of cushions, and a small black table. There's a pot of found things: seeds, stones, a tiny bottle, porcupine quills, an esc key, dice, flakes from a tortoise shell, curling peels of bark. The yellow walls are hung with a few pieces by artist friends and a round slatted wooden light hangs from the ceiling. The window looks down a patched cobbled road toward the fishing harbor and the bay. Outside the door, tangled red and pink hibiscus branches are attended by little white-eyes, sunbirds, and Cape robins. By the gray garden wall, a rusty tin woman sits on her rusty tin swing. Right now, the first rain of the season is pouring down the brick steps and past the open door. This is where people come to talk with me about their lives.

When I began my philosophical counseling practice in 2002, I imagined it as a hostel for travellers who had become fatigued or disoriented. It would offer some shelter, companionship, local knowledge, and direction. A hostel is not a clinic. There is no doctor, no patient, no diagnosis, and no treatment, only engaged conversation about this person's life, about what is happening, what is to be done, and what it all means. In this way, philosophical practice offers both a salutary response to human suffering and a critical response to the professions of clinical psychology and psychiatry. In this chapter, I want to suggest that philosophical practice can also be a therapeutic and critical response to the profession of philosophy.

THE END OF PHILOSOPHY

In 2010, physicist Stephen Hawking announced the death of philosophy:

> What is the nature of reality? Where did all this come from? Did the universe need a creator? . . . Traditionally these are questions for philosophy, but philosophy is dead. Philosophy has not kept up with modern developments in science, particularly physics. Scientists have become the bearers of the torch of discovery in our quest for knowledge.[1]

No doubt this is so. Martin Heidegger saw it already fifty years ago. In "The End of Philosophy and the Task of Thinking," first published in 1964, he recognized that the "development of philosophy into the independent sciences . . . [is] the legitimate completion of philosophy,"[2] simply because Western philosophy has from the first been primarily concerned with metaphysics. With a broader perspective than Hawking's, he sees this scientific-technological attitude extending into every field of knowledge. "Scientific" here signals a rational, objective methodology of "systematic observation, measurement and experiment, and the formulation, testing and modification of hypotheses."[3] The end of philosophy isn't just that scientists have become torchbearers; it's that every truth must be scientific to be valid, and every knower must have scientific-professional credentials. Heidegger, like Hawking, approves of this:

> [i]t suffices to refer to the independence of psychology, sociology, anthropology as cultural anthropology, to the role of logic as symbolic logic and semantics. Philosophy turns into the empirical science of man. . . . No prophecy is necessary to recognize that the sciences now establishing themselves will soon be determined and steered by the new fundamental science which is called cybernetics. This science corresponds to the determination of man as an acting social being. For it is the theory of the steering of the possible planning and arrangement of human labor. Cybernetics transforms language into an exchange of news. The arts become regulated-regulating instruments of information.[4]

Cybernetics (from Greek κυβερνητικός *kubernetes*, 'steersman') is "the science of communications and automatic control systems in both machines and living things."[5] The traditional aims of social science—to predict and control—are cybernetic aims that require nothing more from philosophy.

> The end of philosophy proves to be the triumph of the manipulable arrangement of a scientific-technological world and of the social order proper to this world. The end of philosophy means the beginning of the world civilization based upon Western European thinking.[6]

We are now living with that world civilization and its social order. For all its evident technological and scientific achievement, it has also yielded cruel inequalities of wealth and opportunity, and cascading social, economic, and environmental crises. All our institutions of state, civic, and religious order are plagued by various forms of corruption. Even so, the scientific attitude and technological character of this civilization cannot be questioned without the questioner appearing naïve or quaintly 'philosophical.' If our institutions are failing us, it must be that we have failed the institutions. Or perhaps we haven't got the technology quite right. It's a problem of leadership or design or regulation or skills. And yet. In this secular, rational, technological world, everything that was meant to serve society now serves to tear us apart. The cybernauts and technocrats shake their heads in perplexity.

Against Heidegger, I would suggest that, under the guise of scientific objectivity, our way of thinking has been depersonalized and dehumanized. In a word: corrupted. Along with philosophy, ethics and politics also end in technologies, rendering them either impotent and ineffective or produced through force and brutality. The rationality celebrated by Europe's Enlightenment has been rolled out to justify the perpetration of slavery, imperialism, and other forms of mayhem across the world. More of the same—more cybernetic technology, more neoliberal capitalism, more social and institutional engineering, more cultural arrogance—will not provide a solution to this corruption and abjection. Only humans can save us now.

THE TASK OF THINKING

There's a certain inevitability that a philosophy that starts from ontological questions about being and the nature of things will end in the triumph of science. As Heidegger notes, "Each epoch of philosophy has its own necessity. We simply have to acknowledge the fact that a philosophy is the way it is."[7] It's not something broken that needs mending, a mistake to be corrected, or a disorder to be cured. We have arrived at our destination.

But doesn't this also open the possibility for a new epoch, one whose necessary task will be to recover its humaneness? We don't need more knowledge; we need the wisdom to understand what we already know. The end of philosophy thus does retain "a task for thinking," as Heidegger puts it. We need to think differently, in a way that will dissolve the overwhelming dominion of scientific—and especially pseudo-scientific—rationalization.

I don't know how to 'think differently,' but I have an idea that philosophical practice is one way to go about it. And even though Heidegger's task of thinking—what he calls 'the thinking in question'—is not the same as mine, it is not different either. This "same difference" suggests a link between philosophy and a philosophical practice.

Heidegger says his essay is driven by a persistent question "more primordial" than that of *Being and Time* about "what the matter of thinking is."[8] My question, equally primordial, is about what being human signifies (and perhaps this is the matter of thinking). And it is the case for both questions that "[i]f the answer could be given it would consist in a transformation of thinking, not in a propositional statement about a matter at stake."[9] Heidegger says we must look back to find something that was said at the beginning of philosophy and "even in virtue of that beginning,"[10] but which has "not been explicitly thought."[11] I think so, too. If the task of thinking is to think differently, this different thinking has to be already present to philosophy, yet unacknowledged. It would be something we already know but don't know that we know. "But above all," writes Heidegger,

> the thinking in question remains unassuming because its task is only of a preparatory, not of a founding character. It is content with awakening a readiness in man for a possibility whose contour remains obscure, whose coming remains uncertain. Thinking must first learn what remains reserved and in store for thinking to get involved in. It prepares its own transformation in this learning.[12]

Heidegger then looks to the philosophical tradition for guidance and finds "the call 'to the thing itself,'"[13] which he traces from Plato through to Hegel and Husserl, who discern that the matter of philosophy is, in fact, subjectivity (variously "the subjectivity of consciousness,"[14] "absolute subjectivity,"[15] and "transcendental subjectivity"[16]): "[i]t is not the matter as such that is controversial for the call, but rather its presentation by which the matter itself becomes present."[17] Using the image of a forest clearing, he notes that both light and an opening are needed for something to present itself to us. "Wherever a present being encounters another present being or even only lingers near it . . . there openness already rules, the free region is in play."[18] He equates this opening of presence with ἀλήθεια (*aletheia,* 'truth'[19]), Parmenides' "untrembling heart of unconcealment."[20] This opening cannot itself be thought, only experienced.[21] Unconcealment is itself self-concealing,[22] but it is the condition for the bond of "Being and thinking, that is, presence and apprehending."[23] Reason cannot think this openness but openness is the ground of reason. In the closing paragraphs, where he will suggest that "Being and Time" gives way to "Opening and Presence" as the task of thinking,[24] Heidegger returns to the "technological scientific rationalization ruling the present age," which justifies itself every day more surprisingly by its immense results. But this says nothing about what first grants the possibility of the rational and the irrational. The effect proves the correctness of technological scientific rationalization. But is the manifest character of what is exhausted by what is demonstrable? Doesn't the insistence on what is demonstrable block the way to what is?

> *Perhaps there is a thinking which is more sober-minded than the incessant frenzy of rationalization and the intoxicating quality of cybernetics. One might aver that it is precisely this intoxication that is extremely irrational. Perhaps there is a thinking outside of the distinction of rational and irrational, more sober-minded still than scientific technology, more sober-minded and hence removed, without effect, yet having its own necessity.*[25] (emphasis added)

My own thinking was not directed by philosophy's call "to the thing itself." It was first directed to philosophy by the sense that I had some responsibility to understand and to respond to the troubles of the world. This led me to the work of Emmanuel Levinas, for whom "ethics"—one's inescapable and infinite responsibility for others—is "first philosophy." In a nutshell: "With the appearance of the human —and this is my entire philosophy—there is something more important than my life, and that is the life of the other. That is unreasonable. Man is an unreasonable animal."[26]

Levinas's view of subjectivity is most comprehensively presented in *Otherwise than Being or Beyond Essence*. I have explored it in depth elsewhere,[27] but here is a rough sketch. For Levinas, subjectivity is always relational and occurs on two levels: 'being' and 'ethics.' The subject is both a term of a relationship (in the common order of being) and the relationship itself (in the transcendent order of ethics). In the order of being, as *Dasein*, *conatus*, *cogito*, *homo oeconomicus*, I am a being that enjoys being and would like to carry on so. I live from the world and am the measure of all things. Things matter as they matter to me.

Then I discover that another person is not just another being for me. The other person breaks through this whatness to accuse me and command my responsibility, to call into question my place in the world. Levinas calls this the revelation of the Face of the Other: "the other man breaks through this composite precisely because his emergence as a Face, which is not just a plastic shape, but which is instantaneously a commitment for me, a call to me, an order to me, to put myself in the service of this Face."[28] This call doesn't come from brute force but through the other's authority—a peculiarly ethical authority that is simultaneously command, destitution, and vulnerability—such that the accusation is not alienating but as if originating from me, like a vocation, without me having done anything to deserve it.

The Face is "otherwise than being," a "non-phenomenon." "It escapes representation; it is the very collapse of phenomenality. Not because it is too brutal to appear, but because in a sense too weak, non-phenomenon because less than a phenomenon."[29] In fact, it acts very much like the self-concealing openness that Heidegger says is necessary for presence.

Levinas rightly speaks of the Face in world-shaking terms, but this exceptional relationship is evident whenever we simply do right by someone, without the *a priori* "because I should" mediation of reason or moral commitments. Even if it's just to let the other pass first through a doorway or to refrain from eating in front of someone who may be hungry, Levinas refers to these moments when our relentless self-interest is brought up short by the appearance of another as "the little humanity that adorns the earth."[30] Turned to the face of the other, I get over myself and find myself in a different light. One can even notice a little gap there, between me-myself and me-I, between being for-myself and being for-the-other. This is the gap in which Levinas works and where he finds the ethical priority in our identity.

As Levinas tells it, if there were only one other person in the world, I wouldn't have a problem: I would just have to accommodate and serve this one. But I do have a problem because the revelation of the Face also reveals my responsibility for all the "other others," all of humanity accusing me with the same immediacy. In responsibility, I am suddenly concerned with justice and peace. I have to figure out who these ones are to me and to each other, and what is owed to each. All these uncertainties push me into consciousness, to thinking and to language, to social institutions, to science and technology, all of which then develop their own necessary substance and logic, and, in the process, cover over the transcendent goodness that inspired them. The movement from presentation to representation is a kind of necessary violence, the reduction of the infinite otherness of the Face to comparisons and categories and totalities: categories and totalities within which the others, each one unique and irreplaceable, continue to provoke and to signify, calling me and my institutions again into question. This interplay of the realms of *ethics* (the Face, infinity, non-indifference, responsibility) and *being* (matter, totality, interest, reason) is something like the *yin-yang* concept in Chinese philosophy: interconnected and interdependent as shadow and light, they continually give rise to and overcome each other, but the weak force, like water, always prevails against the strong. The Face, as Levinas says, is both "what's exposed to murder and what resists murder."[31]

In this way, Levinas's analysis sets out the task for thinking at the end of philosophy that Heidegger sought. The task is not concerned with "man's ecstatic sojourn in the openness of presencing,"[32] but with responding to what that presence reveals to me and about me. This thinking-of-the-other—the thinking in question—is present at and for the beginning of philosophy; it remains implicit to knowing yet cannot be known; it is, as Heidegger predicted, a thinking "accessible neither to philosophy as metaphysics nor, and even less so, to the sciences stemming from philosophy;"[33] it is precisely "a thinking outside of the distinction of rational and irrational, more sober-minded still than scientific technology, more sober-minded and hence removed, without effect, yet having its own necessity."[34]

By locating the Other at the center of subjectivity, Levinas's work rocks Western philosophy the way that Copernicus's heliocentric solar system did astronomy. The stars and planets still cross the heavens as they always have, but their patterns now signify differently. People still go about their business, for better or worse, but it turns out we are oriented by the grace of love as fundamentally as we are by the gravity of self-interest. That is, if Levinas is right.

PHILOSOPHICAL PRACTICE

At the end of an era, we're looking for a way to think differently, to reason differently, to awaken "a readiness . . . for a possibility."[35] Levinas's exploration of thinking's subjective ethical origins opens a way to do that. But this thinking doesn't want to abandon reason or science or philosophy. It doesn't take anything on faith. So how can we test Levinas's findings? Not objectively in a laboratory. Not abstractly in a book. Only through direct practical experience. As in phenomenology, as in Goethean science, this thinking is not some sequestered interiority looking out at some object of knowledge. To use John Shotter's distinction, it is not "thinking-about" but "thinking-with."[36] We find ourselves and each other caught up in the midst of life. We participate. We take part.

My counseling practice has developed alongside a growing field of Levinas-inspired psychotherapy.[37] If Levinas is right, then we could expect that a civilization like ours, based on the idea that we are only isolated and self-interested beings, would certainly drive people to distraction and despair, and we could expect that relief might be found in a relationship that honored and relied upon our originary ethical inter-relatedness.

In a 2008 essay called "Levinas in Practice: Face-to-Face and Side by Side,"[38] I described my work as double-faceted, attentive to both realms of ethics and being. In the face-to-face relationship, welcoming the other is my immediate and ongoing concern. In the side-by-side work of conversation, we try to sort out together whatever needs sorting out. That paper ended with two questions. First was the professional-development question of what philosophical counselors should know in order to be useful to the people who consult us. "What tools should be in our toolbox, what provisions in our cupboard?" I asked, already realizing that it likely couldn't be standardized.[39]

This question has turned out to be an open one. Whatever one knows, it doesn't matter as much as knowing what one doesn't know. I don't know the other's world and what it means to her. I don't understand her. I surely don't know her better than she knows herself. I have to learn from her so that we might come to understanding together. That said, we also share this world and its realities, so I have to be able to draw on my own experience and sensibility, including what I've studied and tried to think through. The broader and deeper my resources, the more I can offer the other and the more I can stir her up. As Gerd Achenbach wrote, "Only as a fellow thinker and fellow feeler is [the philosopher] able to liberate the visitor from his loneliness or forlornness, and by these means help him to change his opinions about life and his circumstances."[40] We have to meet as equals.

In the last few years, by way of Jacques Rancière's *The Ignorant Schoolmaster: Five Lessons in Intellectual Emancipation*, I have reconceived my counseling practice as a practice of emancipation that is grounded in Levinasian ethics and carried out in conversation.[41] It offers conditions in which the other can "conceive of his human dignity, take the measure of his intellectual capacity and decide how to use it," to quote Rancière.[42] As an 'ignorant philosopher,' I have nothing to teach my visitors except that I have nothing to teach them, and that they are perfectly capable of learning for themselves.

My second question asked what the practice of philosophical counseling would bring to the discipline of philosophy.

I would now say that there are several things the counselor could tell the academician: that philosophy didn't begin just once, once upon a time in Greece. It begins anew with each person who is caught up in a question. It begins each time in restlessness, disappointment, frustration or wonder. Meaning is always meaning *to someone*. That the measure of the work is pragmatic: how useful it is for that person in terms of that question. Is it emancipatory? Does it cut through the tangles of confusion? Does it affirm our dignity? Does it enhance our ability to live, love, and work well? That there isn't much call for abstract or universal terminology, but poetry comes naturally. In each relationship that struggles to name or express *this* particular experience, a fresh dialect (like lovers' pillow talk) sprouts and shoots up. Even the most commonplace words generate layers of metaphor and meaning as they pass between us.

It isn't yet philosophy proper—and may never be—but this is how philosophy begins: in practice, in relationship, in conversation, in desire and struggle. We come to our senses. We awaken and develop our ability to know for ourselves what is true and what is right and what is good. This work reconnects us to the ancient appreciation of philosophy as direct and personal, as a way of life, and of its importance for a life well lived and for the alleviation of suffering.

Beyond the one-to-one of philosophical counseling, this reconnection with Western philosophy's perpetual beginning as a personal and human concern—and especially the theoretical and practical reconnection of knowledge to ethics (via Levinas)—opens a path toward another possibility for philosophy itself.

THINKING DIFFERENTLY

All this talk of philosophy's proper dissolution into the "empirical science of man" refers only to the dominant mainstream of Western philosophy, which is also the philosophy of Western domination. If Levinas is right about goodness and Heidegger is right about the triumph of the cybernetic technology, and if this so-called 'scientific' attitude is actually dehumanized zombie-think, then we would expect to find animated human opposition and resistance to that corruption cropping up all over. As we do.

Since Heidegger's time, the academy has seen developments in interdisciplinary critical thinking, notably in feminist and gender studies, postcolonial studies, and critical race theory: different thinking by and for philosophy's historically excluded 'others.' Drawing resources from specific embodied identities and histories—*qua* black, *qua* woman, *qua* native—they work to restore the dignity and worth of forms of life and ways of knowing that have been misunderstood, misrepresented, and debased by 'European civilization.' Another line of critique comes from within, from philosophers who carry on the lineage of Western critical theory and Europe's own struggles for liberty, equality, and fraternity (which should not be forgotten). These theorists are busy stealing fire at the line drawn between center and periphery, pointing out crossovers and co-dependencies and exposing the workings of coercive force.

But, if Levinas is right, all this critical thinking in the realm of being—of politics, power, and interest—is also at risk of forgetting its latent origin in the responsibility of the one for the other. If we think that justice is a principle or an ideal to strive for, we are at risk of instituting further violence and injustice in our struggle against injustice. If we don't find a way to remember (to unconceal) that justice is first of all justice for the other, and first of all my responsibility, then this work will not take us all the way to a new thinking and to a human philosophy (rather than another philosophy of the human).

For Levinas, as a Jew and a philosopher, the Nazi Holocaust is "the key experience" of his life and his thought.[43] How could twenty centuries of European culture lead to Auschwitz? France Guwy gives a condensed answer:

> Despite his respect and admiration for European civilization, the experience of fascism prompted Levinas's fundamental criticism of Western thought. Because, he says, Western thought places the Self in the middle of all things, [it] tends to become totalitarian by the very fact that it ignores the radical experience of the Other.[44]

In this interview with Guwy, Levinas describes his research:

> as governed by what I consider to be an imbalance within this civilization between the basic theme of knowledge and the basic theme of the relationship with the Other. . . . But I don't think that the solution consists in a change in the principles of this civilization. I think that, within this civilization, by giving a central role to elements that were on the sidelines, there might be a solution.[45]

This is new thinking for the West, which thrives on the logic of dualism and identity, good and evil, black and white, A is not B. But if consciousness itself has its hidden origin in goodness, then all of our thought has to contain a trace of that, however corrupted or concealed.

Levinas suggests something similar in *Totality and Infinity*: "Like a shunt every social relation leads back to the presentation of the other to the same without the intermediary of any image or sign, solely by the expression of the face."[46] And this, from *Otherwise than Being or Beyond Essence*: "Philosophy is called upon to conceive ambivalence, to conceive it in several times."[47] Along with the logic of reason, there is also this ambivalence between being and otherwise-than-being, synchrony and diachrony, presence and proximity. Which is to say, there is nothing wrong with the pursuit of abstract or productive knowledge, but there is something wrong when it is out of balance with our concern and responsibility for others, and for the harm that is done to them. To correct the balance, we conceive ambivalence, trace our social relations back to the other, and bring to the center elements that have been sidelined. We put our thinking in question. It's a practice.

DERRIDA'S MOTHER?

I don't know what a human philosophy would be, but it starts with a sense of having lost our way. It starts with a call to responsibility, to think differently, to think for and with others, which means taking part, in person. It means coming to our senses. It calls for conversation and collaboration and solidarity, which means equality and respect. As good scientists, we will judge our truth by the effects of its application. As seekers, by where it leads us. "If the answer could be given it would consist in a transformation of thinking, not in a propositional statement about a matter at stake."[48]

Writing this chapter has provided an opportunity for appraisal. As a practitioner, I have learned to find my own way and I have helped others to do so as well. None of us, I would guess, has ended up where we would have predicted or by the most 'efficient' route, but we have kept company with ourselves and each other, and something deep and trustworthy has been learned.

As a philosophical thinker—and as a woman—I am intrigued to notice that this practice runs on qualities that are not celebrated in Western philosophy: passivity, willingness, care, humbleness, discretion. Feminine qualities. Which is to say, qualities that the fathers of philosophy assigned to Woman, qualities scorned and dismissed as 'slave morality.' But when people come to this small hostel, when they are beside themselves with hurt and fear and confusion, it is these soft virtues that allow me to be present usefully and without harm.

What would it mean to give these elements a central role in philosophy? Is the task for thinking "women's work" (no matter who does it)? When Levinas proposed that the Feminine is philosophy's Other or when he described the basis of ethical subjectivity as radical passivity and Passion, I wonder if this isn't what he was indicating. Jacques Derrida had a similar idea in deconstruction, which was also mobilized in the name of justice. Derrida was once asked which philosopher he would like to have been his mother. I will close with his charming reply, as an invocation of that "possibility whose contour remains obscure, whose coming remains uncertain":

> A philosopher couldn't be my mother . . . Because the figure of the philosopher is, for me, always a masculine figure . . . All the deconstruction of phallogocentrism is the deconstruction of what one calls philosophy which, since its inception, has always been linked to a paternal figure. So, a philosopher is a Father, not a Mother. So the philosopher that would be my mother would be a post-deconstructive philosopher . . . An inheritor. A woman philosopher who would reaffirm the deconstruction. And consequently, would be a woman who thinks. Not a philosopher. I always distinguish thinking from philosophy. A thinking mother—it's what I both love and try to give birth to.[49]

NOTES

1. Stephen Hawking and Leonard Mlodinow, *The Grand Design* (London: Transworld, 2010), 5.
2. Martin Heidegger, "The End of Philosophy and the Task of Thinking," in *Basic Writings from "Being and Time" (1927) to "The Task of Thinking" (1964)*, ed. David Farrell Krell, trans. Joan Stambaugh (San Francisco: Harper San Francisco, 1977), 376.
3. *New Oxford American Dictionary*, Mac OS X 10.6, n.d.
4. Heidegger, "The End of Philosophy and the Task of Thinking," 376.
5. *New Oxford American Dictionary*.
6. Heidegger, "The End of Philosophy and the Task of Thinking," 377.
7. Ibid., 375.
8. Ibid., 373.
9. Ibid.
10. Ibid., 378.
11. Ibid., 379.
12. Ibid., 378.
13. Ibid., 379.
14. Ibid., 381.
15. Ibid., 382.
16. Ibid.

17. Ibid., 383.
18. Ibid., 383–84.
19. Formed from privative prefix ἀ- (*a-*, privative alpha meaning "not" + λανθάνομαι (*lanthanomai,* "forgetfulness," "oblivion").
20. Heidegger, "The End of Philosophy and the Task of Thinking," 387.
21. Ibid., 388.
22. Ibid., 390–91.
23. Ibid., 387.
24. Ibid., 392.
25. Ibid.
26. Tamra Wright, Peter Hughes, and Alison Ainlie, "The Paradox of Morality: An Interview with Emmanuel Levinas," in *The Provocation of Levinas: Rethinking the Other*, ed. R. Bernasconi and D. Wood (London and New York: Routledge and Kegan Paul, 1988), 172.
27. Helen Douglas, *Love and Arms: Violence and Justification after Levinas* (Pittsburgh: Trivium, 2011).
28. France Guwy, "You who are looking at me [*Toi qui me regard/Jij die mij aanziet*]: IKON Interview with Emmanuel Levinas" (Netherlands Interdenominational Broadcasting Company (IKON), 1986).
29. Emmanuel Levinas, *Otherwise Than Being or Beyond Essence*, trans. Alphonso Lingis (The Hague: Martinus Nijhoff, 1981), 88
30. Ibid., 185.
31. Levinas in Guwy, "You who are looking at me [*Toi qui me regard/Jij die mij aanziet*]: IKON Interview with Emmanuel Levinas."
32. Heidegger, "The End of Philosophy and the Task of Thinking," 390.
33. Ibid., 378.
34. Ibid., 392.
35. Ibid., 378.
36. John Shotter, "Understanding Process From Within: An Argument for 'Withness'—Thinking," *Organization Studies* 27, no. 4 (April 2006): 585–604, doi:10.1177/0170840606062105.
37. See, for example, Edwin E. Gantt and Richard N. Williams, eds., *Psychology for the Other: Levinas, Ethics and the Practice of Psychology* (Pittsburgh: Duquesne University Press, 2002); G. Kunz, *The Paradox of Power and Weakness* (Albany, NY: SUNY Press, 1998); D. Loewenthal and G. Kunz, eds., "Special Issue: Levinas and the Other in Psychotherapy and Counselling," *European Journal of Psychotherapy, Counselling and Health* 7, no. 1–2 (June 2005).
38. Douglas, "Levinas in Practice: Face to Face and Side by Side," *Philosophical Practice: Journal of the APPA* 3, no. 1 (March 2008): 226–34.
39. Ibid., 233.
40. Gerd B.Achenbach, "A Short Answer to the Question: What Is Philosophical Practice?," trans. P. Neubauer, accessed May 9, 2013,http://igpp.org/?page_id=169.
41. Douglas, "Philosophical Counseling as a Practice of Emancipation," *Philosophical Practice: Journal of the APPA* 9, no. 1 (March 2014): 1312–19.
42. Jacques Rancière, *The Ignorant Schoolmaster: Five Lessons in Intellectual Emancipation*, trans. K. Ross (Stanford, CA: Stanford University Press, 1991), 17.
43. Guwy, "You who are looking at me [*Toi qui me regard/Jij die mij aanziet*]: IKON Interview with Emmanuel Levinas."
44. Ibid.
45. Ibid.
46. Emmanuel Levinas, *Totality and Infinity: An Essay on Exteriority*, trans. Alphonso Lingis (Pittsburgh: Duquesne University Press, 1969), 213.
47. Levinas, *Otherwise Than Being or Beyond Essence*, 162.
48. Heidegger, "The End of Philosophy and the Task of Thinking," 373.
49. Kirby Dick and Amy Ziering Kofman, *Derrida* (Jane Doe Films, 2002), www.kirbydick.com/derrida/DerridaTRANSCRIPT.doc.

BIBLIOGRAPHY

Achenbach, Gerd B. "A Short Answer to the Question: What Is Philosophical Practice?" Translated by P. Neubauer. Accessed May 9, 2013. http://igpp.org/?page_id=169.

Dick, Kirby, and Ziering Kofman Amy. *Derrida*. Jane Doe Films, 2002. www.kirbydick.com/derrida/DerridaTRANSCRIPT.doc.

Douglas, Helen. "Levinas in Practice: Face to Face and Side by Side." *Philosophical Practice: Journal of the APPA* 3, no. 1 (March 2008): 226–34.

———. *Love and Arms: Violence and Justification after Levinas*. Pittsburgh: Trivium, 2011.

———. "Philosophical Counseling as a Practice of Emancipation." *Philosophical Practice: Journal of the APPA* 9, no. 1 (March 2014): 1312–19.

Gantt, Edwin E., and Williams Richard N., eds. *Psychology for the Other: Levinas, Ethics and the Practice of Psychology*. Pittsburgh: Duquesne University Press, 2002.

Guwy, France. "You who are looking at me [*Toi qui me regard/Jij die mij aanziet*]: IKON Interview with Emmanuel Levinas." Netherlands Interdenominational Broadcasting Company (IKON), 1986.

Hawking, Stephen, and Mlodinow Leonard. *The Grand Design*. London: Transworld, 2010.

Heidegger, Martin "The End of Philosophy and the Task of Thinking." In *Basic Writings from "Being and Time" (1927) to "The Task of Thinking" (1964)*, edited by David Farrell Krell, translated by Joan Stambaugh, 373–92. San Francisco: Harper San Francisco, 1977.

Kunz, Geroge. *The Paradox of Power and Weakness*. Albany, NY: SUNY Press, 1998.

Levinas, Emmanuel. *Otherwise Than Being or Beyond Essence*. Translated by Alphonso Lingis. The Hague: Martinus Nijhoff, 1981.

———. *Totality and Infinity: An Essay on Exteriority*. Translated by Alphonso Lingis. Pittsburgh: Duquesne University Press, 1969.

Loewenthal, Del, and Kunz, George. Eds. "Special Issue: Levinas and the Other in Psychotherapy and Counselling." *European Journal of Psychotherapy, Counselling and Health* 7, no. 1–2 (June 2005).

New Oxford American Dictionary. Mac OS X 10.6, n.d.

Rancière, Jacques. *The Ignorant Schoolmaster: Five Lessons in Intellectual Emancipation*. Translated by Kristen Ross. Stanford, CA: Stanford University Press, 1991.

Shotter, John. "Understanding Process From Within: An Argument for 'Withness'-Thinking." *Organization Studies* 27, no. 4 (April 2006): 585–604. doi:10.1177/0170840606062105.

Wright, Tamra, Hughes, Peter, and Ainlie Alison. "The Paradox of Morality: An Interview with Emmanuel Levinas." In *The Provocation of Levinas: Rethinking the Other*, edited by Robert Bernasconi and David Wood. London and New York: Routledge and Kegan Paul, 1988.

Open End Notes: My Journey with the Authors and an Invitation

Luisa de Paula

My journey with the authors starts with "Listening to Whispers:" women whispering to one another, helping each other find their voices in countries where they are systematically ignored, smothered, or silenced. But whispers also refer to women from theoretically equal rights countries who have unlearned to listen and been left to die within, their voices either renounced or neglected as they fail to speak out and assert their value in the ongoing improvement of human life in its entirety.

The whispers are a chorus of stifled voices striving to bring their richness to the world: the muffled and subdued voices of Turkish girls and young women in the first essay; the voices that would rather remain silent than say anything outside the script of gender roles witnessed by Racovanovic, the multidimensional voice of *Anima* bringing out her silent words in Bakirdjian's contribution, the hidden and marginalized voices of dying people coming alive in the closing chapter of the section.

In "Women Think in Whispers in a Developing Country: A Glance Through The Lens of Philosophical Counseling," Riella Morhayim gives an account of the obstacles women from many countries in Africa and Middle East face when they begin to question their identity and dare assert their true potential as free subjects, masters of their own life choices. Taking real case histories from her philosophical counseling in Turkey as the point of departure, Morhayim paints a lively picture of women's experience as they bend their lives to the customary and statutory subjugation of their fathers, husbands, and other male members of their family. Working with these women, Morhayim argues, the philosophical counselor has to take due account of their counselees' social and cultural context and understand their acquired value system while working to dismiss any prejudice and preconception which might arise. As pointed out by James Hillman, and one of the main reasons for his own shift in perspective from psychoanalysis toward philosophy, the focus on the individual self, as if separable from their socio-cultural and economic environment, is one of psychology's original sins.

The need to take context into account is thrown into sharp relief by the specific circumstances of women in countries where not even in theory or law do they enjoy equal rights with men. Philosophical counseling broadens the scope of action with an in-depth analysis of the counselee's acquired—and often imposed—value system. Its aim is to widen and enhance the counselee's awareness of their received values, and their understanding of which of these need to be either smothered or strengthened, quietly accepted or patiently reworked to make them acceptable. The process allows the counselee to work on their friction points and intersections with the generally accepted values of their family, community, and cultural background so as to reassess and recreate them within a personal ethic.

Morhayim's essay shows the need for philosophical counseling to fine-tune its toolbox and strategies according to the very different and specific contexts in which it applies them. It also bears witness to the crucial role women philosophical counselors can and should play in countries where gender inequality and discrimination appear to be the norm. In such contexts, women philosophical counselors are called on to both help other women value themselves and make themselves be valued. The stories Morhayim reports and her philosophical approach provoke the reader, providing abundant food for thought and further discussion.

Further testimony in similar but somehow analogous circumstances is provided in "Therapy in Serbia from a Gender Perspective." Here the Serbian philosophical counselor and schoolteacher Natasa Radovanovic paints a disconsolate but passionate portrait of a country where rigid gender roles and patriarchal values still hold a firm grip on social and family institutions, and where the people's mentality blocks the beginnings of equality and change.

Working as a school counselor with pupils from age seven to fifteen and with parents and teachers, Radovanovic observed developmental trends in counseling from childhood to adulthood. Realizing that the gender gap in attitudes to therapy and counseling increases with age, she devised an interview-based qualitative inquiry to find out how women and men conceive of kinship forms of intervention, standard forms of (psycho)therapy, and philosophical counseling.

Apart from its originality and the light it sheds on the situation in Serbia, Radovanovic's research moves away from the fenced-off interests of philosophical counseling insiders, as it focuses on the general field of therapy rather than on the specific approach offered by philosophy. This may rattle sensitivities in places where philosophical counseling seems to have developed more in competition with—and in polemical opposition to—psychoanalysis and psychotherapy, rather than engaging in a mutually enriching dialogue.

As the author explains: "The Serbian layperson would not be able to distinguish philosophical counseling from psychotherapy . . . in Serbia the rise of philosophical counseling can be regarded as part of the revival of psychotherapy, as it was conceived of in antiquity: therapy of the soul."

Irrespective of the issues of self-interest, turf battles, and trivial controversy, there is an important lesson here: psychology and philosophy can and should be allies: in a historical moment where many of the boundaries between different disciplinary fields are being redefined are undergoing a paradigm shift, psychology and philosophy can and should be allies.[1]

This ancient Soul revival, with a capital 'S,' is also the protagonist of the third and central chapter of the section, where the classical tradition of Anima, 'Soul' is given new life through the sensitivity and listening skills of the philosophical counselor, bringing to light dimensions of thought that mainstream theoretical philosophy has condemned to oblivion.

In her "The Awakening of 'Anima' in Philosophical Counseling," the Argentinean philosophical counselor Silvia Bakirdjian argues that even if "spiritually elevated activities have no sex," gender differences can generally be observed in the practice of philosophical counseling. She identifies an enhanced capacity for listening as the core peculiarity of a 'she' style. Here, the act of 'listening' is not just attentively and sensitively taking note of what is said, but also the ability to detect what is revealed in the 'in-between' of words and silence, the reading of gestures and body language, and the capacity to stay open and vigilant to the present moment so as to recognize and receive the transcendent manifesting itself. This kind of listening gives a glimpse of a difference in approach on the part of women, particularly with regard to received notions about truth and care relationships as conceived within the male-oriented hegemonic model: an epistemology and a therapy that differ from the monotheistic conception of reality and the paternalistic approach to care that prevails in mainstream cultural patterns.

Women tend to experience truth more as a gray area, while men tidy up gray areas into black-or-white zones with the proud, dazzling light of reason banishing all doubt. Inversely, doubt shelters women's way to knowledge, which multiplies its forms and colors at every step: the truth always stands within a particular position and particular relations. This partly accounts for the way men counselors tend to straightaway seek a clear understanding of the situation, and use that deductive understanding to guide their counselee. Women, by contrast, "take a long time reaching full awareness of a subject's inherent complexity, and upon reaching it, many times prefer to leave various doors open to allow the other to advance at his own pace," as Bakirdjian writes.

The importance of leaving doors open and renouncing any claim to reach a secure and final understanding is the essential priority when dealing with incurable pain, approaching death, and preparation for mourning. In "Philosophical Counseling at the End of Life: A Gender Perspective," the Italian philosophical counselor Luisa Sesino draws on her more than twenty years of experience in support of the dying and the people around them to bring out what the terminally ill most need to be really cared for and accompanied in their most difficult life passage: the humility to strip oneself of all presumed knowledge and be prepared to learn from others,[2] the skills and willingness to listen, the courage to raise questions that have no answers, the strength to maintain one's own presence until the last moment. In order to be up to this task, the philosophical counselor has to prioritize the act of being-there over the claim to do something, and to listen with open heart and raised antennae while exposing their naked and vulnerable self. With this mindset, they can guide the terminally ill person along a path of dialogue and self-understanding where they learn what really matters to them, to focus on the essential, and finally to come to see that, at least, they "can actually live their illness and, maybe, death."

Through her experience, Sesino sketches the importance of skills traditionally regarded as feminine for pushing philosophical thought to its borders, where there is no certainty or final answer.

In parallel with hospice and palliative care—perhaps the only predominantly feminine branch of medicine—end-of-life philosophical counseling represents a privileged space to develop an awareness of the limit of human life within its lived experience. In contrast to the painful conspiracy of silence surrounding the dying person, a philosophical engagement with the end-of-life experience can meet a need peculiar to our secularized society, where pain and death are usually relegated to ghettos and hidden as a shameful scars on the positive face of the world. As a matter of fact, philosophical counseling can serve as a militant laboratory for rethinking pain and death as constitutive limits and an inherent and essential part of life.[3]

The recovery of vulnerability from its relegation to a stereotyped feminine identity[4] is one of the threads that connects the first section with the second, "Enhancing Doubt." Here doubt is not a paralyzing state of indecisiveness or a difficulty in assessing a given state of affairs, but rather an existential opening to the situations in which people find themselves from time to time.

In "The Eros of Doubting," the German philosophical counselor Heidi Salaverría points toward doubt as one of philosophical counseling's essential resources for helping both women and men untie themselves from the culturally induced model of a fixed and rigid identity. The reward for a systematic philosophical ἦθος (*ethos*) of doubting is the personality's permeability to the flow of experience. This means not being dragged away and dispersed by the current,[5] but gaining the skill to take advantage of the situations life exposes us all to, and to evolve one's identity structure toward an increasing complexity. Again: the practice of philosophical counseling faces us with the need for an epistemological and therapeutic framework essentially different from the epistemology and the conceptions of self-identity that underlie both mainstream therapeutic approaches and common sense assumptions of the self as well as their reflections in common behavior.

The 'self' of modern medical and psychological therapy is primarily the individual, according to Latin etymology: *in-* (not) and *dividuus* (divisible), "that which cannot be divided," but also—and in parallel—"the one that is by itself," differentiated and apart from the rest of the world by virtue of stable and firm boundaries. It is not by chance that the Greek equivalent to the Latin *individuus*, the ἄτομος (*atomos*), was chosen to name what for centuries has been thought of—before it could even be seen—as the smallest particle that can be isolated.[6]

Today, after that atom has been split and re-split into smaller and smaller components, and science has left behind the myth of an object independent and separated from the observing subject,[7] we still assume an autonomous impermeable self, and let that idea proliferate throughout our lives. Such an assumption is not only outdated: it is also uncomfortable and even cumbersome. Reflecting on different cases of individual and collective discomfort, from alcohol dependence to military violence, Salaverría argues for the need to raise permeability and heteronomy from their devalued position within feminine stereotypes where they are no more than the reverse image of the allegedly steady and autonomous masculine identity, to serve instead as prerequisites for a more flexible and integrated image of the self.[8] How this has to be done is incumbent on the philosophical counselor, in accordance with every irreducibly specific case.

The author offers some insights into a situation that—with the consent of a strong autonomous self—everyone hopefully finds themselves in more than once in a lifetime: falling in love. The *Hegel-Hollywood Model* of falling in love illustrated by Salaverría may provide the reader with some useful tips to understanding a situation that, from the standard perspective of the male super-ego, is as little understandable as it is embarrassing. It is sure to make readers smile, preparing them to savor the next essay.

The Israeli philosophical counselor Lydia Amir's *Philosophical Humor for Women—(and Men): Fighting Shame and Disgust* counters both the die-hard prejudice against women as humorless and the assumed lack of feminist interest in the subject in order to restore the philosophical dignity of the comic, the ironic, and the humorous. These are powerful tools for helping us to accept those aspects of our humanity that are either condemned to shame or rejected with disgust on a daily basis, due to deeply rooted patterns of civilization that segregate the allegedly shameful and disgusting within the construct of an all-needy and all-vulnerable femininity.[9] Because of the undisputed priority that autonomy enjoys in mainstream culture, neediness is another hypostasis of femininity that we often have to strive to integrate. The author suggests that is an aspect of our human condition we can face with humorous strategies.

Amir invites the philosophical practitioner to be aware of humor's extraordinary potential to maintain a positive tension between different aspects of personality, to bear the frustrations, conflicts, and inconsistencies of everyday life, and to understand and accept ambivalence as an integral part of life. Last but not least, humor possesses an intrinsically therapeutic power to challenge the establishment and taken-for-granted power hierarchies. It promotes mobility, flexibility, and change, both outwardly, in terms of social and interpersonal relations, and inwardly, within the different components of the self. Drawing on an extraordinarily rich repertoire of thinkers, Amir develops a multistep philosophical path that does not fail to inspire the reader to face shame, disgust, and other discomforts with the subtle weapon of a smile.

In her chapter *The Need to Be Needed,* the Israeli philosophical counselor Ora Gruengard also takes up neediness, here from the perspective of women subjected to the double bind of being needed and needing, on one hand, while, on the other, having to appear emancipated and not in need of support and protection from others, especially from men, and especially from their male partners.

Gruengard draws together threads from her philosophical counseling case histories in an "associative journey" that reveals some of the slow-burning questions lying beneath the apparently calm surface of what we call "women's emancipation." Her protagonists are six women and two men who have received philosophical assistance from the author, some of them while hospitalized with some form of psychiatric diagnosis. Their stories are presented in tandem with sketches of other cases as Gruengard investigates a problematic issue that has come to light over her long experience as a philosophical counselor, and which she puts at the core of her chapter. When trying to justify their lack of effort to change whatever it is that is causing them discomfort, she finds that women often claim they are needed by other as *a reason* to act or not act in a certain way, while men tend to be more concerned with what they do and how they act than with their own needs and those of the people closest to them. But there are also women who adopt the opposite strategy: they pretend not to be needy and not to care about the needs of others, when in fact their attitudes show they are both needy and need to be needed.

The emerging picture is neither simple nor univocal. But among its many nuances, it is clear that, while it might be that women are on average more inclined to need and be needed than men are, this does not amount to a reason (or an explanation) for a dualistic moral psychology which assumes women value mutual care and interdependence and men value independent action and self-affirmation.

Philosophical counselors should be both critically well informed about studies dealing with gender differences, especially when they present themselves to the general public in the sacred robe of 'science.' Already evolutionists many centuries before Darwin, philosophers have always worked on and with a human 'nature' that is both a product and raw material for ongoing change and adaptation, so there is no way for them to avail themselves of any hypostatization on 'Nature' or 'the Natural' to explain, justify, and perpetuate the *status quo*.[10]

Differences between women and men come with an evolutionary history, which is today at an unprecedented turning point. The traditional patterns of gender evolution have undergone an abrupt change. In the words of the psychologist John Gray: "the complex mosaic of traditional roles and expectations for men and women, fashioned and refined for thousands of years, has been shattered, and we are still picking up the pieces."[11]

After the scattered pieces have been measured and identified by researchers in neuroscience and evolutionary biology, they can be either reassembled or attentively imagined in new and different combinations The work of reassembling pertains to those sociologists and psychologists who are committed to grasping and adjusting human reality according to their own specific frameworks and objectives. But the task of recombining and re-imagining the new in open and multiple perspectives pertains instead to philosophical counselors who are ready to risk abandoning any given theoretical framework in favor of systematic doubt. In their commitment to bring forward the evolution of human 'nature,' philosophy has always spurred women and men to discover their unexplored potential and to realize their own unique and irreducibly singular life. From the time of the Ionic naturalists, philosophers with a commitment to improving the human condition have freely taken advantage of experimental research. Philosophical counselors today can restore a constructive and reciprocally stimulating dialogue with biology and the natural sciences.

In *Sex, Dating and Love: Differences Between Men and Women,* the Argentinean philosophical counselor Roxana Kreimer shows how this dialogue can significantly enrich the toolbox of philosophical counselors and provide background information on deeply rooted evolutionary drives that can play tricks on us, even if they underlie some of our most apparently reasonable intentions.

For example: are we really sure that our female tendency to be hyper-skeptical and highly selective with respect to potential partners still works to increase our chances of finding a faithful ally and a provider of great genes? As a good philosopher, the author leaves this and other questions rigorously open, but the examples she draws on from her counseling suggest that is probably not the case.

The sketches of dialogue Kreimer provides from her philosophical counseling bureau illustrate a range of moods and states of mind which many women have no problems identifying with as they seem to be dictated by deep, pressing, and unintelligible impulses. But once a woman realizes, for example, that her attraction to her boss is at least partly due to an instinctual drive toward alpha males widespread among most species of greater apes, she can rescale what she might have felt to be inappropriate in her attraction and raise her awareness in order to take a better course of action according to circumstances.

The critically constructive dialogue with the field of science that Kreimer's philosophical counseling appeals to is very relevant now, since mass culture and education do not encourage critical thinking and spread an (over)simplified and often deformed version of scientific findings and dominant theories which tends to pass for *the* Truth. As a consequence, laymen are bound to frame their life issues with ready-made theoretical perspectives that fit the standards for their own socio-cultural context. Firmly adhering to these, they transform an open question into a theoretical belief, a relationship issue into an emotional imbalance, an existential concern into a disease. Which is why, paradoxically, philosophical counselors can find themselves grappling with the delicate task of "de-psychoanalizing" the life of a counselee, giving it back its fluidity, and returning to the counselee her or his own potential to think about it.[12]

But what does it mean 'to think life,' and why should philosophical counseling feel entitled to help people embark on such an enterprise?

It is often argued that psychoanalysis is mostly focused on emotional conflicts, while philosophy prioritizes rationality and cognition, in this respect being akin to cognitive-behavior approaches in psychotherapy. The perspective arising from the overview of this book is different, much more complex and nuanced.

Like Socrates in Plato's dialogues, philosophical counselors do not appeal to reason as opposed to emotion, nor do they assume the one or the other to be separate 'real things,' each working independently. What they aim to work with is the overall capacity to think, which encompasses both the emotional and the rational as constitutively interwoven dimensions.[13]

When emotions and reason are encouraged to work separately, it cripples thought's growth. To break with this disabled paradigm which has run for so long in parallel with Western civilization, philosophical counselors train their counselees to cultivate and exploit the capacity to think their emotions and feel their thoughts.

This capacity is discussed in the third and central section of the book, "Thinking emotions."

In *Rational Emotions in Philosophical Counseling*, the Norwegian philosophical counselor Marianne Vahl challenges the deeply rooted assumption that emotions are irrational and as such should be subservient to reason. It comes as no surprise that, from Aristotle to Freud, this has been theorized along a path that parallels the assumed gender relation between women and men.

It is no small challenge that Vahl chose to face, and yet it is a crucial one. Already the formula of the essay's title, "rational emotion," strikes us as oxymoronic, bringing to light how difficult it is to circumvent the dichotomous assumptions so deeply ingrained in our historical-cultural patterns, such that they are implicit in the language which informs our thoughts and discourse.[14]

Today, however, "emotional intelligence"[15] has experimental researchers on its side, working on the anatomy and physiology of the brain. According to them, "the word 'emotion' does not refer to something that the mind or brain really do. 'Emotion' is only a label, a convenient way of talking."[16]

Emphasizing the ethical overtones of this shifting paradigm that neuroscience has brought to public attention, the author rejects shortcuts and avoids every simplification in order to face the issue in all its complexity. She calls for a re-reading of philosophers who have long been pilloried as endorsing an abstractly rational all-male paradigm of thought. In particular, she invites us to re-read Kant's conception of respect as both a value and a dimension that constantly nurtures and renovates the relationship within the philosophical couple. Derived from the Latin *re-* (suffix for 'again, back') and *spicio* ("I look"), to respect means, etymologically, 'to look at again and again.' This suggests that respect is rooted in giving attention and refusing to objectify the other to a given identity, being ready to look at him or her again and again. It is significant that the idea of respect originates from the sensible act of looking.

The other rational emotion essential to philosophical counseling Vahl explores is empathy.

Empathy and respect are both dialogical skills: they appeal to interpersonal exchange, where philosophical thought renews its original commitment to confront public issues, people's concrete problems and everyday life situations.

In *Philosophical Practice and the Call for Traditional Female Values,* the Norwegian philosophical counselor Camilla Angulten calls for revival of ancient φρόνεσις (*phronesis*), the practical wisdom praised and cultivated by ancient philosophers in the ἀγορά (*agora*) public space.

Angulten writes in the first person, taking as a point of departure her personal discomfort within the institutional settings of philosophy and her struggle to assert philosophy's potential as a resource in real life situations. She argues that the detachment of philosophers from practical contexts and practical issues not only marginalizes values traditionally regarded as feminine, but also paralyzes the voice of male philosophers, confirming stereotypes that dry up thought and life, setting each apart from the other.

Raising walls, separating and suspending every form of dialogue between two entities never gets us very far. Angulten calls for a "both/and" capability to express a full and lively human voice beyond the standard "either/or" of female and male constraints. For this we need to restore a new virtual circle between practical wisdom (φρόνεσις, *phronesis*), action (πρᾶξις, *praxis*), and ethics (ἦθος, *ethos*). This path involves a rediscovery of ethics and care as an essential dimension of thought in real existence.

Here we come to a very important point. To rebalance and return to dialogue what has been crystallized into *the* feminine and *the* masculine, we not only have to reshape the pretensions of an allegedly pure and objective reason, but must also move in a positive direction: to give back to philosophy the tools it has lost by marginalizing them to the feminine, inessential side of humanity, and to reintroduce the dimension of care and affection into the dignity of thought.

This is Angulten's challenge as she develops a heterodox and fertile combination between the concept of care in Heidegger's existential ontology, and Gilligan's ethics of care. Along the way, we meet the core values and working tools of a living, practical, and experimental philosophy: in-depth analysis of lived situations, the identification and exploration of moral dilemmas, open listening, and sensitivity to context.

In the fourth section of the book, "Sharing insight," we re-encounter practical wisdom (φρόνεσις, *phrònesis*) at the core of philosophical strategies aimed to value and capitalize on one's own peculiar sensitivity.

In *He Comes to My Practice: Sharing Sensibilities*, the Spanish philosophical counselor Rayda Guzmán González shows how philosophy can deal with the personal problems that are entangled with gender codes, and how they can turn into restraining roles, internalized norms and rigid identity schemes. The reader becomes deeply involved with the case of a young man whose sensitivity clashes with the internalized social model of a male identity marked by pragmatism, assertiveness, and results. When he first met González, he suffered from severe psychosomatic symptoms, apparently due to the fallout from a painful breakup with a woman who misinterpreted his gestures of attention as the jealousy of a control freak, did not appreciate his job as a musician and composer, and wanted him to manage activities that were completely at odds with his character. In short: she wanted him to be what he was not and did not want to be(come).

The choice of this particular case provokes the reader to consider the drawbacks of gender stigmas for men, who tend to pass non-critically as privileged within the social hierarchy, advantaged by their stance at the positive pole of the established value system, and accorded status by cultural identifications with a strong masculinity.

The philosophical strategies set out in this case point to a radical innovation in the relational dynamics of therapy and a departure from the standard classical models. The philosophical counselor abandons the claim to neutrality and does not deny herself authentic exchange and genuine reciprocity, turning on its head the fear of commitment and obsession with independence of the male code. Since she applies her philosophical skills and knowledge to the service of the other, the philosophical counselor maintains a position of asymmetry with respect to her counselee, but still cares for the problems dealt with during the sessions.

Responsibly and willingly assuming a genuine involvement, the philosophical counselor is not afraid either to express her feelings and impressions or to occasionally share stories from her own experience in order to help the counselee, for example, to distance themselves from an overwhelming involvement in their own situation, or to shift or broaden the counselee's perspective.

As they strip off the impersonal mask of the traditional therapist, philosophical counselors may also overcome the restrictions of the classical philosopher's toolbox of conceptual analysis and logical argument and build their own repertoire of analysis techniques, thought styles, and communication registers.

In *How Might Philosophical Counseling be in Garments from Simone de Beauvoir's Armoire, The Second Sex?*, the Australian philosophical practitioner, Narelle Arcidiacono, describes her *Just Story* technique as an original method to explore, question, reconsider, and empower personal attitudes in order to hold the individual at an proper distance between the extremes of exasperated and blind-to-otherness individualism and renunciation of self-assertion with its consequent fall into bad faith.[17]

Taking advantage of her twin careers as actress and philosopher, Arcidiacono guides people in group and individual sessions to give an illustrative story of their life in the form of a narrative text with certain criteria. This is the starting point for questioning and analysis that draws inspiration from existential thought, in particular Simone de Beauvoir, who, as a woman philosopher, remains far removed from the recognition she deserves.

What Arcidiacono is most concerned with here is the scant following accorded to de Beauvoir's radically original and resonant style of philosophizing, in contrast to the abstract, logical, and conceptual guise that philosophy usually assumes in institutional contexts and that seems more congenial to men than women. De Beauvoir developed a subtle and sophisticated narrative style, which tailored deep and incisive thought in firsthand, real-life situations. She left us a philosophical handbook from which women and men can fully draw on in training "to think their life and live their thought."

As Arcidiacono proposes practical exercises to enhance one's attitude in the light of the existential value of authenticity, she also warns the reader against the authoritative pitfalls to which both therapy and group practice are prone when not supported by a truly philosophical critical awareness, genuine opening to otherness, and respect for the unique potential inherent in each individual. Passionately concerned with the affirmation of a balanced individual freedom, the author expresses her disappointment with the dominant ultra-liberal paradigm, unfaithful as it is to the tangible freedom that constitutionally implies the relation to the O/other(s).

Here the question of difference comes to the fore as a fundamental and problematic issue to be reconsidered: to what extent are we allowed to express difference as a primary source of our personal identity? This question is particularly relevant with respect to gender, because it involves the whole structure of personality, and also because gender studies can be—and have already been—the pivotal ground for rediscovering the essential value of difference to offset the present trend of homologation and forced equalitarianism in line with the push toward globalization.

In *Young Women and the Strengthening of One's Moral Character*, the Canadian university professor and philosophical counselor Marie-France Lebouc tackles the question of difference, drawing on her teaching experience in business ethics and international aid ethics classes. Like Arcidiacono, Lebouc uses a method based on personal histories, one that she developed herself and has improved over years of professional practice.

The particular tool takes the form of a personal log. At the beginning of the semester, she asks students to identify a situation in their life that has raised moral dilemmas or ethical issues, give a narrative account of it, and detect and define emerging core issues. Students commit themselves to regularly updating their log with any insights and reflections offered by experience or circumstance over a period of time, giving them the opportunity to shift or broaden their original perspective.

Lebouc observes the different reactions of young women and men to this assignment. The most remarkable revolve around body perception, the topics chosen, and the degree of involvement in such issues as parenthood, pregnancy, and abortion. She also remarks on how genders show differing tendencies in their general perception of the truth and, correlatively, in their orientation toward doubt and ambivalence. She finds divergences from established gender patterns, evidence which should not be overlooked as it offers the chance to find alternative paths for gender orientation.

Resisting the prevailing trend for homologation, the author calls for observing and endorsing diversions, for striving to single out and value the multiple paths that disappear under superimposed mainstream patterns.

The time has come to give voice to difference and to differences: to resist the temptation to passively fit into dichotomous gender roles and to take a critical distance from the fixed gender code as a strategy for softening their rigidity and opening a free space for a wide range of differences to emerge and flourish. In Lebouc's essay the reader will find a cogent example of how the recently born movement of philosophical practices is recovering difference within relationship as both a value and a methodological principle, while returning philosophy to its original dialogic orientation.

Modern philosophical practice, in common with ancient Greek and Roman philosophy, acknowledges dialogue as the royal road to authentic confrontation and μετάνοια (*metànoia*): a "change in opinion," an "upheaval of thought" which involves the entire personality and way of life. The Latin translation for *metànoia* is *conversio* ("change, transformation, conversion"), which results from the combination of *cum-* 'with' and *versus* 'turned, inclined.'

This etymology shows the common root between the 'conversion,' which we usually think of an exceptional life-altering event, and 'conversation,' to which we do not attach such an importance since it has fallen into ready-made patterns of daily use. The training offered by professional philosophers, like that of the ancient schools, can help people develop techniques for improving everyday conversations, to make them a space for real confrontation, genuine exchange, mutual enrichment, and (inter)personal development.

This sense of 'conversation' is championed by the U.S. university professor and philosophical counselor Marilyn Piety in her article *The Talking Cure or Conversation with Women.* Here the therapeutic potential inherent in conversation is explored through a comparison between different conversational models which have informed our culture.

The author's reflection revolves around the 'talking cure' born from Breuer's experiment with Bertha Pappenheim and later developed into a more systematized pattern of psychoanalytical 'conversation.' In Piety's sensitive analysis, the Freudian conversational framework shows itself to be firmly lodged within the therapist-patient relationship model, inclined to fall into an authoritarian and prescriptive dynamic in which conversation is doomed to distortion. First of all, it is invisibly armed with veiled assumptions and unquestioned claims; secondly, it kept the values and stance inherent in the therapist's role aloof from a genuine confrontation with the other; third, it fails to engender a shared process of questioning; lastly, it has been stripped of authentic reciprocity.

Appealing to Diotima as the mother of philosophy and the all-female image of genuine conversation, Piety singles out the stance of the philosophical counselors from other therapists in that they do not claim anything more than an "epistemic advantage" over the people they counsel, avoiding the dangers of covert authoritarianism, pretended neutrality, or the dismissal of primary responsibility for their counselees. Instead, they readily involve themselves in the soul-searching exchange that is the real process of conversation.

The fifth and final section of the book, "Acting to Change," focuses on the shift in therapeutic paradigms that has been triggered by philosophical counseling. It endorses a critical approach toward the forced and elaborate standards which go hand-in-glove with an underlying structure of dominance. It discusses an approach that lends a humble and attentive ear to the *différance* within the infinite number of irreducibly different life stories.

In common with Piety, the American philosophical counselor Dena Hurst argues that a paradigm change in therapy ought to run in parallel with a recuperation of the feminine roots of care. In her article, *Woman as Healer*, Hurst paints a masterly picture of how the outstanding problems facing broader humanity are entangled with gender issues.

The author is well aware of the potential danger of a structured discourse based on inequality that, with its very calls for rejection of gender divides, actually seeks to reinstate them.[18] This is one reason that she does not fit neatly into the gender perspective, but makes clear that her appeal to the archetype of Woman as healer is (also) a strategy to overcome the constraints of a language that is "limited to man and woman, male and female."

Hurst interweaves mythology and anthropology to shed light on key elements in healing and therapy that have been banished to the outer darkness, and which philosophical practice wants to regain for the potential benefit of today's multicultural society.

The Woman-as-Healer archetype goes beyond modern assumptions about the mind-body issue and the individual self. Philosophical practitioners can draw on it to see each person as a concrete human subject within the context of their relations with others, without pretending to treat their body or psyche as different parts of an autonomous self. In doing so, they express their responsibility toward their community, the natural environment, and society as a whole.

In their role as healers, philosophical counselors endorse, invest in, and capitalize on the differences in values and perspectives of people from a wide variety of cultural backgrounds. They are committed to their counselees' needs as perceived, felt, and expressed, rather than trying to translate them into standardizing categories that follow a so-called scientific agenda of "true needs."[19]

Kate Mehuron's article, *Relationship Violence: How Philosophical Counseling Can Help* echoes the claim in Hurst's article for listening to different voices. In choosing to deal with the unpopular topic of violence in lesbian relationships, the U.S. university professor and philosophical counselor turns to a particularly marginalized group within the more generally marginalized class of women.[20] It is doubly provocative insofar as we unwittingly take for granted that violence is male rather than female, and that it is exercised within intimate relationships by men against women.

Working for government-funded agencies as a counselor for survivors of domestic violence, Mehuron was frustrated with the way that domestic violence has become a conceptual template for gender oppression: a universal model of a violent, overbearing, and overpowering man, *versus* a battered, fragile and submissive woman.

In her article, we hear the voices of women abused and battered by other women as they struggle to find words to account for experiences that our present interpretational framework cannot handle.

The sociological and the legal lexicons abound in ambiguities and confusion, tailored as they are to a paradigm of the heterosexual couple. As a result, very real acts of domestic violence fall outside of all categories with which judicial courts deal. The same paradox applies where a man struggles to find the legal and the psycho-sociological support he needs when subjected to threats and assaults by his wife.

By overgeneralizing, the current social and legal framework covertly endorses the stereotypical association between violence and masculinity, pushing men into the role of 'bad guy' instead of allowing them space for more positive image of themselves. The media acts as chorus to this allegedly manly image, to the point where the screen offers us an exaltation of the criminal enterprises of various husbands and male lovers. By contrast, men who have actually passed through such violence and want to help others to understand and deal with violent inclinations come up against institutional barriers that prevent them from giving such badly needed help and counsel—and prevents potential beneficiaries from receiving it.

Again, we have to face the fact that the binary hierarchy of the sexes penalizes not only women, but also—and sometimes more severely—men who, whether hetero- or homosexual, do not fit the compulsorily strong, overbearing hegemonic image of masculinity they are expected to embody.[21]

Society does not encourage men to talk about pathways toward emotional maturity, from showy machismo to an internalized masculinity, authentically strong and tender, and not terrified by bonds and feeling. In this respect, the bias found in the legal and social code is equally present in school programs and university research.

In *Sexism and Gender Issues in Academic Philosophy: Philosophical Practice as a Balancing Act*, the Dutch philosopher Marleen Moors tells of her early disillusionment when, as a graduate student, she was haughtily denied permission to work on Heidegger's metaphysics of feeling, as this was not deemed a topic relevant to a degree in philosophy.

Feelings have never enjoyed a good reputation in mainstream academic philosophy. For sure, a budding researcher who aims to make a university career would gain no benefit in choosing this kind of topic—even less if this budding researcher happened to be a woman. Her colleagues in the faculties of neuroscience and psychology would have had a better chance. The first would be welcome to chase love and fear through entangled brain circuitries, while the second would do only as long as they kept faith with the assumption that feelings belong in the closed theater of the psyche. But when a philosopher proposes a research project which aims to question the role and impact of feelings on reality itself, she jeopardizes her academic credibility and is dismissed with a scornful laugh. Why?

From Moore's perspective, academic philosophy suffers from a "hierarchy of thinking." Only what is deemed impersonal, consistent, and rational according to the old-fashioned model of rationality can gain legitimate entrance to the dignity of philosophical thought. By contrast, all thought which carries emotion, lived experience, ambiguities, conflict or contradiction, is not given free or easy entry to philosophy's inner sanctum.

What academic thought suffers from is a kind of pathological disease whose symptoms include a delirious mania for pure rationality, an obsession with neutrality and objectivity, and a phobia of the distorting effects of subjectivity and emotion on thought. The etiology of the disease can be traced back to the dramatic imbalance between a hypertrophic theory and an atrophic practice that has been the hallmark of Western mainstream philosophy from the sixteenth century onward.

Today, not only do ontology, metaphysics, and epistemology have absolute priority over ethics and moral philosophy, but they have also erected such rigid boundaries that at least half of the world's philosophers are better off outside academia, since inside they would be hard put to find anything that would be of any real interest to them.[22]

Philosophy's banishment of so many issues and dimensions relevant to human existence from the certified field of its thought and the marginalization of women within mainstream philosophy are not separate phenomena. They run in parallel as two of the many aspects of one and the same story, which started with the triumph of Cartesian *cogito* and culminated with the Freudian *Ego* pretending to take over the *Id* as a civilizing act.[23]

Where and to whom can we look to for some fruitful deviation from the straight and narrow path ahead?

In *Giving Birth do Derrida's Mother: Philosophical Practice at the End of Philosophy*, the South African philosophical counselor Helen Douglas ponders the future of philosophy.

She starts her reflection in her philosophical counseling room in Cape Town, which has been imagined as a hostel for travelers in need of rest, guidance, and sustenance. Its atmosphere is rendered so vividly and intensely that the reader can almost sense the warm smell of wood and the gentle harmony of light and colors shifting through the open door.

She recalls the key stages in the long passage of philosophy to its present day end-of-career nemesis: the death announced by Nietzsche theorized by Heidegger, established as a *leitmotifv* by twentieth-century philosophers, eventually becoming fashionable even among non-philosophers, scientists *in primis*.

Reading between the lines of this litany, the reader begins to wonder whether all these enthusiastic mortuary proclamations are merely self-serving grist to the mill for those eager to relieve their agendas and worldviews from the burden of proper analysis. A picture emerges of philosophers, from Socrates onward, being a bunch of wet blankets, with all their admonishments on human limitations and their killjoy critiques of scientific progress. For those who comfortably and non-critically believe in what seems obvious, or from the other direction, those proud positive scientists who toil for new discoveries, philosophers are a pesky nuisance. However, it is not necessarily this critical disquieting spirit of philosophy that has been diagnosed as terminally ill. Before joining the wake at philosophy's bedside, it might be better to ask ourselves: what precisely it is that is dying along with philosophy? Or, to put it another way: which philosophy is it that is dying? Is this dying philosophy the only one we humans—women and men—have produced in the past and could possible produce in the future?

Douglas suggests that what is dying might only be the fetish of an abstract and dehumanized reason: the allegedly pure and objective rationality which the Enlightenment *philosophes* ingeniously devised and handed down to their sons, who refined and elevated it to a universal measure for the human, to the cost of different and imperfect peoples and individuals, with all their contingencies, vulnerability, and precarious lives.

What is supposed to be dying might simply be the hegemonic thought patterns propagated by the dominant power, always conniving for the affirmation of inequality, subjugation, ideology, famine, injustice It might also include any and all forms of slavery, from those legitimized by Aristotle or reported loud and clear in history textbooks up to the current variety, with its legitimization part of its disguise, hardly recognizable and largely ignored for what it actually is.

If this is the case, letting the old philosophy die is not only an inevitable fatality, but even a worthy enterprise, a task to be critically and proactively promoted, an act of mercy for this overage and irretrievably outdated patient who is consumed by an endless agony. Not that we should necessarily assist in its demise, but rather work toward a new way of thinking from its ashes.

Philosophy has to learn from life itself those gestures that biology and history have preferentially, but not exclusively, assigned to women: *to let die* and *to give birth.* It is to these apparently simple gestures that we have to look at to achieve a renewed thought in step with life.

As Douglas puts it, what is needed is a human philosophy rather than the umpteenth philosophy of the human. We need to expose philosophical thought to everyday frustrations and human fragility, open its doors to the slippery and erratic folds of difference and confrontation rather than leaving it as the seduced captive of a sovereign rationality, relegated to a wasteland slum of indifference.

Enhancing difference from within and in relation to others and the world is an essential step for both women and men today. We need to leave behind the stifling enclosure of our self-identical *Ego* whose *alter* cannot be but an *alter-Ego*: a mirror of the Ego's reflections and projections, rather than an inexhaustible source of wonder, knowledge, and discovery.

Regaining our voices as both women and philosophers is the first fundamental step to regaining our ability for dialogue on the royal road to thinking differently: to think the difference and to think differently, or to think the difference as a means to thinking differently.

This is what this book wishes for and wants: to be a starting point for thinking about difference and the differences camouflaged in indifference. It is a process that has been denied over time with the construction and maintenance of identity philosophy. It is still only an indication along an unbeaten path, an invitation whose appeal rests on the (re)actions it will be able to elicit, always within the unpredictability of the future.

NOTES

1. Thomas S. Kuhn, *The Structure of Scientific Revolutions* (Chicago: Chicago University Press), 1962.

2. Drawing from Idries Shah, it can be said that working at the deathbed, more than everywhere else, the philosopher has to "know how to know" and "learn how to learn." See Idries Shah, *Learning How to Learn: Psychology and Spirituality in the Sufi Way* (New York: Harper & Row, 1981) and Idries Shah, *Knowing how to Know* (London: Octagon Press, 1998).

3. Ancient philosophy and the examples given by Greek and Roman philosophers of their own ease of dying demonstrate both for the relevance of death and mortality in ancient philosophy and for a confidence and familiarity with it that it is striking to our modern mentality. Artistotle's definition of life (βίος, *bios*) as "the capacity to feed on one's own, grow and perish" (Περὶ Ψυχή, *Peri Psyke,* B 1, 412a [Milano: Rusconi 1996], my trans.) leaves us to think that ancients perceived and conceived death as the constitutive and essential limit of life itself rather than being contrary and in opposition to life, as we tend to assume and feel today.

4. On the exorcism of human frailty and vulnerability through their projection on woman's body see Dowling Colette, *The Frailty Myth* (New York: Random House, 2000).

5. According to the Polish philosopher and sociologist Zygmunt Bauman, the destructuring and dissolving of the subjective is the main character of modern "liquid identity." See Zygmunt Bauman, *Liquid Modernity* (Cambridge: Polity, 2000); *Liquid Love: On the Frailty of Human Bonds* (Cambridge: Polity, 2003); *Liquid Life* (Cambridge: Polity, 2005); *Liquid Fear* (Cam-

bridge: Polity, 2006); and *Liquid Times: Living in an Age of Uncertainty* (Cambridge: Polity, 2006).

6. The model of the atom is a perfect mold and reflection of the modern individual. As a matter of fact, the atom is primarily conceived as standing for itself, not changing and not dying, nevertheless having exchanges with other atoms.

7. See f.i. Heisenberg Werner, *Physics and Beyond: Encounters and Conversations* (New York: Harper & Row, 1971).

8. Didier Anzieu, *Le Moi-Peau* ([Paris: Éditions Dunod, 1995] Eng. Trans. Chris Turner, New Haven: Yale University Press, 1989).

9. Dawling, *The Frailty Myth.*

10. For example, to be in hormonal balance, women require a higher proportion of oxytocin, the 'cuddle-hormone' which is related to childbirth, maternal bonding, and lactation, and whose release is prompted, among others, by sharing, constructive interconnections, help and care activities, fulfilling relationships. See Gray John, *Why Mars & Venus Collide* (London: HarperCollins 2008), 31–75.

11. Gray, *Why Mars & Venus Collide*, XVI.

12. Schuster C. Schlomit, *Philosophy Practice: An Alternative to Counseling and Psychotherapy* (Westport: Praeger 1999), 15.

13. A major challenge to the deeply rooted dualism of emotion and rationality is today represented by experimental studies on brain and body functions. See Jospeh LeDoux, *The Emotional Brain: The Mysterious Underpinnings of the Emotional Life* (New York: Simon & Schuster 1996).

14. Michel Foucault, "The Discourse on Language," in *Archaeology of Knowledge*, trans. Alan Mark Sheridan-Smith (New York: Pantheon, 1972), 215–237.

15. Daniel Goleman, *Emotional Intelligence: Why It Can Matter More than IQ* (New York: Bantam Books, 1995).

16. LeDoux, *The Emotional Brain*, 16.

17. John Start Mill, *The Subjection of Women* (University of Oxford Text Archive, University of Oxford).

18. "In the phallogocentric system . . . women's 'otherness' in relation to each other remains unrepresentable because the peripheral 'other' is conceptualized in function of and in relation to a masculine center. . . . Beauvoir's 'emancipationism' or 'equality-minded thought' is perceived as naive insofar as it assumes that women can simply 'grab' transcendence as a point of exit from the paradox of femininity as a systematically devalued site of otherness. . . . The theory of sexual difference rather banks on the politically subversive potential of the margins of eccentricity that women enjoy from the phallogocentric system . . . feminists need to revalue discourses and practices of difference." Rosi Braidotti "Sexual Difference as Political Cartography," in Alison M. Jaggar and Iris Marion Young (eds.), *A Companion to Feminist Philosophy* (Malden-Oxford: Blackwell, 1998), 301–2. Luce Irigaray and Michael Foucault's lesson is recognizably running between the lines here. See Luce Irigaray, *Thinking the Difference: For a peaceful Revolution* trans. Karin Montin (New York: Routledge, 1994); Luce Irigaray, *Je, Tu, Nous. Towards a Culture of Difference* (London and New York: Routledge, 1993).

19. The presumption that all human attitudes and mental activity can be translated into allegedly universal patterns of rationality underpins Freudian psychoanalysis both as theory and practice. The metaphor of translation from one language to another is at the foundation of the method for the interpretation of dreams which marks the birth of psychoanalysis. See Sigmund Freud, *The Interpretation of Dreams*, in *The Complete Psychological Work of Sigmund Freud*, trans. Alix Stratchey and Alan Tyson (London: Hogarth Press, 1953), Vol. IV, 96–108.

20. That early feminism spoke on behalf of white, upper-class women, and did not take into due account the voices of lesbians, women of color, or lower-class women has been the subject of debate in more recent feminist work. See Sarah Lucia Hoagland, "Lesbian Ethics," in Jaggar and Young (eds.), *A Companion to Feminist Philosophy*, 402–410; Linda Martín Alcoff, "Racism," in Jaggar and Young (eds.), 475–484.

21. See Boni Federico, *Men's Help. Sociologia dei periodici maschili* (Roma: Meltemi 2004), 7–30. The author highlights how society pressures men info conforming to a single

model of masculinity, the hegemonic model, while many others tend to be depreciated and pushed to the margins, even aggressively mocked and despised. "There are different masculinities: hegemonic and subaltern, marginalized, subordinated, stigmatized, which is the case of homosexuals" (p. 18, my translation). The notion of hegemonic masculinity was brought to the fore by the Australian sociologist Raewin Connell. See her groundbreaking book in the field of men's studies: Connell Raewin, *Masculinities* (Sydney: Allen & Unwin 1995).

22. "Mainstream academic philosophy has effectively ignored half the human population: women." Raabe Peter, *Issues in Philosophical Counseling* (Praeger: Praeger Pub, 2002), 8.

23. "Where id was, there ego shall be. It is a work of culture—not unlike the draining of the Zuider Zee" Sigmund, *Introductory Lessons on Psychoanalysis*, in *The Complete Work* Vol. XXII, 80. In the last chapter of *The Ego and the Id*, (Vol. XIX, 56), Freud had already explicitly referred to the ego's subjection of the instinctual and impulse-driven id as the proper task of psychoanalysis: "Psychoanalysis is an instrument to enable the ego to achieve a progressive conquest of the id."

BIBLIOGRAPHY

Alcoff, Linda Martín. "Racism." In Jaggar and Young (eds.) *A Companion to Feminist Philosophy.* Malden and Oxford: Blackwell, 1998, 475–484.

Anzieu, Didier. *The Skin Ego*. Translated by Chris Turner. New Haven: Yale University Press, 1989 [1985].

Aristotle. Περὶ Ψυχή (*Perì Psykė,* "On the Soul"). Edited by Giancarlo Movia, Milano: Rusconi 1999.

Bauman, Zygmunt. *Liquid Times: Living in an Age of Uncertainty.* Cambridge: Polity, 2006.

———. *Liquid Fear*. Cambridge: Polity 2006.

———. *Liquid Life*. Cambridge: Polity 2005.

———. *Liquid Love: On the Frailty of Human Bonds*. Cambridge: Polity, 2003.

———. *Liquid Modernity.* Cambridge: Polity, 2000.

de Beauvoir, Simone. *The Second Sex* [1949]. Translated by Constance Borde and Sheila Malovany-Chevallier. New York: Vintage Books, 2011.

Braidotti, Rosi. "Sexual Difference as Political Cartography." In Alison M. Jaggar and Iris Marion Young (eds.) *A Companion to Feminist Philosophy.* Malden and Oxford: Blackwell, 1998.

Brizendine, Louann. *The Male Brain.* New York: Harmony, 2011.

———. *The Female Brain.* New York: Harmony, 2007.

Connell, Raewin. *Masculinities*. Sydney: Allen & Unwin, 1995.

Dowling, Colette. *The Frailty Myth: Redefining the Physical Potential of Women and Girls.* New York: Random House, 2000.

Gilligan, Carol. *In a Different Voice*. Harvard: Harvard University Press, 1982.

Descartes. *Meditationes Metaphysicae*. Edited by Lucia Urbani Ulivi. Milano: Bompiani, 2001.

Foucault, Michel. *The Care of the Self.* Translated by Robert Hurley. New York: Random House, 1986 [1984].

———. The *Use of Pleasure*. Translated by Robert Hurley. New York: Random House, 1985 [1984].

———. *The Will to Knowledge*. Translated by Robert Hurley. New York: Random House, 1978 [1976].

———. "The Discourse on Language." *Archaeology of Knowledge*. Translated by Alan Mark Sheridan-Smith. New York: Pantheon, 1972 [1969].

Freud, Sigmund. *Introductory Lessons on Psychoanalysis* [1930]. In *The Complete Works,* Vol. XXII Edited by James Strachey. London: Hogarth Press, 1956–74.

———. *The Ego and the Id* [1923]. In *The Complete Works,* Edited by James Strachey. London: Hogarth Press, 1956–74.

———. *The Interpretation of Dreams* [1900]. In *The Complete Works,* Edited by James Strachey. London: Hogarth Press, 1956–74.

Goleman, Daniel. *Emotional Intelligence: Why It Can Matter More than IQ*. New York: Bantam Books, 1995.
Gray, John. *Why Mars and Venus Collide*. London: HarperCollins, 2008.
Heisenberg, Werner. *Physics and Beyond: Encounters and Conversations*. New York: Harper & Row, 1971.
Hoagland, Sarah Lucia. "Lesbian Ethics." In Jaggar annd Young (eds.) *A Companion to Feminist Philosophy*. Malden and Oxford: Blackwell, 1998, 402–410.
Hillman, James. "From Mirror to Window: Curing Psychoanalysis of its Narcissism." *City and Soul*. Irving: Spring Publications, 2006, 62–75.
Irigaray, Luce. *Je, Tu, Nous: Towards a Culture of Difference*. Translated by Alison Martin. London: Routledge, 1993 [1990].
———. *Thinking the Difference: For a Peaceful Revolution*. Translated by Karin Montin. London: Routledge, 1994 [1989].
LeDoux, Joseph. *The Emotional Brain: The Mysterious Underpinnings of the Emotional Life*. New York: Simon & Schuster, 1996.
Mill, John Stuart. *The Subjection of Women*. Oxford: University of Oxford Text Archive [1869].
Schuster, C. Schlomit. *Philosophy Practice: An Alternative to Counseling and Psychotherapy*. Westport CT: Praeger, 1999.
Shah, Idries. *Knowing How to Know*. London: Octagon Press, 1998.
———. *Learning How to Learn: Psychology and Spirituality in the Sufi Way*. New York: Harper & Row, 1981.

Index

About the Authors

Lydia Amir teaches philosophy at the College of Management Academic Studies in Israel and at the Department of Philosophy of Springfield University, in Springfield, Illinois. She is also an adjunct researcher at the Institute of Advanced Humanistic Studies, at Hubei University, in Wuhan, China. Apart from authoring books and articles on ethics and the practice of philosophy, she is coeditor of Practicing Philosophy for Cambridge Scholars Publishing and on the editorial boards of several international peer-reviewed journals, the President of Joyology, an association for the promotion of humor, and the Founding President of the International Association for the Philosophy of Humor. A seasoned practitioner of philosophy attending to individuals, couples, groups, and organizations in Israel, she travels regularly for workshops and lectures on philosophy and its practice, and airs a weekly radio program on philosophy in everyday life. Her website is: http://www.lydiaamir.com.

Camilla Angeltun holds a BA in retail management (BI) and a MA in philosophy from the University of Oslo. She is an active member of the Norwegian Society for Philosophical Practice, where she trained and got her certification as philosophical practitioner. In the last years Camilla has managed several projects on philosophical dialogue, acquiring an expertise in facilitating both group and one-to-one dialogue sessions. Along the same lines she has engaged herself in dialogue facilitation in a wide range of Norwegian libraries, and carried out training programs for teachers wishing to apply Socratic dialogue in school settings. She has also been *philosopheronline*, offering philosophical dialogues to clients from a secure online office. Last but not least, she has contributed in the last years to the Norwegian festival, inspired by the Norwegian philosopher Arne Næss "Tankeranglingsfestivalen," with both philosophical dialogues and presentations. Her website is: http://www.dialogpraxis.com.

Narelle Arcidiacono holds a Masters of Arts (philosophy), a Graduate Diploma in special education, a Bachelor of educational studies, and an Associate Diploma of performing arts, and has extensive teaching, theatre, and philosophy experience. Through the use of her 'Just Story' technique she creates, together with clients, scenarios that can be explored through dramatic representations to reach constructive philosophical outcomes on issues critical to the client. The author of many papers on dramatic philosophy and its implications for philosophical practice, she has presented and conducted workshops at major conferences throughout the world. Her diverse background as actor, director, writer, researcher, corporate consultant, trade union official, arts administrator, political advisor, and parent, alongside her passion for focused philosophical exploration and discourse, enables her to work effectively with clients of differing ages and social, cultural, and economic backgrounds. In 1994 she co-foundered Lupus Australia, Queensland Inc. providing volunteer counseling services. She established her Australian-based philosophical practice in 2009. Her website is: http://www.dramaticphilosophy.com.

Silvia Bakirdjian was born in Buenos Aires. She studied with the Jesuits at the Salvador University (Universidad del Salvador), where she graduated with a Diploma of Honor in philosophy. She became a teacher in philosophical anthropology, metaphysics, cultural anthropology, ethics, theodicy, and epistemology and a researcher at the National Council of Scientific and Technical Research, and she held senior posts of university level. She worked for ten years at the Institute of Eastern and Western Comparative Sciences. She has authored numerous essays and two books on issues of metaphysics, theory of knowledge, and theory of education, as well as three books on philosophical counseling, a discipline she is professionally dedicated to at present. She also worked for four years as consultant for the United Nations Development Program specializing in ecophilosophy issues, producing numerous reports as a result of her theoretical and field research. Her website is: http://www.consejeriafilosofica.com.

Luisa de Paula has been working with philosophy at all levels of public and private schools, psychiatric clinics, general hospitals, social cooperatives, and managed experimental philosophy projects with the marginalized. Experienced in maieutic-orientated tutoring, team- and dream-work, and end-of-life counseling, Luisa had the opportunity to lecture at departments of philosophy, psychology, economy, and arts both in Italy and abroad, and to give conferences in Italian, English, and French worldwide. Her background includes BAs (*magna cum laude*) in Philosophy and Journalism, a three-year specialization MA in Psycho-philosophy and Philosophical Practice, a French-Italian PhD in Ethics, and an international certification in Philosophical Counseling. So far, she has contributed to two international publications, authored four books, fourteen scientific papers in internationally accredited journals, and more than one hundred articles of general interest. Her website is: http://luisadep.wix.com/philoconsulting.

Helen Douglas (MA Stellenbosch 2002; BGS Simon Fraser 1997) began her practice in Cape Town, South Africa in 2002, offering counseling for individuals and couples and a monthly philosophy café. A longtime activist, she is interested in philosophy as a relational practice of ethics and emancipation, drawing particular inspiration from the philosophy of Emmanuel Levinas. Her first book, *Love and Arms: Violence and Justification after Levinas* (Pittsburgh: Trivium), was published in 2011. She has also published essays on such diverse topics as addiction, madness, and postcolonialism, and blogs regularly about philosophy in everyday life. Her website is: http://www.philosophy-practice.co.za.

Ora Gruengard studied philosophy at the Hebrew University of Jerusalem (Israel), PhD, 1976, Universities of Lille and Paris (France). She also studied economics (MA, 1966), cognitive psychology (Tel Aviv University (1982–1986)), family therapy (1989–1992), and was trained in psychotherapy (1991–1992). She worked mainly at The Hebrew University of Jerusalem and Tel Aviv University and is still teaching philosophy at some Israeli colleges. She has been practicing philosophical counseling since 1992, with the conviction that philosophy provides a richer arsenal of tools than clinical psychology and a wider range of theories that are relevant to the understanding of conflicts and dilemmas and the ability to cope with them.

Rayda Guzmán, *Summa Cum Laude* PhD in contemporary philosophy (University of Barcelona, Spain) with a research on fiction and hermeneutics. She has taught in many universities in Venezuela and Spain. As International Affairs Vice Dean, she coordinated an European program on narrativism and decision making to attend children on risk of exclusion. She planned and coordinated the first master's degree in Spain on philosophical practice (University of Barcelona), where she taught: dialogical skills for philosophical practice, tools for creativity and critical thinking, and hermeneutical devices for consultancy. She was the first one on introducing Cafés philo in Barcelona. In 2007, she published "La Mujer Serena," which was presented at several conferences in Spain (Madrid, Sevilla, Barcelona), México, and Venezuela. She belongs to a postdoctoral research team (CIPOST-FACES-UCV, Caracas). As a painter she is working now on a project linking art and philosophy. She has had her practice in Barcelona since 2003. Her website is: http://www.raydaguzman.net.

Dena Hurst received her PhD from Florida State University. Her area of specialization is social and political philosophy, specifically class and gender issues. She teaches a variety of philosophy courses in applied ethics, philosophy of race/class/gender, philosophy of technology, and philosophy in popular culture. She works as a special projects manager for Florida State University and is a certified philosophical counselor and consultant. She has authored journal articles, international conference presentations, and workshops in areas of applied philosophy. She serves as associate editor of *Philosophical Practice* and is on the board of the International Society of Philosophers and the Florida Association for Volunteer Action in the Caribbean and Americas. Her website is: http://www.denahurst.com.

Roxana Kreimer has a degree in philosophy and a PhD in social sciences (University of Buenos Aires). She published her first book of Philosophical Counselling originally written in Spanish. She has published four other books and since 2002, has organized four Philosophical Cafés each weekend, besides working as a philosophical counselor. She has given courses and lectures at various universities in Argentina and abroad. She has organized the first Seminar of philosophical counseling in an Argentinian University (UCES, 2005). She often appears in the media and in social networks, and her research on social inequality contributed to implement the "Universal Child Allowance" in Argentina, which enabled more than three million children to go out of extreme poverty. Her website is: http://www.filosofiaparalavida.com.ar.

Marie-France Lebouc is associate professor of Business Ethics at Laval University, Quebec, Canada. A certified affiliate of the American Philosophical Practitioners Association (APPA), she uses techniques of philosophical counseling as teaching tools in her graduate and undergraduate applied ethics classes to help students better face up to the ethical challenges that they encounter and to learn from those challenges. Indeed, her teaching philosophy is that in addition to the classical method of case-study analyses, students should have the opportunity to learn more about themselves, something rarely taught in business schools. Presently, Marie-France Lebouc works on several teaching and research projects, including the paradoxical project of introducing a reflexivity-based approach to ethics in a bureaucracy.

Kate Mehuron is professional philosophical counselor, Associate Dean of Programs, and professor. She received her PhD in Philosophy from Vanderbilt University in the United States for her research in nineteenth- and twentieth-century continental philosophy and French feminist theory. Her teaching interests include ancient philosophy, phenomenology, nineteenth and twentieth century European philosophy, feminist philosophy, and social ethics. She is the author of numerous published articles in feminist and social ethics anthologies. Her current research focuses on philosophical practice and philosophical critiques of medical mental health paradigms. She is a philosophical counselor certified by the American Philosophical Practitioners Association. She is employed as the Associate Dean of Programs and professor of philosophy in the College of Arts and Sciences, Eastern Michigan University. Her website is: https://emich.academia.edu/KateMehuron.

Marleen Moors (BA, Mphil) studied philosophy and religious studies at the University of Saskatchewan in Canada (BA) and received her Mphil on the late work of Martin Heidegger at the department of philosophy at Radboud University Nijmegen, the Netherlands. Her areas of expertise are existentialism, existential phenomenology, and metaphysics. After her graduation, Marleen worked as a junior researcher at the department of medical humanities (specialization medical ethics) at University Medical Center Utrecht (2011–2012), where she worked on the ethically sound inclusion of palliative care patients in scientific research. Marleen has given lectures on ethics, metaphysics, applied phenomenology, existentialism, and cultural theory and is currently writing for several journals and magazines. Besides running her philosophical practice in Amsterdam, she also teaches philosophy at the Fontys University of Applied Sciences in Tilburg and is a board member of the Netherlands Institute for Logotherapy and Existential Analysis. Her website is: http://www.marleenmoors.com.

Riella Morhayim received her BA in philosophy from Bogazici University in Turkey, MA in organizational psychology from Interdisciplinary Center Herzliya in Israel, and another MA in philosophy from Tel Aviv University in Israel. From the second year of her BA, she became interested in philosophical counselling and philosophical practice in which she improved her knowledge by online, onsite, educational, practical courses, and seminars. By the meantime, she has participated and given conferences in Turkey, Bulgaria, Budapest, Greece, and Israel about philosophical practices. So far, she has contributed some articles to philosophy journals (in Turkey). In addition, she has been practicing philosophy with individuals, groups, and organizations. She offers online philosophical practices to Turkish speaking clients for the Australian Consulting Philosopher Association and Turkish Immigrant Association in Israel. She is doing her counseling sessions with English, Turkish, and Hebrew speakers. Her website is: www.unlockingpractices.wix.com/unlockinpractices.

M. G. Pietyis an associate professor of philosophy at Drexel University. She's translated two works by the philosopher Søren Kierkegaard for Oxford University Press and published many articles on Kierkegaard and philosophy more generally in both scholarly and popular journals and magazines. She emphasizes the practical and therapeutic value of philosophy in all her courses and has been engaged in private counseling on a pro bono basis since she was first certified as a philosophical counselor in the summer of 2010. Her website is: http://www.mgpiety.org.

Peter Raabe received his PhD from the University of British Columbia in Canada for his research in philosophical counseling. He teaches a variety of philosophy courses at the University of the Fraser Valley, including reasoning, metaphysics and epistemology, philosophy of mind, philosophy of psychiatry, and a specialized upper-level course of philosophy for students of counseling and psychotherapy. He facilitated a public philosophy café in North Vancouver for eight years, and established three mental health discussion groups. He is the author of several books, many journal articles, international conference presentations, and workshops in the area of philosophical mental healthcare, and is on the editorial boards of several international peer-reviewed journals. He lives in North Vancouver where he has a private practice offering philosophy as mental healthcare. His website is: http://www.peterraabe.ca.

Natasa Radovanovic holds a MA in pedagogy and education from the University of Belgrade. She has been working as a school counselor for eleven years with pupils, parents, and teachers. She won the Serbian National prize for the advancement of creative teaching in 2008. After being trained in philosophy for children, she has had the opportunity to carry out workshops on the upbringng of children and teaching advancement, as well as international research with European philosophical practitioners. Beside pedagogy and psychology, her main field of interest is philosophy. More in particular, she is interested in philosophy as a constructivstic approach to life and learning, and a powerful tool for women's empowerment. In the last years, she has placed a constant effort in the attempt of implementing the traditional school teaching approach with philosophical counseling and philosophical practices. At present, she is engaged in a research publication on personal willpower in relation to personal freedom.

Heidi Salaverría, has a PhD (SCL) in philosophy with a work on pragmatism and is a freelance author, lecturer, counselor, and performance artist living in Hamburg. Her study and research stays in Buenos Aires, Hamburg, and Philadelphia, and her childhood was in Mexico City. Salaverría was born in Caracas, Venezuela. Lecturer at various German universities (Flensburg, Hildesheim, Heidelberg, Lueneburg, Music conservatory Nuremberg, et. al.), she has been researcher at the Institute of Philosophy, University of Hildesheim, and Scholarship holder of the Ev. Studienwerk Villigst, and has also held leadership trainings, consulting, and workshops in Germany and Austria. She speaks in English, German, and Spanish at numerous conferences in Europe; and so far she has published three books, and numerous articles, some of them in English. She has been involved in philosophical performances and philosophical art projects since 2002 (in Hamburg, Stuttgart, Karlsruhe, Munich, et. al.). Her research areas include: the relationship between politics and aesthetics, philosophy of agency and recognition, pragmatism, poststructuralism, and the philosophy of everyday life. She is currently writing a book on the Aesthetics of Doubt. Her website is: http://www.salaverria.de.

Luisa Sesino received her MA (*summa cum laude*) in philosophy from the University of Turin. She has been practicing as a professional philosophical counselor since 1991. From 1996 onward, she has been working in the public healthcare system, particularly in the area of palliative care, where she gained cutting-edge experience which is unique and unprecedented in Italy as well as in Europe. Besides individual counseling to the ill and their families, Luisa leads groups in philosophical practice and existential reflection among healthcare professionals and volunteers engaged either in hospice or home care. She is the scientific director and lecturer in training courses of Bioethics and Medical Humanities for health professionals in several Italian hospitals. Her approach is documented in several publications, long essays and papers in scientific journals included.

Marianne Vahl holds a BA in mathematics and an MA in philosophy from the University of Oslo (UiO). As a trained philosophical practitioner, certified by the Norwegian Society for Philosophical Practice (NSFP), she has facilitated philosophical dialogues at a medical office and has also worked with philosophy in school. She has completed the teacher education programme at UiO and is a qualified lecturer in music and philosophy. One of her main fields of interest is how to use philosophy in singing and in teaching music. She is a certified singer from the Complete Vocal Institute (CVI) in Copenhagen, having also studied musicology at UiO. Her website is: http://www.mariannevahl.com.

www.ingramcontent.com/pod-product-compliance
Ingram Content Group UK Ltd.
Pitfield, Milton Keynes, MK11 3LW, UK
UKHW012035150926
475560UK00001B/28